CHILDHOOD FRIENDSHIPS AND PEER RELATIONS

In the second edition of his unique overview of peer relationships in childhood, Barry Schneider re-examines this fundamental aspect of childhood. Taking the work of Jacob Moreno as its starting point, the book provides an up-to-date and accessible understanding of how children develop social competence in different environments, from school to cyberspace. It is informed by a cross-cultural perspective that examines how peer relationships vary in different cultures, as well as among children who have migrated to new cultures, whilst also providing increased coverage of how bullying is perceived and managed within peer groups. The book is informed, too, by new research techniques, both qualitative and quantitative, which mean we know far more about how children relate to each other than ever before.

Childhood Friendships and Peer Relations is a fascinating and very timely overview of what we know about making friends and enemies in childhood, showing how these relationships can have lasting effects. It will be essential reading to all students of Developmental Psychology and Educational Psychology, as well as anyone training towards a career working with children and young people.

Barry H. Schneider is Professor Emeritus at the University of Ottawa, Canada, now teaching at Boston College.

International Texts in Developmental Psychology

Series editor: Peter K. Smith, Goldsmiths College, University of London, UK

This volume is one of a rapidly developing series in *International Texts in Developmental Psychology*, published by Routledge. The books in this series are selected to be state-of-the-art, high-level introductions to major topic areas in developmental psychology. The series conceives of developmental psychology in broad terms and covers such areas as social development, cognitive development, developmental neuropsychology and neuroscience, language development, learning difficulties, developmental psychopathology and applied issues. Each volume is written by a specialist (or specialists), combining empirical data and a synthesis of recent global research to deliver cutting-edge science in a format that is accessible to students and researchers alike. The books may be used as textbooks that match on to upper-level developmental psychology modules, but many will also have cross-disciplinary appeal.

Each volume in the series is published in hardback, paperback and eBook formats. More information about the series is available on the official website at: www.psypress.com/books/series/DEVP, including details of all the titles published to date.

Published Titles

Child Development: Theories and Critical Perspectives, 2nd edition
By Rosalyn H. Shute and Phillip T. Slee

The Child at School: Interactions with Peers and Teachers, 2nd edition
By Peter Blatchford, Anthony D. Pellegrini and Ed Baines

Children's Literacy Development: A Cross-Cultural Perspective on Learning to Read and Write, 2nd edition
By Catherine McBride

Childhood Friendships and Peer Relations: Friends and Enemies, 2nd edition
By Barry Schneider

Forthcoming

Aging and Development: Social and Emotional Perspectives, 2nd edition
By Peter Coleman and Ann O'Hanlon

CHILDHOOD FRIENDSHIPS AND PEER RELATIONS

Friends and Enemies

Second Edition

Barry H. Schneider

Routledge
Taylor & Francis Group
LONDON AND NEW YORK

First published 2016
by Routledge
2 Park Square, Milton Park, Abingdon, Oxon OX14 4RN

and by Routledge
711 Third Avenue, New York, NY 10017

Routledge is an imprint of the Taylor & Francis Group, an informa business

British Library Cataloguing in Publication Data
A catalogue record for this book is available from the British Library

Library of Congress Cataloging in Publication Data
Names: Schneider, Barry H.
Title: Childhood friendships and peer relations : friends and enemies / Barry H. Schneider.
Other titles: Friends and enemies.
Description: Second Edition. | New York : Routledge, 2016. | Revised edition of the author's Friends and enemies, 2000. | Includes bibliographical references and index.
Identifiers: LCCN 2015031917| ISBN 9781848723245 (hardback) | ISBN 9781848723252 (softcover) | ISBN 9781315727042 (ebook)
Subjects: LCSH: Peer pressure in children. | Peer pressure in adolescence. | Interpersonal relations in adolescence. | Interpersonal relations in children.
Classification: LCC BF723.I646 S36 2016 | DDC 155.4/192—dc23
LC record available at http://lccn.loc.gov/2015031917

ISBN: 978-1-84872-324-5 (hbk)
ISBN: 978-1-84872-325-2 (pbk)
ISBN: 978-1-315-72704-2 (ebk)

Typeset in Bembo
by Keystroke, Station Road, Codsall, Wolverhampton

To all my friends, especially those who have also been my teachers and students

CONTENTS

FIGURES AND TABLES

Figures

Tables

PREFACE TO THE SECOND EDITION

It was with both delight and trepidation that I accepted Peter Smith's invitation to prepare a volume on children's peer relations for the *International Texts in Developmental Psychology* series in 2000. It was with even greater delight, but almost as much trepidation, that I undertook the writing of this second edition. I took up these challenges because I had often searched in vain for a comprehensive text to help me introduce my own area of research to students in courses I have taught. The assortment of excellent chapters and review articles I assigned them failed to provide a coherent presentation of theory and research on children's peer relations, or of their practical applications. I have found that students without extensive background in the behavioral sciences particularly need an integrated overview of the field.

In addition to providing the teaching resource I felt was so lacking, I had several main objectives in mind as I wrote. First of all, I wanted to convey to both the beginning and advanced students the historical, social and intellectual context that has stimulated the scientific study of relationships among children since its inception. It is important to me that students appreciate that the questions asked by researchers and the methods researchers use are vitally intertwined with the history of ideas and with the socio-political currents of the times and places in which the research is conducted.

My second goal was to foster an appreciation of the profound commitment to empirical science that has characterized research and practice in children's peer relations since the days of its pioneers. To accomplish this, I emphasize not only *what* has been learned, but also *how* it has been learned. I would not have done justice to the empirical traditions of the field had I glossed over the inconsistencies and limitations of research on fundamental issues by providing oversimplified summary pronouncements backed up by isolated examples.

Indeed, one of the pronounced strengths of the peer-relations field is the close link between research and applied practice. I am well aware that many students approach the field with a thirst for solutions to the difficulties faced by children who do not enjoy satisfactory relations with their peers. I also know very well that some scientists are skeptical of the applied interventions that have been developed. I have attempted herein to describe in sufficient detail the many ways in which peer-relations research has been translated into practice. I have also attempted to be authoritative and clear about the extent to which these interventions have been successful.

In writing this book, I have kept in mind the world-wide interest in children's peer relations that has burgeoned over the past few decades. The problems tackled by peer-relations scholars have always been matters of international concern, though their cross-cultural relevance is not always evident in the most influential books or articles.

I would like to acknowledge the invaluable assistance of the colleagues in many countries who have taught me and welcomed me in my international exploration of children's peer relations. They have become friends who have supported me throughout my writing of this book.

Barry H. Schneider
Boston, June 2015

1

THEORETICAL AND HISTORICAL ROOTS OF PEER-RELATIONS RESEARCH

This chapter is a sketch of the social and intellectual contexts of research on children's peer relations from its inception to the present day. Pioneer theorists explored peer relations as part of their search for an alternative to psychoanalysis. The political climate of the 1930s and 1940s resulted in sustained interest in the childhood roots of leadership and intolerance. During the years after World War II, the community mental-health movement provided strong impetus for the development of social-competence interventions in schools and communities and for research to help shape these efforts and document their success. The digital age and rapid urbanization since the 1980s has brought modes of relating to others that are qualitatively different from the face-to-face interaction styles of all previous eras. Some social critics maintain that relationships grounded in the new technology are lacking in the intimacy that is at the core of human social relationships.

Far more than any other species, humans seem programmed to form relationships with others, to rely on their relationship partners for support and assistance in times of trouble and to derive a sense of well-being from the relationships they create and cultivate. In the words of gifted playwright Tony Kushner, 'the smallest individual human unit is two persons, not one' (1993, p. 307). On the most fundamental level, human beings are driven to engage in sexual cooperation. The needs of children also reveal a biological preparedness to cooperate. Research suggests that cooperation between children begins to emerge at approximately two years of age, at the latest. Some of the cooperative behaviors that emerge include general abilities aimed at coordinating interaction around a set goal, behaving reciprocally and communicating effectively (Brownell and Brown, 1992). In addition, cooperative problem-solving, evidenced by children coordinating their actions with those of other children in order to achieve an otherwise unattainable goal occurs quite frequently among 24-month-olds (Brownell and Carriger, 1990). Theorists in several of the social sciences emphasize that the needs to belong and to relate are universal among humans and drive them to seek rewarding bonds with other people (Baumeister and Leary, 1995; Deci and Ryan, 2012).

Evolutionary psychologists have traced a progression starting with what they regard as genuine friendship among animals. In a convincing review paper, Seyfarth and Cheney (2012) note that behaviors interpretable as 'friendship' can be observed among horses, elephants, hyenas, dolphins, monkeys and chimpanzees. These behaviors involve cooperative interactions that recur at intervals separated in time. The animals appear to recognize these friendships. Importantly, the individuals who engage in these friendly, cooperative behaviors derive many benefits from them. They are more likely than other animals to reproduce successfully, to live longer and to have infants that survive.

These connections between children's peer relations and the adaptation of the human species are the core of *ethological theory*. This intriguing theory brings developmental psychology into close contact with social anthropology and biology in studying the adaptive functions of different ways of relating to others (Benenson and Alavi, 2004). Peer-relations researchers have embraced the ethnographic methods used by ethologists to only a limited extent. These methods include observing children in interaction in natural settings, sometimes using detailed field notes (Rubin *et al.*, 2013; Vaughn and Santos, 2009). Although its roots can be traced back to the work of Charles Darwin on human evolution in the nineteenth century, the field of human ethology experienced a resurgence in the 1970s. Its evolutionary approach represents an alternative to the classic behaviorism that was prominent at the time, which focused on observable stimuli and responses to them. The essence of the ethological approach is captured by four questions articulated by Tinbergen (1963, p. 410; see elaboration by Burkhardt, 2014):

1 How is it caused physiologically?
2 What is its survival value?
3 How has it evolved?
4 How does it develop in the individual?

The volume entitled *Human Ethology* by prominent ethologist Irenaeus Eibl-Eibesfeldt (1989) provides the most complete statement of the human ethological position. Human ethology as it exists today is sometimes considered a discipline of its own. Ethological ideas are also a fundamental part of *attachment theory*, which is discussed later in this chapter and in Chapter 3 (van der Horst, van der Veer and van Ijzendoorn, 2007).

The field of neuropsychology also brings peer-relations researchers into contact with biologists. Brain scientists are beginning to demonstrate a neurological basis of the centrality of relationships in human development and human well-being. The newest fMRI (functional magnetic resonance imagery) techniques are providing exciting evidence, although most of it pertains to relationships among adults. For example, Keysers and Gazzola (2014) review evidence from several studies on brain activity and empathy. These studies show that viewing the actions of others triggers mental images of performing similar actions ourselves, leading the individual to experience sensations similar to those of the person whose actions are experienced, perhaps leading the 'witness' to experience empathy. Hari and her colleagues (2013) discovered patterns of brain activity during face-to-face interaction. A series of studies by Eisenberger and her colleagues have shown neural responses by adolescents and adults to the experience of being socially rejected and even to witnessing another person being rejected (Eisenberger, 2013; Masten *et al.*, 2013). The amygdala has been implicated in the developmental shift that results in the increased importance of peer relations that coincides with the onset of adolescence. Scherf, Smyth and Delgado (2013) propose that the amygdala, influenced by adolescent sex hormones, affects the adolescent's perceptual, cognitive, emotional and motivational systems in ways that increase the relevance of such stimuli as the facial expressions of adolescent peers as the salience of such experiences as physical separation from parents is reduced.

As early as infancy, children are aware of their peers and recognize them in such ways as offering them objects (Underwood and Rosen, 2011; Williams, Ontai and Mastergeorge, 2010). Adorable and innocuous as these interactions among infants usually are, the roots of social dominance and some early forms of conflict among peers can also be traced back to the infant years (Plusquellec *et al.*, 2007). This juxtaposition of pleasure and problems, this 'paradoxically positive and negative nature' (Perlman, 2007, p. 7), characterizes peer relationships throughout the lifespan. When negative emotions are tracked over periods of hours or days, sharing the experience with another person seems to reduce the duration of the negative experience (Brans *et al.*, 2013). Even a brief positive social exchange with a stranger can change a person's mood for the better, according to a laboratory study by Epley and Schroeder (2014). These researchers observe that strangers on a street or public-transportation vehicle often make the mistake of seeking solitude, when they might be happier if they evoked even a superficial positive social exchange with those around them. Unfortunately, many of these revolutionary studies on the species-wide basis of social interaction were conducted with adults. But there is no reason to doubt that the results apply to children, too; future researchers will hopefully find out how.

In many societies, children spend a great deal of time in each other's company, although the age at which this starts varies considerably. Spending long periods of time with other children has been the standard way of growing up in many agricultural societies for centuries: while adults work together, children play together; and older siblings have responsibility for the care of their younger brothers and sisters (Whiting and Edwards, 1988). In contrast, children in the United Kingdom, the United States and Western Europe are depicted as having spent most of their time with their families until the late nineteenth century and early twentieth century. The Industrial Revolution and the resulting rapid societal change led to the decline of the family as the fundamental economic unit, as people of all ages began to work in factories together with co-workers outside their families. As a result, children began to congregate in play groups in the streets of large cities, without any substantial supervision by adults. With the advent of compulsory public education, school emerged as the venue in which children form peer relationships, and these are often continued outside of school. Contemporary patterns of school and community life vary from place to place and home to home. However, sophisticated technological advances, such as the sampling of children's time using electronic pagers, has revealed that, at least in the United States, older school-age children and adolescents spend most of their free time in the company of peers (Larson, 2014).

If children are so intensively involved in interaction with their peers, it is logical to expect that children would have a major influence on the development and personalities of other children. The desire to understand that influence – and put it to good use – is the reason sometimes given for the earliest interest by scholars of many disciplines, such as psychology, sociology and education, in the scientific study of peer relations: that is, of children's relations with other children (Renshaw and Parke, 1992). The debate as to how much of children's behavior and personality is determined by peers and how much by family continues to rage. Such comparison of the weights of parent and peer influences has perhaps never received as much public attention as it did after Judith Rich Harris (1998) published her controversial bestseller entitled *The Nurture Assumption: Why Children Turn out the Way They Do* (see Chapter 3).

The first major theories of personality and child development also emerged at the end of the nineteenth century and the start of the twentieth. The theorists of the time speculated extensively about the importance of peer relations in child development. G. Stanley Hall, the pre-eminent psychological theorist of that time, believed that children's association with other children was part of a process wherein ontogeny recapitulates psychology – in going through the stages of development, children repeat the process of evolution from more primitive species to more sophisticated ones. Hall saw herd-like association with other children as an important expression of an inborn 'social instinct'. He maintained that following the social instinct by associating with other children during the primary years enabled children, especially boys, to achieve independence from their parents and prepare themselves for the trials of adult life. Most of the other major theorists of the late 1800s and early 1900s offered theories that were not as bold as Hall's, but they too emphasized children's peer relations as an important element in child development. Another major psychological theorist, James Mark Baldwin, was interested in the ways children change as they grow from independent, separate individuals into cooperative members of society. He believed that being a member of a team in childhood play was an important part of that process. In a similar vein, the influential educational theorist John Dewey emphasized the value of children's informal learning though play, with social experience a major source of the benefit. He believed that playgrounds should be run as miniature, democratically governed towns, with mayors, policemen and other civil servants, so that children could prepare for their roles as adults in a democratic society.

Jacob Moreno and the focus on social reputation

The importance of interpersonal relationships seems so obvious that one would expect relationships to be core elements of any and all theories of personality and human development. Therefore, it is surprising that many of the early scholars interested in the peer relations of children and adults felt that they were regarded as heretics in a psychology that was dominated in the 1920s by a fascination with events occurring inside single individuals – their feelings, instincts, drives and complexes. In the writings of peer-relations researchers in the 1920s, Freudian psychoanalysis is depicted as a tyrannical force that suppressed interest not only in interpersonal relationships but in systematic research about human behavior in general. Nowhere is this clearer than in the provocative writings of Jacob Moreno (1889–1974), the flamboyant founder of sociometry and psychodrama, two techniques that will be described later. Moreno was a physician of Romanian origin who trained in Vienna and was interested in social relations and inter-group and international problems. He dubbed psychoanalysis 'the vengeance of mediocrity' (1953, p. xxxiv), because of its passivity, its stifling of creativity, and its insistence that healthy, creative, everyday events were the sources of sickness. If God had been no more active or creative than a psychoanalyst, taunted Moreno, the world never would have been created. However, God could well have been a psychodramatist, analysing from on high the relationships between the things he had created and endowing them with new ways of relating to each other (1953, p. xvi). It is thought that Moreno met Freud only once, at a lecture given by the latter in 1912. After the lecture, Moreno spoke briefly with the founder of psychoanalysis: 'Well, Dr. Freud, I start where you leave off. You meet people in the artificial setting of your office, I meet them on the street and in their homes, in their natural surroundings. You analyze their dreams, I try to give them the courage to dream again' (Moreno, 1972, cited in Hare and Hare, 1996, p. 7).

Mary Northway, the Canadian pioneer of peer-relations research with children, echoed the call for a counter-revolution against the psychoanalytic revolution and for a theory based on interpersonal relationships:

> Consciously known living relationships are of major importance to the individual. The early relationship to his mother in infancy or to his father at his Oedipal stage has historical rather than dynamic meaning. The early psychoanalytic doctrine which considers society as an oppressing and stultifying prison is replaced by a view of society as a potentially rich soil out of which the individual derives nutriment for his growth and the sustenance necessary for an enriched life.
>
> *(Northway, 1952, p. 49)*

Obviously, such ideas were unwelcome in the community of mental-health professionals that was still in a state of euphoria because of the recent major contributions of Freudian theory: the acceptance of psychiatric problems as natural, human phenomena that were to be understood rather than as manifestations of evil forces that had to be defeated (Goodwin, 1990). Moreno's assault against what he saw as the uselessness of psychoanalysis ('stillborn to start with'; 1953, p. liv) reached a climax when he belittled a psychoanalytic description of the personality of Abraham Lincoln that appeared in an American newspaper in 1932 (cited in Hare and Hare, 1996). Moreno felt that more could be learned by analyzing the reasons why modern psychoanalysts chose to dissect particular historical personalities than by analyzing the personalities of dead people whose social relationships could not be studied meaningfully from historical documents: 'neither transference [the direction of positive feelings and desires towards a new object or person] nor resistance [the often unconscious refusal to admit to one's awareness of potentially useful insights] can be expected from a dead person' (1953, p. xlvi).

From that point on, Moreno and his followers became outcasts in the community of mental-health professionals, outcasts who themselves studied people who were outcasts. Instead of studying people's feelings, instincts and drives, as psychoanalysts did and do, Moreno and his followers focused on the roles people play in groups. Relationships and roles in them were to become the major unit of analysis. By no means were relationships to be considered a surface by-product of primitive sexual drives, as they are in Freudian theory, as it was interpreted by Moreno and his followers. Moreno used the term 'role' as it is often used in social psychology – to refer to the privileges and responsibilities that accompany a given position in society. One can have the *role* of teacher, leader, scapegoat, supporter of unpopular individuals, and so on. In Moreno's 'spontaneity theory', an individual's personality is a reflection of the roles he or she plays in life. A psychologically healthy person is one who, in relating to others, can assume healthy roles in a flexible and spontaneous way (Hare and Hare, 1996; Moreno, 1953).

Learning from the relationships of 'normal' people

Inattention to the social world was not the only flaw in Freud's approach to which Moreno and his followers objected. Early peer-relations researchers also objected vociferously to the Freudian preoccupation with the exclusive study of abnormal behavior without learning, if only for comparison purposes, how the 'normal' individual thinks, feels and relates. The study of both normal and abnormal development is another feature of early peer-relations research that has survived to the present day. As in the past, many contemporary peer-relations researchers believe that, in order to understand and help children who cannot get along with others, it is important to understand the social behavior of children who have no problem with their relationships with others. Northway (1956, p. 3) maintained that:

> From the days of Freud on, investigations of the neurotic and the psychotic, of emotionally disturbed or retarded children, of criminals and delinquents, of deprived infants, have been made. On the basis of these discoveries, theories of mental health have been established, but these have not told us the whole and may have told us a distorted story. Mental health is not simply a lack of mental illness and a theory of mental healthiness can hardly be completed by saying that mental health is what these patients do not have. Mental health can only become understood by observing mental healthiness.

In the years since this criticism was voiced, much more research has been conducted on the development of normal children – although, according to many influential contemporary social scientists, still not enough. It has been remarked that the study of peer relationships in its early years was predicated on the assumption that the relationships themselves were superficial reflections of dispositions internal to the child. Therefore, until the longitudinal evidence mentioned later in this chapter became known, the relationships themselves were not considered very important to psychological adjustment. Once awareness of the link between relationships and life outcome was established, researchers resumed in earnest the study of the peer relationships of maladjusted individuals. Rubin *et al.* (2013) remark that this thrust comes at the price of excessive neglect of developmental differences.

The early behavioral scientists' infatuation with psychoanalysis was seen at the time as a suppressor not only of interest in interpersonal relationships but also as an inhibitor of objective, scientific research about human development. The peer-relations research community felt that the psychoanalytically inspired researchers of that period refused to design studies and discuss the results in a scientific way that was free of jargon and unproven theoretical explanation. It would be unfashionable to observe and describe exactly what children did in specific situations – for example, whether they cried, laughed, hit, approached others – and how they did these things. Such unfounded pronouncements as 'Jeffrey exhibited attention-seeking behavior, demonstrating regression to an early stage' would have been much more respectable. In a perhaps overzealous reaction to the ubiquity of such unscientific thinking, many members of the first generation of peer-relations scholars set out deliberately to describe exactly what children did in the company of other children in plain, everyday language. They felt it premature to offer elaborate theories to explain the relationship-building behaviors they observed. In particular, they wanted to use precise, direct observations to corroborate their impression that children were not as selfish, insensitive, or even cruel as Anna Freud depicted them in her famous theories about children's psychological defense mechanisms (Renshaw, 1981)

Just as Sigmund Freud's teachings were based on the psychoanalysis of distressed adults, Anna Freud and her colleagues based many of their more pronounced observations about the nature of the child on their study of children who had been evacuated from the Blitz bombings in London. Contemporary scholars who were more skeptical about Freudian teachings took exception to Anna Freud's conclusion that 'children are born as little savages' (Burlingham and Freud, 1942). Blatz (1944), for example, maintained that, even if the child is born as a 'non-social being' (which most present-day researchers of the infancy period would of course dispute), that does not necessarily mean that the child is born 'savage'. To resolve this issue, more intensive and more systematic study of children under normal conditions was needed.

It is important to note that Freudian theories were also seen by some as less harsh and harmful than they were seen by many peer-relations scholars in the early and middle 1900s. For example, Littledale (1946, cited in Renshaw and Parke, 1992) observed that psychoanalytic theories about childhood were of help to parents trying to understand children's instincts, drives and moments of animal-like rage. Instead of trying to stamp out these inevitable aspects of human development by force, parents could learn to accept them as natural and try to channel them.

Because of its traditional emphasis on the precision of measurement and on scientific rigor rather than creativity in explaining behavior, the field of children's peer relations was widely tainted as being atheoretical – not designed to prove any particular theory. This disrepute continues somewhat to the present day. To a considerable degree, this agnosticism about relevant theory is intentional, based on reaction to the highly speculative, elaborate, rich – but largely unproven – elements of expansive theories such as those of Freud and Moreno. Although the objections of critics such as Mary Northway, mentioned earlier, pre-date the heyday of behaviorism in the 1960s and 1970s, the objections share with subsequent behaviorists the reverence for hard facts and the eschewal of jargon and internal mental processes that cannot be observed.

However, there are some important theoretical roots of contemporary peer-relations research. For example, one of the important functions of contemporary research on children's peer relations is to prove or disprove attachment theory or Sullivan's interpersonal theory of psychiatry, which will be discussed in Chapters 2 and 3. Even though peer-relations researchers of all periods have shown little regard for theories that are not supported by evidence, the scientific methods of peer-relations research such as sociometrics and direct observation (see Chapter 6) were used as early as the 1930s by scholars such as Isaacs (1933) who wanted to demonstrate the validity of Freud's and others' theories.

The child study movement and the respectability of observational research

The need to see phenomena in front of one's own eyes is consistent with the reaction against what some see as unnecessary and unproven theory. However, Darwin's evolutionary theory can be seen as a broad inspiration for the observational approach, traceable back to his observations of his own children (Conrad,

1998). The universal, species-wide nature of the stages of development that would be discovered was more or less understood but was not emphasized by most subsequent researchers.

The child study movement of the late nineteenth and early twentieth centuries emphasized direct observation of children's behavior for the purpose of seeing how development unfolded. Detailed standards for observational research were proposed by William Preyer, a scientist at Jena University in Germany who has been described as 'careful, precise, compulsive and pedestrian' (Cairns and Cairns, 2006, p. 98). Preyer's main theme was the insistence on direct observation by the scientist rather than second-hand accounts. The behaviors observed were to be recorded immediately and directly. The child was to be observed in an unobtrusive way so as not to constrain the behaviors of interest artificially. Importantly, the child was to be observed on repeated occasions before conclusions were drawn (Cairns and Cairns, 2006). Any of these principles would be obvious and unexciting to a contemporary researcher interested in observational work.

As chronicled by Coplan and Rubin (2010), observational research on children's peer relations began to flourish in the 1920s and 1930s. Researchers of that period developed typologies for classifying different types of social interaction in children's play groups. Researchers classified, first of all, whether the child played alone or in the company of others. In the case of social play, were the children involved in a common purposive activity, such as construction or acting out a story? Were the children watching each other's play? Were they exploring new objects or people? Are there children who play alone in the presence of peers, or peers who engage in solitary activities similar to the solitary activities of those around them (Bott, 1928; Verry, 1923; Lehman, 1926)? These observational categories, especially those of Parten (1932), remain highly influential.

Putting peer-relations research to work: helping individuals in distress

Proving or disproving theories has never been the only reason for studying peer relationships. The field of peer relations has always attracted scientists and practitioners with particular interest in the practical applications of their work. This has been evident since the 1920s. Moreno's main purpose in developing highly technical methods for finding out what roles people play in groups was to help people understand their roles in groups and try out new roles. Within his theory, this enactment of roles is seen as enabling reduction of stress.

One of the first 'real-world' problems that inspired peer-relations research was the observation that a substantial number of children and adolescents were alienated from schools and schooling (Renshaw, 1981). The writings of peer-relations researchers who worked during the interval between the two world wars indicate their desire to take up the challenge posed by predominant theorists of the time, including Piaget (1932), who criticized the emphasis on rote learning in the school curriculum (Renshaw, 1981). Piaget saw rote memorization as stunting children's social development along with their academic achievement. Troubled peer relations were rarely contemplated as a pressing educational need at the time but as a problem that would either disappear naturally with the course of development or respond to guidance to parents regarding their child-rearing practices. However, there were a few embryonic efforts at intervening directly to improve children's peer relations (Coplan and Rubin, 2010; Craig, 1922). Lowenstein and Svendsen (1938) conducted what was likely the first planned intervention to improve problematic peer relations of children. They identified thirteen boys aged between six and eight whose social withdrawal seemed problematic. These boys participated in a six-week summer camp that was viewed as very successful.

Concern about the massive problem of unemployment among adolescents and young adults led to research on interactions between members of street gangs. This started in Chicago with the advent of Thrasher's (1927) methods for scientific observation from the vantage point of members of the group being studied. These methods are similar to the field-study methods used by some subsequent researchers to study interpersonal interaction in different cultures around the world.

Moreno was deeply concerned about the social and political problems of the inter-war years, especially the conflicts between nations and between racial, religious and ethnic groups. He believed that the world could be fixed from the ground up – by fixing one interpersonal relationship at a time and, especially, by helping individuals such as chronic outcasts to obtain different positions and roles in their peer groups. He proposed *psychodrama*, also known as *sociodrama* – a therapeutic technique that is the very antithesis of Freudian psychoanalysis – as a way to achieve this. In his work on psychodrama, Moreno went so far as to design special theaters in Vienna for psychodrama. In psychodrama, people experiencing distress could achieve insight about the roles they played in their interpersonal relationships and practice the enactment of new roles. The trusting, empathic relationship (called '*tele*') between the person whose roles were being played out and the other participants in the psychodrama enabled the enactment of new roles in an atmosphere of flexibility and spontaneity. In a typical psychodrama, the protagonist is the person whose roles and relationships are being analyzed. Other actors play the various persons involved in the relationships. Yet other players act as auxiliaries, who follow the main players about the stage, expressing the inner feelings and perceptions of the main players. There might be several sequences in which a critical conversation is first enacted exactly as the protagonist remembered it, followed by repeat enactments in which the actors change roles. The session might end with a soliloquy during which the protagonist reflects on what has happened during the session.

Moreno defended with great vigor the emphasis on action in his psychodramatic movement. Psychodramas were to be staged with spontaneity and creativity. However, Moreno also wanted the therapeutic techniques of psychodrama to be informed by the scientific study of peer relationships. Therefore, he devoted much energy not only to the development of his psychodramatic technique but also to the refinement of precise sociometric techniques for measuring individuals' reputations in their peer groups. He also devoted some attention to 'living sociometrics' – that is, studying relationships by observing them directly – as in his studies of children's interactions in a state primary school in New York.

Psychodrama is still practiced today, although it has declined in importance among the major therapeutic techniques. Rich and vivid as it is, psychodrama never inspired the hard-core empirical validity research that has become important in the current era of professional accountability. However, elements of it live on in many of the social-skills training techniques that will be discussed in Chapter 12. Furthermore, the fundamental idea that an individual's symptoms relate to events and disturbances in interpersonal interaction is the basic underpinning of contemporary interpersonal psychotherapy, which does indeed enjoy considerable empirical support (e.g. Weissman, Rabinovich and Verdell, 2013). Moreno emphasized the therapeutic value of getting to know an interpersonal situation from the perspective of the other person or persons involved. This is achieved in psychodrama by role reversal, acting out the situation from the perspective of the other person. The cognitive and emotional processes involved in role reversal remain the focus of many cognitive psychologists who study theory of mind, which has been seen as having important applications within psychotherary (Boyd, 2008).

Putting peer-relations research to work in the service of society

Moreno emigrated to the United States before World War II to avoid Nazi persecution. By the time of his arrival, the pioneers of peer-relations research in the United States had already established laboratory schools on the grounds of several universities in order to study human development in great detail. They managed this despite the fact that by then Freudian psychoanalysis was deeply entrenched in the country as the main theory of human behavior. Psychodrama had attracted a loyal following among therapists working with adults in institutions and the community. Nevertheless, peer-relations researchers felt the need to venture beyond the niche they had carved for themselves in the research community and the helping professions and to use what they had learned to construct a less troubled world.

It is not difficult to understand this concern with real-world social and political problems when one considers the turbulence of the times. Leadership is a frequent theme in the articles published in the 1930s on relationships between children, reflecting the widespread alarm in the United States, Canada and the United Kingdom about the appeal of the charismatic leaders of Germany and Italy at that time (Jack, 1934). Discovering the childhood precursors of effective leadership became a pressing scientific concern. Of course, when one studies leadership, one studies not only the leaders but also the followers and the relationships between the two. These researchers were well aware that similar research was being conducted in Germany at the time, for many of the same reasons. Blatz (1944), who was the leading Canadian scholar of child development at the time, offered the observation that one can become a leader of a group by either direct or indirect means. 'Direct' means include becoming proficient at activities that are central to the purpose of the group and relating to others in a friendly, persuasive and sensitive manner. 'Indirect' means include securing leadership by force and bullying, as displayed by the Nazis. The problem of bullying continues to preoccupy scholars interested in children's peer relations, as will be discussed in Chapter 5.

One can also trace to the writings of the war years some of the principles that are used to this day in teaching children how to get along with other children (see Chapter 12), although the reasons for wanting to help children in this way have changed dramatically. For example, Blatz (1944) attributed Hitler's leadership to the fact that the latter's messages contained no ambiguities: there was only one way of behaving. In a democracy, children and adults have many choices in their relationships with others; that is what makes it a democracy. Blatz noted that it is more difficult to be effective socially in such a climate of choice and that individuals need help in understanding their choices and deciding which of their options to select in managing their interpersonal relationships. This is, essentially, the basis for social problem-solving lessons, which are often used to prevent children from suffering social failure (see Chapter 12).

Many theorists and researchers around the time of World War II attempted to determine the type of parenting that might lead to children becoming cooperative citizens within democratic societies. Running a home democratically was often seen as the way to do this. Arnold Gesell, one of the foremost child-development theorists of the mid-twentieth century, was influenced by the work of Kurt Lewin, the social psychologist, on the effectiveness of democratic leadership in social and work groups. Gesell advocated democracy in child-rearing (Gesell and Ilg, 1943; Renshaw and Parke, 1992). This theme would be continued many years later in Baumrind's research into the type of parenting that is associated with children being socially successful and cooperative. Baumrind began her longitudinal research at a time when all child behaviors, good and bad, were understood to be reflections of the parenting the children had received. Baumrind continued her follow-up data collection, however, for several decades as awareness of genetic, peer and media influences increased (Baumrind, Larzelere and Owens, 2010). Her work, discussed in Chapter 3, remains influential. Parent training is now one of several components of *multi-modal interventions* that have been proven effective in enhancing the social competence of children at risk for social and emotional maladjustment.

Determining the long-term importance of peer relations in childhood

In their therapeutic work, the pioneer scholars in the peer-relations field insisted on finding out exactly which problems of children would lead to psychological problems in later life and which might disappear as children mature. They felt that this information was needed in order to decide which children required treatment and how to treat them. Therefore, in the 1930s, a number of longitudinal studies – studies in which the same individuals were followed from childhood into their adult years – began (e.g. Walcott, 1932). Undertaking expensive, long-range studies of this type required some skepticism about yet another assumption made by Freud: namely, that it was impossible to predict psychological health over the long term.

> So long as we trace development from its final outcome backwards we feel we have gained an insight which is completely satisfactory or even exhaustive. But if we proceed the reverse way, if we start from the premises inferred from the analysis and try to follow these up to the final result, then we no longer get the impression of an inevitable sequence. Hence the chain of causation can always be recognized with certainty if we follow the line of analysis [i.e. backwards], whereas to predict it . . . is impossible.
>
> *(Freud, 1920, p. 167)*

If, as Freud maintained, it is impossible to predict adult mental health from aspects of children's lives, it becomes difficult to understand when, how, and, indeed, whether to provide help to troubled children (Kohlberg, LaCrosse and Ricks, 1972). However, the results of many longitudinal studies, as summarized in Chapter 2, have shown that some degree of prediction is indeed possible and, as will be detailed in that chapter, that success in early relationships with other children is a reasonably good predictor of doing well as an adult. This has become the reason most scholars of peer relations cite nowadays to explain why they conduct their research. It has also inspired the development of techniques to assist young children to improve their relationships with other children.

Practical techniques for helping children improve their relationships with others achieved enhanced respectability as mental-health practitioners wanted to work more extensively in communities, homes and schools rather than confine their activities to hospitals, clinics and professional offices. The peer-relations researchers of the 1930s went so far as to publish books of advice for parents on how to raise their children to be self-reliant but effective in establishing relations with others. A classic example is Isaacs' (1933) concise interpretation of child development research, which was a bestseller in Britain. In order to place such value on the dissemination of psychological information to the general public, yet another Freudian precept had to be debunked: the idea that transference (the transfer of previous relationship attachments by the patient in psychoanalysis on to the analyst) was the only serious mechanism for achieving therapeutic change and, furthermore, that transference could occur only in the relationship with the analyst. In classical Freudian terms, helpers in the community (as well as supportive friends, parents and teachers) can serve, at best, as secondary, outside adjuncts to treatment, if they do not sabotage the therapeutic process entirely

(Nietzel, Guthrie and Susman, 1991). Interestingly, some contemporary psychoanalysts have discovered the value of 'transfer of the transference' to important people in their clients' lives (Wallerstein, 1989). But how can one conduct psychoanalysis in a working-class neighborhood or inner-city school? It is not surprising that most of the techniques that have been developed to assist children in relating to their peers do not involve analysis of deep, repressed feelings, but, typically, the practical teaching and learning of the ways that lead to being accepted by potential relationship partners. This was attempted, with some success, as early as the 1930s, when Jack (1934), a scholar at the University of Iowa, found that children who were disliked by other children could be helped by simply teaching them to follow the basic rules of a game. Contemporary techniques for improving the peer relations of children and adolescents are considered in Chapter 3.

Thus, by the end of World War II, the gap between peer-relations scholars and psychoanalysts was clear and wide. There were acute differences in terms of the basic understanding of the nature of child, the methods used to learn about child development and the techniques used to assist individuals in difficulty. Since then, the traumatic breach with psychoanalysis has healed only somewhat. Perhaps the best example of recent interest in psychoanalytic ideas in relation to children's peer relations is the growing acceptance of attachment theory in explaining the origins of individual differences in children's ways of relating to other children. Attachment theory, which has been called an 'ethological adaptation of psychoanalytic models' (Rubin, Stewart and Chen, 1995, p. 259), is considered more fully in Chapter 3.

Other than its flirtation with attachment theory, contemporary research on children's friendships and peer relations has largely eschewed complex theories such as those of Moreno and Freud to the point where some prominent researchers are vociferously expressing a need for new ideas and new models. In counterpoint with the attenuation of theoretical richness has come unprecedented methodological sophistication. A contemporary peer-relations researcher looking at a study published fifty years ago would probably understand the subject matter but would find the article odd and primitive only because of its simplistic methodology (Rubin *et al.*, 2013). Longitudinal studies have proliferated; large samples have become the norm. Statistical methods are sophisticated. These refinements are highly valued, although they have come at a price. Direct observations of social interaction and analysis of children's narratives about their relationships do not fit well within the impressive array of statistics in today's publications, to the dismay of some important researchers and theorists. It is likely that new ideas will only emerge when these more time-consuming and more subjective methods are granted a reprieve (Ostrov *et al.*, 2015). These remarks should be complemented with recognition that some of the most sophisticated recent research on peer relations involves physiological processes that we almost completely ignored a generation ago. Indeed, these ventures into psychobiology may lead to very intriguing new theories and insights.

Peer-relations research and the community mental-health movement

Although their rupture with the psychoanalytic community resulted in many peer-relations scholars becoming outcasts in the mental-health community in the 1930s, their popularity surged in the post-war years. Their emphasis on rigorous research techniques and real-world applications was a good match for many of the ideas about child development and mental health that emerged after World War II. Psychological examinations of men reporting for wartime military service in the United States indicated that mental illness was far more widespread than had ever been thought. Over a million men had been rejected from the armed services because of mental-health disturbances. Furthermore, 40 percent of those who were discharged from service were discharged because of mental or neurological disorders (Brand, 1966). It became apparent that such traditional modes of treatment as psychoanalysis would never minister to more than a tiny fraction of those in need (Albee, 1959).

As early as the 1930s, psychiatrists in Western Europe began to experiment quietly with alternatives to institutional care of psychiatric patients, including family care. However, large-scale de-institutionalization did not become a matter of public policy in many Western countries until the 1960s (Brand, 1966). In the United Kingdom, the population of psychiatric hospitals fell from 151,400 in 1954 to approximately 60,000 in 1993, as community service provision became a tenet of national policy (Weller, 1993). More sweeping policy changes occurred in Italy, leading to the almost total abolition of psychiatric hospitals and schools for children with special learning needs (Donnelly, 1992; Dosen, 1994); similar reforms took place in the Scandinavian countries.

Some sources assign part of the credit for the de-emphasis on institutions to the emergence of psychoanalysis, which sensitized both professionals and the general public to the possibility that institutional care was not the only viable mode of treatment for individuals with psychiatric disorders (Brand, 1966). It soon became clear that the most viable and useful treatments that could probably be offered to the individuals being released from institutions would be oriented to the 'common problems of common existence' (Galdston, 1965, p. 462), despite the fact that the psychoanalytic emphasis on in-depth personality change and growth had received widespread acceptance, especially in America. One of the most important of these common problems is, in the words of the prominent community psychologists Albee and Gullotta, how to obtain 'simple sustained human friendship' (1997, p. 18). Unfortunately, many of the psychiatric patients released from institutions, or never admitted to institutions, could not form the interpersonal relationships in the community that were envisaged by proponents of the de-institutionalization movement. Therefore, the need arose for research on the social skills required for community living and the ways of teaching them.

Inclusiveness in schools and the social interaction of pupils

The de-institutionalization movement was extended to school systems in most Western countries. Until the 1960s, it was commonly held that the best way to provide a sound education for children with learning and behavioral problems was to establish special classes or special schools for them. In those self-contained settings, special education techniques could be used to maximize learning. It was a common belief that after a few years of such intensive, needs-specific learning, children would return to regular classes and schools near their homes. However, this assumption was challenged vociferously by ardent critics in the 1960s and the 1970s. Wolfensberger (1972; Wolfensberger and Tullman, 1982), for example, attacked separate special-education classes and schools as a vehicle for the oppression of children with handicaps and for ensuring that their conditions would be perpetuated. In response to such criticisms, legislation in the United States, Italy, Sweden, and many Canadian provinces regulated the placement of children with learning and behavioral problems. Attempts to educate those children in regular classes and schools increased even where they were not required by law.

Critics such as Wolfensberger emphasized the advantage to children without handicaps of receiving education alongside peers who have special learning needs. They hoped that children without disabilities would become familiar with children who have disabilities. Proponents of *mainstreaming* – educating pupils with handicaps in regular schools and classes, rather than in separate, self-contained facilities – expected that, once children with and without disabilities came into regular contact with each other, they would form relationships with each other. The stigma attached to having a disability was also supposed to decrease in these circumstances. These expectations were based on the contact hypothesis, which was formulated by the personality theorist Gordon Allport (1954) in the 1940s and 1950s. Simply stated, this hypothesis holds that contact between majority and minority groups should lead, in general, to reductions in prejudice. However, it is often forgotten that Allport specified that only certain types of contact with a minority group would lead to diminished prejudice. The contact must be regarded by the members of the majority as pleasurable. They must feel a sense of common goals with the members of the minority, and they must regard the individual with whom they interact as a positive exemplar of the minority group.

Sadly, despite many successes, it was quickly determined that many of the mainstreamed children with special learning needs were rejected socially by the peers who were supposed to benefit from their presence (Gresham, 1982; McCoy and Banks, 2012). Many peer-relations researchers took up the task of studying and helping to promote acceptance of children with disabilities as companions in work and play and as friends by children without disabilities. This challenge applies to children with such problematic interaction patterns as bullying and social anxiety as well as children whose social-interaction problems relate to such underlying conditions as intellectual challenge, learning disorders and autism. Recent years have seen a dramatic increase in the numbers of children with autism spectrum disorders, for reasons that are not fully understood (Schneider, 2014). There is, therefore, an unprecedented need for new and better interventions to counter the social-relations deficits that are at the core of autism spectrum disorders.

Cultural diversity in schools and relations among pupils

The contact hypothesis also applies to relationships between children in schools and neighborhoods composed of persons from different cultural heritages. Much attention was paid world-wide to the racial desegregation of US schools in the 1960s. Massive immigration resulted in many families from Asia, Africa, Eastern Europe and Latin America moving to the United States, Canada, most countries of Western Europe, Australia and Israel. Daily contact between children with such diverse backgrounds has never been more possible.

As attention throughout the world centered on the civil rights movement in the United States, which insisted that the separation of the races in schools, on public transport, and in universities be brought to an end, Northway (1967, pp 51–2) urged peer-relations scholars to increase their attention on relationships between members of different racial and cultural groups:

> In this era of the 1960s, when violence has erupted in the North American continent in race riots, senseless murders, tragic assassinations and the like, has sociometry no more to say than it has on this point? . . . Has it neglected its potential contribution to the understanding of groups precipitated into violent action? . . . Would it not be profitable for sociometry to investigate the structure of the huge apartment block, the sprawling vast industry, the suburban neighborhood, the ghettos, the separatists and indeed the Eskimos and Indians of Canada and the Negro–White relationships of the United States? As social chaos has increased, have sociometric relationships broken down? What, for instance, would a sociogram of the hippies look like? . . . The [sociometric] technique is now ready to be used to gain insight into a society living under the threats of extinction by a nuclear bomb . . . and by the pollution of its interpersonal relationships from within.

Thus, thirty years after Moreno had first called on peer-relations scholars to address problems of the world in the throes of world wars, Northway implored the post-war generation of researchers to address real-world social phenomena. Her call was heeded. Although some peer-relations studies seem to focus on matters of theoretical interest only, others have directly examined such issues as the social relations of children living in poverty and the friendships between children of different races and cultural backgrounds, as will be discussed in detail in Chapter 10. Contacts among people of different cultures have increased substantially since Northway's time. There has been unprecedented immigration to North America and Western Europe. Relationships between immigrants and their peers of the majority host culture are seen as fundamental in promoting tolerance and post-immigration adjustment (e.g. Cherng, Turney and Kao, 2014). Hence, Moreno's goal of improving inter-group relations by improving individual interpersonal relationships one by one may have a new home, one that is easier to build and improve than the perfect world for which he strove.

The digital age and the possible decline of intimacy in relationships

Recent societal changes have sometimes been seen as attenuating the intimacy inherent in peer relationships, especially close friendships. Goodwin (2009) notes that intimacy may be incompatible with the individualism that accompanies the 'modernizing' transformation of many contemporary societies. It should be noted that individualism is increasingly intruding into several classic bastions of collectivism, such as East Asia and Latin America (Chen, 2014; García, Rivera and Greenfield, 2015). In their sociological treatise on trends in the history of friendship since World War II, Peel, Reed and Walter (2009) argue that the last half of the twentieth century witnessed the historic peak of the importance of voluntary close friendships, at the expense of the clan and the extended family. It is not clear, however, that friendship ever became as important to boys and men as it did to girls and women. One reason cited for a possible more recent decline is that social interaction increasingly occurs in larger, more anonymous and lonely communities, schools and other institutions than previously. The lack of rich social interaction at the group level fails to spawn intimate relationships at the dyadic level.

However, the most salient reason for the possible decline in intimacy is that, especially for young people, a greater portion of social interaction is occurring by means of electronic communication. Turkle (2011) presents an influential treatise on online relationships entitled *Alone Together: Why We Expect More of Technology and Less of Each Other.* She observes that, although it has become easy to dub online interactions 'friendships', these relationships bear little resemblance to the traditional notions of friendship and are, in particular, devoid of intimacy. If intimacy is declining, attachment theory may be less relevant to relationships than when it was first formulated. The distinction discussed earlier between narrow and broad outcomes of attachment becomes less compelling. However, Schneider and Amichai-Hamburger (2010) observe that the internet may in fact facilitate close interpersonal relating by individuals who have trouble being intimate in face-to-face encounters. In any case, Fletcher *et al.* (2013) hasten to highlight that intimacy is programmed into the interpersonal relationships of humans as a result of a lengthy evolutionary process that is not easily modified.

Chapter 11 includes additional information and speculation about the fate of intimacy in current society. If society is increasing the obstacles in the way of humans pursuing their inherent needs for intimacy and relationships, peer relations have more of a role than ever before in changing the world, relationship by relationship. Indeed, it has been speculated that 'old', close, intimate friendship may be on the increase, despite the digital revolution, because of several other social upheavals.

Urbanization often entails less frequent contacts with family members than in previous eras, which, in turn, means that individuals are more likely to seek from friends they have chosen the social support that came from family members in earlier times. As children are increasingly relegated to social contacts within their own age groups, they are more likely to seek out companionship and support from their age mates than, for example, their siblings or cousins (Peel, Reed and Walter, 2009).

Interpersonal relationships and the search for happiness in life

Although not mentioned as frequently as the other reasons reviewed in this chapter for studying peer relationships, there is some interest in studying and promoting peer relationships for the simple reason that relationships make people happy. Perhaps the quest for happiness is universal or perhaps it is a form of indulgence that can be afforded only by individuals who have no need to be preoccupied with their survival in spite of adverse economic, social and political conditions. The second half of the twentieth century saw massive economic progress in North America, Western Europe, Japan and Australia, although, even in those privileged places and especially elsewhere, a great many individuals still need to be concerned with their own survival. Some authors maintain that a major shift in people's priorities occurred in North America and Western Europe during the 1960s (e.g. Hewitt, 1998). Striving for economic or educational advancement was no longer as strong or ubiquitous a goal as it was in the years immediately after World War II. Happiness and personal fulfillment have become important objectives for many. Many parents became concerned with their children's happiness, achievement of their own goals, and self-concepts. Helping improve children's social relationships is an excellent way to achieve these goals and many others that have not declined in importance, despite arguable changes in society. The many and diverse benefits of relationships to children are outlined in the next two chapters.

2

THE IMPORTANCE OF PEER RELATIONS: COPING WITH THE STRESSES OF LIFE

The dynamics by which peer relations are thought to affect adjustment and maladjustment across the lifespan are outlined, with particular attention to the role of social competence in fostering resilience in the face of adverse early experience. Longitudinal research documenting the links between childhood social competence and subsequent psychological adjustment is critically reviewed, as is research addressing the importance of social competence as a protective factor for children at risk for maladjustment.

The reasons for studying children's relations with their peers mirror the reasons for studying child development in general. Adler and Adler (1998, p. 6) divide the reasons for studying childhood into two main categories. The first category is the study of children because they are considered 'incomplete adults' (see also Qvotrop, 1990). From that perspective, one studies children's lives in order to understand how childhood experiences contribute to the understanding of the same individuals as adults. According to Adler and Adler, this involves the assumption that adulthood is the most important period of life. Childhood is just a transitional period from which one graduates into 'real life'. Adherents of this point of view typically devote considerable attention to how adults prepare children for their future roles in adulthood. They often view children as passive recipients of the teachings of adults.

The alternative is to study childhood because it is an important period, worthy of attention in its own right. Proponents of this position offer the image of childhood as a permanent feature in society: although individuals grow out of childhood, childhood remains an ever-present feature of human existence. Therefore, children's peer relations should be studied as an important aspect of life itself, not as a part of preparation for life (Sutton-Smith, 1982). Those who advocate direct attention to the study of children for its own sake are influenced by the fact that children are quite active in developing independent ways of thinking and functioning quite independently of adults.

Having introduced the distinction between these two categories of reasons for studying child development, Adler and Adler point out that the distinction can be carried only so far because it is not really possible to study children without studying the adults in their social worlds at the same time. The history summarized in Chapter 1 suggests many reasons for studying children's relationships with their peers specifically. However, even the most cursory scan of articles and books in the field will confirm that one of these reasons is widely seen as the most important: namely, the fact that successful peer relations during childhood are linked with general psychological well-being throughout life. It is perhaps human nature that causes parents and teachers to contemplate the behaviors of young children and use what they see as the basis for predicting those children's futures. When it becomes apparent that an adult has not turned out to be the well-adjusted individual that was envisaged, it is also human nature to look back at that person's childhood years in an attempt to find out what went wrong. In the peer-relations field, forward and backward predictions of these kinds serve crucial purposes. First and most fundamentally, they confirm that it is important to study children's peer relations. Second, they indicate which childhood social behaviors are of greatest importance because they are most likely to lead to problems later. For example, there have been many efforts to compare aggressive behavior with shyness/withdrawal during childhood years in order to determine whether either or both remain stable and whether they are equally connected with problems during the adolescent and adult years (studies on that issue will be considered shortly). Such efforts at predicting adult mental health are particularly useful in determining the content of special programs aimed at preventing and treating mental illness. They also help to identify children who are showing early signs of maladjustment, so that early assistance can be provided to minimize the negative outcome.

As noted in Chapter 1, Freud was quite pessimistic about the possibility of predicting the future adjustment of an individual from his or her current behavior. However, considerable knowledge has accrued since his time as result of the work of scholars who have taken up the challenge of prediction, despite Freud's admonitions. Nevertheless, it turns out that Freud was quite perceptive in sensing the pitfalls in making long-term predictions of adjustment. It is a slow and costly enterprise to collect data about the functioning of large groups of children and follow them into adolescence and adulthood. One of the problems in making predictions from longitudinal studies is that some of the children who participate may move to other schools or even other cities. Of course, this is more of a problem in places where there is high population mobility. However, it is conceivable that, in any location, persons with psychological problems relocate more frequently, perhaps because they are unable to find work or keep jobs, or because of strained interpersonal relationships in other settings. In some studies, individuals who reveal to researchers that they had personal problems refuse to participate in subsequent phases of the same study, which they could experience as uncomfortable. The possibility that dropout from longitudinal studies is not a random phenomenon was confirmed by Spiel, Weixelbaum and Spiel's (1999) comparison of the data from participants who agreed and refused to continue in a longitudinal study in Vienna. Those who refused to continue were far more maladjusted than those who remained in the study. Thus, the possibility of losing the most maladjusted individuals before the intended follow-up study is real, and this may be a more acute problem in places such as the United States, where adults tend to change homes and communities more often than in most other places.

In recent years, statisticians have perfected techniques for analyzing longitudinal data sets with many dropouts (e.g. Han, Song and Wang, 2015). However, these sophisticated techniques cannot repair the lack of representativeness if participants with specific characteristics, such as being more maladjusted than most of the sample, drop out in disproportionate numbers, which often happens.

Another major challenge is selecting the child behaviors that one thinks will be associated with adjustment and maladjustment later. It is impossible to change the measures of a longitudinal study retroactively to accommodate improvements in measurement or new thinking about the sources of problems that may emerge as the participating children are growing up. Rubin, Bukowski and Parker (1998) provide some notable examples of longitudinal studies that have been influential and valuable, but that do not provide all of the important information one would now want about the participants' early peer relations. One of them is a longitudinal study by Roff, Sells and Golden (1972), an influential survey in which 38,000 children, aged eight to eleven at the start of the study, were followed for several years. They assessed peer acceptance by asking the participants to indicate the schoolmates whom they would choose as companions (see more detailed discussion of sociometric methods in Chapter 6). Those children who tended not to be chosen as companions displayed a significantly greater chance of becoming juvenile delinquents by age fourteen. However, as did many (although not all) researchers at the time, Roff and his colleagues did not ask for 'last choices' – children who were not chosen. The 'last choices' are likely to be actively disliked, not just ignored. More recent research has confirmed that being actively disliked presents a far greater risk for later maladjustment than simply not being chosen or liked (Rubin, Bowker, McDonald and Menzer, 2013). Furthermore, the combination of being actively disliked (rejected) by peers and displaying aggressive behavior has been found to increase the risk even further (e.g. Coie *et al.*, 1995a; Kupersmidt and Coie, 1990).

Follow-back studies are an alternative to the costly and difficult strategy of collecting data about children and following them into adulthood and adolescence. In follow-back studies, adults or adolescents who are known to have such difficulties as juvenile delinquency or psychiatric disturbance are the participants. The researchers study their backgrounds based on recollections or on information about their childhoods that can be retrieved from archives, such as school records. For the most part, this alternative is decidedly inferior for several reasons. First, the vagaries of the human memory make recollections a very unsatisfactory source of information. People experiencing current problems may try to read the origins of their problems into their recollections of the past, or, like anyone else, they may fail to have recognized or fail to remember important information about their social relations during their childhoods (Ayjan and Isiksal, 2004). Moreover, school or clinical records often do not contain the information the researcher is looking for about childhood peer relations, because they were not designed to include such information systematically. Finally, and most importantly, follow-back studies may be biased because they usually fail to include children who may have had problems during childhood, but managed to overcome them. It is not surprising, then, that these studies generally indicate that adolescents and adults experiencing maladjustment are more likely than others to have had problems getting along with their peers during their childhood years (Parker and Asher, 1987; Rubin, Bukowski and Parker, 1998).

Despite the problems with follow-back studies, probably the most influential existing longitudinal study of children's peer relations used a follow-back strategy. Cowen and colleagues (1973) gained access to a registry of persons receiving psychiatric services in their county in New York State. They were able to compare the names with those of participants in a study they had conducted in the schools between eleven and thirteen years earlier. The names of children who had been identified by their classroom peers during the earlier study as either aggressive or withdrawn were much more likely to appear in the psychiatric register. In fact, of all the information available, it was *only* peer-relations problems that predicted the later use of psychiatric services.

Gender differences in the correspondence between childhood social competence and adult adjustment have often been neglected in the interpretation of longitudinal data, even though such gender differences are often considerable. For example, the results of the Jyvaskyla Longitudinal Study of Personality and Social Development, in which 160 males and 151 females in Finland were followed from age eight to thirty-six, indicate substantial differences in both the childhood behaviors that are forerunners of later difficulty and in the specific difficulties they predict. Overt behavioral problems during childhood predicted later maladjustment for males, whereas more internal emotional problems were the risk factor for females. Having many social problems during childhood predicted 'outer-strand' problems, such as career failure, for both males and females, but the overall accumulation of social problems also predicted an inner sense of failure for females only (Pulkinnen, 1999).

Childhood aggression and long-term adjustment

Aggression among children is highly salient, alarming and disruptive. It is not surprising, therefore, that longitudinal researchers have invested heavily in finding out how stable aggression is and what problems it leads to.

Many of the studies confirm that childhood aggression leads to adult delinquency. These include studies conducted in North America (Brook, Whiteman and

Finch, 1992; Brook *et al.*, 1996; Fite *et al.*, 2010; Fontaine *et al.*, 2008; Kupersmidt and Coie, 1990; Roff, 1990; Rolf and Wirt, 1984; Vitaro *et al.*, 1998) and Europe, especially Scandinavia (Stattin and Magnusson, 1989). Some of the studies also reveal links between childhood aggression and later academic problems (Chen, Rubin and Li, 1995; Ledingham and Schwartzman, 1984; Moscowitz and Schwartzman, 1989; Kupersmidt and Coie, 1990), including the study conducted in China by Chen, Rubin and Li. There is also ample evidence of a link between early aggression and subsequent substance abuse (Brook *et al.*, 1996; Martin-Storey *et al.*, 2011) and with a variety of health problems (Moscowitz and Schwartzman, 1989; Serbin *et al.*, 1991). Longitudinal research has been fundamental in distinguishing the long-term consequences of conduct problems that begin in childhood and late-onset conduct problems that begin during adolescence (e.g. Moffitt and Caspi, 2001).

Some longitudinal studies have focused on the distinction between aggressive children who are and those who are not rejected by their peers (Cillessen *et al.*, 1992; Miller-Johnson *et al.*, 2002; Sandstrom and Coie, 1999). In most of these studies, it has been found that rejection by peers exacerbates the long-term prognosis.

Longitudinal studies of shyness, behavioral inhibition and social withdrawal

It was once believed that childhood shyness is largely an ephemeral phenomenon that disappears with development (Asher, 1985; Coie, 1985). Longitudinal research has challenged this. Although many young children do outgrow their shyness and wariness, there is a group of children who do not. Despite this awareness, there has been less longitudinal research on the long-term consequences of shyness and withdrawal than on aggression. This is not surprising, because shy children are not disruptive. Shyness by itself rarely makes the headlines of newscasts and newspapers. However, it is linked to depression, depression is linked to suicide, and suicide is a drastic outcome that does merit and does receive attention and concern. This has been found in a number of influential longitudinal studies (Burks *et al.*, 1995; Prior *et al.*, 2000; Rubin *et al.*, 1995). Martin-Storey *et al.* (2011) found, at thirty-year follow-up, that male participants who were socially withdrawn in childhood had higher rates of substance abuse than other participants. Social withdrawal in childhood has also been linked to problems in interpersonal and romantic relationships later (Caspi, Elder and Bem, 1988; Kerr, Lambert and Bem, 1996) and with schizophrenia (Frazee, 1953). As detailed in Chapter 9, much of the longitudinal research on the long-term outcomes of childhood social withdrawal has found a new home in China, where rapid social change has altered people's perceptions of socially withdrawn, inhibited children. In contemporary China, these children are not as valued as they were a generation ago.

Much of the longitudinal database on children's social withdrawal suffers from a lack of detail about the withdrawal itself. It is now known that the implications of social withdrawal may depend on its features, such as whether the withdrawal is accompanied by wariness and fear, whether it indicates a general lack of interest in social participation, fear of negative evaluation, and so on. Unfortunately, the researchers cannot travel back in time to collect additional information about the social withdrawal of the participants in longitudinal studies that began decades ago.

Children's friendships as the foundation for intimate relationships in later life

By far, most of the attention in longitudinal studies of peer relations has been devoted to the long-term consequences of being disliked, aggressive, or withdrawn in large groups, such as classrooms or schools. However, it has been argued that this emphasis on rejection by the peer group as a whole obscures a potentially vital link between early peer relations and later adjustment that occurs because of the benefits of having even a single close friend (e.g. Furman and Robbins, 1985). Nowhere are the advantages of friendship assigned as much weight as in the influential theories of the American psychiatrist Harry Stack Sullivan (1953). Sullivan was born in the small agricultural town of Norwich, New York, in 1892. Appalled by the 'waste of human abilities' (Perry, 1982, p. 5) that he observed in his work as a psychiatrist, researcher and consultant for Selective (conscription) Service during World War II, Sullivan became determined to increase the available base of knowledge about raising children. He developed an interpersonal theory of development in which friendships play a key role, and posited that friendships are necessary because they satisfy the human need for interpersonal intimacy and help develop vital social skills and competencies (Bagwell and Schmidt, 2011). More specifically, he proposed that the formation of close, one-on-one relationships during pre-adolescence is crucial to the acquisition of these social competencies (Kerns, 1996). These relationships, called 'chumships', prevent loneliness and enhance children's sense of self-worth. Their relationships to their chums provide children with a means to develop sensitivity to others' problems and perspectives of mutuality in their interpersonal relations. According to Sullivan, this relational base is reflected in later, intimate heterosexual relationships.

Popularity and friendship may contribute in different ways to children's well-being, although children who are generally popular with peers also have a greater likelihood than others of cultivating close friendships. There are convincing reasons why close friendships might have particular implications for coping with life's challenges. As will be detailed in Chapter 7, a relationship with a close friend is characterized by intimacy, unlike children's more superficial relations with the classmates who might regard one as popular. Learning how to form and manage close, intimate relationships may lead to having a close friend to serve as confidant(e) during moments of stress and to having someone who would provide considerable time and practical help when these are most needed.

Participation in a close friendship is also thought to foster flexible thinking in many ways; flexible thinking is known to relate to successful coping with stress (Cantor and Harlow,1994). One of the modes of flexible thinking that is associated with adaptation in the face of adversity is the ability to understand how other people think about things and appreciate that they may have views about a specific situation that are quite different from one's own (see Selman, Levitt and Schultz (1997) for a detailed exposition of how this might occur). It has been emphasized that friends not only gain more knowledge about interpersonal relationships from their friendships than from their contacts with acquaintances, but that one gains in friendship qualitatively different knowledge about relationships, knowledge and skills that are particular to close, supportive bonds (Barr, 1997). Having a close friend has been shown to predict self-concept (Mannarino, 1978; Vandell and Hembree, 1994).

There is much less longitudinal research documenting the long-term implications of friendship during the childhood years specifically than there is with regard to acceptance or rejection by peers in large groups. Indeed, Sullivan emphasized chumship at the very beginning of adolescence; perhaps for that reason, more longitudinal research documenting the benefits of friendship has followed individuals from adolescence into early adulthood. Most of the longitudinal studies conducted with children involve follow-ups for relatively short periods of time, typically less than two years. The range of outcome measures of adjustment is also limited, with more data available about the implications of friendship for adjustment to school than with regard to any other aspect of well-being.

One important exception is a very convincing illustration of the protective power of friendship by Bukowski, Laursen and Hoza (2010). These researchers followed 431 children each year during their first three years of primary school. They focused specifically on the participants who were found to avoid contact with peers and who were also excluded by their peers from group activities at the start of the study. In general, depressed affect increased dramatically over the three years of the study for members of the high-exclusion, high-avoidance group. Importantly, however, this effect was moderated by friendship: there was much less evidence of an increase in depressed affect among children of the high-exclusion, high-avoidance group who had friends. This study is particularly revealing because it demonstrates how one form of peer interaction – namely, having a close friend – can protect from deficits in another aspect of peer interaction – that is, participation in the larger peer group and acceptance by its members.

Another important study on the influences of both close friends and the larger peer group was conducted with Swedish adolescents by Marion and colleagues (2013). These participants were recruited when they were fifteen years old and enrolled in high school. They were subsequently followed for approximately thirty years. Among the participants who were rejected by their high school peer groups, those who had close friendships reported greater satisfaction in life and in their interpersonal relationships than did participants who were rejected by their high school peer group and also did not have close friends at the time.

Another important longitudinal study featured repeated measurement of early adolescents' friendship relations and their depressed moods. Brendgen and colleagues (2010) followed 201 fifth graders (age eleven) for three years. They collected self-reports of depression and friendship nominations each year. The benefits of having a mutual friend depended on whether that friend was depressed. If the friend was not depressed, the self-reported depression was lower. However, participants with depressed friends became more depressed. The depression scores of the few friendless participants were somewhere in between.

Several excellent studies have been conducted to gauge the importance of friendship in the transition to a new school, either at the beginning of primary school at age five or six years (e.g. Ladd, Kochenderfer and Coleman, 1996), or between primary and middle school, at about age twelve years (e.g. Berndt and Keefe, 1992). In general, the supportiveness or closeness of friends seems to facilitate successful adaptation to the new school, whereas 'head counts' of the number of friends one has, regardless of how close they are as friends or how positive they are as models of behavior, seem to be unrelated to adjustment (Hartup and Stevens, 1997). Much more will be said about ways of assessing friendship in Chapter 7, and about friendship and school adjustment in Chapter 4.

Some research has confirmed that friendship serves as a protective factor contributing to the resilience of youngsters considered at risk because they were raised in adverse environments. Conrad and Hammen (1993) found that friendship served as a protective factor for the children of medically ill mothers, though not depressed mothers. Similarly, Pryor-Brown and Cowen (1989) found that social support from both friends and family mediated the relation between stressful life events and adjustment in a large sample of American children in the late elementary school years. In an important study with particular implications for intervention, Schwartz and colleagues (1999) found that friendship helped break the cycle of victimization by bullies: children with good friendships at age five or six years were less victimized by bullies three years later. These important findings have been replicated a number of times, including in a recent longitudinal study by Kendrick, Jutengren and Stattin (2012). Wasserstein and LaGreca (1996) reported that the quality of support from friends mediated the relationship between child-reported parental marital conflict and teacher reports of behavioral problems.

Thus, although there are many inconsistencies, limitations and problems with the available data, and far more longitudinal studies in particular are needed, there is some basis for accepting the contention that friendship is associated with adjustment, particularly among children at risk for maladjustment.

Successful peer relations and children's happiness

As summarized until this point, exhaustive efforts have been made to prove that peer relations in childhood are linked with maladjustment in general, with psychiatric conditions, and with such blatant indications of maladjustment as criminality. This investment of research resources has brought very satisfactory returns, although much still remains to be learned about the long-term course of children's peer relations and their psychosocial adjustment. However, it is important to remember that interpersonal relationships are a major source of satisfaction in their own right. When asked to indicate the people that are important to them, children almost always name friends, though not quite as often as they name parents (Bagwell and Schmidt, 2011; Blyth, Hill and Thiel, 1982; Kiesner, Kerr and Statin, 2004).

There has been very little research on what makes children happy, but there are a few relevant studies. Westman (1990) asked young adults to recall what made them happy when they were children. She was interested particularly in determining whether it was contact with people or the receipt of toys or other gifts that would remain more salient in their memories. Interpersonal contact was cited as the main source of childhood happiness. Contrary to folk wisdom, 89 percent of the participants in the study mentioned specific persons in their responses, compared with only 39 percent who mentioned gifts they had received (most frequently a bicycle). Although many of the interpersonal contacts that were recalled as sources of happiness involved family members (parents 60 percent; brothers and sisters 17 percent; other relatives 24 percent), friends were involved in as many of the happy recollections as parents were: 60 percent. (Totals exceed 100 percent because many of the university students recalled more than one happy childhood experience.) Several Canadian studies conducted with early adolescents have demonstrated that pupils who consider themselves socially withdrawn or introverted also indicate that they are unhappier than other pupils in the same classes (e.g. Young and Bradley, 1998).

Children's peer relations: cause or effect of life-long adjustment or maladjustment?

It is very important to remember that the longitudinal evidence reviewed in this chapter provides no proof that positive or negative peer relations in childhood are the cause of mental health or mental illness. This issue is discussed in detail by Parker and Asher (1987) in their very influential review article. The difference between causal and incidental models is depicted in Figure 2.1, reproduced from Parker and Asher's paper. As suggested by the title of their figure, these models represent implicit assumptions made by the authors of the original research, who often skirt the issue of causation. According to the causal model, poor peer relations result directly in maladjustment. As depicted in Figure 2.1, this may occur because children who do not relate well with peers may be excluded from social interactions where important new skills are learned and practiced. In contrast, the incidental model maintains that the maladjustment is already there at the time of the child's difficulties with other children. The peer-relations deficit is but one of many manifestations of the disorder.

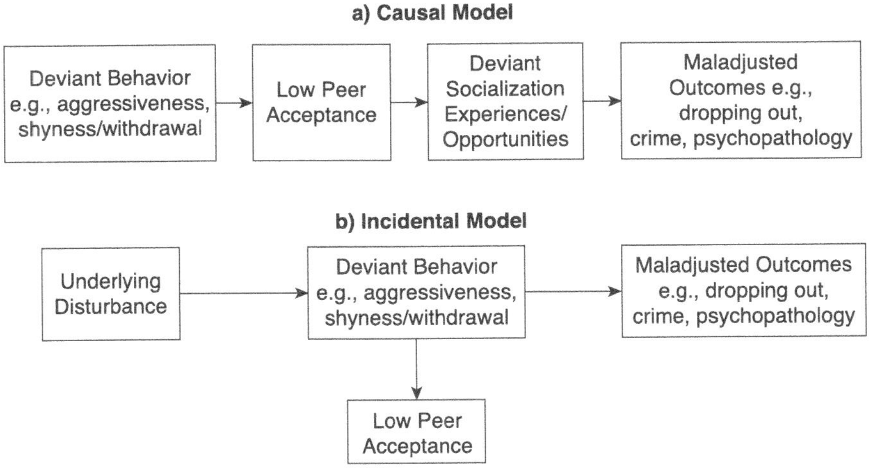

FIGURE 2.1 Implicit models concerning the link between peer relationship problems and later maladjustment (Source: Parker and Asher, 1987)

Of course, most peer-relations scholars and most teachers and parents who advocate the promotion of social competence in schools and communities probably ascribe, if only implicitly, to the causal model. Sophisticated statistical techniques, called *structural equations modeling*, can be applied to longitudinal data in order to determine how likely it is that patterns of peer relations cause psychological well-being or distress. However, even that technological advance cannot provide conclusive proof of causation. Therefore, it is important not to overinterpret the very convincing longitudinal evidence.

Current status of longitudinal research on children's peer relations

Like any other studies, longitudinal studies can be interpreted only as products of the eras in which the research was conducted. Pioneering studies began in the period between the two world wars. The developmental psychopathology movement emphasized longitudinal research to trace and to determine the trajectories of normal and abnormal development across the lifespan. This led to many longitudinal studies beginning in the years between 1960 and 2000. Developmental psychopathologists emphasize life-long development. Some of the landmark longitudinal studies have continued their follow-ups into the old-age years of their original participants and even into the next generation, studying the offspring of the original participants. Most of the developmental psychologists conducting longitudinal research, however, felt that their job was complete once they had followed their childhood participants into adolescence and adulthood. Because of the social changes that have occurred since then (see Chapter 1), it seems important to track the future development of today's children with high and low levels of social competence. However, given the enormous cost of longitudinal studies, it is understandable that many researchers may not wish to invest so heavily in research that may lead merely to replication of previous findings. Replication of research is an essential and important aspect of the research process, but, unfortunately, it is not valued highly in the academic world. Therefore, the existing database of longitudinal studies, which consists disproportionately of now-dated information, must be accepted as the best proof available of the long-term importance of rewarding peer relationships during childhood and adolescence.

In brief, the many longitudinal studies have documented that problems in early peer relationships *do* predict adjustment difficulties in later life. It is important to remember that this prediction is not perfect: many individuals who experience problems in relating to others during childhood overcome these problems in later stages of their development. Nevertheless, the longitudinal evidence of the predictive power of early peer relations has inspired many programs for the prevention and early correction of social-skills deficits in schools, as will be discussed in Chapter 12.

3

WHERE DOES SOCIAL COMPETENCE COME FROM?

This chapter provides a capsule sketch of the antecedents of children's social competence. Genetic factors appear to explain individual differences in social behavior to a substantial degree. Social learning theory maintains that children learn much of their social behavior by observing others, including peers and adults alike. Attachment bonds between parents and children are also linked to children's peer relations, as are parents' styles of child-rearing. Relatively little is known about the potentially important influences of siblings, schoolmates and neighbors in influencing the social interactions of children. The chapter closes with a challenge to popular thinking about the causes of social behavior by insisting that variations in social behavior probably have multiple roots, rather than single causes that can be pinpointed.

For a species that is supposed to be programmed for cooperation in order to survive, humans show remarkable variation in their cooperativeness and in many other aspects of their social behavior. As detailed in the previous chapter, individual differences in social behavior have been traced longitudinally from early childhood through adulthood. The differences are often stable and are related – to some extent – to individual differences in well-being. Hence, determining the origins of individual differences in patterns of relating to others is not only important because it satisfies our curiosity, but, to the extent that the differences stem from causes that can be controlled or modified, such research can lead to meaningful measures aimed at preventing maladaptive social behavior. This book would be incomplete without some discussion of the origins of children's peer relations. However, space permits only a cursory treatment of these issues.

Parents' genetic contribution in interplay with the environment

Figure 3.1 depicts the major theories offered in the developmental literature to explain individual differences in social behavior. The central issue in the debate

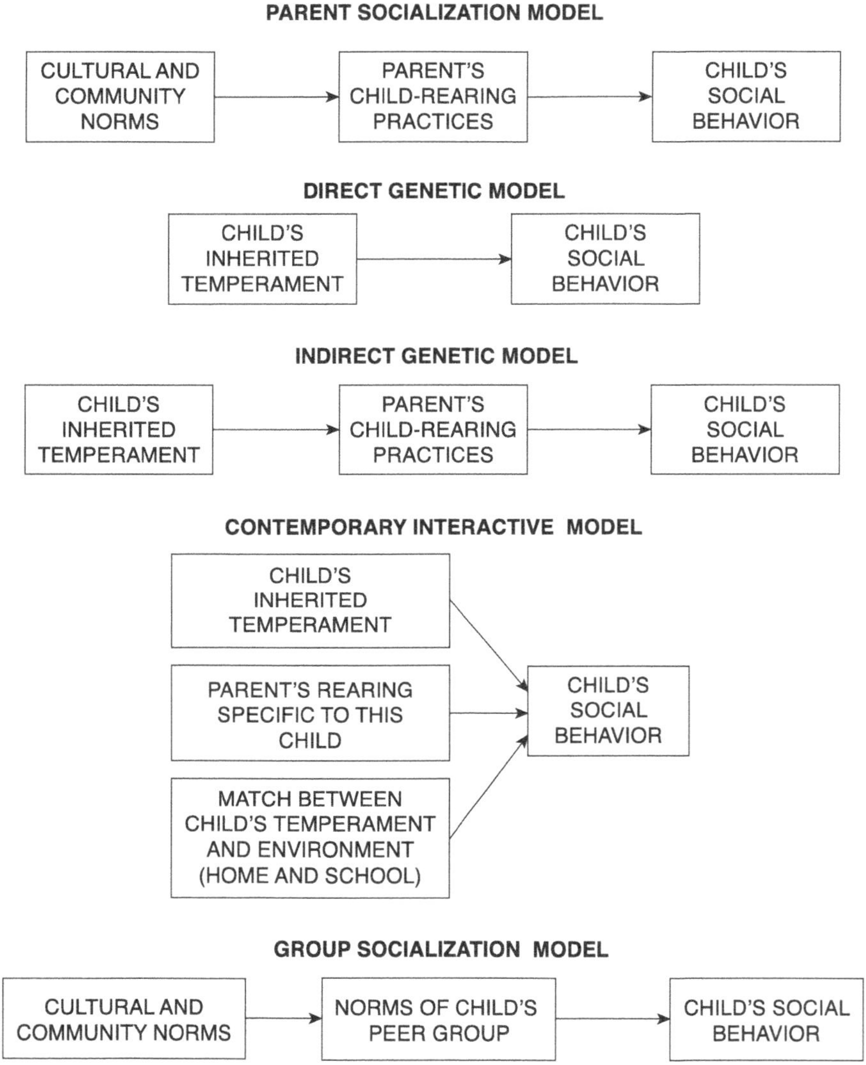

FIGURE 3.1 Causal links discussed in the developmental literature

about the relative validity of these theories is how much of children's social behavior is caused by heredity versus how much can be explained by the environment, especially the environment provided by parents. The concept of temperament has been useful in research designed to determine whether patterns of social behavior are inherited or acquired from the environment. Temperaments are stable modes of responding in social situations; and temperament can be considered the childhood equivalent of the notion of personality, which is used more frequently in reference to adults. There are wide differences in temperament among children, ranging from approachable and sanguine to colicky and distant. These wide differences in sociability and temperament and their relative stability have led some authorities to suspect that children are, at least to a certain extent, pre-wired to behave a certain way.

The field of behavioral genetics aims to tease out the effects of inborn, dispositional influences and the effects of the human environment on children's temperament and social behavior. In order to do this, behavioral geneticists focus their study on genetic influences and environmental influences that are and are not shared by family members. Much of that research must, of necessity, be conducted with atypical family situations, such as twins who were separated at birth and reared apart, or adopted children. This is because, when studying children who are not twins and who come from intact families, it is difficult to separate the genetic and environmental influences, precluding any quantitative estimate of hereditability. Nevertheless, studying these exceptional populations is not without its problems: for example, if the innate temperament of the adopted child determines in some way the family environment into which he or she is adopted.

Brendgen (2012) offers an authoritative and very accessible review of research on the genetic basis of children's peer relations. She begins with a sweeping statement that would have been very controversial a generation or two ago but probably is not now, contending that there is wide consensus that *both* genetic and environmental influences determine virtually every aspect of human development. No longer do scientists believe that genetic and environmental factors work independently of each other for the most part, only rarely acting in concert or influencing each other. Researchers are now very aware of both *gene–environment correlations* and *gene–environment interactions.* These two forms of gene–environment interaction are depicted in Figures 3.2 and 3.3

The term 'gene–environment correlations' refers to situations in which heritable factors co-occur with specific environments. This can arise when genetically determined traits or behaviors influence the nature of the environment the person may have. For example, very athletic children may end up in sports clubs chosen by parents who see and wish to develop their children's athletic ability. *Selective* gene–environment correlation arises when part of the environment is influenced by an individual trait of genetic origin. This occurs, for example, when aggressive children seek out other aggressive children as friends, resulting in a peer culture that is highly aggressive. *Evocative* gene–environment correlation occurs when an individual characteristic that is of genetic origin leads to specific reactions from the social environment. This happens, for example, when the aggressive behavior of a child leads to rejection and scorn by his/her peer group.

Besides gene–environment correlation there is *gene × environment interaction.* This may occur when the effects of heredity depend on the nature of the environment. The environment may *trigger* the inherited trait or the environment may *suppress* the inherited trait. A trigger may be pulled, for example, when a child who is genetically predisposed to being aggressive is harassed in a peer group.

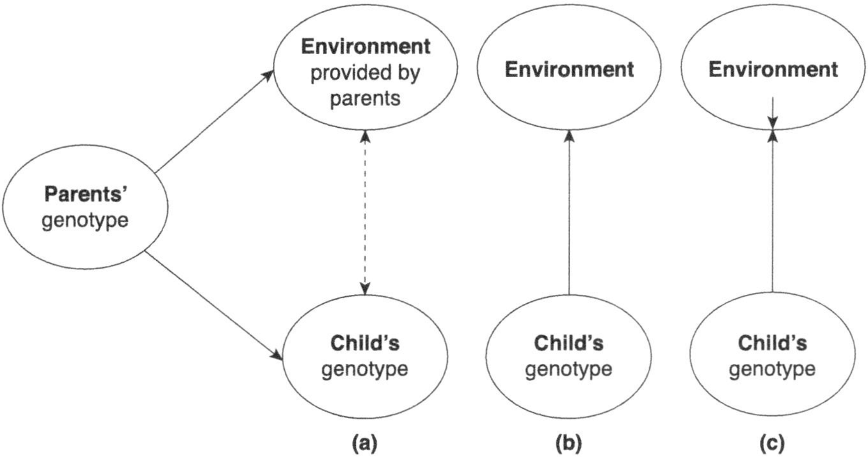

FIGURE 3.2 (a) Passive rGE. A Passive rGE between the child's genotype and the environment arises as a by-product because both are influenced by the parents' genotype. (b) Selective rGE. A Selective rGE between the child's genotype and the environment arises because the child actively shapes his or her environment in accordance with his or her genetically influenced characteristics. (c) Evocative rGE. An Evocative rGE between the child's genotype and the environment arises because the child's genetically influenced characteristics elicit a reaction from the environment (Source: Brendgen, 2012, used with permission of John Wiley and Sons)

Genetic influences have long been studied quantitatively in twin and adoption studies. Comparing monozygotic (identical) twins, whose genetic endowment is identical, with dizygotic (fraternal) twins has provided invaluable evidence of the genetic basis of children's peer relations. Additional information is added by comparing, where possible, twins reared together and twins who have been reared apart for some reason. In addition to these twin studies, quantitative genetics research has relied heavily on adoption studies, in which adopted children are compared to their natural and foster parents. In recent years, quantitative genetics has been supplemented extensively by exciting new techniques in *molecular genetics*, in which genetic material is examined directly.

Brendgen (2012) cites a number of studies in which gene–environment interplay has been documented. In this literature, the relative contributions of genetic and environmental factors are often reported in terms of a hereditability index, expressed as an estimated percentage of causation. For example, quantitative genetics studies on the genetic basis of antisocial young people becoming friends reveal that genetic factors are responsible for anywhere from 20 to 64 percent of the causation of such affiliations, depending on the sources of information about the behavior. Substantial genetic causation of affiliation with deviant friends has recently emerged from molecular genetics research, in which genetic material

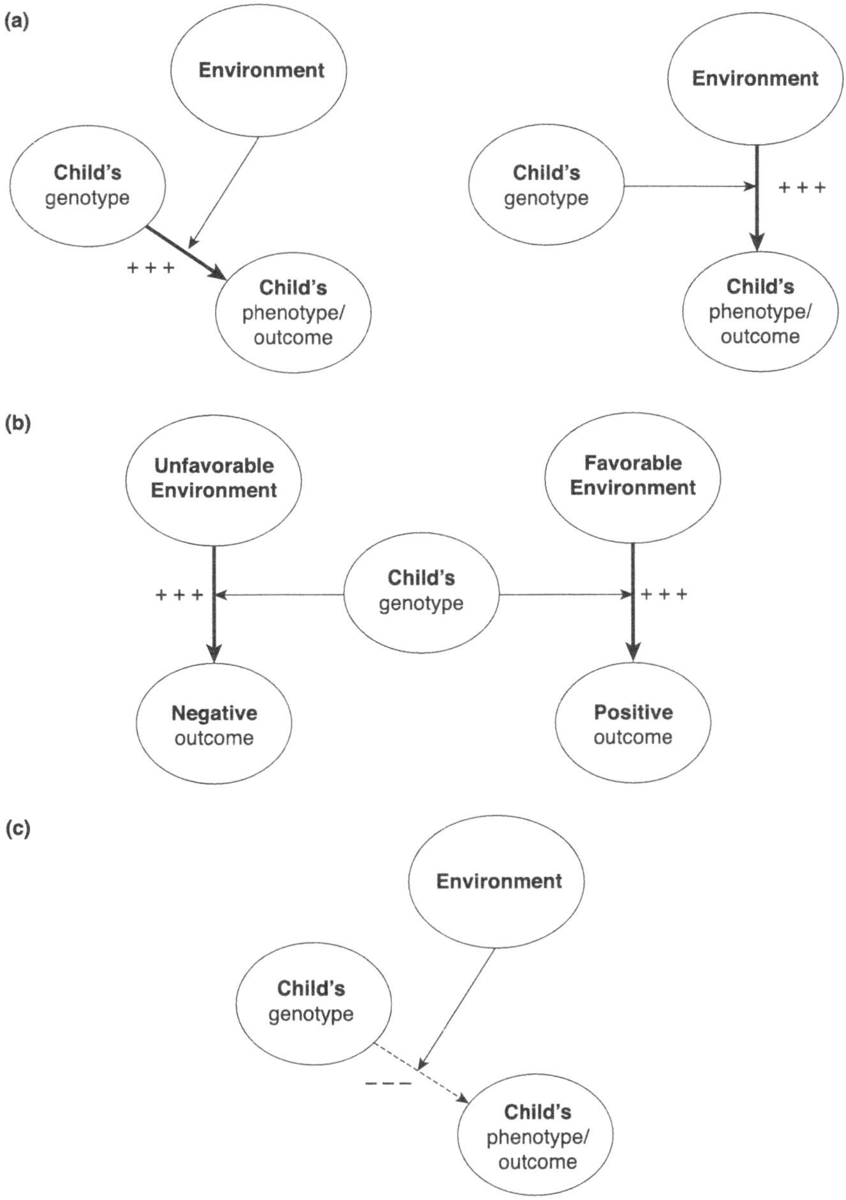

FIGURE 3.3 (a) Trigger process of GxE. A Trigger process of GxE arises because the environment exacerbates the influence of genetic factors on developmental outcomes or because the child's genotype exacerbates environmental influences on developmental outcomes. (b) Differential susceptibility process of GxE. A Differential susceptibility process of GxE arises because some genotypes exacerbate the effect of unfavorable and favorable environments on developmental outcomes. (c) Suppression process of GxE. A Suppression process of GxE arises because the environment reduces the influence of genetic factors on developmental outcomes (Source: Brendgen, 2012, used with permission of John Wiley and Sons)

is examined directly (Brendgen, 2012; Fowler, Settle and Christakis, 2011). Acceptance or rejection by peers may also act to suppress or trigger internalizing behaviors, such as depressive feelings (Brendgen, 2012). There is ample evidence of a substantial genetic basis of children's shyness (see A.K. Smith *et al.*, 2012), but this may vary depending on the form of shyness (e.g. self-conscious or fearful; Eggum-Wilkins *et al.*, 2015). The genetic basis of aggressive behavior is very well established but recent research also demonstrates a genetic basis for children being *targets* of aggression (DiLalla and John, 2014).

Observational learning

It will come as little surprise to caregivers who work with groups of children that the processes of observation and imitation have been found to influence individual patterns of relating to peers. This is part of the more elaborate *social learning theory* pioneered by Bandura and Walters (1963), which became prominent in the 1960s and 1970s. One of the tenets of social learning theory is that peers are important influences on each other's social behavior, as was emphasized by Judith Rich Harris, whose views will be discussed shortly, although she does not identify specifically with social learning theory.

Social learning theory can be regarded as a successor to classic reward-and-punishment behaviorism because it added important dimensions of observational learning and vicarious learning or punishment. A child does not have to be rewarded specifically for a particular behavior in order to adopt it but may be influenced by seeing one of his/her peers reinforced for it. Although the heyday of social learning was the 1970s, the theory is still regarded as a major influence on peer-relations research to this day (Rubin *et al.*, 2013).

Child–parent attachment

Attachment theorists profess that an attentive caregiver provides a 'secure base' to support the child in its exploration of its objective and interpersonal environment. Bowlby (1969, 1978, 1990) suggested that infants create 'internal working models' of themselves, their world and social contacts within their world. This follows from Craik's assertion that 'the organism carries a small-scale model of external reality and its own possible actions within its head' (1943, p. 61). 'Internal working models' are essentially mental pictures of relationships that the child uses to understand and predict others' behavior. As the child matures, his or her models broaden and evolve to incorporate the expanding social world.

Internal working models are adaptable to environmental change, but their modification is not an easy task. This is because the models are centered on conservative expectancies which can govern behavior so as to confirm these expectations. An example of this would be an individual who expects repudiation and consequently invites such an attack, thereby confirming prior, ingrained expectations. Because models of others' behavior are sculpted by a child's particular environment, they may be resistant to change regardless of their incompatibility with and inaccurate reflection of the reality of the child's peers.

The basic assumption that security of attachment influences a child's adjustment has been challenged by several investigators. For example, Grusec and Lytton (1988) questioned the causal nature of attachment, proposing that attachment reflects the child's overall adaptation and adjustment; these forms of resilience may have other sources. Arguing that the internal working model has been used as a catch-all, Hinde (1988) contended that it is used in attachment theory to explain stability too generally. Hinde maintained that the existence and role of internal working models have not been determined convincingly and that temperament and other non-attachment models may explain stability just as effectively. Lewis and Feiring (1989) also maintained that there is weak empirical evidence for the major suppositions of attachment theory. They asserted that non-parental figures may be crucial to a child's socialization, but that theorists often fail to acknowledge this. Belsky and Cassidy (1995, p. 383) suggested that theorists should be cautious when applying internal working models to developmental processes: 'the notion of internal working models as the causal process explaining the associations between attachment security and the developmental sequelae remains a useful interpretive heuristic in need of empirical evaluation'. Parent–child attachment bonds are sometimes thought to be the result of the parent's sensitivity and responsivity (Spieker and Booth, 1988). In addition, the child's temperament, the parent's personality and the stress under which the parent lives may also influence the attachment bond. Together with the infant's emotionality, the infant's sociability is assumed to influence the security of the attachment between children and parents.

Attachment is usually measured with either the Strange Situation technique or the Q-sort method, with the former the better known of the two. This procedure involves studying the interactions of mothers and children in an unfamiliar situation – the laboratory – that can produce some stress. At the beginning, the mother and the child become familiar with the laboratory room, which contains several chairs and some toys so that the infant is free to explore his or her new surroundings; the infant's initial willingness to explore is carefully noted by the researchers from behind a one-way mirror. A stranger then enters the room and, a minute later, begins a conversation with the mother. Next, the mother leaves the child alone with the stranger. Then the stranger leaves and the mother returns. At the end of the procedure, the baby is left alone for a short time; then the stranger returns and finally the mother returns for a reunion with her child (Ainsworth and Whittig, 1969). The situation is probably no more stressful than numerous separations and reunions that occur in a typical infant's life, but, of course, the more stressful sessions are shortened if the baby shows a very strong reaction to the procedure, which can be aborted totally in the rare case of an extreme reaction. The child's behavior in the Strange Situation is used to classify his/her attachment bonds. If he or she is secure enough to explore the new surroundings before the mother leaves, becomes distressed when the mother leaves and welcomes her cheerfully upon her return, the infant is securely attached, which characterizes about two-thirds of the child population. Secure attachment is believed to serve as a healthy foundation for exploring the world and the vagaries of close personal relationships later (Bowlby, 1980). More than 20 percent of children are typically classified as anxious-avoidant in their attachment bonds because they are not anxious when the mother leaves and avoid her when she returns. About one child in ten is classified as anxious-ambivalent: they show signs of distress during the whole procedure, but especially when separated from their mothers (Ainsworth *et al.*, 1978). Cross-cultural studies indicate substantial similarity in the proportions of children assigned to the various groups, although the proportions of babies in the two categories of insecure attachment vary somewhat in non-Western cultures (e.g. van Ijzendoorn and Kroonenberg, 1988).

Although the Strange Situation technique has been the predominant tool in attachment research, there has been some call for alternatives that would allow for the measurement of attachment in more natural situations and without stress induction. Of course, this is more than a matter of measurement: instruments designed for use outside the laboratory and under different conditions may not be measuring attachment in the same sense as the Strange Situation. The Attachment Q-set (Waters and Deane, 1985) is a scale of ninety items, with each pertaining to attachment, that can be used by observers of the interaction between parents and their children. There is some evidence that observers' scores correlate with Strange Situation data, although mothers' own ratings when using the Q-sort items appear not to (Tarabulsy *et al.*, 1997).

Inspired by this intriguing theory, a number of researchers have conducted studies comparing children's parental attachment histories with their peer relationships. Some of these studies measure attachment and peer relationships at the same point in time. Others are longitudinal studies, in which the researchers try to predict the nature of children's peer relationships from earlier attachment data. Of course, the latter provides the better test of the theory, but even longitudinal studies documenting the link between early parent–child attachment and children's peer relations at later stages cannot rule out the possibility that some other cause is responsible for the children's successes or failures in their relationships with other children. Schneider, Atkinson and Tardif (2001) conducted a meta-analysis (a statistical summary of the results of all the research conducted to date) of the studies on attachment and children's peer relations. Their database consists of sixty-three studies, about half of which are longitudinal studies. The average correlation between mother–child attachment scores and data pertaining to children's peer relations is .20, which is significant but by no means large. This statistic supports the validity of attachment theory only to some extent and seems somewhat incongruous with the sweeping causal statements made by attachment theorists. Importantly, the average correlations seem not to differ substantially between studies in which Strange Situation and

Q-sort methods were used. However, Schneider, Atkinson and Tardif noted that the correlations were somewhat higher in studies where the indicators of peer relations pertained to close friendships rather than to relationships in large groups; the correlations between parent–child attachment and indicators of friendship were substantially higher than the overall average (in the .30 range). The authors maintained at the time that because a primary intimate relationship is more likely to be mirrored best in subsequent intimate relationships, the data on friendship may be the more relevant indices of the predictive strength of attachment theory.

This effect was no longer evident in a follow-up meta-analysis conducted thirteen years later by Pallini and colleagues (2014). The new meta-analysis was based on forty-four new, original studies conducted between 1998 and 2013. The average effect size for the overall correlation between child–parent attachment and all measures of children's peer relations was within a few decimal points of the effect size in the 2001 meta-analysis. This provides reassuring support for one of the most basic tenets of attachment theory. However, the effects for measures of friendship were no longer different in any substantial way. The reasons for this are not clear, although the authors speculate that the possible decline in intimacy in close relationships, discussed in Chapter 1, may explain the differences between the original review and the update.

It is important to note that the contribution of child–father attachment to the emergence of children's peer relations remains relatively unexplored according to the data reported in both of these meta-analyses. However, one important recent longitudinal study has documented the importance of child–father attachment in the emergence of dyadic friendships. Verissimo and her colleagues (2011) followed a group of pre-schoolers from age two to age four years. Attachment to fathers was highly correlated with attachment to mothers, as it often is. However, it was child–father attachment, not child–mother attachment, that predicted the child's engagement in dyadic relationships with friends at the later age.

Fathers – important but perhaps not in the same way

In many societies, the stereotypical role of the mother includes raising the children. Like many stereotypes, there is probably an element of truth here, despite the progress made in many countries toward gender equity. This does not mean that child–father attachment is unimportant in general. In fact, child–father attachment may have specific importance in shaping the child's interactions with the outside world, including peers. The quality of the time spent together by children and their fathers varies enormously from one family to the next (e.g. Williams and Kelly, 2005). The different but not unequal contributions of mother and father attachment have been summarized by Richard Bowlby, son of John Bowlby, the pioneer 'father' of attachment theory, and reported in an article by Newland and Coyl (2010). One role, typically filled more by mothers than by fathers, is the provision of love and security. Another attachment role, and not an insignificant one, is encouraging the exploration of the outside world and providing exciting and challenging experiences, which, Richard Bowlby maintains, is often the father's job. Thus, the typical father's role is not that of a 'second-class, alternate attachment figure' (Newland and Coyl, 2010, p. 26). In helping children prepare for interactions with the outside world, fathers may play a vital role in teaching the skills that are involved in adapting to new environments and in coping with the problems that may arise in doing so (Williams and Kelly, 2005). Fathers may encourage the exploration of the outside world by getting involved with their young children in physical activity and social play. In doing so, they assist their children in learning to take judicious risks when leaving the secure home base of the family. Fathers bond with older children during leisure-time activities (Bretherton, Lambert and Golby, 2005; Paquette and Bigras, 2010). Although they might do this in indelicate ways, it has been found that fathers who occasionally engage in frightening play with their children may not damage attachment bonds with their children if they are generally sensitive in their interactions with them. This does not apply to mothers, whose frightening behavior has been linked with disorganized attachment bonds (Hazen *et al.*, 2010).

Many attachment experts maintain that father involvement is associated with positive outcomes for children and that father absence has devastating consequences. Pleck (2007) argues that time spent with fathers is not, by itself, an appropriate variable that merits the attention of researchers. Studies must go on to consider what the father brings to the relationship and how the time is spent. Lucassen and her colleagues (2011) add that sensitivity to the child's feelings and needs is not nearly as strong a correlate of attachment to fathers as it is to maternal attachment. Thus, the constructs used in studying child–mother attachment may not be as useful in studying child–father attachment or, indeed, other aspects of parenting that may relate to children's peer relations.

In a study of general parenting style, Meunier, Bisceglia and Jenkins (2012) found some evidence that mothers' positivity may combine with fathers' positivity in a simple additive way, but that the negative influences of mothers and fathers tend to compound in a multiplicative fashion. They also found that the interactive effects of parenting by mothers and fathers in two-parent families differed somewhat according to the age of the child and the nature of the child outcome being predicted. More research into the combined influences of fathers and mothers is strongly needed.

A cross-cultural perspective as well as a focus on changes in Western socieities would make this literature more relevant. In anywhere from 5 to 20 percent of recent case studies, the father emerges as the child's preferred attachment figure, even in the traditional sense of providing love and security (Freeman, Newland and Coyl, 2010). There has been little research on the father role in blended families, single families, and same-sex marriages and unions, which have become far more common. The role of grandparents has changed in many Western societies, where there is often less contact with extended family members than in previous generations. However, grandparents still play an important role for most grandchildren, and even more so for children of teenage mothers (Radin, Oyserman and Benn, 1991; see Dunifon, 2013, for a review of the research on grandparenting).

Child-rearing: the causal factor that is most amenable to change

It was established earlier in this chapter that shared environmental influences, such as parents' child-rearing styles, explain very little of the origins of children's social competence, to the disappointment of many, including the hundreds of researchers who have conducted studies on this topic. Judith Rich Harris (1998), the outspoken American writer mentioned in Chapter 1, mounted a vociferous challenge to the time-honored 'nurture assumption' – the belief that children's behavior is caused by the way their parents raise them. She insists that many people – university researchers, religious leaders and psychologists who give advice to parents – possess a passionate need to believe in the nurture assumption. Their fervor blinds them to the scientific fact that, although many children do resemble their parents, it is not necessarily the parents' child-rearing that accounts for the similarities. In rejoinder, several critics, such as the Harvard University professor Jerome Kagan (1998), have lambasted Harris for attending selectively to evidence that supports her position while ignoring other data. More will be said about Harris's group socialization theory later in this chapter.

Even if child-rearing does not have as causal a role, as once thought, there remain important reasons for studying it. Perhaps the most important of these is that, of the various causes of children's social competence, parents' child-rearing is one of the most amenable to change. Science may yet develop methods for altering genetic material on a large scale. Effective interventions based on attachment theory have been introduced (e.g. Marvin *et al.*, 2002). Attachment theorists recognize that exceptional positive life experiences can mitigate the negative effects of insecure attachment bonds between parents and children. However, most attachment theorists maintain that such effects tend to be relatively stable (Ainsworth and Marvin, 1995). In contrast, parents' ways of raising their children are, at least in theory, under their own control. Although changing those ways is not easy, it can be accomplished, as evidenced by the success of many systematic parent-training programs, such as those of Gerald Patterson, whose structured parent training intervention has proven successful in managing the antisocial behaviors of predelinquent youth (Forgatch and Patterson, 1998). Even if a trait is genetically determined to a considerable extent, an appropriate environment may mitigate the effects of the genetic pre-programming on the observable behavior of the individual child. This is the core of Chess and Thomas's (1996) concept of goodness of fit, which emphasizes that children's overt behavior and adjustment depend on the abilities of families and schools to provide them with an environment that 'fits' their temperaments – that is, an environment that offers the degree of structure, predictability and support needed by individuals of one's particular temperament. It is also very important to remember that much of the heated nature-versus-nurture debate about the origins of children's social behavior centers on individual differences – deciding, for example, whether parents' child-rearing practices can explain why some children are more aggressive than others, some children more shy than others, and so on.

Emphasizing individual differences obscures – to some extent – the very important responsibility that parents have in the upbringing of all children: teaching the general values of the culture and the way its institutions and interpersonal relationships work. It is sometimes said that the influence of the family is weakening in contemporary Western societies. However, the Norwegian sociologist Ivar Frones (1995) maintains that the family is more necessary than ever in teaching children about the cultures of adults because institutions outside the family are becoming less guided by tradition and therefore less active and less consistent in promoting its maintenance.

It is also possible that some important effects of child-rearing have been overlooked in research. Scarr (1992) proposed that, within the range of family atmospheres and child-rearing methods that characterize most of the population, differences in family environments may not be very consequential. However, extreme environments may indeed exert a heavy toll on children growing up in them. Such extreme conditions are not adequately represented in behavior-genetics studies. Although extreme negative conditions come first to mind when this concept is discussed, it is also possible that extreme positive environmental conditions may be very important to the child who is prone to maladaptive behavior by virtue of his or her genetic predisposition. Because parents and children share some of their genetic predisposition, research results showing correlations between parents' child-rearing and children's social behavior cannot prove that child-rearing is the cause of the children's social-interaction styles (Scarr, 1992). However, as mentioned previously, research of this type is important in providing guidance for parent-education programs and for the treatment of children displaying atypical patterns of social behavior.

Although parenting practices can be described in myriad ways, Baumrind's classification system has served as the basis for the most comprehensive and influential research on parenting styles. Baumrind (1989; Baumrind, Larzelere and Owens, 2010) distinguishes between authoritarian, permissive and authoritative parenting styles. The authoritarian style involves strict limits, enforced by punishment, whereas permissive parents place very few restrictions on their children. The authoritative style involves parental warmth and clear limits backed up by reasoning rather than punishment; or, as clarified and emphasized in some of Baumrind's writings, reasoning plus the occasional, judicious use of non-abusive forms of punishment within the context of a positive parent–child relationship (Baumrind, 1996).

The child-rearing practices linked to children's social competence are not easy to synthesize. As summarized by Rubin, Bukowski and Parker (1998), parents of socially competent children have been found to be more child-centered, feelings-oriented and warmer than parents of other children; they also tend to use reasoning very frequently in disciplining their children. In contrast, the parents of aggressive children have been found in various studies to be punitive (Eron *et al.*, 1963; Felson and Russo, 1988; Gordon and Smith, 1965; Larzelere, 1986; McCord, McCord and Howard, 1961; Olson *et al.*, 2011; Patterson and Cobb, 1971; Pettit *et al.*, 1991; Sears *et al.*, 1953; Strassberg *et al.*, 1992; Weiss *et al.*, 1992), overly permissive or excessively indulgent (Lesser, 1957; Levy, 1966; Olweus, 1980; Sears, 1961), authoritarian and dictatorial (Becker *et al.*, 1959, 1962), and excessively restrictive or controlling (Harralson and Lawler, 1992; Pettit, Dodge and Brown, 1988). They do not respond adequately to positive expressions of emotion by their children (Dumas and LaFrenière, 1993). Parents of shy/withdrawn children tend to be distant, cold (Rosenthal *et al.*, 1962), protective (Eisenberg, 1958; Engfer, 1993; Lorion et al., 1977), restrictive (Watson, 1957), hostile (Becker *et al.*, 1962; Dumas and LaFrenière, 1993), and domineering (Symonds, 1939). Parents of shy girls (but not boys) who demonstrate active and responsive problem-solving to their children tend to have children who are not rejected by peers even though they are shy (Miller, Brody and Murry, 2010). Finally, parents who are involved with their children (Kennedy, 1990; Ladd and Hart, 1992; Lindsey, Mize and Pettit, 1997; MacDonald and Parke, 1984; MacDonald, 1987; Pettit *et al.*, 1998), encouraging of the expression of emotion (Putallaz, 1987; Roberts and Strayer, 1987), who explain their thinking to them (Franz and Gross, 1996; Hart *et al.*, 1992; Roopnarine and Adams, 1987), who provide democratic households (Baldwin, 1948; Dekovic and Janssens, 1992), who are fair and consistent (Dishion, 1990) tend to have children who are competent socially. Parents who support the development of their children's social skills and their children's relationships at school have children who are less likely to be bullied than others (Healy, Sanders and Iyer, 2015). Thus, most research is consistent with Baumrind's (1989; Baumrind, Larzelere and Owens, 2010) well-known longitudinal studies that indicated the superiority of authoritative parenting over permissive or authoritarian styles, by showing that the children of authoritative parents grew up to have more positive peer relations.

It is almost a reflex to infer that the parents' behavior is the cause of the child's behavior, but that is not necessarily so; the child's aggressiveness could be the cause of the parents' punitiveness rather than vice versa (e.g. Besnard *et al.*, 2013). These child-rearing behaviors may interact with the parent's relationship with his/her spouse or partner in influencing child behavior (Gallagher, Huth-Bocks and Schmitt, 2015) and with child–parent attachment (van der Watt, 2014).

In addition to their roles as disciplinarians, parents act as managers of their children's access to social contacts with peers. Parents may actively initiate peer contacts for their children either on an ad hoc basis, such as inviting neighbors' children to their homes, or by enrolling the children in organized extracurricular activities. They may also provide direct guidance and informal 'coaching' to their children regarding ways of making friends. These modes of parental facilitation have been linked to the peer participation of young children (e.g. Ladd and Hart, 1992). Guidance and coaching are characteristic of parents of middle and upper socio-economic status. Socioeconomic status (SES) and the related concept of social class refer to the prestige of a person's occupation, the education needed to prepare for it, and the salary one earns. Within a given country or society, differences between the beliefs and behaviors of members of different SES levels have often been found to be greater than the differences between countries. One of the reasons why lower SES is associated with social withdrawal among younger children is that parents from lower SES backgrounds are less active than others in facilitating peer contacts for their children, at least in the United States (Ladd *et al.*, 1988).

Older children may be less dependent than younger children are on parental structuring of their social lives (Rubin and Sloman, 1984). Parents may 'coach' their adolescent sons and daughters and provide appropriate guidance; this may facilitate some aspects of social competence (e.g. assertion) but not necessarily cooperative behavior with peers (Mounts, 2011). As issues of autonomy become more important to the maturing child and adolescent (Krappmann, 1989), parental structuring of peer contacts may become less acceptable than it is to younger children. Thus, there are several reasons for believing that the managerial role of parents is pivotal mostly for young children and may be important only in Western countries, rather than in societies where child-rearing is guided more extensively by tradition and where raising children is considered much more the collective responsibility of the community and society. Some support for this comes from an intriguing cross-cultural study by Hart and his colleagues (1999), conducted with five-year-olds from Utah, China and Russia and their parents. The Chinese mothers were more active in facilitating peer contacts for their children, perhaps because there were relatively few children in the immediate neighborhood with whom the children could play. However, only in Russia did such facilitation relate in any way to children's social competence (the lack of findings in Utah represents a failure to replicate the results of the US studies mentioned earlier in this paragraph). Two studies, one conducted in Germany (Krappmann, 1989) and one in Canada (Schneider *et al.*, 2001), indicated that direct facilitation by parents is no longer important in fostering the peer contacts of children once they reach the middle years of primary school.

In summary, very extensive research demonstrates that children who display competent and incompetent social behavior receive very different treatment from their parents. As mentioned earlier, the children's own temperaments could affect the parents' behavior as much as the parents' child-rearing affects the children; it is impossible to corroborate the common belief that the parents' child-rearing *causes* the children's positive or negative social behavior with their peers. Nevertheless, interventions aimed at improving the child-rearing practices of parents whose children display maladaptive patterns of relating to other children may be a promising avenue of intervention for those children.

Socialization by peers

As discussed in Chapter 1, the amount of time children spend in the company of other children has fluctuated through history and depends heavily on the organization of adults' work activities. In agricultural societies, boys often work together with adult men, whereas girls often work with adult women, resulting in relatively little contact between children (Frones, 1995). Most other economic activities result in children spending large amounts of time in each other's company, with older children taking responsibility for supervising younger ones and, in doing so, participating very extensively in child-rearing (Edwards *et al.*, 2006; Whiting and Edwards, 1988). The great potential of peer socialization was recognized historically by several peoples, who went as far as having children live separately from adults so that the older children could inculcate the values of the society unfettered by the distracting influences of parents; this occurred more frequently among warrior peoples, such as the Aztecs and the ancient Spartans. In contemporary Western societies, organized childcare and recreational activities account for many children being together for much of their free time (Frones, 1995).

Although peers influence each other in many ways, both positive and negative, social scientists study peer influence most extensively when they attempt to determine why children become aggressive or antisocial. Some of this literature will be discussed in Chapter 7, in the section pertaining to the sometimes negative influences of friends.

In Judith Rich Harris's (1998) group socialization theory, peers, rather than parents, are seen as the major socializing agents who determine the ways in which children relate to others, in counterpoint with a definite but not unlimited degree of genetic causation. Harris correctly points out that children are innately 'wired' to imitate other children and that they also seem to seek out the company of other children, even in cultures where children spend much of their time with their parents. According to the theory, children acquire their styles of social interaction by attempting to conform to the norms of their peer group, or the norms of children who are slightly older than themselves. Harris cites a variety of extreme situations in support of group socialization theory. These include the children of deaf parents, who learn both language and culture, and the children of immigrants, who learn the languages and cultures of their host countries, even though their parents could not have taught them.

When Harris's book first appeared, it was anticipated that her strong advocacy of group socialization theory and her outspoken attacks on the 'nurture assumption' would stimulate more – and better – research on the influence of peers. However, her work came to be recognized as a somewhat isolated challenge to the centuries-old assumption that parents determine almost completely how their children turn out (Rubin *et al.*, 2013). Over fifteen years since the publication of her provocative theory, Harris remains the outsider she was when her book was first published. Not surprisingly, some of the most prolific researchers in the area of child-rearing lambasted her for ignoring the enormity and methodologically eclectic evidence of the influences of parents (Collins *et al.*, 2000). Eisenberg (2008) remarked that what Harris regards as peer influence may really be peer influences that are essentially programmed by adults but not necessarily parents. This programming includes determining the social contexts of peer interaction and the messages that adults transmit to peers through mass media.

Siblings as peer-relations coaches

There are many literary accounts of older siblings coaching their younger brothers and sisters in the social skills needed to get along in the world of peers. If one compares interaction with siblings to interaction with parents, learning to relate to siblings is more similar in many ways to the skills needed to relate to peers (Ross and Howe, 2009). Sibling influences per se have been somewhat overlooked in literature on the origin of children's social competence although, of course, siblings have been studied extensively in order to establish the hereditability of temperament from parents to children. There have, however, been a few very careful studies in which the social interactions of the same children with their siblings and peers were compared. This research has been conducted with young children and has featured observational methods that provide rich detail on social interaction. There is some evidence that children display similar styles in interacting with siblings and with peers, although the results of the few studies available are not entirely consistent (Abramovitch *et al.*, 1986; Mendelson, Aboud and Lanthier, 1994; Volling, Youngblade and Belsky, 1997). However, the fact that the interaction styles are similar does not necessarily mean that the children learned the patterns of relating from their siblings, then applied them to peers. The reverse could have occurred, or they could have acquired the relationship styles from their parents. Given the amount of time children spend with siblings and their closeness in age, the amount of research on sibling research seems minuscule in comparison with the extent of the possible influences of siblings.

The end of the nature–nurture debate appears imminent

Although much has been learned about the origins of childen's social competence, much work remains to be done. New advances in behavior-genetics methodology now permit improvements on the methods used in existing twin and adoption studies. Hopefully, more geneticists will make fuller use of the range of methods for studying children's behavior that have been developed by scholars specializing in children's social development. Moreover, there may be many advantages in specifically targeting the influences of families who provide unusually positive and negative environments for children already at risk for social maladjustment to test the limits of environmental influence. It is unlikely, however, that the massive evidence indicating a genetic component in the origin of children's styles of relating to peers will be refuted. More intensive intervention studies (see Chapter 11) will hopefully determine how amenable to change problematic patterns of social behavior really are, despite the fact that those patterns derive in part from genetic preparation.

Much more needs to be learned about the influences of community (as opposed to school) peers on children's social competence. In that specific regard, much has already been learned about the influences of aggressive peers on aggression and delinquency in studies starting with Thrasher's classic work on street gangs at the beginning of the twentieth century (see Chapter 1), but little is known about neighborhood peers' influence on sociability, friendship or leadership behaviors. Research on socialization by siblings remains sorely neglected, too.

Most people have their own theories about what causes children and adults to relate to others in their individual ways. Probably few of these personal theories implicate genetics to the extent that it is featured in child-development research on the origins of children's social competence. Folk wisdom assigns parents most of the credit for their children's achievements and most of the blame for their weak points. As noted above, that may not be justified; but improving parenting practice may still be a very fruitful way of helping children who display atypical patterns of peer relations, such as problematic aggression and social withdrawal.

Changing the habitual thinking pattern of searching for the supposed single cause of any problem is no easy matter. However, there is good reason to believe that, for the most part, individual differences in children's social competence have several causes, both genetic and environmental. The environmental influence, in turn, consists not only of parents but also of peers, siblings and teachers. It may be difficult or impossible to identify '*the* cause' of any single case of maladaptive social behavior. Therefore, it is time to declare an end to the nature–nurture debate that has raged among scientists for decades and to recognize that both sides have won.

4

PEER RELATIONS AND SUCCESS AT SCHOOL

Philosophers and laypersons often debate the relative virtues of teaching academic subjects at school and preparing children for responsible social interaction. This misguided debate assumes that these two purposes of schooling are incompatible. This chapter begins with a review of research on the links between social and cognitive development. It continues with a section on the existing research on the links between peer relations and academic success, in terms of both achievement and personal adjustment to the school setting. The final portion of the chapter is devoted to the influence of school climate on children's peer relations.

There has been heated debate as to whether the main priority of the school should be to teach children social skills or to foster their academic achievement. Proponents of the latter goal maintain that the role of the school is to educate its students in various disciplines and to maximize academic achievement. This 'back to basics' position gained some prominence in the 1980s, which brought a general conservatism to the field of education in many Western countries, resulting in an emphasis on the acquisition of facts and academic skills – called 'Thatcherism in education' by Johnson (1989). Social development was seen as the family's domain. One of the more recent participants in this debate is *Washington Post* columnist Mari-Jane Williams, who commented:

> Everyone graduates from high school knowing how to read, write and do basic math (hopefully). But to be a self-sufficient adult, those skills are not enough. In fact, they're nowhere close to enough. Advanced skills in academic areas aren't going to help a young adult out of every jam he is likely to face in the next few years. Most of those predicaments probably will have nothing to do with Shakespeare, trigonometry or world history. What will he do when his car breaks down or he

> gets sick? Does she know how to navigate a job interview or a lunch with co-workers.
>
> *(Williams, 2013)*

However important academic achievement may be, proponents of the social role of education argue that the school should be responsible for teaching children social skills and encouraging social and emotional learning. Elias *et al.* (1997), who are the developers of one of the best-known social-skills curricula for schools, maintain that the goal of the school is to produce knowledgeable, responsible, caring individuals; promotion of social development, they assert, is unfortunately absent from agendas of school reform. The influential pioneer educationalist John Dewey (1900) claimed that the child was a product of the social world, and that the school should reflect the goals of the home and community. Early humanists such as Dewey hoped that the school might buffer the effects of a stressful family environment. To do so, the school had to be sensitive to the child's needs. There have been some attempts to translate Dewey's ideas about schooling into practice and to study the effects. Peres and Pasternack (1991) compared the adjustment of Israeli primary-school children of divorced parents in six structured, traditional schools and one experimental school. Results indicated that the children from the traditional schools were less accepting of other children than control-group participants from the experimental school. Relations among children were better in the experimental school, which was characterized by more student participation and by a longer, more diverse school day.

Elias *et al.* (1997, p. 1) assert that there may also be academic gains to fostering social and emotional learning in children: 'when schools attend systematically to students' social and emotional skills, the academic achievement of children increases, the incidence of problem behaviors decreases, and the quality of the relationships surrounding each child improves'. The Canadian educationalists Isherwood and Ahola (1981) maintain that instrumental and expressive socialization can coexist peacefully within the classroom setting. They, like Bloom (1977), the prominent US educator, refer to two modes of school influence and socialization: *instrumental objectives* emphasize adherence to school rules and learning of the academic curriculum; *expressive socialization* places importance on less formal learning that is facilitated by peer group and peer culture.

This debate about social and academic priorities has less substance than is apparent at first. Research indicates that academic success and social competences are interdependent, that achievement may facilitate social development and vice versa (e.g. Chen, Rubin and Li, 1997; Gresham, Vance and Chenier, 2013).

The effects of social interaction on cognitive development and learning

The social world of the child has a monumental influence on his or her development. Traditionally, research has addressed the role this social context plays in the development of the child's social competence. However, there is a growing field of research that explores the links between social interaction and cognitive development as well as academic achievement. Indeed, numerous findings have illustrated the positive effects of social interaction on cognitive development. It has even been suggested that social competence is a more accurate indicator of achievement than measured intellectual capacity (Wentzel, 1991). Such findings imply that social forces within the classroom are integral to children's academic achievement.

Chen, Rubin and Li (1997) studied the correlation between academic achievement and social functioning in ten- to twelve-year-old children from four Shanghai schools. They identified three different models useful in explaining the relationship between academic and social competence. The first maintains that children's prosocial behavior fosters a positive attitude toward the school experience, which, in turn, compels them to succeed academically. Children who display positive social behavior may be more likely to receive requested teacher help, and this may affect their academic results. The second model is essentially the converse of the first: children's academic success is seen as causing their social adjustment. Finally, the third – 'bidirectional' – model combines the first two, and asserts that academic achievement and social competence are interactive and mutually influential.

The findings from this study indicated that academic achievement was influenced by social competence and peer acceptance, which were in turn affected by levels of academic success; this supports the bidirectional model. Results also showed that aggression and externalizing behavior were negatively correlated with later academic achievement. The researchers found that popular children surpassed unpopular children in Chinese language and mathematics. They suggest that the peer group could have a positive effect on academic performance by acting as a social resource.

A number of influential studies in the United States have also demonstrated that positive peer relations are correlated with academic achievement but that negative peer relations are associated with poor academic progress (Altermatt and Pomerantz, 2003; Juvonen, Graham and Schuster, 2003; Li *et al.*, 2011; Wentzel, McNamara-Barry and Caldwell, 2004). Going further, Steinberg, Brown and Dornbusch (1996) showed that peer culture can in some cases be more influential than parenting.

There is speculation as to what specifically must occur during interaction between children in order for cognitive gain to occur. Piaget (1932) asserted that cognitive growth could occur only between peers of more or less equal status. Although he emphasized the child's interactions with the physical world and did not focus on the social world as a developmental force, he did maintain that, through interaction and conflict, children encounter disequilibrium which causes a restructuring of their logic and cognitive growth. Smith (1996, p. 119) likened Piaget's line of reasoning to Aristotle's analysis of economic transactions: 'Two partners to an economic exchange may have different products and so a decision about their equality, or lack of equality, requires the construction of a common scale so that either product can be compared with the other.' In her study of peer interaction and problem-solving, Margarita Azmitia (1988) first paired children into novice, expert, and novice/expert (mixed) dyads and then determined which children were subsequently able to generalize the skills learned while working on a task. She found that generalization depended on the quality of the discussion between the children, the amount of observation and imitation, and the provision of instruction by experts.

The eminent Soviet psychologist Lev Vygotsky also maintained that the ability of expert peers (or adults) to provide guidance was a key factor in cognitive development, for, within the 'zone of proximal development', the expert provides the scaffolding needed to support the novice's attempt to perform new and higher-level skills. The child is then able to internalize new knowledge and apply it independently: 'What the child can do in cooperation today, he can do alone tomorrow' (Vygotsky, 1962, p. 104; see also Bearison, Magzamen and Filardo, 1986). Rogoff (1991) found that children learned more from an adult than a peer, whether the peer was skilled or unskilled at the task to be mastered, confirming the importance of experts who represent the adult culture. Lin and colleagues (2012) conducted a particularly rigorous study that demonstrated the benefits of social interaction in children's use of analogy during collaborative reasoning.

Socio-cognitive conflict is an important component of social interaction that may modify the extent of cognitive growth. Bearison, Magzamen and Filardo (1986) examined the effects of socio-cognitive conflict on cognitive change and hypothesized that dyadic interactions characterized by salient disagreements and opposing solutions would foster more cognitive growth than those characterized by compliance. The researchers found that there was a curvilinear relationship: small and large amounts of conflict did not promote significant cognitive growth, whereas intermediate amounts did. They stressed the importance of 'interindividual reequilibration', wherein disagreement between children is followed by some sort of consensus. Mugny, Giroud and Doise (1979) also maintained that socio-cognitive conflict is a major spur for cognitive growth. They showed that pairs of children engaged in conflict were able to solve cognitive tasks at a more advanced level than singletons. Cooper, Marquis and Edward (1986) suggested that the importance of socio-cognitive conflict emerges in middle childhood, when children possess the skills necessary for maintaining effective, task-related conflict. Peers act as 'attentional anchors' for younger children, helping them to focus on the task at hand.

These ideas have been extended by a number of influential Italian educationalists who have inspired the renowned Reggio-Emilia approach to pre-school education. Social interaction, discovery learning and applied problem-solving are prominent features of the Reggio approach. As summarized by Pontecorvo and Arcidiacono (2010, p. 19):

> For researchers who embrace [the] socio-cultural theoretical framework – who thus acknowledge the interaction root of higher psychic functions – and

> conceive cognitive growth as a progressive mastering of participation in sociocultural activities – the exploration of cognitive processes in their spontaneous contextual occurring constitutes one of the most intriguing and challenging enterprises. Cognitive development and learning are not seen as taking place within the individual mind, but rather as processes of improving contribution to interactional activities. It follows that the basic unit of analysis cannot be the isolated novice. It is the whole activity, including not only all of its participants but also the cultural artifacts they make use of, that becomes the focus of researchers' analysis.

Kim and Darling (2009) conducted an analysis of the benefits of cognitive classrooms in a study of the constructive conversations of pre-schoolers in a Reggio-inspired classroom in Canada.

There are a number of studies in which it has been demonstrated that children and adolescents learn better when they are in social interaction than when they are alone. In a classic experiment using Lego blocks, the influential Swiss researchers Doise, Mugny and Perret-Clermont (1975) found that children learning together were better at reconstructing a Lego village than children working alone. This finding was replicated in several follow-up studies, now also considered classics, using other tasks (Doise and Mugny, 1984). Similar results emerged in another Lego study conducted in the United States (Azmitia, 1988). Children working in pairs have also been found to display better problem-solving than children working alone with a computerized version of the logic-based game Mastermind (Light and Glachan, 1985). Focusing on thinking skills more directly, Roazzi and Bryant (1998) found greater gain in logical inferential skills among children who worked together on a balance-scale task than among children who worked alone. Goldbeck (1998) reported similar benefits of working together in terms of improvement on a spatial-knowledge task. Larkin (2009) demonstrated the benefits of collaboration in learning to write in a study conducted with five- to seven-year-olds which featured extensive analysis of the children's meta-cognitive talk. Finally, Bulotsky-Shearer and colleagues (2012) demonstrated the benefits of interactive peer play for problem-solving and learning among urban children from low-income homes.

Montessori schooling: planned social interaction in learning

The findings discussed above indicate that the structure and organization of the classroom, independent of the actual classroom curriculum, may influence children's development. It has been found using direct observation that children engage in much more social interaction in Montessori classrooms than in others (Reuter and Yunik, 1973). In their case study of interactive learning, Cooper, Marquis and Edward (1986) conducted naturalistic observations on children aged five to twelve in a Montessori elementary school. This form of schooling encourages collaboration and recognizes its impact on cognitive growth. Whereas imitation might be negatively labeled as 'copying' or 'cheating' in a more traditional school environment, children in Montessori schools are urged to learn skills and techniques directly from observation of their peers. This offered Cooper, Marquis and Edward a unique opportunity to study the effects of peer interaction on cognitive development. They identified several different types of peer learning that occurred in the classroom environment. *Onlooker learning* consisted of a child observing another rather than engaging in work of his or her own. Onlookers tended to be younger children or children who did not work effectively in collaboration with other students. In *parallel-coordinate learning*, a group of two or more children work independently but refer to each other for help or information. *Guidance* involves one child actively teaching and guiding another child to help accomplish a task. *Executive guidance* is a more elaborate form of guidance, in which one child helps a peer by instructing a third child. *Collaboration* consists of equal sharing of power, whereby children share teaching roles or do not adopt a well-defined leader–follower formation. This taxonomy should be useful in future research studying the implications of patterns of social interaction among children in learning environments.

Friendship and cognitive growth

In most of these tasks, the children working together may not know each other or feel connected in any way. However, there may be some benefit in working together with friends. DeLay and colleagues (2014) found that adolescents working together in a dyadic computer instructional setting learned computer skills from their partner only when the partner was a friend. This effect was especially strong when the paired friends were both confident in their computer skills.

Working with eight- and nine-year-olds, Nelson and Aboud (1985) found that friends explained their opinions and criticized their partners more often than did non-friends. Higher levels of disagreement led to more cognitive change than did compliance. Nelson and Aboud concluded that friends who experience conflict undergo more social development than non-friends do in conflict. Their work supports other findings that friends who work together are more prosocial and share more information than do non-friends (Berndt, 1981; Newcomb and Brady, 1982; Newcomb, Brady and Hartup, 1979). In contrast, Swenson and Strough (2009) found no difference between the work of friends and acquaintances who worked together on a project in their classrooms.

It is likely that some children profit more than others from collaborating with peers. Current knowledge provides little basis for distinguishing them. In an interesting initial exploration of this issue, Ladd and colleagues (2014) encouraged elementary school students to describe peers who were good and poor collaborators on academic tasks. Those who corresponded to the students' categorization of good collaborators fared better academically, according to teachers' reports.

The contribution of friendship to adjustment following school transitions

Research into the relationship between children's friendships and school adjustment has indicated that social relations may positively influence adaptation after stressful school transitions, in which children are thrust into new and often daunting environments. Howes (1983, 1988) maintained that children may influence each other and thus facilitate school transitions by substituting for the parental/caretaker attachment that is lost at least temporarily when children leave home. Her work also indicates the importance of attachment to the teacher or caregiver, who were not mentioned at all in Bowlby's or Ainsworth's classic attachment theories (see Chapter 3). Schwartz (1972) explored the effect of close attachment between children on their reaction to novel situations. In Schwartz's experiment, children were paired with a close friend or an unfamiliar peer, or left alone, to explore an unfamiliar environment. One may infer that this setting mimics the new world of a child's first kindergarten or junior high school class. Schwartz found that those children who were paired with a close friend were more willing to explore the environment and exhibited more positive affect than their counterparts in the other experimental conditions. Furthermore, such an effect was more evident among children paired with an unfamiliar peer than among solitary children. This suggests that even the presence of an unknown peer may lower a child's stress level and facilitate adjustment to a new environment.

In a case study of four African-American students who underwent the transition from a regular program to a special program for gifted students, Slanina (1996) highlighted certain factors that may facilitate adjustment. Prominent among these were positive peer influences. Three of the students continued to associate with their neighborhood peer groups after they had transferred from their home schools to the gifted program. After these students took time to adjust to their new situation, there did not appear to be negative effects of the transition. However, the student who did not maintain contact with his neighborhood friends found it difficult to adjust to the new program. This suggests that having a stable peer group outside the classroom may facilitate adjustment after a transition.

Classroom structure may also affect adjustment to school transition, for children who remain together throughout the day may find that a stable classroom composition facilitates their adjustment. In a study by Berndt, Hawkins and Jiao (1999), self-esteem declined for students who were organized into traditional junior high school classrooms, where the composition of the classroom varied throughout the day, according to subject. However, in 'teacher–student teams', in which the classroom rotated as a whole from teacher to teacher according to subject, permitting the peer group to remain together, there was little change in general self-esteem.

McDougall and Hymel (1998) examined the transition to middle school, which occurs in Canadian schools at age twelve or thirteen. The participants were

160 students from Ontario who were entering a single middle school from a number of different primary schools. McDougall and Hymel postulated that, in schools where students remain with the same classmates throughout the day and change location from subject to subject, the transition to middle school should be relatively smooth due to the formation of a stable peer group. Findings from this study supported this hypothesis, and indicated that those participants who reported a difficult transition also reported poor social adjustment and self-concept.

The transition from elementary to middle school is often seen as particularly problematic. In many places, pupils transition from a familiar, relatively small school where they have become the oldest pupils and where teachers relate to young pupils warmly to a larger and more anonymous school that is oriented to academic learning. In many middle schools, there are different teachers for the various subjects, which is sometimes a new experience for pupils. This transition has been studied several times in well-designed longitudinal research. A recent example is a study by Kingery, Erdley and Marshall (2011), who studied 365 pupils undergoing this transition in the United States. Measures of pre-transition peer relations included peer acceptance, number of friends and quality of friendships. These indices of social competence were correlated with post-transition loneliness, school involvement and academic achievement. Interestingly, the largest correlations were between peer relations and academic achievement. In another study focusing on friendship quality, Berndt, Hawkins and Jiao (1999) studied the influences of friendship on adjustment to school transition. Using peer nominations, self-reports, teacher ratings and school records, they assessed adjustment levels of students entering junior high school, which in the United States also occurs at about age twelve or thirteen. These students were interviewed in the spring of the year before the transition and again in their new schools in the fall and spring of their subsequent school year. The researchers postulated that the quality and stability of friendships would relate to school adjustment and that students' adjustment would relate to, and be influenced by, their friends' adjustment (Berndt, 1996; Hartup,1996). Results indicated that those students who had high-quality friendships increased their social and leadership skills across the transition period. Also, students with friends who perceived themselves as competent socially in the fall of the year following the school transition reported that they consolidated their social competence even further during the school year.

Friendship may not be as fundamental a factor in post-transition adjustment in countries where ties to nuclear and extended family members are particularly strong. Schneider and colleagues (2008) studied the transition from elementary school to middle school in central Italy. This transition is particularly drastic because children move from elementary schools that practice the Reggio-Emilia approach described earlier to traditional, academically oriented middle schools. The results indicated that only family support, not the support of friends, bolstered post-transition adjustment. The same might apply to the very family-oriented Latino/Latina community in the United States (see Chapter 9).

Another important transition occurs in early childhood. In their study of peer relations and adjustment to kindergarten, Ladd, Kochenderfer and Coleman (1996) also hypothesized that the nature of friendship influences children's adaptation to school transition. They postulated that positive friendships that included validation and self-disclosure would bolster children and facilitate their adjustment; conflictual friendships were expected to have a negative effect on children's adjustment. The findings indicated that boys who perceived their friendships as characterized by conflict were more lonely and avoidant than others, and liked school less. The researchers suggested that this gender difference may be attributable to the fact that boys tend to be more negatively affected by conflict, and/or tend to be slower at resolving conflicts than girls. Boys and girls who perceived validation and aid in their friendships also perceived support from classmates; aid was predictive of improvement in attitudes regarding school.

How many friends are needed for a good transition and how good do the friendships have to be?

There have been some attempts to determine whether it is the number of friends or the frequency of contact with them that best explains the facilitative effects of friendship on schooling. In their longitudinal study of 410 students, Fenzel and Blyth (1986) examined the benefits of supportive peers on adjustment to junior high school (age twelve to fifteen years, approximately). There was a gender difference in the nature of the link between friendship and adjustment. Boys whose self-esteem levels increased after the transition to junior high school had more frequent peer contact and were somewhat more intimate with their friends than boys whose self-esteem diminished after the transition. However, girls who attained higher levels of self-esteem had equal or lower intimacy levels with peers than those who declined in self-esteem. Fenzel and Blyth speculated that females who gain in self-esteem may receive family rather than peer support. Alternatively, it may be the case that girls who face new roles and changes may be more involved with their peers, but these peers may not offer them adequate emotional support. Results from this study indicated that facilitation of school adjustment is not affected by the *number* of important peer relationships. However, significant findings suggested that the *frequency* of contact with peers did affect the adjustment of boys, because boys who gained in their perception of their social integration in the school had more frequent contact with same-sex peers than did boys who declined in their perception of school integration; there were no such benefits of contact for girls.

In contrast, Ladd and Price (1987) found that kindergarten children's initial school adjustment at about age five was positively correlated with the number of their classroom friends. Moreover, children with classroom friends who had been their friends prior to the start of kindergarten displayed more positive attitudes towards school and less avoidance of school. In a subsequent study, Ladd (1990) found that children who maintained their friendships with their prior friends acquired more positive attitudes toward school than those who did not.

Peer influence on school engagement

Children and youth vary enormously in their commitment to the school experience. *School bonding* refers to the connections students have with their schools, the school personnel and the academic ideals espoused by the school (Maddox and Prinz, 2003). Beyond its confirmed association with academic performance (e.g. López, Ehly and García-Vázquez, 2002), school bonding can deter social deviance (Murray and Greenberg, 2001) and compensate for stressful life events (e.g. Hawkins *et al.*, 1992). *School engagement* is a related term. As noted by Li and colleagues (2011), there are two types of school engagement: *behavioral engagement* includes enthusiastic participation in school activities, refraining from disruptive behavior and being generally helpful; *emotional engagement* refers to pupils' feelings about the people they meet at school – peers, teachers and administrators. In their longitudinal study of school engagement in early adolescence, Li *et al.* found that peer support was positively linked to both forms of school engagement. These effects increased with age and applied to both boys and girls and across socioeconomic levels.

School climate and pupil interaction

According to an advocacy group in the United States that strives for better schools, *school climate* 'refers to the quality and character of school life. School climate is based on patterns of students', parents' and school personnel's experience of school life and reflects norms, goals, values, interpersonal relationships, teaching and learning practices, and organizational structures' (www.schoolclimate.org/climate/, retrieved May 17, 2015). The definition of school climate has been debated widely in academic journals. The details of this debate are beyond the scope of this chapter, but the definition cited above captures its essence.

School climate is known to influence peer relations in schools in a number of ways. One of these is regulation of the social participation of shy, withdrawn children. Several studies indicate that the warmth of the welcome by peers and teachers influences the extent to which shy, withdrawn children withdraw further into their loneliness or increase their social participation. Gazelle (2013) provided a useful review of studies confirming this contention. Some research has shown that teacher sensitivity and peer acceptance may work interactively in regulating shyness in school (e.g. Buhs *et al.*, 2015).

Another important influence of school climate is on rates of bullying; there is extensive research on this issue, summarized in a recent paper by Azeredo and colleagues (2015). As an example, it has been shown that pupils' perceptions of school climate influence decisions about their choice of action during a bully–victim confrontation – to upstand, bystand, or join in the bullying (Ferrans and

Selman, 2014). In an interesting elaboration of teacher effects, Oldenburg and colleagues (2015) found that bullying was highest in classrooms taught by teachers who believed that the bullying was beyond their control. It has been shown a number of times that it is possible to reduce bullying, though not eliminate it, by improving the school environment (e.g. Kyriakides *et al.*, 2014).

Applying the findings: cooperative learning

The cooperative learning movement represents a major effort at organizing education in order to capitalize on the facilitative effects of positive peer interaction. Single-case research on the academic benefits of peer tutoring is aptly summarized by Bowman-Perrott and colleagues (2013). Many studies have indicated that there are numerous positive effects of cooperative learning, compared with the traditional competitive learning method that exists in many classrooms. Stevahn and colleagues (1996) define competitive behavior as working against a person to achieve an individual goal. As they define it, competition is motivated by self-interest and is short term in nature. Individualistic learning involves working individually toward personal goals. Cooperation, however, is defined as individuals collaborating for mutual gain. Compared with competition, cooperation is more long term in nature. It is important to note that other conceptualizations of competition also exist. For example, Tassi and Schneider (1997) differentiate between task-oriented competition, in which a person competes with others with the goal of measuring his or her own achievements, and other-referenced competition, which is aimed at proving that one is better than other individuals in one's social context. Their concept of task-oriented competition is different from the individualistic learning defined by Johnson and his colleagues, because it still involves competition, albeit good-natured competition: the person is in a competitive situation and is not working individually. Of course, Tassi and Schneider believe, and provide some data to demonstrate, that it is other-referenced competition, not task-oriented competition, that damages harmonious social relationships.

There are many different forms of cooperative learning, but they do have common elements. Cooperative learning not only means that students sometimes work together in groups, which happens in most schools. It means that students must have an active stake in each other's learning. In some cases, this extends to not competing with each other for individual marks in their subjects. This requires a total overhaul of traditional styles of teaching and of classroom instructional materials, to achieve the optimal combination of 'group goals and individual accountability' (Slavin, 1991, p. 112).

Hertz-Lazarowitz (1995) provides a rich, multidimensional model consisting of six interrelated 'mirrors', depicted in Figure 4.1, to illustrate the aspects of classroom life that can reflect competition or cooperation. Only by focusing on the first four mirrors – physical organization, learning and task structure, teacher's instructional style, and patterns of communication – can one predict what the

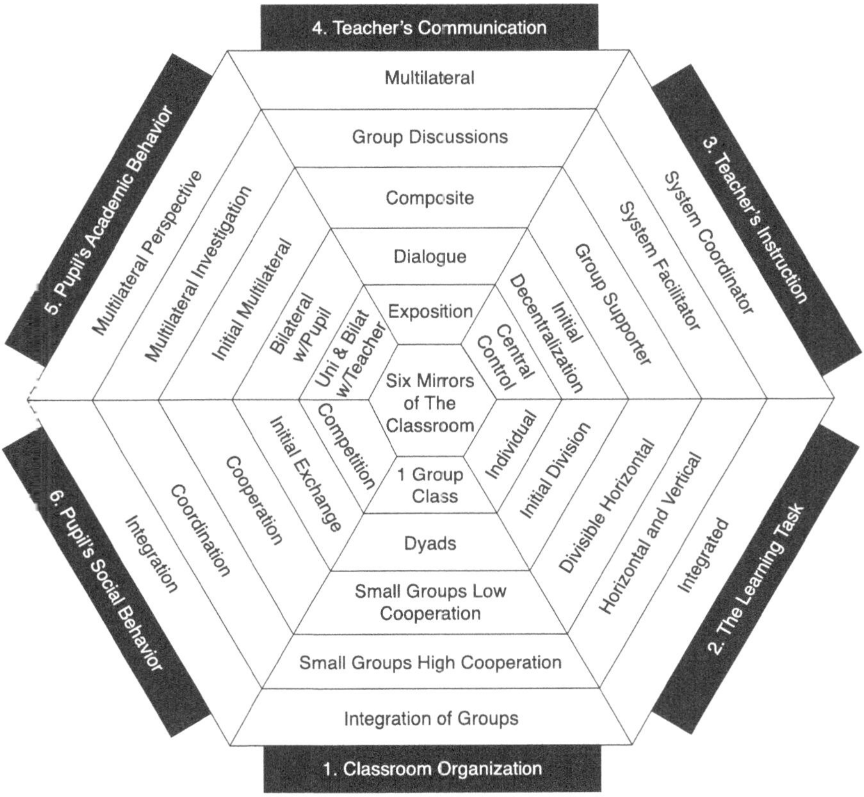

FIGURE 4.1 Six mirrors of the classroom (Source: Hertz-Lazarowitz, 1995)

images in the fifth and sixth mirrors – student academic achievement and social behavior – will look like.

Slavin (2015) argues in a recent review of theory and practice that cooperative learning is practiced most extensively in primary school but that it is also applicable to older students. Cooperative learning has been linked with academic gains (Slavin, 1987), improvement in self-esteem (Johnson and Johnson, 1989), prosocial behavior (Lloyd *et al.*, 1988) and other benefits. Many studies have focused on the academic gains offered by cooperative learning, comparing planned group collaboration to the traditional, competitive learning that exists in many classrooms. Such research is essential in order to confirm that the cooperative, non-competitive context does not stunt learning, and may, in fact, facilitate it. For example, Klinger, Vaughn and Schumm (1998) examined whether collaborative learning has an effect on reading comprehension. In the cooperative condition, students were taught collaborative strategic reading (Klinger and Vaughn, 1996; Palinscar and Brown, 1984), which provides instruction in reading comprehension strategies in a cooperative learning context. Students in the competitive condition learned from their social studies texts, but the instruction was teacher led and did not incorporate collaborative strategic reading. Findings indicated that the students in the collaborative condition improved in reading comprehension more than their non-collaborative counterparts; both groups improved equally in understanding of content. Klinger, Vaughn and Schumm (1998) concluded that this form of learning is especially appropriate for classrooms that are heterogeneous in terms of the cultural origins or ability levels of the students.

Peer tutoring

Another major way of harnessing the effects of peer interaction on academic achievement is to enlist the help of competent peers in tutoring other children who need help. Greenwood, Carta and Kamps (1990) highlighted some important requirements of peer tutoring in order for it to be effective: it must be highly structured; tutors must be trained; teachers must monitor and provide feedback; and students must know who their partner is, what material is to be taught, and how to correct their partner, prior to the tutoring session.

Accounts of children teaching other children can be traced back as far as the first century AD; the formal designation of peer tutoring as an educational technique dates back to the late eighteenth century (Goodlad and Hirst, 1990). Several theories have been used to explain the possible benefits of peer tutoring to the tutors (see Kennedy, 1990). According to role theory, children who assume the role of the teacher may develop empathy for their teachers; this could help improve classroom behavior (unless, of course, they develop the belief that teachers are not really necessary). Cognitive-dissonance theory would lead to the expectation that the role of teacher is incompatible with the belief that one is incompetent in the subject matter to be taught; therefore, peer tutoring should modify the feeling that one is ineffective as a learner (Kennedy, 1990).

The benefits of peer tutoring have been confirmed in many studies. Gumpel and Frank (1999) examined the effects of peer tutoring on social interactions using a case-study method. Two twelve-year-olds tutored two socially rejected/isolated five-year-old boys in social skills. The investigators postulated that, even though the tutoring focused on the younger children, there would be reciprocal positive effects. Results supported this hypothesis: there was a maintained increase in prosocial behavior among all four boys. Indeed, benefits to the tutor as well as the tutee are emphasized throughout the literature.

Recognizing the potential benefit to the tutors, there have been many studies of peer tutoring by children with immature social skills, behavior disorders and learning problems. The benefits to secondary school students with mild disabilities are summarized in a review article by Stenhoff and Lignugaris-Kraft (2007). Most studies demonstrate positive effects, but sometimes the results are mixed or even negative (Kennedy, 1990). Hogan and Prater (1998) paired tutors with behavior disorders and tutees with learning disabilities and found that, during peer tutoring, there was improvement in the tutees' academic achievement and on-task behavior.

Disappointingly, though, there were no improvements in disruptive behavior. Summarizing the extensive research on peer tutoring using children with special learning and emotional needs as tutors, Osguthorpe and Scruggs (1990) conclude that there is usually academic gain, but the evidence for social and emotional growth is inconsistent.

Putting learning first

I hope that the research discussed in this chapter is ample evidence that one of the best ways of putting learning first is to arrange for cooperative, rewarding social interaction among pupils. Abundant data indicate that fostering positive peer interaction and fostering basic academic learning are not at all in competition with each other but are fundamentally interrelated. Despite the strength of this database, I recognize that not all parents and teachers are as convinced by research as are scholars within the social sciences. One important way of translating research into practice may be to train new teachers in ways of helping pupils relate better to each other, besides teaching them to harness the power of cocperative interaction in their teaching.

5

DEFINING SOCIAL COMPETENCE AND DETERMINING WHAT IT LOOKS LIKE

Divergent concepts of social competence are introduced here. These derive from a wide range of theoretical roots, ranging from behaviorism to the psychology of motivation to moral education. Consideration is given to the criteria for determining that a given behavior or ability pertains to social competence. These criteria have been used to determine the behaviors that are linked with both social competence and social incompetence. Recent researchers have introduced a distinction between social competence based on patterns of liking and disliking in the peer group and being considered popular. The chapter concludes with deliberation on the merits and consequences of this distinction.

In musing about the problems that plague researchers in defining friendship, Contarello and Volpata (1991, p. 49) remembered Louis Armstrong's comment about the difficulty of defining jazz: 'If you have to define it, you cannot possibly understand it.' Indeed, the greatest jazz musicians have not been deterred from making music by the lack of a common definition of jazz. Nor has the absence of a clear definition of social competence stopped researchers from studying the phenomenon. However, it is often believed that much of the research lacks focus because there is no clear, common understanding of where social competence begins and ends. Deciding how to define 'social skill' and 'social competence' has consumed vast amounts of energy. Nevertheless, a commonly accepted definition has failed to emerge, which has been a source of agony for many scholars. Because there are so many different reasons for studying peer relations (see Chapter 2), it is not surprising that there are so many diverse concepts of what it means to be socially skilled or socially competent.

In a classic essay published in *American Psychologist*, Zigler and Trickett (1978) lambasted the community of researchers and theoreticians for their inability to agree on a definition of social competence. The intervening decades have not brought agreement among theorists and researchers regarding an exact definition.

However, there seems to have emerged an appreciation of the multiple, heterogeneous components that can be seen as different facets of social competence. Most authors now maintain that social competence must extend beyond observable behavior to include internal processes related to the overt behavior as well as the coordination between the individual and the social environment. This coordination may achieve such outcomes as having friends or being accepted in a social group. Coordination may also be conceptualized in terms of processes internal to the child, such as achievement of one's own goals, enhanced self-esteem, self-efficacy, or confidence in oneself as a social being (Denham, 2006; Ladd, 2005; Shin *et al.*, 2011). Halberstadt, Denham and Dunsmore (2001) introduced the notion of *affective social competence*, which consists of sending affective messages, receiving affective messages, and experiencing affect. *Information processing* relative to social exchange is the core of Crick and Dodge's (1994) influential model, in which social competence and incompetence are distinguished according to children's abilities to interpret and react appropriately to the social cues contained in exchanges with other children.

A very useful way of recognizing the multifaceted nature of social competence has emerged in writings about the distinction between social competence and social skills. The latter can be defined as 'the molecular responses necessary for

TABLE 5.1 An incomplete list of social tasks

Entering a Group	Helping
Responding to Ambiguous Provocation	Asking for Help
Managing Conflict	Responding to Cheating/Unfairness
Coping with False Accusations	Resisting Distraction by Others
Listening	Persuading
Negotiating Rules	Achieving Equity/Fairness
Retrieving Belongings	Complimenting
Generating 'Fun' Ideas	Coping with Frustrating Situations
Sharing Resources/Belongings	Getting Picked for Teams/Activities
Maintaining Interaction	Expressing Affection
Making Requests	Coping with Teasing
Eliciting Disclosure	Avoiding Dangerous Peer Contexts
Self-Disclosure	Comforting
Responding to Requests	Defending Self
Expressing Appreciation	Communicating Contingently
Coping with Public Failure	Sticking up for a Friend
Coping with Rejection	Refusing a Dare
Dealing with Losing	Responding to Winning/Success
Apologizing	Keeping Secrets
Forgiving	Terminating Interaction

(Source: Asher and McDonald, 2009)

socially competent responding in a given situation' (Nangle, Grover and Fales, 2011, p. 40; see also Nangle *et al.*, 2010). Accordingly, social skills are seen as the observable facets of the larger construct of social competence, which is seen as deeper and broader in a number of ways that vary considerably from author to author. Asher and McDonald (2009) present a useful table (Table 5.1) with many examples of molecular units of behavior that pertain to competent social interaction. They note that only a few of these 'social tasks', as they refer to them, have been studied by researchers. Therefore, they emphatically include the qualifier 'incomplete' in the title of the table.

It is important to note that some of the earlier writings on the conceptualization of social skill and social competence emanate from a behavioral perspective in which processes internal to an individual were often not considered. Social skills are still seen as components within a hierarchical model of social competence, but social competence does not include or emphasize affective or cognitive components that many contemporary theorists regard as indispensable. For example, in Gresham's (1986) model, social competence has two elements: social skills and adaptive behavior. Social skills include appropriate play behavior and cooperativeness, expression of feelings, positive self-concept, and conversational skills. Adaptive behavior includes language development, academic functioning, physical development, and self-care skills, such as grooming. McFall (1982) refers to social skills as specific behaviors performed well, whereas social competence is an evaluative term based on others' judgements of the adequacy of task performance. It should be noted that yet other authors use the terms 'social skills' and 'social competence' in ways that are essentially synonymous.

The next sections are devoted to several approaches that are useful in delineating the components of the broad construct of social competence that contribute to the well-being of children and adolescents, recognizing that, although ideas about the nature of social competence have changed over the years, consensus remains elusive.

Trait versus situation-specific approaches

Definitions of social competence may be seen as adhering to either a trait or a situationally specific perspective. Trait approaches assume, at least implicitly, that a socially competent person (as defined by inherent personality characteristics) will be equally competent in all social situations. This mirrors a classic debate in psychology as to whether enough human behavior is similar across situations to warrant the use of such concepts as 'personality' (Mischel, 1983). Greenspan (1981) outlines two major trait approaches: the *bag of virtues strategy* and the *factorial strategy*. In the former, all possible behaviors that the theorist considers desirable are included, making it difficult to make any distinction between social and other forms of competence (such as physical or intellectual competence). In contrast, the factorial strategy delimits a number of behavioral dimensions that relate more strictly to interpersonal behavior. For example, an individual might be considered highly sociable or very shy, with the understanding that the person is likely to be sociable or shy to a considerable degree in most social settings, such as school, home, neighborhood, or work. It should be noted that the few studies on the topic indicate a significant if small concordance between social withdrawal inside and outside of school (see Schneider, Richard, Younger and Freeman, 2001), contrary to Mischel's position.

Theorists who emphasize the situational specificity of social competence emphasize the need to take into account the extent to which children's ability to function in socially appropriate ways is contingent on specific contexts. In contrast with trait theorists, they are more likely to refer to behaviors rather than individuals as socially skilled or socially competent. Opponents of trait theories resist the categorization of individuals as generally aggressive or generally sociable, for example. Most of the limited data on the situation specificity indicate some degree of cross-situational stability in the social behavior of individuals, but probably not enough stability to provide incontrovertible support for trait theories. For example, Schneider, Richard, Younger and Freeman (2001) found that children considered shy by their schoolmates were somewhat less involved than other children in social contacts outside of school. Similar findings emerged in a study of withdrawn pre-schoolers by Coplan and colleagues (2009). A possible confounding factor is the familiarity of peers in different settings, as shy children are less withdrawn in social situations containing other people they know (Gazelle, 2013). In any case, the correlations reported in these and a few other studies are not very large. Importantly, the number of studies on the situation specificity of social behavior are few, especially when one considers the amount of rhetoric on the issue. Given the lack of clear, convincing data, critics of trait approaches decry the proliferation of trait theory in the assessment of behavior over the thirty years since Mischel first mounted his attack on that approach (Nangle, Grover and Fales, 2011).

Social competence versus conformity

Some definitions of social competence have emphasized personal needs and goals. From this perspective, social competence hinges on fulfilling one's own needs for affiliation or social support. Parks (1985, p. 177), incorporating personal goals into his model, defines social competence as 'the degree to which individuals have satisfied their goals in a given social situation without jeopardizing their opportunity to pursue other subjectively more important goals'. Ford (1982, p. 323) also stressed an individual's goals when defining social competence as 'the attainment of relevant social goals in specified social contexts, using appropriate means and resulting in positive developmental outcomes'.

Contrary to these theorists' conceptions, many researchers base their concepts of social competence on the opinions or reactions of peers. For example, Libet and Lewinsohn (1973) defined social skills as the ability to emit behaviors that are reinforced by others and to refrain from emitting behaviors that are punished by the group. Bellack and Hersen (1979) also defined social skills as being normative or socially sanctioned. Basing one's notion of social competence entirely on the reactions of groups may be seen as empowering deviant sub-groups to define behaviors or persons as socially competent that the majority would consider antisocial or that might simply be 'wrong', from a moral standpoint.

Social competence as capacity or as demonstrated knowledge

Definitions and models of social competence differ with regard to whether social competence should be seen as the theoretical capacity or ability of an individual to behave in a socially competent manner, or as the individual's actual performance in a social situation. One solution is to propose that social competence or social skills refer to abstract ability in social situations, or in handling social situations adequately, irrespective of whether one actually uses these abilities. In many cases, this distinction is limited because it may only be possible to assess what one is capable of doing according to what one does. Nevertheless, it is important to make a distinction between individuals who are capable of initiating social contact but choose not to do so and those who experience distress because of their social isolation and inability to remedy it. Despite the inherent value of social contact in human society, isolation may constitute no problem if that is a person's choice, made on the basis of personal preference rather than an inability to form relationships, and if the isolation does not cause distress to the individual.

Social competence as dependent on development stage

The seminal work of Jean Piaget illustrated that children's ideas about their social worlds change radically as they proceed through different stages of development. From that standpoint, it becomes difficult to accept a notion of competence that is composed of discrete skills, few of which would be relevant across developmental levels. Some 'skills' that may be assets at certain levels of development can become liabilities at other stages. For example, rote imitation of peers' play behavior, though important in achieving interpersonal contact in early childhood (Nadel and Butterworth, 1999), may become a liability in achieving social relations at later stages, as in early adolescence when that 'skill' could lead to imitating risky or antisocial behaviors at school. Nevertheless, there are examples of skills that have potential for application across developmental levels. Going over to and joining in a game in an appropriate way may be competent both for very young children and for adults, even if its importance is not equal across all ages.

Social competence as relational competence

Schneider (1993, p. 19) proposed an emphasis on relationships in his definition of social competence as 'the ability to implement developmentally-appropriate social behaviors that enhance one's interpersonal relationships without causing harm to anyone'. Some social behaviors, such as the ability to greet others in an appropriate, friendly way, are common to both close and superficial relationships. Other behaviors, such as disclosing one's private experiences in an appropriate way, at the right time, and in relationships where self-disclosure is accepted and wanted, could be overlooked in applying definitions of social competence built on the unelaborated contingencies of peer acceptance or reinforcement.

The social competence of groups

It is undeniable that social competence, or lack of it, is treated as a characteristic of individuals in the overwhelming majority of studies in the recent literature. Groups, however, can be considered socially competent or incompetent depending on the values that cement them and the behaviors they hold in high esteem.

The best-known contemporary technique for studying patterns of associations within groups was developed by Robert Cairns and his colleagues (Cairns and Cairns, 1994; Kindermann and Gest, 2009). They constructed a 'social map' of the group by asking children to indicate which peers they associated with most frequently, and then determining in interviews with children the reputations each group had in its school or community. This research has revealed that distinct groups are very easy to identify; the children often refer to them by names such as 'jocks', 'nerds' and 'preppies' (for readers unfamiliar with North American slang, these terms refer to athletically inclined people, bookish people, and young followers of fashion, respectively).

The person–group similarity model (Stormshak *et al.*, 1999) considers the interface between the characteristics of individuals and those of the peers in their immediate groups. In a study conducted with an enormous sample (2,895) of six-year-olds in the United States, Stormshak and colleagues tested the predictive strength of the person–group similarity model. They found some support for the model, because the acceptability of aggressive and shy, withdrawn behaviors increased with the number of behavior problems found in the children's school classrooms.

In an interesting extension of the social-group approach to pre-schoolers, Brighi and colleagues (2015) found that children with similar behavioral features tended to cluster together in cliques characterized by common behavioral patterns from the age of four onwards. These researchers identified cliques of socially competent young children, of children prone to anger and aggression, of children with strong language skills, and of children who became inhibited in novel situations, among others.

What social competence looks like: behaviors associated with social competence and incompetence

A more empirical approach to understanding the nature of social competence is to examine in detail the social behaviors that are correlated with acceptance and rejection by peers. Research on the behavioral basis of acceptance and rejection constitutes a major component of peer-relations research from the 1930s to the present day. As summarized by Asher and McDonald (2009), the basic strategy is to determine the behaviors children find 'rewarding' in their peers. The candidate behaviors are usually based on the researchers' intuitions and knowledge of child development rather than any formal theory. The methodology almost always includes a sociometric choice measure (see Chapter 6) as well as a measure of the behavior being studied as a possible correlate of popularity, acceptance and/or rejection. Asher and McDonald emphasize the advantages of studying the target behavior directly using an observational methodology whenever possible, as opposed to having the behavior rated by third parties such as teachers, convenient as rating-scale measures may be. Such observations may be conducted in the settings where children normally interact, such as school playgrounds. Structured game situations contrived by the researchers have also been used. These analogue methods sacrifice the advantage of studying behavior where it occurs naturally. However, they may be more feasible in many cases and may ensure that the situation the researchers want to study, such as one that might trigger aggression, actually occurs during the observation time.

The characteristics of children who are liked and disliked in their social groups have been studied extensively for about ninety years. A wide array of behaviors and personal characteristics can lead to being accepted or rejected in children's peer groups. Almost all of the studies have been conducted on social groups in schools rather than neighborhoods or settings where extracurricular activities take place, with the exception of a few that were conducted at summer camps. The school setting probably provides the most representative samples, although, as Asher and McDonald (2009) emphasize, children and adolescents also interact extensively in the understudied community settings.

Within the realm of social behaviors, peer-directed aggression and social withdrawal have been studied most frequently as indicators of social incompetence. Unfortunately, many of the studies are quite dated now and may not reflect any recent changes in the correlates of acceptance and rejection in the communities that participated. However, there has been important progress in another respect because many of the more recent studies have been conducted in cultures that are very different from the Western countries that constitute most of the existing database, as will be discussed in greater detail in Chapter 9.

Behaviors linked to being well liked and well accepted

Many of the individual characteristics of the sociometric 'stars' identified by researchers are not social behaviors at all. These include physical attractiveness (Adams and Roopnarine, 1994; Dion and Berscheid, 1974; Dodge, 1983; Krantz, 1987; Spence, 1987; Tuddenham, 1951; Vaughn and Langlois, 1983), athletic ability (Buchanan, Blankenbaker and Cotton, 1976; Daniels and Leaper, 2006; Tuddenham, 1951), academic achievement (Buchanan, Blankenbaker and Cotton, 1976; Coie and Dodge, 1988; Hortaçsu, 1994; Vosk *et al.*, 1982; Wentzel and

Asher, 1995) as well as trying hard at school (Kosir and Pecjak, 2005). Tassi and Schneider (1997) found that competitive children were sometimes well liked, depending on their motivation in competition. Those who compete to win at any cost tend to be rejected whereas those who compete to become more skilled earn the esteem of their peers. Well-liked children remain on task during classroom lessons (Schaughency *et al.*, 1992; Vosk *et al.*, 1982).

Researchers interested in identifying behaviors useful in social-skills training have found that well-accepted children are proficient at knowing just when and how to enter a group game or conversation (Bonn and Kruger, 1996; Dodge *et al.*, 1983, 1990; Gelb and Jacobson, 1988; Putallaz, 1983). Well-liked children are also known for their general friendliness and positive dispositions (Dodge *et al.*, 1990; Tuddenham, 1951) and for being cooperative (Cillessen *et al.*, 1992; Coie and Dodge, 1988; Dodge, 1983; Tomada and Schneider, 1997). They are not meek but make their feelings and wishes known in appropriate, assertive ways (Dodge *et al.*, 1990; Rubin, Bukowski and Parker, 2006). Children who are well liked by their peers also provide positive reinforcement to those peers in several ways (Adams and Roopnarine, 1994; Erwin, 1994).

In almost every study, well-liked children have been found to be helpful, cooperative and prosocial (Attili, Vermigli and Schneider, 1997; Chen and Tse, 2008; Coie and Dodge, 1988; Dekovic and Gerris, 1994; Gazelle, 2008; Wentzel and Asher, 1995; Wright, Giammarino and Parad, 1986). The rare exception may be some groups in which prosocial behavior is not the norm (Asher and McDonald, 2009; Boivin, Dodge and Coie, 1995; Chang, 2004). Even so, the size of the correlations suggests that group norms for prosocial behavior appear to have less to do with being liked or disliked in the same groups than group norms for aggression and social withdrawal. Several authors suggest that the weaker group-norm effect for prosocial behavior indicates that prosocial behavior is almost universally valued, more so than the absence of aggression or social withdrawal (Asher and McDonald, 2009; Chang, 2004).

Researchers have also identified a cognitive substrate to being well liked. The well-liked student is one who is able to understand the perspectives of his or her peers (Dekovic and Gerris, 1994; Nowicki and Duke, 1992; Spence, 1987) and to solve interpersonal problems competently and well (Erwin, 1994; Mendelson, Aboud and Lanthier, 1994; Troop-Gordon and Asher, 2005). These cognitive skills form the basis of many intervention programs (see Chapter 12).

Aggression as an obstacle to peer acceptance in most cases

Although children can be rejected by their peers for myriad reasons, aggression is probably the most frequent, at least until the early adolescent years. Detailed studies have indicated that at least half of the school-age children who are rejected are aggressive (Cillessen *et al.*, 1992; French, 1988). In this chapter, as in most other writings on the subject, aggression is discussed as leading to rejection by peers. However, the converse is also true, as noted by Rubin and colleagues

(2013): peer rejection probably acts in most cases to inhibit and reduce aggression; rejection can provoke aggression. The data are, of course, correlational, and correlation does not indicate causation. Whatever the causal direction, though, the correlational database is massive (Alvarez Valdivia *et al.*, 2005; Attili, Vermigli and Schneider, 1997; Bonn and Kruger, 1996; Cantrell and Prinz, 1985; Carlson, Lahey and Neeper, 1984; Chen, Rubin and Li, 1995; Chen, Rubin and Sun, 1992; Cillessen *et al.*, 1992; Coie and Dodge, 1988; Coie and Kupersmidt, 1983; Dodge, 1983; Dodge, Coie and Brakke, 1982; Dodge *et al.*, 1990; Dubow and Cappas, 1988; French, 1990; Green, Vosk and Beck, 1981; Ladd, 1983; Parke *et al.*, 1997; Prinstein and Cillessen, 2003; Rubin, Chen and Hymel, 1993; Rubin, Daniels-Beirness and Hayvren, 1982; Rubin, Hymel, Lemare and Rowden, 1989; Spence, 1987; Tseng *et al.*, 2014; von Salisch and Uhlendorff, 1998; Wentzel and Asher, 1995; Wolters *et al.*, 2014).

Ledingham (1999) notes that because there is so much overlap between peer rejection and aggression, many of the longitudinal studies that purport to investigate the consequences of peer rejection may actually be portraying the effects of aggression. She speculates that aggression may be a more potent predictor of later maladjustment than is rejection by peers. There is some evidence for her contentions. Several careful studies have been conducted in order to distinguish the consequences of being rejected by peers, being aggressive, and being both. Cillessen and colleagues' (1992) longitudinal data – collected in the Netherlands – showed that children who are both rejected and aggressive were much more likely than non-aggressive rejected children to be rejected by peers again at the time of follow-up. Longitudinal studies conducted in the southern United States by Coie and colleagues (1995b) and by Kupersmidt and Coie (1990) indicated that aggression was more closely associated with subsequent juvenile delinquency than was rejection.

The unambiguous findings that aggression is the leading correlate of peer rejection among school-aged children do not mean that every aggressive child is rejected by all or most of his or her peers. If that happened, the aggression might in fact diminish, because it would be discouraged by the peer group. However, the general rejection of aggressive classmates by most children often propels them toward cultivating associations with cliques of antisocial peers who value both their company and their aggression (Cairns and Cairns, 1994).

Researchers have focused not only on overt, physical aggression but also on covert, verbal and relational forms of aggression. In a research program spanning several decades, Crick and her colleagues have demonstrated the importance of studying relational aggression along with the overt forms of aggressive behavior (e.g. physical, verbal aggression) that have traditionally been the subject of investigations in this area (e.g. Crick and Grotpeter, 1995; Kawabata, Tseng and Crick, 2014; Mathiesen and Crick, 2010). Relational aggression consists of behaviors such as threatening to terminate a friendship in order to attain a goal, or excluding peers from activities in order to get back at them (Crick, Bigbee and Howes, 1996). Grotpeter and Crick (1996) compared the friendships of relationally aggressive (i.e. inflicting harm through the manipulation of others' peer relationships, for instance by spreading rumors), overtly aggressive (physical or verbal aggression), and non-aggressive children. They reported that the friendships of relationally aggressive children included more instances of relational aggression and more frequent intimate exchanges than those of other children, whereas those of overtly aggressive pupils involved less intimacy and a greater frequency of overtly aggressive acts against other peers. The friendships of aggressive and non-aggressive students were similar in many respects, including comparable degrees of conflict, effective conflict resolution, caring and validation, help and companionship. Perhaps the intimacy in the friendships of relationally aggressive children makes the relationship a more potent instrument of aggression.

Tomada and Schneider (1997), in a study conducted in Tuscany, confirmed that relational aggression was common among Italian girls in middle childhood. They found that boys used both overt and relational aggression, indicating that relational aggression should not be considered the female form of aggression. Nevertheless, they insisted that it is important to study relational as well as overt aggression, because if researchers include only overt aggression in their studies, they will often conclude that females are not aggressive. Research with seven–eight-year-old children in Minsk, Belarus, confirmed that overt aggression occurs almost exclusively among boys, whereas verbal and relational forms of aggressions were far more frequent among the girls in the study (Alexandrovna, 1999). These cross-cultural extensions of the work of Crick and her colleagues indicate the potential importance of studying relational aggression in various cultures, because cultural prohibitions against self-expression by females may differ, as may cultural condoning of overt aggression by males.

Situations in which aggression may lead to popularity

Aggression does not always lead to rejection by peers, even if that is the general pattern found in most of the studies. It has been known for some time, for example, that aggression is not linked with peer rejection in the exceptional social settings where aggression is the norm, as may occur in some disadvantaged neighborhoods (Asher and McDonald, 2009; Boivin, Dodge and Coie, 1995; Chang, 2004; Stormshak *et al.*, 1999; Wright, Giammarino and Parad, 1986). Aggression is more likely to lead to peer rejection of and by girls than boys, especially with increasing age, probably because aggression by girls is incongruent with stereotyped sex roles (Garandeau, Wilson and Rodkin, 2010). Some forms of aggression may lead to rejection more readily than others. Peers seem to tolerate planned, calculated, instrumental aggression more than impulsive acting out (Price and Dodge, 1989), perhaps because they understand the purpose of the aggression, perhaps because the perpetrators are skilled enough to target their victims strategically without alienating others.

Some contemporary researchers have gone further than their predecessors in examining the situations in which aggression is linked to popularity or acceptance rather than rejection by peers. It is tempting to speculate that the more recent research reveals societal changes that have caused aggressive children to be better liked than in earlier years. Although that contention cannot be totally discarded in the absence of comparable data from different historical eras, the probable reason for the emergence of aggressive research participants who are not outcasts is simply the result of current researchers doing a better job of looking beyond the overall average, which may not tell the whole story. Statistical techniques such as cluster analysis facilitate the identification of groups of participants whose data do not replicate the general trend in the entire sample.

Exploring this process depends on certain relatively recent modifications by some researchers of the question used to determine which participants are popular and which are unpopular, as opposed to liked and disliked. Traditional sociometrics are based on the selection of work and/or play companions using such questions as 'Which of the children in your class are you most likely to choose as a partner to work [or play a game] with?' It has been discovered, however, that very different results emerge if the question is changed to 'Which of the children in your class are very popular [or considered popular]?' This new twist on the classic sociometric method has led to many novel and interesting findings, as discussed in the next few paragraphs. However, it is imperative to remember that there is far more evidence that peer acceptance and rejection in the traditional sense are related to well-being over the lifespan than being considered popular at school.

It has been proposed that the sub-group of group members who are *populistic* (i.e. popular but not necessarily well liked) should be distinguished from the sub-group who are *prosocial-popular* (De Bruyn and Cillessen, 2006). It may seem paradoxical that a substantial portion of the sample may be perceived as popular but is not chosen by many peers as companions for common play or work activities, but this happens quite often. Researchers have also found it valuable to refine the stimulus question further by asking the participants to separate pupils who are considered popular among boys from those who are popular among girls (Asher and McDonald, 2009; Cillessen and Mayeux, 2004; Parkhurst and Hopmeyer, 1998; Rodkin *et al.*, 2006; Rose, Swenson and Waller, 2004; Rubin *et al.*, 2013). When the sample is broken down in this way, it has been found that aggressive, strong boys may indeed be popular with other boys, even if they might not be anyone's first choices as potential friends (e.g. Rodkin *et al.*, 2006). Some of the aggressive, popular boys display desirable characteristics such as athletic skill that may outweigh their aggression in determining peers' perceptions of their popularity. The popularity of the sub-group of strong, aggressive boys may make them more aggressive over time; conversely, their aggression seems to make them more popular. Aggressive children perceived as popular may be characterized by their dominance over others and their 'upward mobility' – their desire to move up the hierarchy of popularity and prestige, even through the use of force (Cillessen and Mayeux, 2004; Parkhurst and Hopmeyer, 1998; Rubin *et al.*, 2013). Consistent with this conclusion are recent data by Cillessen and his colleagues (2014) showing that adolescents, especially adolescent boys, who are both popular and who consider popularity a personal priority are often considered group leaders.

Social incompetence as a factor in bully–victim problems

Bullying is a particularly vicious sub-category of aggression that has aroused particular concern around the world. Smith and colleagues published an interesting compendium of research on bullying in fifteen European countries, Canada, the United States, Japan, Australia, New Zealand, and the developing world (Smith, 1999). As noted by Slee (1999), an Australian researcher, people in many countries often initially believe that bullying is a problem elsewhere, only to be awakened by a shocking and saddening incident of it close to home. Bullying is aggression directed repeatedly and specifically toward a specific victim who is, in most cases, known to be weaker than the bully (Vaillancourt *et al.*, 2010). Bullies exploit their stronger status to prove their own strength or to exact possessions from the victim (Olweus, 1999, 2010; Smith, 1999). Bullies may use physical force or threats of physical force. They may also employ verbal and relational tactics. Although bullying has been found to exist in every country and community that has been studied, there are cross-national differences not only in the reported prevalence rates but in some of the tactics used. For example, bullies in Japan often use verbal and relational tactics more often than the physical aggression that seems to be prevalent in English-speaking countries (Murray-Harvey and Slee, 2010; Taki, 2010).

Questionnaire responses from around the world indicate than anywhere from 5 to over 40 percent of children report that they have been bullied, although some reports place the figure as high as 70 percent (Björkqvist and Osterman, 1999; Fonzi *et al.*, 1999: Jimerson, Swearer and Espelage, 2010). Jimerson, Swearer and Espelage (2010) offer an authoritative estimate of one in five US pupils who are victimized by bullies, with about the same number bullying other children. A similar figure, about one in five, has been reported as the average across European countries (Analitis *et al.*, 2009). More convincing than estimates based on questionnaires are direct observation studies of children's playgrounds, such as those made by Pepler and her colleagues in Toronto. On average, they observed an incident of bullying every seven minutes (Craig and Pepler, 1997). In recent years, cyberbullying has emerged as a threat that is just as substantial as face-to-face bullying but probably more difficult to study, contain and control. In many cases, the same pupils are bullied using both online and face-to-face modalities (Lonigro *et al.*, 2015; Smith and Slonje, 2010)

Bullies are often rejected, on the whole, by their peers (Coie, Dodge and Kupersmidt, 1990; Slee, 1999) but may still abuse victims in an attempt to cultivate reputations of strength. Sometimes, their bullying may make them solidly popular within a minority sub-group of antisocial peers, even if they are despised and feared by most others (Boulton and Smith 1994; Cillessen and Mayeux,

2004; Slee, 1999). In an interesting study of the motivations of bullies, Olthof and Goossens (2008) found that some children engage in bullying in order to become more popular among strong, popular boys. It has been found that many early adolescent bullies who are not well liked by their peers are still perceived as 'popular' in the sense that they are visible, dominant and prestigious in their peer groups (De Bruyn, Cillessen and Wissink, 2010).

Victims are often less popular than the bullies, even in the early childhood years (Alsaker and Gutzwiller-Helfenfinger, 2010; Godleski *et al.*, 2015). This may occur because bullies are quite proficient at targeting peers who will probably not be supported or protected by others. With increasing age, desirable features such as physical attractiveness, athletic or academic proficiency may reduce the likelihood that even a rejected pupil will become a victim of bullies (Knack *et al.*, 2012). Moreover, although few rejected pupils are athletic, 'cool' and popular, those who are may become bullies, perhaps taking advantage of their ability to cultivate the companionship of socially prominent peers (Farmer *et al.*, 2011). Bullies of this type may be considered popular even though they may not be considered well accepted according to sociometric measures of pupils chosen by others to be play or work companions (De Bruyn, Cillessen and Wissink, 2010; Dijkstra, Lindenberg and Veenstra, 2008).

Sutton, Smith and Swettenham (1999) observed that, in contrast to the popular stereotype, many bullies are not socially unsophisticated individuals. Many bullies need and have strong understanding of others and their thinking, without which they would be less efficient at selecting vulnerable victims and manipulating people. Thus, bullying is surely antisocial, but it may not be indicative of social incompetence. In retort, Crick and Dodge (1999) cited studies showing that bullies are deficient in many basic social-cognitive processes. Further evidence of the social competence of aggressive children was provided by Hawley (2003), who analyzed the control strategies used by pre-schoolers. These strategies were classified as prosocial or coercive (aggressive). Hawley identified a group of 'bistrategic' pre-schoolers who are expert users of both prosocial and coercive strategies. Members of this group were very popular; their control strategies worked very well.

In the years since this issue was raised, some researchers have studied the 'theory of mind' abilities of bullies: that is, their awareness that other people may see a situation from their own distinct perspective. In a review of the research on this issue, Smith (in press) found that many, but not all, bullies do demonstrate sophisticated theory-of-mind skills. Thus, these skills may be applied to either prosocial or antisocial behavior.

Shyness and social competence

Although shyness among young children may not be stable and is not always problematic, shyness/social withdrawal begins to interfere substantially with children's social relationships and peer acceptance at the stage when they begin formal schooling, when their withdrawal becomes noticeable and clearly atypical (e.g. DeRosier and Mercer, 2009). It has been estimated that 10–20 percent of rejected school-age children are socially withdrawn and that 25 percent of withdrawn children are socially rejected (Cillessen *et al.*, 1992; Rubin, Chen and Hymel, 1993; Rubin *et al.*, 2013). Although both boys and girls may be shy and socially withdrawn, social withdrawal is often linked with peer rejection of boys because it violates stereotypical expectations for outgoing, extroverted behavior by males (e.g. Coplan and Weeks, 2010; Doey, Coplan and Kingsbury, 2014; Gazelle, 2008).

Despite exhaustive efforts extending over several decades to define and clarify the nature of shyness/social withdrawal, much confusion remains. As noted by Schmidt and Coplan (2014), the term 'shyness' is used interchangeably with other constructs such as 'behavioral inhibition', 'social reticence', 'social anxiety', 'social withdrawal', 'solitude' and 'introversion'. It is unclear whether social withdrawal is a unidimensional or multidimensional construct – that is, whether children identified as exhibiting socially withdrawn behavior are a homogeneous or heterogeneous group. Although there is little consistency in the names of the sub-types used by various authors, there are some commonalities in their properties. *Fearful shyness* (Buss, 1985) or *unfamiliar-inhibited shyness* (Asendorpf, 1986) is characterized by an early onset during the toddler years, a possible biological predisposition toward inhibited behavior; social wariness, especially in novel, unfamiliar situations; and a propensity to withdraw from the peer group to engage in solitary, passive play. *Self-conscious shyness* (Buss, 1985) or *social evaluative inhibition* (Asendorpf, 1986) typically emerges between four to six years when the child acquires cognitive awareness of the self as a social object. It is accompanied by social anxiety.

Rubin and his colleagues (2013) delineate three forms of social withdrawal: *solitary-passive*; *solitary-active*; and *reticent*. Solitary-passive behavior consists of solitary exploratory or construction play occurring in the company of other children, as in a pre-school classroom. Solitary-active play refers to solitary dramatic or sensorimotor play. Reticence refers to the active avoidance of social contact; reticent children may be seen watching other children without engaging in social contact. The different forms of social withdrawal may be differentially associated with peer rejection at different developmental stages. Solitary-passive play may be perfectly normal in a pre-school setting but it is not typical or adaptive in an elementary or secondary school. In contrast, solitary-active play is atypical and maladaptive in pre-school and throughout childhood and adolescence. Reticence is linked with social anxiety (Rubin, Coplan and Bowker, 2009) and has been found to correlate with rejection by peers as early as the pre-school years (Gazelle *et al.*, 2005; Hart *et al.*, 2000).

There is some evidence that children are aware of different forms of shyness in other children. For example, Coplan and colleagues (2007), working with a sample of five- and six-year-olds, described children who were either shy – meaning that they wanted to play with others but were afraid to – or unsociable

– not interested in playing with others. These descriptions were followed by interview questions designed to determine whether the child depicted in the vignette wanted to play or not, acted the way they did on purpose, and would be liked by most other children. Other interview questions probed the respondent's desire to be a friend of the described child and whether the respondents felt sorry for them. The respondents seemed very aware of the difference between these two sub-types of shyness. In particular, they understood the intentionality described in the vignette about the unsociable child. The respondents indicated that they would prefer to play with a shy child who wanted to play but was too anxious in comparison with an unsociable child who didn't want to play. Even so, an aggressive playmate was rated even lower as a likeable classmate or a potential friend.

Correlations between shyness and peer rejection have emerged in many, if not most, studies conducted in North America and Western Europe (Attili, Vermigli and Schneider, 1997; Green, Vosk and Beck, 1981; Cantrell and Prinz, 1985; Cillessen *et al.*, 1992; Coie and Kupersmidt, 1983; Dodge *et al.*, 1990; Rubin *et al.*, 1989). There have been a number of cross-cultural replications, many of which indicate that shyness/social withdrawal can be a liability in terms of peer acceptance even in very collectivistic societies and places where children have traditionally been expected to be quiet, deferent and modest. Cultural issues in the role of shyness in children's peer groups have been studied in considerable detail, as is discussed in Chapter 9. The cross-cultural findings are particularly interesting because they include the possible effects of cultural change within the same cultures.

Individual shyness is thought to interact with the classroom climate and teacher supportiveness in influencing both peer rejection and the child's engagement in all aspects of the school experience (e.g. Arbeau, Coplan and Weeks, 2010; Buhs *et al.*, 2015). Such interactions between genetic and environmental factors were discussed in greater detail in Chapter 3.

Models of social competence: a brief guide for the perplexed

The debate about how to define social skills seems likely to continue for the foreseeable future. I will not end this chapter with a facile attempt at proposing a definition of my own but with a few remarks that should be helpful in delineating – to some extent – the behaviors, processes and skills that should and should not be included in the concept of social competence.

Cillessen and Bellmore (2011) speculate that there may be more than one form of social competence, based on the outcome that the competent behaviors are supposed to achieve. The first of the two forms of competence they discuss consists of being prosocial and cooperative, understanding the feelings and social messages of others, being kind, supportive and empathic, and solving problems effectively and without conflict. They believe that these are the skills needed to achieve acceptance, as research does indeed suggest. I might add that the same skills are also likely to lead to close, rewarding relationships, as research has indicated as well. The same skills are also very consistent with the humanistic values and goals of research on the behavioral correlates of peer acceptance, as noticed by Asher and McDonald (2009). Cillessen and Bellmore do not mention the cognitive and emotional processes that might underlie this first form of social competence. However, most contemporary peer-relations researchers would likely consider these less visible processes components of their understanding of social competence.

Cillessen and Bellmore discuss a second form of social competence consisting of behaviors that will probably lead to popularity, visibility and prestige but perhaps not to acceptance or close relationships. The components of this form of social competence include effective ways of achieving one's goals and asserting oneself. They remark that some children use aggressive means to achieve their goal of becoming popular and powerful. If one's goals are achieved in cooperative ways that harm no one – which is the intent of most assertiveness training – there is probably nothing wrong with pursuing one's own objectives and acting in one's own interest. If this is what one does to become popular and powerful, there may be no need for this second form of social 'competence' because it is probably not very different from the first. Invoking Asher and McDonald's statement of the goals of this body of inquiry suggests, however, that antisocial means of achieving personal prestige might be considered socially impactful or even socially effective but perhaps not socially competent. Competence can be understood as doing what is effective to achieve rewarding, prosocial relationships without harming anyone (Schneider, 1993), not merely achieving what one wants in a social situation.

What would the pioneers of peer relations, such as Moreno and Sullivan, think of a construct of popularity that consists of an understanding by group members that a certain member is of high status but might not be wanted by any or many group members as a companion? Or of being considered popular but not being really *liked* by anyone? To the degree that high status is achieved at the expense of individuals of lower status, this idea is not consistent with the general tone of Moreno's remarks on social acceptance, which he viewed as a manifestation of goodwill for both individuals and society. A divorce between the constructs of popularity and liking would more likely offend later theorists, such as Harry Stack Sullivan, whose notion of social competence is rooted in close interpersonal relationships. The idea of being popular but not close to anyone would, of course, resonate with the thinking of contemporary social critics, such as Sherry Turkle (see Chapter 1), who decry the decline of intimacy in modern Western society.

6

TECHNIQUES FOR ASSESSING CHILDREN'S PEER RELATIONS

This chapter contains descriptions of the major tools used to assess social competence: sociometrics, direct observation, reports by adults and self-reports by children. The purposes, advantages and disadvantages of each are considered. Recent innovations have enabled researchers to probe social interactions that occur in places previously considered out of reach.

There is no perfect way of gathering information about children's peer relations, which is not to say that the methods available are all equally good. Amazingly, virtually all of the tools used in present-day peer-relations research were known in Moreno's time and were described and debated before 1950 in a journal called *Sociometry*. Of course, very substantial technical improvements have been made to each method in the intervening half-century. The major techniques are peer reports or sociometrics, direct observation of children's social interaction in a variety of settings, reports by adults who know the children well, and self-ratings by participants in the research.

Sorting out the validity and usefulness of the measures can be a confusing exercise, but it must be undertaken whenever one tries to compare different studies in the field, design a new study, or interpret a study one is reading. This task is made more trying by the fact that the different sources of information – peers, teachers, parents, observers and participants – will, more often than not, provide somewhat discrepant information about the same children. As will be illustrated by a few examples in the following paragraphs, even a slight change in the wording of a question may affect the results. One fundamental principle of research design must always be remembered: a study is no better than its measures, however brilliant the underlying theory. It is probably better not to do a study at all than to do one with unsound measures.

There are several ways of deciding among the potentially useful instruments for the assessment of children's peer relations. One is to assign a premium to one of the methods on a substantive basis. Following a tradition established by Moreno, information provided by peers is often considered more valuable than any other method. Peers are assumed to be in the best position to evaluate the relationship behaviors of others from the perspective of potential relationship partners. Although Moreno's dedication to sociometrics pervaded his career and his writings, he did toy with all of the other methods – direct observation, reports from informed persons in the social network, and self-reports – at different points in his career. He found some correspondence between these methods and sociometrics, but also many appreciable differences, and concluded that observations and the other methods provided superficial information that would not reveal the 'deep structure' of a social group. The 'alternative' or 'supplementary' methods could be useful, however, in circumstances where the 'real test' (sociometrics) could not be administered (Moreno, 1960).

This premium on sociometrics has survived to the present day in many circles. However, some investigators trained in behavioral psychology place a premium on direct observation because of its inherent nature. When the social interaction being described occurs in front of one's own eyes, there is no denying that it happened. Given sufficient time and appropriate equipment, the event can also be described in as detailed a manner as is prescribed by the researcher, who can also direct the attention of the observer towards a particular aspect of the social interaction.

Sociometrics can be used to identify the role played by individuals in their social groups – their social status, for example, be it rejected, popular, neglected (ignored). Sociometric ratings can also be used to learn about the people who play these roles. For example, peers might be asked about the friendliness, shyness or hostility of fellow group members. Other methods, including but not limited to direct observation, may also be used to determine the characteristics linked with each role in the group.

Finally, in order to understand these processes best and use them in the true spirit of Morenian sociometrics, one might delve into *remedial sociometrics* – trying to help a person enhance his or her position in a group, perhaps by changing the behavior of an individual who is rejected by his or her peers:

> We cannot adequately comprehend the central direction of an individual in his development either through observation [of], for instance, a child, through watching its most spontaneous expression, its play life, or through partnership [observing as a group participant in order to learn about the individual's relationship style]. We must make him an experimenter.
>
> *(Moreno, 1960, p. 101)*

If the intervention succeeds in improving the 'diagnostic' status of the person receiving it, then the particular process or trait that was targeted in the intervention is important.

A third basis for deciding among the measures of children's peer relations is to consider the purpose of the study being planned or interpreted. Some measures may be best in particular situations but not in others. Teachers' and peers' ratings, for example, might be particularly useful in a study of bullying behavior at school. In that situation, one might not want to go to the expense of observing children's play directly, because one might observe for weeks and still miss the few, but psychologically important, incidents of bullying that occurred in the school's rest rooms or on the way home. Other studies might be focused on the mental space associated with peer relationships: for example, the feeling of closeness in friendship. The best way of accessing these feelings is by directly interviewing the friends or asking them to complete a questionnaire.

Advances in research methodology provide yet another perspective that is useful in gauging the value of the different measures, one that was introduced to methodologists in the 1950s (Campbell and Fiske, 1959) but is featured more prominently in studies appearing in the past few decades. The multi-method approach assumes that each method available for studying a particular social or psychological process is of some value, but that each is also hampered by some bias or error in measurement. Therefore, it is important to measure the same processes by several measures. In a study of children's social behavior at school, for instance, one might use teacher ratings, peer ratings *and* direct observations. Hopefully, each of the measures will provide similar information about how disruptive, friendly and cooperative each pupil is. Measurement problems would be evident, on the other hand, if the same pupils were rated positively by teachers, for instance, on all of the traits or characteristics being studied, but not rated positively on any of them by other pupils. This might happen if a pupil is particularly proficient at academic subjects, which might please the teacher so much that it affects all aspects of his or her perception of that pupil.

If the different methods provide the same information about individuals, this bolsters confidence that the study is authoritative in explaining the process it is attempting to explicate. Often, however, the different measures will lead to contradictory conclusions. A child who seems to be shy according to his or her peers may seem less so in data obtained from teachers. In that situation, frustrating as it can be, there may still be an important story to tell, perhaps that the child's 'shyness' is not evident in all situations, but only during social play outside of the classroom where the teacher is less directly involved. Interestingly, different informants, such as teachers and peers, may concur much more in providing information about the social status of individuals – that is, how liked or disliked they are in general – than in describing the details of their behavior (van den Berg, Lansu and Cillessen, 2015).

The 'real test'

Sociometry has always been based on the assumption that human beings cannot like or love each other equally, even if some might wish that they did, should or could. Therefore, studying patterns of preferences among the companions of children or adults is assumed to be a useful study of a process that is universal and natural. Both children and adults are assumed to be conscious of their preferences for play and work companions, even if they are not conscious of the reasons for those preferences (Northway, 1967). In other words, by asking children or adults to indicate which schoolmates or workmates they prefer to associate with, researchers are not creating patterns of acceptance or rejection, like or dislike. They are only measuring patterns that already exist within play or work groups. It is important to remember that sociometric methods cannot measure a group's collective opinion about any individual; rather, they can only provide a global picture about how well that individual is liked by each of his or her associates (Northway, 1967). Indeed, some children – called 'controversial' – can be liked by many and simultaneously disliked by many others.

Within most children's peer groups, some children are popular or well liked by most of the other children, whereas other children are unpopular or disliked by their peers. Standard classification systems developed by Coie, Dodge and Coppotelli (1982) and by Newcomb and Bukowski (1983) have made it possible to develop a more fine-grained identification of children's social status among their peers and to assess more accurately the consequences of rejection and acceptance. Because of their widespread use, these systems permit meaningful comparison among different studies. They stem primarily from Peery's (1979) taxonomic model, which is built upon the distinct dimensions of *social preference* and *social impact*. The former refers to the extent to which children are liked or disliked by their peers. The latter represents how noticeable in a group the child is or how the group is influenced by the presence or absence of the child. Of course, a child can be noticeable because others either value or dislike his or her companionship. Therefore, social preference is the clearer of the two dimensions and hence it is used more frequently in analyses.

The dimensions of social preference and social impact can be determined by the use of positive and negative sociometric nominations. Negative nominations – asking children to indicate which of their associates they would be *least likely* to choose as play or work companions – were used in the very earliest sociometric tests. However, 'last choices' were often omitted from research conducted in the 1950s and 1960s because some researchers found that they resulted in negative comments in the group (Northway, 1952). Furthermore, remembering that one of the main uses of sociometrics in the earlier years was in the study of leadership (see Chapter 1), many of the earlier users of the technique found no pressing need for negative nominations: 'Insofar as most people are not actively interested in those with whom they do not associate, the question itself was artificial' (Northway, 1952, p. 7). As discussed later in this chapter, any negative comments about last choices appear to have no enduring negative consequences, so last choices are now included routinely because they enable a far more precise designation of the individuals who are at risk because they are actively disliked by many of their peers, as Moreno and other pioneers intuitively sensed (Kidd, 1951; Moreno, 1960). As is also discussed later in this chapter, very careful research has since confirmed that being actively disliked is stable over time and uniquely linked to maladjustment (Asher and Coie, 1990).

Moreno (1960) maintained that it was wrong to indicate to respondents exactly how many choices they should make. He believed that some individuals had one very important best friend and few others; they should not be forced to name three or five. Other people may really have five or more people in their social environments with whom they would genuinely wish to play or work. Some versions elicited anywhere from one to eight choices of play or work partners, or 'as many as you like' (Northway, 1952). As sociometrics became more widespread, a concern arose that because of the different questions being asked, and especially because of the different number of nominations allowed, the results of different studies were not really comparable (Northway, 1952). Until recently, researchers usually asked children to identify the three or five children from their class or grade whom they would most and least like to have as play or work companions (e.g. Coie, Dodge and Coppotelli, 1982; Newcomb and Bukowski, 1983).

Today, many researchers are questioning the practice of arbitrarily predetermining the number of peers that children may designate as peers they like or don't like to play with (i.e. typically three or five). The use of unlimited nominations is spreading rapidly, not only because it permits children to make the number of choices that corresponds best with their social realities but also because the inclusion of a peer on a particular child's list does not depend on the nomination of other peers (Parkhurst and Asher, 1992). Unlimited nominations are now probably used more often than limited nominations. In other words, if a child equally likes to play with four peers and is allowed to identify only three, the inclusion of the first three will arbitrarily force the absence of the fourth peer from the list of nominees. The fourth peer may be almost as popular (or as rejected or controversial) as the third, but the researcher will never know that. In early sociometric research, the wording of the question used in eliciting the choices, including any restriction on the number of choices, was left to each investigator, who was presumed to be in the position to design the question on the basis of the group being studied. It should be noted that, in practice, limited and unlimited nominations yield very similar information most of the time (Gommans and Cillessen, 2015).

In contemporary sociometrics, most researchers ask children to indicate the classmates with whom they would or would not choose to play or work. It has been pointed out, however, that the exact wording of the question may color the findings more than is sometimes thought. Vaughn and Haager (1994), commenting on the use of questions like 'Who would you be most likely to choose to work with at school?' in studies of the peer relations of children with learning disabilities, pointed out that some children with learning problems might not be disliked, but still may not be chosen as partners to work with on school assignments. A male student who is not athletically inclined might be the last choice as a play partner, but might not be totally ostracized if he has other positive attributes. Sociometrics are very suitable for use with pre-school children

(Gazelle, Faldowski and Peter, 2015), but the wording of the question must be consistent with their language development. Computerized administration of sociometrics is a very recent innovation that appears to enhance validity (Endedijk and Cillessen, 2015).

Based on his or her social preference and social impact scores (the number of positive and negative nominations received), each child is classified as belonging to one of the following groups:

(a) *popular* (having many positive nominations and few negative nominations – which translates into high preference and high impact scores);
(b) *neglected* (few positive and few negative nominations – average preference and low impact scores);
(c) *rejected* (few positive and many negative nominations – low preference and high impact scores);
(d) *average* (average amount of positive and negative nominations – average preference and impact scores); or
(e) *controversial* (many positive and many negative nominations – average preference and high impact scores).

(Coie, Dodge and Coppotelli, 1982)

Some sociometric instruments involve *peer nominations* (e.g. Coie, Dodge and Coppotelli, 1982), whereas others are based on *peer ratings* (e.g. Asher and Dodge, 1986). There has been considerable debate about their relative merits (e.g. Asher, 1985; Frederickson and Furnham, 1998). Nominations, consistent with the original practices of Moreno and his contemporaries, have already been described as involving the naming of individuals who correspond to characteristics indicated in the question asked. In contrast, as depicted in Figure 6.1, children who participate in sociometric ratings are asked to rate each of their associates, often on a scale of 1 to 5, in terms of a question such as 'How much do you enjoying playing with each of the following classmates?' Rating scales have a number of attractive features. First of all, information is obtained on all members of the group, not just the extremes. Perhaps because of this, sociometric ratings are more stable over time than nominations, though nominations are also quite stable (see below). Second, rating scales are better if one wants to use the direct question 'How much do you like each of the following?' in sociometric procedures. As noted by Vaughn and Haager (1994), that is the clearest sociometric question and the most likely to lead to clear information about social relationships. However, most researchers would not want to use it in the nomination format, where negative nominations would be elicited by the blunt 'Name the classmates you do not like.' In completing rating scales, children are free not to rate anyone as a classmate who they do not like or do not enjoy playing with by avoiding the lower extremes of the rating scale. The latter is an advantage only if, in reality, the respondent enjoys playing with *all* of his or her classmates; it is all too easy to avoid indicating dislike when it is really there. For this reason,

Name ______________________

EXAMPLES: How much do you like to play with this person at school?

	I don't like to				I like to a lot
Louise Blue	1	2	3	4	5
Russell Grey	1	2	3	4	5

John Armon	1	2	3	4	5
Andrea Brandt	1	2	3	4	5
Sue Curtis	1	2	3	4	5
Sandra Drexel	1	2	3	4	5
Jeff Ellis	1	2	3	4	5
Bill Fox	1	2	3	4	5
Diane Higgins	1	2	3	4	5
Harry Jones	1	2	3	4	5
Jill Lamb	1	2	3	4	5
Steve Murray	1	2	3	4	5
Jo Anne Norman	1	2	3	4	5
Pam Riley	1	2	3	4	5
Jim Stevens	1	2	3	4	5

HOW MUCH DO YOU LIKE TO PLAY WITH

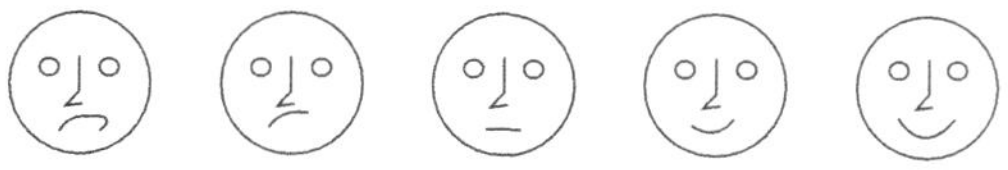

THIS PERSON AT SCHOOL?	1	2	3	4	5
	I don't like to				I like to a lot

FIGURE 6.1 Sample rating-scale sociometric measure (Source: Asher, 1985, used with permission of Springer Science and Business Media)

nominations are believed to be better than ratings in identifying children who are at risk because of peer rejection (Asher and Taylor, 1981; Gresham, 1981). Another decided disadvantage of rating scales is research time: it takes children much longer to go down a list of all their classmates and assign ratings to each one than it does to name the few associates who match a specified characteristic.

Psychometric properties and main characteristics of nominations

Measures of sociometric acceptance and rejection have been shown to be quite stable, especially for short-term intervals between measurements. Researchers have frequently obtained short-term stability correlations ranging from .60 to .80 (e.g. Asher and Dodge, 1986; Jiang and Cillessen, 2005). The majority of studies that have investigated the long-term stability of sociometric nominations (e.g. Bukowski and Newcomb, 1984; Hymel, Rubin, Rowden and LeMare, 1990; Roff, Sells and Golden, 1972) have indicated slightly lower stability coefficients than those pertaining to short-term stability. For example, Hymel, Rubin, Rowden and LeMare (1990) reported a stability coefficient of .56 for ratings of peer acceptance conducted three years apart (age seven to ten years).

The classification of children in the various social status groups (i.e. popular, average, neglected, rejected, and controversial) is less stable than the overall stability of nomination scores (e.g. total 'liked most' nominations, total 'liked least' nominations, social preferences scores). For instance, Terry and Coie (1991) compared the classification outcomes using four similar but distinct formulae for classifying peer status – those of Coie, Dodge and Coppotelli (1982), Newcomb and Bukowski (1983), Asher and Dodge (1986) and French (1988, 1990). The first two of these systems feature positive and negative nominations; the third is computed with the scores from a five-point rating scale; and the final system involves a cut-off score applied to positive nominations only, as could be computed with many data collected in the 1950s and 1960s, when many researchers used only positive nominations. In general, the authors found only moderate agreement between the different classification systems, with considerable confusion between the neglected and rejected peer status groups, as well as between the popular and controversial groups. Nevertheless, the one- and two-year stability of status classification for the various measures was roughly the same. Stability coefficients for all four procedures ranged from low stability for the average (ranging from $k = 0.01$ to $k = 0.20$ across the four methods), neglected ($k = 0.01$ to $k = 0.20$) and controversial ($k = 0.04$ to $k = 0.17$) peer status groups, to low–moderate stability for the rejected group ($k = 0.19$ to $k = 0.41$), and moderate–good stability for the popular group ($k = 0.20$ to $k = 0.52$). Thus, there appears to be greater stability in the more general peer nominations for acceptance and rejection than for membership in social status groups. For that reason, global acceptance and rejection scores, 'liked most' and 'liked least', are preferable in many analyses. The stability of rejected status may be sufficient to indicate that peer rejection poses a long-term risk for children's adjustment, as many have emphasized (e.g. Asher and Coie, 1990). However, since many children may be rejected only at some points in their development, Vitaro, Gagnon and Tremblay (1990) have suggested that researchers interested in studying rejection as a risk factor should use longitudinal data that permit the identification of children who are chronically rejected by their peers at several measurement points. Several studies have shown that chronic ostracism by peers increases the odds of later behavioral problems (DeRosier, Kupersmidt and Patterson, 1994) and the risk of boys developing feelings of loneliness and depression (Burks, Dodge and Price, 1995), over and above the odds of a maladaptive outcome by children rejected at only a single point in time.

The major index of the validity of sociometrics is the poor long-term prognosis of rejected children, which has been documented in longitudinal studies, as discussed in Chapter 2. A recent and very creative addition to the validity data has emerged from a study by Lansu, Cillessen and Karremans (2014), who discovered that high-status children were the objects of much more visual attention by their peers than other participants. Much has been written about the validity of nominations by peers of the child's own sex. Opinions vary, but the nominations of opposite-sex peers can be surprisingly valuable for the assessment of some forms of behavior (Frazier *et al.*, 2009). Many experts believe that sociometric methods are not valid if only a small number of the reference group (e.g. a school class) consents to participate in the nominations or ratings. Sociometrics are more reliable if the consent rate is high, but some useful information can be obtained from sociometric measures of some constructs even with a relatively modest consent rate (Babcock *et al.*, 2013).

Ethics in sociometric methods

Although sociometric measures are among the most widely used assessment tools in peer-relations research, there has been considerable debate concerning the possible negative consequences of their use with children. As discussed above, in order to achieve a more precise peer status categorization when conducting peer-relations research, it is important to include negative peer nominations ('Name the children you do not like to play with'), along with positive nominations ('Name the children you like to play with'); otherwise the identities of children at risk of maladjustment because of rejection by peers will not be determined. Despite their importance in determining peer status, it is these negative peer nominations that have sometimes brought researchers, ethics committees, parents and school authorities to question the appropriateness of sociometric measures (Bell-Dolan, Foster and Tishelman, 1989; Bell-Dolan and Wessler, 1994; Child and Nind, 2013; Mayeux, Underwood and Rissser, 2007). The major concerns are that by asking children to identify the peers they do not like, researchers may implicitly encourage participants to make negative statements toward those peers (Hayvren and Hymel, 1984) and to perceive or interact with unpopular and rejected peers in an even more negative manner (Asher and Hymel, 1981; Foster and Ritchey, 1979).

Given the importance of gauging the risks involved in conducting research, especially with children, some researchers have studied in very careful and systematic ways the effects of sociometric measures on the children participating in their studies (e.g. Bell-Dolan, Foster and Christopher, 1992; Bell-Dolan, Foster and Sikora, 1989; Hayvren and Hymel, 1984; Mayeux, Underwood and Risser, 2007). Overwhelmingly, these studies have provided no support for the contention that sociometric measures place children at greater risk than they encounter in everyday life. After children participated in sociometrics, no increase in negative peer interaction was noticed by trained observers (Hayvren and Hymel, 1984) or by parents and teachers (Bell-Dolan, Foster and Christopher, 1992; Mayeux, Underwood and Risser, 2007). In all studies on the effects of sociometrics, the majority of children reported that they enjoyed participating in the research. In one particular study (Bell-Dolan, Foster and Christopher, 1992), in which thirteen girls (7.5 percent of the participants) learned that a peer had identified them on the negative question nomination, only one of the thirteen stated that she did not enjoy participating in the research.

Thus, the limited data available on the effects of sociometric testing on children clearly suggest that the benefits of this type of research outweigh the potential risks. However, proper steps must be taken by researchers in order to ensure that a minimum amount of distress is present (i.e. no more than in the children's other daily activities, such as chores and homework). Bell-Dolan and Wessler (1994) provide suggestions on how to minimize risks. For example, it is advisable to add distractor questions such as 'Who is the tallest pupil in the class?', 'Who is the best at arithmetic?', 'Who tries hardest at sports?' so that the questions about disliking are imprinted less prominently in the child's memory. In Schneider's research in Canada, sociometric data are not collected on a group basis, although that method would save time. Children are brought individually to a small seminar room in their schools when they participate. If only sociometric data are collected during these individual sessions, the added privacy costs only a few minutes of research time per child.

A decision about the ethical acceptability of a research project is based on an appraisal of the relative benefit of the project in comparison with an estimate of any possible harm. In commenting on the benefits of sociometric methods, Leadbeater (2006) invokes Jesse Jackson's address to the American Psychological Association in 2000. He ended this address with the parable of the lost sheep:

> A shepherd called in his sheep in the evening; 99 came but one did not. He was worried about it, wanted to go look for it. But some argued that 'You can't save everyone,' and the 99 sheep said, 'What about us? We came when called.' As they argued about whether he should go find the lost sheep, the sun went down. Maybe the one who stayed behind had an auditory problem; maybe it stepped on glass and was bleeding; maybe it was kicked by a bigger sheep, or was lost, or in distress, or had been abused. You, as good psychologists, as teachers, bring your light to dark places. Help us find all the lost sheep, and leave no one behind.
>
> *(Jackson, 2000, p. 330)*

Observational methods

Peer nominations and peer ratings have been the most important sources of data about children's peer relations since research in the area started. However, researchers as early as Moreno were concerned that information from peers was very global in nature, indicating who is liked by whom, for example, but failing to supply detailed information about the social interactions of either the person being rated or the person providing the information about one of his or her peers. Thus, the founder of sociometrics was well aware that sociometrics had its shortcomings and tried direct observation to fill in the missing information. Moreno (1960) abandoned his own flirtation with direct observation once he reached the conclusion that the information gains from it were more superficial than he hoped. He then began to stress the importance of having some relationship with the persons being observed, of observing as a participant within a group rather than as a 'scientific spy' (Moreno, 1953, p. 101), but he did not pursue participant observation very much in his own work or training.

Observation flourished, however, in the laboratory schools in the United States and Canada that had been set up with the help of the Rockefeller Foundation in the 1920s. Those schools were set up at several universities in order to enable researchers to learn about children's development in a more intensive manner than they could as guest observers in other settings. Some of the laboratory schools are still in operation – for example, those at the University of Minnesota and the University of Toronto. Detailed sociometric records were collected at these laboratory schools, but their very nature resulted in an emphasis on direct observations of the children as they interacted at play or at work. Often, the researchers believed that knowledge about child development at that time was too limited to serve as a guide for the observations. Therefore, they often used no categories or codes while observing, and they had no specific hypothesis in mind. They simply hoped that the running narrative logs of children's behavior that they compiled would be useful in illuminating the course of child development, and, therefore, they wanted to ensure that nothing of potential importance would be missed. Many of the observers wrote down *every* event in the child's school day. Consequently, in the end, many of the running narratives were too complex and too disorganized to analyze and were relegated to archival storage after little or no use. The sociometrics, which consumed a small fraction of the research time, were the primary measures reported in journal articles of the time about children in the laboratory schools, along with IQ tests and personality scales.

As interest in behavioral approaches to children's problems increased in the 1960s, observational methods acquired a new lease on life. Direct observation was assumed to be the only acceptable method for studying the problems and tracking changes in the patterns of reinforcement that sustained them. The laboratory tradition that gave rise to behaviorism emphasized objectivity, and direct observations were assumed to be less biased than verbal reports from anyone (Hops, Davis and Longoria, 1995).

In the early stages of inquiry into a specific issue, fairly informal observation methods are still used and are often appropriate. For example, much has been learned about the nature of young children's interactions with their friends from Corsaro's (1988; Corsaro and Rizzo, 2008) and Rizzo's (1992) extended observations in kindergarten classrooms in the United States and Italy. Their observations went on for many months and were unstructured: children were observed in no fixed sequence and the observers were looking for no fixed set of behaviors. Because of this, their results may have been colored by their own subjective perspectives and biases – and by the limitations of human perception and memory, which can result in overlooking an important feature of the behavior being observed. However, previous knowledge did not provide an adequate basis for a formal, structured observational system. Had Rizzo adopted a predetermined list of behaviors to observe and had he observed the children in a predetermined order, his study probably would have contributed less than it did. This research has made a unique contribution to the understanding of the role of friendship rituals and of verbal discourse in the emergence of friendship among young children.

Once there is a sound theoretical basis for developing an observational method, however, it becomes important to convince the research community that the observations have been conducted in an objective manner and to describe very clearly exactly what has been observed. This makes today's observational data very different from the disorganized narrative logs that were collected in the university laboratory schools. The categories of behavior being observed must be defined so that the results of one observational study can be compared with the results of another. Without such definitions, what is considered a 'fight', a 'row', or an 'aggressive' act by one observer may bear little resemblance to another observer's idea of the same phenomenon. An example of a set of definitions for observation categories appears in Table 6.1, which depicts a set of observational categories used by Normand and colleagues (2011) to study the friendships of children with attention deficit/hyperactivity disorder (ADHD). An observer using this system or others similar to it has to decide how to code the social behavior of children being observed at regular, pre-specified intervals (perhaps every ten seconds). In this case, the children are playing a fast-paced game with toy cars. It is important to sample enough behavior to get a representative picture of the typical social behavior of individuals and of the group.

In some observational studies, such as those in which many of the children in a playground are participants in the research, the children's behavior is observed, in rotating order, for specific intervals of time, with coding used to describe their play at each interval. Time-sampling methods are not very suitable for counting specific incidents that have discrete beginnings and ends, such as fights. Event recording involves maintaining a running tally of the number of such phenomena. Duration and latency recording can be used if one is also interested in timing

TABLE 6.1 Definitions of car-race categories

Category (kappa)	*Definition (intra-class correlation)*
Compliance with rules	
Legal maneuvers (0.87)	All legal maneuvers including: avoiding contact with the partner's car legally (e.g., pulling one's car backwards; waiting for the partner before entering the runway); making contact with the partner's car without breaking any rules; car and blocks in proper position at times of loading and unloading. (0.29)
Illegal maneuvers (0.82)	All illegal maneuvers including: avoiding contact with the partner's car by breaking the rules (e.g., lifting one's car in the air); making contact with the partner's car while one's own car is in an illegal position (e.g., driving up the sides of the runway); infraction of rules during loading or unloading. (0.15)
Affect	
Positive (0.80)	The extent to which members of the dyad express nonverbal and verbal positive affect, including positive facial expressions and laughter. 1–3 rating [1 = the child is smiling for most of the segment; 3 = thoroughly positive with extended bouts of giggling or laughter]. (0.57)
Negative (0.81)	The extent to which partners express negativity toward one another or toward the task in their facial affect and speech. Includes orders, threats, reprimands, visible tension and nervousness. 1–3 rating [1 = the child is complaining or exhibits some frustration toward the friend or the task; 3 = extensive negative affect expressed vocally or physically at any point in the segment]. (0.05)
Neutral (0.88)	The extent to which partners manifest neutral affect for most of the segment. (0.57)

(Source: Normand *et al.*, 2011, used with permission of Springer Science and Business Media)

the length of episodes such as fights (Barton and Ascione, 1984; Merrell and Gimpel, 1998). A combination of time sampling and event sampling is often used. Sophisticated software is now available for video-recording, entering the data, and converting them into a computer-readable file for coding and analysis. Noldus OBSERVER software is the most common. Normand and colleagues (2011) used this in their observational research with children with ADHD (see above). It was also used by Charlton and Law (2014) in their recent study of the online behavior of children with behavioral and emotional difficulties.

No matter how simple or complex the observational scheme, no matter where the observations are conducted, it is essential to demonstrate inter-rater reliability, to show that different observers code the same behavior in the same way. Sophisticated statistical formulae have been developed to calculate inter-rater reliability and prove that the agreement among observers is greater than one would expect to occur by chance (Bakeman and Gottman, 1997). Obviously, observations of what is supposed to be hostile aggression, for example, would be of little scientific value if, within the same study, three different observers could not agree as to which of the incidents they observed constituted hostile aggression. It often takes considerable time for observers to be trained for a study to achieve inter-rater reliability. Understandably, this can be frustrating for enthusiastic observers who want to begin data collection as soon as possible. Table 6.1 contains the kappa statistics for inter-rater reliability in the coding of the interactions between children and their friends. Kappa coefficients of .80 are considered acceptable (Bakeman and Gottman, 1997). For additional information on achieving inter-rater reliability in observational methods, the reader is referred to an article by MacLaren Chorney and colleagues (2015) and to a very readable and authoritative methodological primer by Pellegrini (2004).

Despite the recent innovations in observational technology, there remains a lingering doubt as to how the presence of observers affects the behaviors. Children seem to get accustomed to the presence of observers after a short period of time and obvious reactions to the observers' presence seem to dissipate. However, there is no way of escaping the reality that the presence of the observer will affect the behavior being observed to some degree. The observer or the observer's surrogate (e.g. a video camera) is always present and may lead the children being observed to display their most admirable traits and stifle their shortcomings (Sillars, 1991). Nevertheless, it is difficult to stage a style of interacting that is totally unfamiliar for extended periods of time and it is unlikely that children being observed even attempt to do so. Despite the inevitable reactivity to the observer, researchers are able to capture by direct observation many of the most unattractive aspects of children's social behavior as well as their more pleasing features. Suggestions for minimizing observer bias are made in an article by Burghardt and colleagues (2012).

There are many advantages to observing children in the settings where they normally interact with each other, especially the obvious fact that the observations are conducted under normal conditions that are typical of children's lives. However, some of the most influential studies of children's peer relations have featured observations in groups set up by the experimenters, especially studies of the peer relations of aggressive and rejected children (e.g. Dodge *et al.*, 1990). Artificial as they may be, these contrived play groups can be very useful because they permit the intensive, efficient observation of specific situations of interest. For example, one could set up a play group with one aggressive, one shy/withdrawn, and two other children. It is true that interactions between aggressive and shy children do take place in school playgrounds and elsewhere from time to time, but one might have to wait so long to witness such exchanges in the midst of so many other social contacts that it might not be feasible to station observers to look for them. In the examples cited earlier, Normand and colleagues

(2011) used contrived situations: a fast-paced car race game played by two children while visiting the laboratory and negotiations during the same session about how to share an object and which game to play at the end of the session.

Observational data are rich. Observers learn first hand and in living color about children's peer relations played out in behaviors ranging from generous and helpful all the way to vicious and vindictive. However, this comes at a price. Conducting and coding observations are slow, costly and painstaking processes that are far more expensive than any of the other assessment methods considered in this chapter.

Children's self-reports: a distorted mirror?

Some peer-relations research relies on children accurately responding to self-report measures referring to various aspects of their behavior with peers. Unfortunately, the accuracy of self-report measures is often questioned (e.g. Furman, 1996), with the prevailing consensus that children may not be the most reliable informants on their own behavior. Many children may harbor no active wish to deceive when completing self-reports on their interactions with peers, but their reports may be distorted because they may be unaware of shortcomings in their own behavior, or may be unable to compare their own behavior with that of the 'typical' child at their stage of development. Aggressive and rejected children and adolescents, in particular, are known to underestimate their problems and provide in their self-reports distorted – often inflated – impressions of their social competence (e.g. Patterson, Kupersmidt and Griseler, 1990; Zimmer-Gembeck *et al.*, 2013).

Despite these reservations about self-reports on behavior itself, self-reports can be invaluable in providing important information concerning children's feelings, thoughts and impressions. Useful data have been gathered by many researchers using self-report measures for topics such as feelings of loneliness and social dissatisfaction (e.g. Asher, Hymel and Renshaw, 1984; Asher and Wheeler, 1985; Weeks and Asher, 2012), feelings about friendships, understanding and perceptions of friendship (e.g. Bukowski, Boivin and Hoza, 1994; Neal and Neal, 2014; Parker and Asher, 1993b), goals and strategies for peer interaction (e.g. Asher, MacEvoy and McDonald, 2008; Renshaw and Asher, 1983; Rose and Asher, 1999), social cognitions (e.g. Crick and Dodge, 1994), and so on. For example, it is through the use of self-report measures that researchers have found that aggressive children often have the biased belief that other people are intent on causing them harm (Crick and Dodge, 1996; Dodge and Coie, 1987). It is also through the use of self-report measures that Rose and Asher (1999) have shown that children who have friendships of poorer quality tend to endorse more social goals involving revenge than do children who have friendships of greater quality. Self-reports are the best source of information about children's feelings of loneliness and about their confidence in their abilities to be effective in social situations.

Thus, although self-report measures may lack reliability or accuracy when an objective report of the child's social behavior is desired, it is important not to underestimate their relevance to many aspects of the study of children's peer relations. Only children know what is happening inside their private mental space and, therefore, they are the best sources of information about their thinking with regard to social situations.

Information from individuals in the child's social world

One alternative to conducting high-cost observations is to obtain reports from people who spend extended periods of time in interaction with the children one wishes to study and who know them well in a variety of situations. Therefore, reports about aggressive, withdrawn and socially competent behaviors of participants in research are routinely obtained from teachers, parents and peers. Each of these informants will rate any individual's behavior through a particular lens. Teachers, for example, have experience with large numbers of children to use as a reference point. However, they cannot reasonably be expected to rate children's peer relations from the perspective of a potential friend, work companion, or relationship partner; and their ratings of many of a child's traits may be colored by that child's level of cooperation in class and academic achievement (Schneider and Byrne, 1987; White and Kistner, 1992).

Parents know their own children intimately, which means that they may be aware of aspects of their social behavior that teachers are unaware of. However, it is difficult for parents to be objective about their own children. Aside from the difficulty inherent in being objective about a loved one, parents may not have enough experience with children of a particular age to use as a reference point. In many cases, they may also have little first-hand access to information about their children's social behavior at school or in other community settings.

Not surprisingly, in light of their different perspectives, reports from teachers, peers and parents often provide discrepant information about an individual. The extent of the discrepancy depends on the particular behavior being rated and the age and gender of the child participants. There may be greater agreement with regard to a very visible behavior, such as physical aggression, than in reports about more subtle aspects of interaction (Schneider and Byrne, 1987). However, it is usually best to obtain reports from as many informants as possible and to interpret the information derived from each source with an understanding of the strengths and weaknesses of its particular perspective. Some of the major instruments for obtaining reports from informants are designed for use with several informants. These tools offer the advantage of having each of the informants rate the same behaviors using the same items as far as possible. Leading examples are the Self-Description Questionnaire (Gomez, 2014) and the Social Skills Improvement System (Gresham *et al.*, 2011).

Studying peer relations in contexts that are difficult to access: peer-relations research goes high tech

With any of the methods mentioned thus far, there is a risk that the data collected do not really represent the real-life social interaction of children and adolescents at times and at places other than those surrounding the data collection. A researcher might want to know, for example, how often a child is alone and/or feels lonely in the hours between the end of the school day and the family evening meal. So the researcher might include an item in a questionnaire to ask the child how lonely he or she feels after school. As outlined by Laursen, Denissen and Bjorklund (2012), such questionnaire content is limited by the capacity of the child to remember accurately, retrieve and recount the events that have occurred during the time frame specified in the instructions provided for responding to the questionnaire. If the researcher wants some subjective accompanying data, such as the emotions accompanying the event, the questionnaire method is surely influenced not only by the limitations of human memory but also by defense mechanisms used by humans to protect themselves from negative feelings and by the emotion experienced at the time the questionnaire is being completed. This problem applies equally to questionnaires that are collected in group settings and to online questionnaires, which have become very common. For many years, a few researchers have used diaries and logs to add precision, as in the study of social withdrawal in school, home and neighborhood contexts by Schneider, Richard, Younger and Freeman (2001).

The experience sampling method (Csikszentmihalyi and Larson, 1987; Hektner, Schmidt and Csikszentmihalyi, 2007) is a very useful way of studying children's daily activities and the fluctuations of their emotions in naturalistic settings. This technique has been used primarily with adolescents, but successful use has been reported with children as young as seven years old (Manning, 1990). These methods entail communication with the research participant at regular intervals over the course of several days, a week, or longer. Originally, the participant carried an electronic pager, but cellphone and smartphone links are now quite common. When signaled by the experimenters, the children fill out reports about how they are feeling at that moment, what they are doing, what they are thinking, and so on, depending on the purpose of the study. The random time sampling allows for measurement that is far more precise than the data recorded in diaries or running logs of children's activities, although these 'low-tech' measures have also proved useful and valid (Duck, 1991; Ladd and Golter, 1988; Schneider, Richard, Younger and Freeman, 2001).

Pepler and Craig (1995; see also Pepler, Craig and O'Connell, 2010) were concerned that traditional methods of direct observation were inadequate for their observations of school playgrounds, where they study incidents of violence. They believed that many incidents of verbal abuse, threats and aggression occur so rapidly and are so concealed from adults that they are missed by adults observing the playground under the normal limitations of human vision and hearing. Furthermore, observers are unlikely to be able to capture verbalizations among children while observing a school playground without special equipment. This is a particular disadvantage in studying aggression among girls, who tend to be verbally rather than physically aggressive (Björkqvist, Osterman and Kaukiainen, 1992; Pepler and Craig, 1995; Pepler, Craig and O'Connell, 2010).

Therefore, Pepler and Craig developed a method for remote audiovisual observations, using microphones and video cameras that enabled them to see and hear all the events occurring in the playground. The children who are participating in the study wear a wireless microphone and a lightweight transmitter. The researchers can then hear the conversations of the child wearing the microphone as well as those in his or her immediate proximity. Using the zoom lens of the camera, the researcher can also compile visual records of the same events. These records are then preserved for later observation and coding. The microphones are too expensive to hand out to every child in the playground, but some degree of anonymity is preserved by putting the microphone and transmitter in a 'fanny pack' which the child who is being observed then wears. Other children are given similar 'fanny packs', so the identity of the child under observation is not obvious. Pepler and Craig (1995) suggest that this method allows the observed children to interact with each other far away from the observers; and, at a distance, the more subtle observers' presence may have less of an effect on the children's behavior than is the case when using traditional observational techniques.

Another way of accessing the natural environment is the electronically activated recorder developed by Mehl and Robbins (2012). This recorder is small enough to be carried in a handbag, briefcase or purse. It records fifty-second excerpts of ambient sound. Mehl and his colleagues have used the recorder in health-psychology research, including a study on anger. Other recent applications of experience sampling include a study of children's after-school activities as correlates of their social and academic competence by Shernoff (2010), who used a logbook method to collect almost 5,000 recordings of specific events. Steca and colleagues (2007) used a digital diary to prompt Italian adolescents to report on what they were doing and how they were feeling when beeped at specific intervals during the day. They used the data to compare the quality of the participants' daily lives with their parents' perceptions of their self-efficacy in the parental role. Intriguing as these experience-sampling methods are, they represent only a tiny fraction of the research on children's and adolescents' peer relations.

What is new and exciting in the assessment of children's peer relations?

The fact that most of the assessment techniques used today were known fifty years ago does not mean that everything has remained static. Relatively small but important technical improvements have been made to sociometrics, observational methods and questionnaires. However, the most dramatic changes have to do not with the techniques themselves but with what is done with the data (Laursen *et al.*, 2010).

Advances in statistical-analysis strategies now facilitate inferences that emerge from data that represent the vagaries of the social lives of many, if not most, children, and especially those at risk for life-long maladjustment. Data from or about these children may not be complete and may not correspond to a normal curve. New techniques have emerged to test hypotheses that go well beyond the prediction of a simple, linear link between peer relations and some form of outcome. Peer relations may be one of many causes of a phenomenon. They may also be an indirect cause or may influence some form of outcome in an indirect way (Laursen *et al.*, 2010). New strategies have been developed to analyze data that violate the assumption of independent measurement in many basic statistical procedures. Such data reflect the realities of children's intimate dyadic relationships with friends (see Ackerman *et al.*, 2012) and their tendency to aggregate in cliques (Cillessen and Borch, 2008).

Importantly, contemporary data on peer relations are more likely than data from previous generations to be combined with information that is best described as 'biological'. This includes data on genetics (Brendgen, 2012; see Chapter 3) and underlying physiological processes. An excellent example is the research on children's anger, in which it is not uncommon to combine physiological data with self-reports, observational data and data from teachers, peers and/or parents (e.g. Hubbard *et al.*, 2004).

7

RELATIONSHIPS AT THE DYADIC LEVEL

Interactions with friends offer children and adolescents the opportunity to relate on a more intimate level than interacting within a clique or large group. Antipathy can also be experienced very strongly at the dyadic level. Concepts of friendship are often borrowed from philosophy and religion before being scrutinized with empirical research tools. Much has been learned about the basic features of friendships at different levels, including features linked to antisocial behavior and substance abuse. Both the rewards of good friendships and the costs of bad ones have been studied intensively over the past thirty years. Very little has been learned, however, about how to help facilitate friendships for children who have trouble making and keeping them. Enemyship is known to be a powerful social context, one that sometimes emerges when a friendship goes wrong.

Researchers studying children's peer relations have grown up in several substantial ways over the past twenty or thirty years. They no longer engage in the debate that pervaded the literature of the 1990s about whether it is more important for children to have close friends or to get along well with most of their classroom peers. In retrospect, this debate can be seen as paralleling deliberation by parents as to whether children should be fed vegetables or fruit. In both cases, children need both, probably for different reasons. As knowledge has increased, so has awareness of the fact that friendship is quite often an integral part of interaction in groups. Rodkin and Ahn (2009) discovered that some larger social groups consist essentially of several dyads of friends who 'hang around together'. Much of the time, close friends are also members of the same larger social group with which one identifies (see also Urberg *et al.*, 2000). When asked to name the people who are important to them, children mention friends very frequently, along with parents (Kiesner, Kerr and Stattin, 2004).

As was mentioned in Chapter 1, there is probably a species-wide inherent, genetic basis for friendship between humans and in other higher species. The friendship bond is related to cooperation, reproduction, vitality and freedom from stress, for many animal species as well as humans (Seyfarth and Cheney, 2011). Children and adolescents do vary in their motivation to befriend others, but those who are intrinsically motivated toward friendship are generally better adjusted than those who are more indifferent about having friends and feel that they are more in control of things (Ojanen *et al.*, 2013; Richard and Schneider, 2005).

Friendship can be defined in several ways, depending, in part, on the scholarly discipline behind the definition. Many psychologists define it as an interpersonal relationship in a dyad, 'a close relationship between two individuals' (Rubin, Bukowski and Parker, 2006, p. 605). The relationship is defined by certain dyadic properties such as equality or 'horizontality' and reciprocity (Bagwell and Schmidt, 2011). Sociologists emphasize to a greater extent the ways in which friendships are embedded in larger social structures, how friendship is rooted in symbolic interactions and how friends reproduce routines they adopt from adult culture (Bagwell and Schmidt, 2011; Corsaro, 2003), probably as part of the process of becoming part of the culture. Some anthropologists have studied how children understand friendship in different cultures. They have found that, in some societies, there are formal rituals that mark a mutual declaration of friendship (Bagwell and Schmidt, 2011).

Children spent vast amounts of time together in groups during earlier periods in the history of Western societies, even more than they do now. For much of the day, they provided for many of each other's physical and emotional needs, in situations where children now receive support from parents and teachers. Cross-cultural studies indicate that this social arrangement still prevails in many non-Western societies. In those circumstances where children live primarily in a world of children, 'friendship', as Lopata (1981) aptly explains, is just an ordinary relationship taken a bit further. However, in contemporary Western society, there are certain distinguishing features of close friendships that have been emphasized by philosophers and scientists alike. As noted by Ginsberg, Gottman and Parker (1986, p. 10), 'intimacy and affection are, of course, the hallmark of friendship at any age, the facet that most clearly distinguishes close friends from distant friends, acquaintances and activity partners'. The pivotal role of intimacy in friendship, typically seen as having its roots in Sullivanian theory (Sullivan, 1953; see Chapter 2), mirrors the reflections about friendship in age-old philosophical, literary and theological writings. This is perhaps most explicit in some of the work of the Augustinian philosophers. Aelred, for instance, maintained that one owes loyalty, trust and support to all other humans; the essential difference between one's relationships with friends and those with acquaintances is that the friend is the person to whom one confides the secrets of one's heart (Entralgo, 1985).

Most psychological theories and many major authors in Western literature have insisted, mistakenly, on the temporary nature of children's friendships, which cannot really be considered friendships at all because they change so quickly and lack depth. Traditionally, childhood relationships have been characterized as fleeting alliances precipitated principally by the momentary pleasure of sharing enjoyable activities. Enright and Rawlinson (1992) and Grayling (2013) follow the path of friendship as a literary theme. Emphasizing the transient nature of children's friendships, Aristotle observed in the *Nichomachean Ethics* that:

> their affection alters as their taste in pleasure alters and pleasure of that thought changes rapidly . . . Consequently they form attachments quickly and break them off quickly, often changing over the course of twenty-four hours. But young people who are friends, unlike the old, do want to pass their time in one another's company; that is how their friendship is carried on.
>
> *(Rackham, 1945, p. 461)*

In contrast to earlier theorists emphasizing the quick changes in children's friends, more recent evidence confirms that many children do have enduring relationships with their friends, as will be discussed later in this chapter.

The beginnings of friendship in early childhood

Refuting the many claims that young children do not have friends in the true sense of the word is no easy matter; the inherent difficulties are reviewed in detail by Howes (1996, 2009). Children who are two, three or four years of age do not have the vocabulary to communicate to researchers who their friends might be or to describe the nature of any relationships they might have with them. Therefore, in studying friendship among pre-schoolers, external sources of information must be used: reports from parents, impressions of teachers or caregivers, or observations of play behaviors. These sources do not provide ready access to the mental space of the children or of their possible friends, although only the children involved can construct the internal idea that they have a relationship as each other's friends. Nevertheless, some important conclusions can be drawn from the data that can be gathered.

First of all, by the time they have reached two years of age, children who have the opportunity to play on a regular basis with peers do form specific relationships. In other words, they are able to select from among their group of peers an individual or set of individuals with whom they play more frequently and ask to associate with more frequently. They also respond more positively to invitations to play from that particular child or those children. Observations of the play of pre-schoolers indicate that children involved in specific relationships act out elaborate scripted play sequences from as early as thirteen to eighteen months. Such scripts do not appear until the age of two years in the play of unacquainted children (Dunn, 1993; Howes, 1996). By the age of two years, children become involved in play sessions arranged by parents for children whom the parents believe to be friends (Ladd and Golter, 1988). According to the best data available, the specific relationships of children aged two to four years can remain stable for as long as one or two years (Dunn, 1993; Howes and Phillipsen, 1992; Unger, 1991, cited in Howes, 1996). This rate of stability (e.g. 75 percent over one year among two-year-olds in Unger's study) is essentially the same for children up to the age of ten (Berndt, Hawkins and Hoyle, 1986; Schneider, Fonzi, Tani and Tomada, 1997).

When playing together, toddlers who are friends display more complex and more mature play than others (Howes, 1996; Werebe and Baudonniere, 1991). Although most pre-schoolers ignore classmates who cry, friends are more likely to try to comfort each other if they cry (Howes and Farver, 1987). Importantly, friends are likely to experience distress should one of them move away or change pre-schools. When peers with whom children are well acquainted accompany them to new pre-school settings, their adjustment appears to be smoother than that of children who make the transition alone (Howes, 1988).

Several characteristics of children's relationships correspond to the criteria often used to define adult relationships (Howes, 1996, 2009). Children, like adults, seek to satisfy their needs for companionship, affection and intimacy in their interactions with one another. Companionship can be operationalized as the close proximity that children maintain to their preferred play partners, the stability of their choices of playmates, and simply having fun or playing together. There is evidence that children identified as friends display shared positive affect and that their social pretend play functions to explore trust and intimacy. Children's play activities indicate that they recognize the need for sensitivity to others if they want to solve problems (Howes, 1996, 2009). In addition, children of nursery school age have shown tendencies to organize into social peer groups for which 'friendship' is a basis for inclusion (Corsaro, 1981).

Thus, according to the best information it is possible to obtain, children as young as two years seem to have relationships that can be thought of as friendships. The quality of the play interactions between friends and friends' responses to each other's distress can be interpreted as early signs of what Hinde (1979) considers the distinguishing feature of a relationship – mutual commitment.

What causes friendships to form and be maintained?

Proximity

Being in a location that is physically near one's friends is a main factor of friendship, for it increases the likelihood that children will become companions and reduces the effort needed to maintain the relationship (Clark and Drewry, 1985; Spurgeon, Hicks and Terry, 1983); this may be more important for younger children than their older counterparts due to their restricted mobility (Epstein, 1989). Evidence for the importance of propinquity comes from classic findings, known since Furfey's (1928) early work, in which children are found to be more likely to form friendships with peers from their own neighborhood or school.

This tendency is recognized readily by children themselves (Furman and Bierman, 1983; Neal, Neal and Cappella, 2014; Spurgeon, Hicks and Terry, 1983).

Shared activities

The substance of childhood friendship is usually considered to be the sharing of common pastimes (Radmacher and Azmitia, 2006; Rubin *et al.*, 2013; Selman and Schultz, 1989), although the salience of this as the cement of relationships with friends decreases with age. For instance, shared play activity is more important in the relationships of pre-schoolers than those of older children. The relative importance of shared activities and interests decreases between the ages of four and seven (Furman and Bierman, 1983) and this continues into adolescence (e.g. Berndt and Perry, 1986; Bukowski and Hoza, 1989; Spurgeon, Hicks and Terry, 1983). Nevertheless, shared activity remains an element even of adult friendships, which are based in part on the common enjoyment of leisure time (Argyle, 1992; Argyle and Lu, 1990; Radmacher and Azmitia, 2006).

Similarity

Similarity, particularly in values and attitudes (Duck, Miell and Gaebler, 1980; Ladd and Emerson, 1984; McDonald *et al.*, 2013) can reduce dissonance in a friendship and increase the chance of agreement (Berscheid and Walster, 1978). Similarity enhances the compatibility that is integral to a relationship and compatibility, in turn, enables the mutual enjoyment of shared activities (Clark and Drewry, 1985). Studies of children's friendships highlight the importance of similarity. Children, at all ages, resemble their friends more than their non-friends in a number of respects (e.g. Erwin, 1985), as do adults. Even thieves can find friendship by befriending other thieves (Flashman and Gambetta, 2014). In a pioneering study conducted by Hartshorne and May in 1928, friends were found to resemble each other in deceitfulness. Thus, the homophily of friendship is not always a good thing. More will be said later in this chapter about the problems that result from aggressive children befriending each other. Some evidence suggests that the dimensions of similarity change according to developmental stage. Emphasis on superficial similarities in age, race and physical appearance declines as children mature (Furman and Bierman, 1983; Ladd and Emerson, 1984). Similarities in tastes, interests and attitudes begin to take precedence (Berndt, 1982; McGuire and Weisz, 1982). This is evidence of a developmental shift that influences the types of similarities children look for in their friends. Although older friends may have more personality-related and less superficial commonalities than younger children, even in early adolescence, friends appear to be more similar in terms of age, sex, race (Berndt, 1982) and social status (Clark and Drewry, 1985). Similarity not only plays an important role in bringing friends together. It has been found that similarity predicts in several respects friendships that remain stable in time (Hafen *et al.*, 2011).

Tangible support, instrumental assistance

Material or instrumental assistance – such as helping a friend by lending something he or she needs or wants – appears to be a key element of childhood friendship. Children report that they expect this type of assistance from their friends (Bukowski and Hoza, 1989; Hartup, 1989; Rubin *et al.*, 2013) and that they receive higher levels of tangible support from friends than from casual acquaintances (Berndt and Perry, 1986). Bukowski and Kramer (1986) found that, when evaluating the likelihood that two children will become friends, children consider levels of helpfulness or sharing. Children are more willing to share with friends than with non-friends, even if this means gaining less reward (Jones, 1985). Children between the ages of four and nine consider the ability of a friend to lend tangible support as especially important in the friendship. In early adolescence, the ability of a friend to stand up for his or her friend in a conflict with a third party attains great significance. Indeed, this has been found to take precedence over engaging in common activities, sharing secrets and discussing private matters in determining friendships for twelve-year-olds (Bukowski, Newcomb and Hoza, 1987).

Of all the features of friendship, it is the support that friends provide at times of stress that is considered the link between friendship and general well-being, as introduced in Chapter 2. There has been some speculation that support from friends can help compensate for lack of support from siblings and parents. However, this has not been confirmed consistently in research. Stocker's (1994) study, conducted with eight-year-olds in the United States, did provide some support for the compensation hypothesis. Participating children who perceived relationships with both their mothers and their friends as lacking in warmth were found to be more maladjusted than children who perceived little warmth in only one of those relationships. Very similar findings emerged in a recent study conducted with early adolescents in China (Tian *et al.*, 2012). Several other studies suggest, on the other hand, that support from friends cannot counteract lack of support from family members and vice versa. Research by East and Rook (1992), conducted with twelve-year-olds in the United States, indicated that support from siblings did not compensate for lack of support from peers. A convincing study by van Aken and Asendorpf (1997), who examined the self-esteem of twelve-year-olds in Germany, demonstrated that lack of support from one parent could be compensated only by support from the other parent. Furthermore, lack of support from classmates was not compensated by supportive relationships with siblings or non-school peers. Because of the inconsistent findings of these studies, it is too early to discard the compensation hypothesis. Adding an interesting fine distinction to the analysis of compensatory effects in social support, Laursen, Furman and Mooney (2006) found that social support in adolescent–mother dyads was related to feelings of self-worth whereas social support by friends was related to better relationships and social competence. Needless to say, outcomes in general were better when both child–parent and friendship relations were supportive.

Intimacy and self-disclosure

The intimate sharing of feelings is an inherent characteristic of childhood friendship; there is more private discussion within close dyads than with non-friends (Waldrop and Halverson, 1975). In many philosophical writings, it is intimacy that distinguishes friendships from relationships with other members of a social group (Entralgo, 1985). Intimacy becomes quite important in middle childhood and early adolescence (Berndt and Perry, 1986; Bukowski and Kramer, 1986; Furman and Bierman, 1983; Gummerum and Keller, 2008; Schneider and Tessier, 2007; Sullivan, 1953). This increase may be based on the ability of youth of these age groups to take others' perspectives into account, as well as their growing awareness of individual differences in personality characteristics among their peers (McGuire and Weisz, 1982). Although it is probably more important to older children, intimacy may still be important to young children, who may be less likely to articulate intimacy-related behavior when explaining their impressions and expectations of friendship to researchers. Some evidence of the intimacy in friendships of younger children comes from a study by Rotenberg and Sliz (1988), in which children aged five and seven conveyed a more personal audio-taped message to friends than non-friends. However, others have found that intimacy is not an important element of friendship until adolescence (Berndt and Hanna, 1995). According to a detailed meta-analysis by Hall (2011), girls and women have greater expectations for intimacy in their friendships than do boys and men. In her study of intimacy in boys' friendships, Way (2013) found that many boys were involved in close, intimate friendships in the early adolescent years but lost these intimate friendships later in adolescence.

Trust

Studies of children from the age of six years (Shannon and Kafer, 1984) through middle childhood (Buzzelli, 1988) highlight the importance of trust in friendship. Research indicates, however, that expectations that center on trust change with age. For instance, younger children tend to rely upon friends to play with them, guard secrets and fulfill promises (Bigelow, 1977; Rotenberg, 2010; Rotenberg and Pilipenko, 1983). These expectations apply to adolescents as well, but, at that developmental stage, emphasis is also placed on honesty, genuineness and the ability to meet interpersonal needs. Reciprocal, dyadic trust – that is, friends trusting each other – has been found to be an important component, particularly, in the friendships of school-aged girls (Betts and Rotenberg, 2008).

Reciprocity

Children who are friends exhibit higher levels of mutual social responsiveness than those who are merely acquaintances. This can surface during play, for best friends tend to be more equal in assuming different play roles than non-friends

(Hartup, 1989; Stoneman, Brody and MacKinnon, 1984). As children grow and become less self-centered, the expectation of reciprocity becomes increasingly explicit (Berndt, 1982; Gummerum and Keller, 2008; Schneider and Tessier, 2007). Rotenberg and Mann (1986) found that, when asked to judge the level of friendship between two age mates, twelve-year-old children considered not only the amount of personal disclosure but also the degree of mutual intimacy. Furthermore, as children mature, trust becomes more reciprocal in dyadic friendships (Rotenberg and Pilipenko, 1983). Laursen and Hartup (2002) report an important developmental progression within the childhood years, from strict equity in giving and taking to reciprocity based on the individual needs of each friend, which, of course, are not always the same.

Exclusivity

Friendships between two children occur against the backdrop of larger social groups containing peers who may also be actual or potential friends of one of the members of the friendship dyad. Most children would like to enjoy the exclusive attention and companionship of the individuals they have selected as friends. Usually, however, each friend has other friends, a reality that often poses substantial challenges to the friendship bond.

Parker and his colleagues have studied the phenomenon of jealousy with regard to child and adolescent friendships in considerable detail (Parker, Kruse and Atkins, 2010; Lavallee and Parker, 2009). Their methods include interviews, a self-report scale specific to friendship jealousy, analysis of children's responses to hypothetical vignettes they hear or read, and case studies. Their findings about jealousy will be reviewed in the next few paragraphs. It is important to remember, however, their contention that outsiders can bring a number of benefits to existing dyadic friendships. The simple act of recognizing the two as friends can cement the friendship. In some cases, outsiders can assist the friends in resolving conflicts between them.

At the same time, outsiders can force members of a friendship dyad to decide among conflicting loyalties at inopportune moments. This often induces intense feelings of jealousy as well as conflict and aggression. The third party is perceived as a threat to a relationship one values greatly. This may occur more extensively at certain periods of development, such as during the stages when children become capable of comparing themselves with others and understanding that there are multiple perspectives on social situations (Parker, Kruse and Atkins, 2010; Selman and Schultz, 1990).

Girls appear to be more sensitive to the threats perceived by a potential competitor for friendship. Both boys and girls with low self-esteem, poor social skills, and inadequate problem-solving abilities may be particularly vulnerable to feeling jealous. Jealousy may be more or less intense, depending on the expectations a child or adolescent has for friendship in general and for the specific friendship. Individual characteristics of the potential interloper may also evoke jealousy. For example, a physically attractive third party may be perceived as a very great threat, especially by an individual with low self-concept or poor body image. The jealousy evoked by a perceived threat to the exclusivity of a friendship can have substantial consequences. Peers often regard this jealousy as unattractive, which may lessen the individual's popularity in general (Parker, Kruse and Atkins, 2010).

Conflict, conflict resolution and competition

Conflicts do occur between friends, although, from middle childhood on, children are known to expect that friends will join them in resolving conflicts as quickly and amiably as possible (e.g. Berndt, 1982). Research results do not provide a precise, consistent image of how these expectations translate into behavior in situations of potential conflict. It has been found that, especially from adolescence on, the two members of a friendship dyad may not be equally aware of the conflict in their relationship. Disagreeableness with friends (as opposed to overt conflict) has been found to be stable across the adolescent years and into adulthood (Hafen *et al.*, 2015).

Sullivan (1953) theorized that competition would lead to conflict and to the dissolution of friendship. However, some empirical findings indicate the diametric opposite, at least for males at certain ages (e.g. Berndt, Hawkins and Hoyle,1986; Buhrmester, 1996; Hartup, 1992). Although he singled out competition more specifically than any other cause of the rupture of friendship, Sullivan (1953) acknowledged that some degree of competition may be normative in male friendship and may do no harm. Laursen and Pursell (2009) point out that conflict can have beneficial effects. In conflict with friends, children and youth develop cognitively by learning that other people have different perspectives on things. Of course, conflict provides practice in resolving conflict, which is a vital life skill. In a recent longitudinal study. Salvas and colleagues (2014) found that conflict in friendship at the beginning of elementary school was linked with physical aggression and maladjustment in subsequent years. However, the effect was attenuated when the conflict was accompanied by a reservoir of positive feeling in the friendship and good conflict-resolution skills.

Everyday decisions, especially regarding such common dilemmas as what to do when only one of the two children can get the first turn or play with a toy designed for one player, lead to the juxtaposition of the individual interests of the two friends and, thence, to potential conflicts. According to some sources, the pursuit of individual needs has often been seen as permissible within the friendships of males only (e.g. Buhrmester, 1996; Maccoby, 1990). Children may also see the context of a close relationship as one in which they might expect to be allowed to pursue their own wishes without fear (Hartup, 1989) and to be accepted without the need to exert the effort inherent in being equitable in each instance. Despite this, reciprocity remains the basis of the relationship. There might be a tendency to concede to the friend's wishes when the inevitable problem arises (Jones, 1985; Morgan and Sawyer, 1967) as a token expression of friendship or, perhaps, out of apprehension of losing the friend. Jones (1985) found that, on occasions when friends wished to argue for their own interests, they felt a far greater need than non-friends to justify their own assertive behavior to each other. Some gender differences have been found in this regard. Hartup *et al.* (1993) found that the tendency of friends to offer more elaborate rationales applied to dyads of girls, but not to boys. Boys tend to use power-assertive strategies rather than seek compromise through negotiation (Thayer, Updegraff and Delgado, 2008). This could reflect the frequent contention that girls are more reticent to promote their own interests in their close relationships (e.g. Buhrmester, 1996). Socially rejected girls, however, seem to negotiate in ways that resemble those of boys the same age. In an intensive observational study conducted with girls only, Lansford and colleagues (2006) discovered that rejected girls use more negative affect and bossiness when trying to resolve conflicts with their friends than socially accepted girls do.

In an observational study of friends and non-friends negotiating how they might share a single toy, Fonzi and colleagues (1997) found that friends worked harder to find a compromise and they displayed greater sensitivity in their discussions than did non-friends. Their most dramatic finding was that dyads of friends spent over twice as much time in their discussions as non-friends did. Friends also responded to each other's proposals with far more novelty; and they tended to accept their friends' offers either partially or conditionally instead of totally accepting or rejecting them. The greater elapsed time could be interpreted in several ways. It might well mean that friends felt the need to offer each other more elaborate rationales for their positions than non-friends did, as suggested by Jones (1985). It might also indicate that, in keeping with the findings of Tesser, Campbell and Smith (1984), friends stood their ground in order to avoid the deflating experience of losing to a close friend.

Dyads of non-friends often spend much time at the beginning of the problem-solving process determining their respective roles rather than tackling the problem (Azmitia and Perlmutter, 1989). With regard to physical aggression between children who are otherwise good friends, it has been found that positive affect and good conflict-resolution skills considerably reduce the likelihood of aggression by friends (Salvas *et al.*, 2014). Thus, although the findings are not entirely consistent, the overall picture is that friends work harder than non-friends to avoid turning everyday problems into heated conflicts. When they do so, their friendship is more likely to continue.

Forgiveness: a double-edged sword?

Conciliatory gestures to repair close relationships have been seen as part of the 'hard wiring' that leads humans and some other species to form interpersonal relationships. Seeking reconciliation is particularly common within relationships that are close and highly valued. Recent research has revealed that valuing the relationship alone may not lead to forgiveness; the forgiving child or adult must also be disposed to display good self-control (van der Wal, Karremans and Cillessen, 2014). Conciliatory gestures may include explicit apologies, offers of compensation, and verbal or non-verbal reminders of the closeness of the friendship bond. In some recent writings, forgiveness is seen as a personality trait or a manifestation of the personality trait of agreeableness (e.g. Tabak *et al.*, 2012).

A developmental progression in forgiveness-seeking has been identified. Older children and early adolescents may start out seeking revenge. They may turn to the pursuit of forgiveness in order to reduce the consequences that the continuing conflict might bring. Subsequently, forgiveness-seeking may be mediated by pressures by the surrounding peer group or the desire for harmony in the group. As development progresses, adolescents develop the increasing capacity to forgive within their own mental space, unconditionally, for its own sake and for the peace it will bring (Girard and Mullet, 2012; Park and Enright, 1997). These concepts have been found to correlate with self-reports of forgiveness-seeking behaviors (Park and Enright, 1997), although their effects on the long-term survival of friendship are not known.

In theory, forgiveness should reduce the hurt that ensues after falling victim to a bully. Some results support this, as in a correlational study conducted with early adolescents by Flanagan and colleagues (2012). However, these positive results are contradicted in other research. In fact, Walters and Kim-Spoon (2014) found that a propensity to forgive may *increase* the likelihood of being victimized by bullies, who may target a victim who is more likely to forgive than defend himself or herself.

Forgiveness therapy is a new and intriguing modality of adult psychotherapy. There have also been some interventions aimed at promoting forgiveness among adolescents. For example, Park and colleagues (2013) demonstrated that a forgiveness intervention with female adolescent victims of interpersonal violence in Korea led to reductions in anger, aggression, hostility and violence both after the intervention and at follow-up. The results for the forgiveness intervention were superior to those of both a comparison social-skills training group and no-treatment control.

The stability of the friendships of primary schoolchildren in a changing peer configuration

In theory, it is easier to study the stability of the friendships of primary schoolchildren than those of pre-schoolers because primary schoolchildren can describe their friendships much better. This provides the opportunity to study how friendships emerge, develop and decline against the backdrop of a peer group context that rarely remains constant.

Children's school lives are punctuated by regular, predictable changes in their network of acquaintances and potential friends, above and beyond those changes that cannot be foreseen. They often form friendships at school; consequently, the network of acquaintances changes at the end of each school year, to a greater or lesser degree depending on the size of the community, the transience of its population, and the organization of the school system. Even if regular contact between friends is still possible, the return to school after summer vacation may provide an opportunity to reevaluate a relationship, consciously or unconsciously, after what is often a period of separation for some or all of the summer. Some friendships may wane as partners mature and change and as new opportunities for friendship with other children emerge; other friendships may be maintained or enhanced. Continuing or renewing a friendship within the somewhat altered peer group configuration that emerges each school year may be an important step, not only for the individual relationships of children with their friends, but also in the developmental unfolding of the ability to form lasting, close relationships in general.

The life cycle of children's relationships

Considerable research has been conducted to determine how the nature of children's friendships changes with increasing age. In virtually all of these studies, each friendship is studied at only a single point in time. It is important to remember, however, that relationships with friends can change over time. Yet the nature of developmental changes in children's relationships with their friends has received very little attention from researchers.

Developmental models of friendship maintain that relationships with friends undergo marked qualitative change over their life course. In these models, the processes related to initial attraction become less potent in cementing the relationship as it continues. Although a number of stage models have been proposed for relationships in general (e.g. Altman and Taylor, 1973; Levinger, 1980; see Fehr, 1996), most of these pertain primarily to relationships between adults. However, a stage model for children's friendships is at least implicit in Selman's work on pair therapy (Selman and Schultz, 1990); its content essentially parallels both Selman's stage model for children's understanding of friendship (Selman, 1980) and most of the developmental models in the adult literature. The reciprocity of the relationship and, in turn, the intimacy of the bond between the two friends characterize the higher stages, replacing the more unilateral benefits obtained from the relationship that are essential elements of the earlier stages.

Ways of studying children's relationships with their close friends

Bagwell and Schmidt's (2011) model for the assessment of children's friendship experiences is presented in Figure 7.1. It is very appropriate that the lines connecting the elements of assessment resemble a precious diamond.

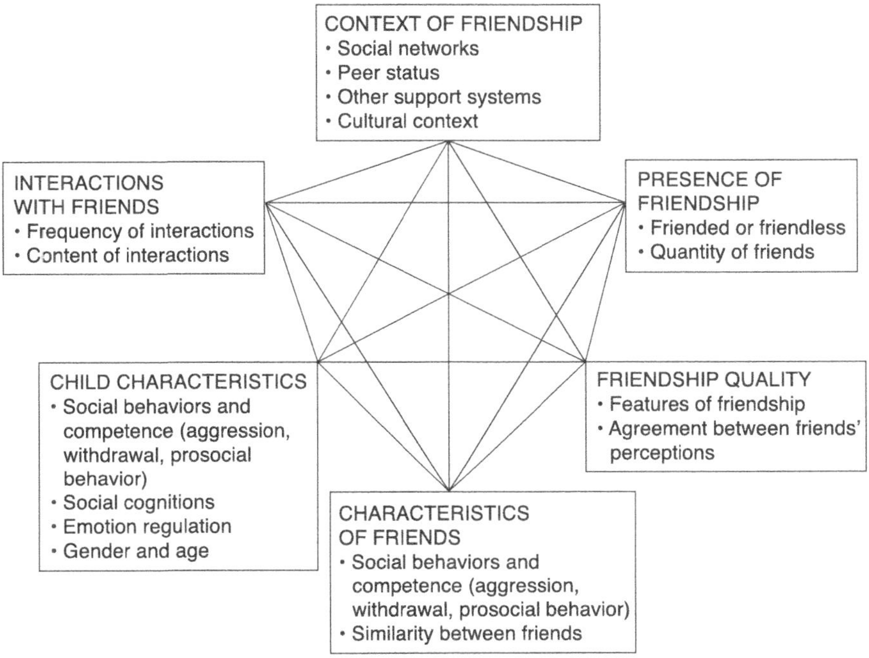

FIGURE 7.1 Model for assessment of children's friendship experience (Source: Bagwell and Schmidt, 2011, used with permission of Guilford Press)

It is essential to remember that children's friendships are private phenomena that often occur at times and in places where adults are not present. This reality imposes certain limitations on all available means for studying children's friendships. The most common methods employed by the widely cited early studies were essay techniques (e.g. Bigelow and La Gaipa, 1975), in which children and adolescents wrote about their conceptions of friendship; or interviews on the topic of friendship. Although these techniques may be of some value, essays and interviews are abstract methods in which certain elements of children's relationships cannot be captured. Because of their limited vocabulary, children may not be able to articulate or identify certain aspects of their friendships fully, even though these may be important dimensions of their relationships. It has been argued that a more direct approach is more useful. Gottman (1983), for example, insisted that it was necessary to observe the interactions of children directly, instead of speculating about them through more abstract approaches; this enables the researcher to identify certain behavior sequences that are crucial to the friendship. However, this may be difficult to implement with older children. Elements that are integral to the friendships of older children, such as self-disclosure, are usually kept from outside observers (Foster, Bell-Dolan and Berler, 1986). Researchers therefore have to assess the impact of their method on the results obtained. In light of this, it is often the case that children exhibit behavior associated with a characteristic of friendship earlier than they articulate the importance of the particular characteristic (e.g. Rotenberg and Sliz, 1988). Different methods are used in contemporary research in order to learn about different aspects of friendship. Not all aspects of a friendship are likely to be included in any single study. Furthermore, the facets of friendship are not independent (Bagwell and Schmidt, 2011). It is important to know which children are friends, how stable the friendship is, and what kind of relationship they have. Furthermore, it is important to know something about each of the friends as individuals. As detailed later, friendship, which sounds quite benevolent, can be quite harmful if one befriends the wrong person.

Reciprocal sociometric choice was the traditional sociometric technique for identifying 'friends' until recently. Users of these techniques (e.g. Northway, 1952), from the early pioneers to many current researchers, have relied on peer nomination as a main criterion for friendship. For instance, if Amy nominates Helen as a play or work partner, and Helen chooses Amy, they would be considered friends. However, there is a certain limitation to this assumption, for the two children may choose each other even though their relationship is superficial. Peer nomination of work or play partner does not necessarily indicate that a friendship has the mutual trust, support and intimacy characteristic of a close childhood friendship. Error can also occur if a child is considered friendless when there is no reciprocal nomination, because that child may have friends outside the classroom.

There have been some useful improvements in sociometric techniques for measuring friendship. One of these is to phrase the stimulus question in terms of friendship rather than choice of play or work partner, using such questions as 'Who are your good friends among the children in this school?' However, there is still ambiguity in sociometric techniques, for children may identify their friends according to their own interpretation of the meaning of friendship. Thus, the definition of 'friends' for one child may not be the same as the definition by which his or her friend lives. Because friendship is by definition characterized by the reciprocal commitment of two individuals to a relationship with each other, it is best to designate friends on the basis of mutual nominations by both. In some studies it is necessary to work with the nomination of only one friend, particularly those conducted with adolescents or those conducted outside of the settings where children meet their friends. This is less than ideal, because it does not permit a distinction between reciprocal friendships and relationships in which only one of two children considers the other a friend (Furman, 1996). The difference between feelings of friendship that are reciprocated and unreciprocated is substantial (Bagwell and Schmidt, 2011). In light of the philosophical writings that have influenced this field, some might not consider a relationship as a friendship if it is not reciprocated.

Another innovation is to retain the sociometric measures for the choice of play or work partners, but to accompany them with ratings of liking. In other words, in addition to indicating their choices of play or work companions, the respondents would be asked to indicate, perhaps on a five-point scale, how much they like each of their classmates or how much they enjoy spending time with each of them.

Different researchers have used different combinations of unilateral nominations, unilateral ratings, reciprocal nominations and reciprocal ratings in designating children as friends for their studies. It is clear that each method will lead to the identification of different children as friends. Nevertheless, each method has its own valid purpose and the friends identified by each are likely to remain stable for several months (Erdley, Nangle and Gold, 1998). In addition to identifying friends, it is essential to find out about the quality of their friendships. Several methods of assessing quality have been proposed, none of which is foolproof.

Friendship-quality questionnaires

Friendship-quality questionnaires provide a standardized way of assessing friendship quality. Several scales have been developed, including the Friendship Quality Questionnaire (Parker and Asher, 1993b) and the Friendship Quality Scale (Bukowski, Boivin and Hoza, 1994). The various rating scales have much in common, though they are not identical (see Furman (1996) or Bagwell and Schmidt (2011) for a more detailed summary of the contents of the scales and their psychometric properties). The questionnaires include items pertaining to the defining features of friendship, many of which were introduced earlier in this chapter: similarity, companionship, help, support, conflict, and conflict resolution. Although questionnaires are usually used with children aged eight years old and older, Ladd, Kochenderfer and Coleman (1996) developed a structured interview version of a friendship questionnaire for use with children aged five to six.

In some situations, it is difficult to obtain ratings from both members of a friendship. However, assessing a friendship by means of the perceptions of only one of the two friends has many limitations, although a unilateral perspective on friendship quality is better than not measuring friendship quality at all. Just as marital or romantic partners may see their relationships differently, friends' perceptions of their relationships are not always similar. This does not necessarily mean that the questionnaires are not valid. The persons involved frequently have different views of the same relationship (Furman, 1996); these differences are an integral and intriguing aspect of the scientific study of friendship.

As noted by Bagwell and Schmidt (2011) and Furman (1996), factor analyses of friendship-quality questionnaires often fail to replicate the factor structure intended by the authors of the scales. Unfortunately, using total friendship scores or total positive quality scores, which often is the only solution, leaves the researcher with a measure that is not satisfying from a conceptual point of view. As noted by Bagwell and Schmidt (2011), not all features of friendship influence outcomes in the same way, correlated though they may be.

Direct observation

Another way of learning about the quality of children's friendships is by observing the friends in conversation at play. This is by no means easy, because it is not likely that an observer will be present during many of the critical moments of a relationship between friends, such as the expression of intimacy or the resolution of a conflict. Moreover, the likelihood of an adult observer having access to such critical moments decreases as children get older. Observations of friends interacting at their pre-schools is very common in studies of younger children, whereas observations of friends of primary school age or older in their natural play or school settings is quite rare.

John Gottman (1983) is one creative, pioneering researcher who was indeed able to observe children in natural play settings. He analyzed children's conversations with peers during play sessions at the children's homes. In one study, thirteen children ranging in age from three to six years played host for one play session to either their best friends or to strangers. A subsequent investigation examined three-year-old to nine-year-old children's conversations over the course of three play sessions. The dyads were recorded on audio tape while the children played in the room where the host child usually entertained playmates. Before the actual play sessions, the parents of the participating children were asked to habituate their children to playing in the presence of the tape-recorder. This was done presumably in order to reduce the potential for awkwardness during the play sessions and to encourage the children to behave just as they would have done if no recording device had been present. From these studies, Gottman generated important information about the social processes that lead to children's friendships.

Jeffrey Parker (1986) used a rather innovative technique to study children's conversations. He knew that it would not be possible to train pre-school children to act as confederates in his experiment because of the complexity of the confederate's task. Yet he wanted to maintain the rich, spontaneous nature of children's conversation while simultaneously exercising a degree of experimental control. Parker utilized a two-foot-tall talking doll called Panduit to solve this problem. Panduit was green, dressed in silver clothing, and immobile, but it stood upright and contained an electronic device that enabled an assistant hidden behind a one-way mirror to talk to the child under the guise of Panduit. Most children responded favorably to the doll. This study, similar to Gottman's (1983), provided significant insight into friendship development in children. Without the creative addition of the Panduit confederate, however, the undertaking would have been impossible.

In working with older children, some researchers have attempted to approximate the conditions of real-life friendship in the laboratory. For instance, Dishion, Andrews and Crosby (1995) invited pre-delinquent youth to bring their best friends to the laboratory. The friends were filmed while discussing how they would resolve various problems that had occurred to them: planning a common activity, resolving a conflict between themselves, and resolving a conflict that they had with other youth. Several other researchers have attempted to simulate conflict and conflict situations for friends. For example, Hartup and colleagues (1993) observed the interactions of pairs of friends in which each member was given a different explanation of the rules of a board game.

Schneider and colleagues (Fonzi *et al.*, 1997; Normand *et al.*, 2011, 2013; Schneider, 2009) have used a simulation task developed by Fulvio Tassi at the University of Florence to measure mild conflict, conflict resolution, and competition. The car-race task simulates interaction between children in a fast-paced, engrossing game. This game requires no previous training and does not favor children with any particular level of ability. The goal of the game is to be quicker than the opponent in transporting five 4 × 3.5 × 5.5cm wooden blocks from one end of the game table to the other. Participants do this by transporting the blocks one at a time in the trunk of a 33 × 21 × 15cm toy truck. The truck must travel down a 180 × 36cm runway with walls 4.5cm high from a starting mark to a finish line and back. The runway cannot accommodate two trucks side by side, and the rules prohibit the players from lifting their wheels from the runway. Thus, a player can:

1 compete energetically but without breaking the rules, e.g. by blocking or pushing against the opponent's car;
2 compete in violation of the rules, e.g. by lifting their own car over their partner's car; or
3 avoid conflicts with their opponent even if this reduces their own chances of winning, e.g. by going in reverse, allowing their partner to proceed.

Integration of measures

Each of the measures discussed in this section provides useful information about an important aspect of children's friendships. Ideally, a single study should include as many of them as possible. Unfortunately, the measures often yield discrepant information. It is difficult to establish why a questionnaire may suggest that a friendship is closer than observers of the friends' interactions may be able to detect. It is a mistake to consider any single measure of friendship quality as the 'accurate' one. What is observed is just that – undeniable behaviors that take place in front of observers. Undeniable as the behaviors may be, they may be affected by the presence of the observer. The questionnaires may measure aspects of friendship that take place only in the mental spaces of the two friends. Individuals' perceptions of their relationships are worthy of study in their own right. Of course, the two friends may not agree on the features of their relationship, just as two spouses may not agree on the quality of their marriage. The concordance or disagreement is another valuable facet worthy of study in itself.

Individual differences in patterns of friendship

Gender differences

Gender has received a considerable amount of attention in the literature on children's friendship. Studies of friendship selection reveal that there is remarkable consistency in choice of friends in terms of gender. Pre-schoolers frequently choose cross-sex friends, whereas elementary school and middle school children make almost exclusively same-sex friends. Studies show that the number of cross-sex choices increases with age for adolescents (e.g. Bukowski *et al.*, 1993a; Eder and Hallinan, 1978). Children's same-sex choices appear to be related to their preferred activities. For example, boys who prefer rough-and-tumble play and girls who dislike this type of activity make more same-sex choices (Bukowski, 1993a; Maccoby, 1988).

Gender differences have been found in the quality of children's friendships. Girls are more likely to report more intimate exchange, validation and caring, help and guidance, closeness and security (Bukowski *et al.*, 1993a; Parker and Asher, 1993a). Girls report receiving more social support from their friends than boys do, just as girls report receiving more support from teachers and classmates (Bokhorst, Sumter and Westenberg, 2010). Their greater caring may be a mixed blessing because it can lead to empathic distress (Smith and Rose, 2011). Although girls have more contact with friends than boys, boys have been found to have greater contact with friends online, perhaps because this entails less intimacy than face-to-face encounters (Baiocco *et al.*, 2011b). Girls, more than boys, expect that talking to their friends about their problems will lead to relief. Boys are more likely to say that they would feel 'weird' in the same situation (Rose *et al.*, 2012).

There has been some suggestion that changes in society affect gender differences in the nature of friendship and in children's accessibility to close intimate friendships. For example, Murray (1999), a columnist in the *American Psychological Association Monitor*, observed that in the United States fathers tend to demand that their boys act 'tough' and that teachers discipline boys with little sensitivity. The mass media now convey images of male heroes as heartless killing machines, replacing the strong but sensitive figures such as the affable cowboy Roy Rogers of the 1950s. For these reasons, Murray maintains, a distrust of other males replaces intimate same-sex friendship as boys enter adolescence. Much more research would be helpful to determine whether Murray's contentions apply to other societies, and, indeed, to confirm that they are true for the United States.

Girls appear more committed to equity in their friendships than are boys. Benenson and Shinazi (2004) found that girls felt uncomfortable if they performed better than their friends at something, whereas boys expressed no such discomfort. It has been found that adolescent boys use more power in their relationships with friends than girls do (DeGoede, Branje and Meeus, 2009). There is, however, a dark side to girls' friendships in that they are more prone to jealousy in their friendships than are boys, and they are more likely to translate that jealousy into conflict, according to a recent study conducted in the Netherlands by Deutz, Lansu and Cillessen (2015). Girls are also more troubled by their friends' violations of friendship expectations than are boys, and more likely to think about revenge and retaliatory aggression (MacEvoy and Asher, 2012). Finally, girls' greater proclivity to intimate relating appears to leave them more susceptible than boys to some negative influences of friends, including the influence of delinquent friends (Haynie, Doogan and Soller, 2014).

Cross-gender friendships

The overwhelming majority of friendships during middle childhood are with members of one's own gender. However, there are distinct advantages and disadvantages to having friends primarily of the opposite gender during the primary school years. Kovacs, Parker and Hoffman (1996) compared eight-year-olds and nine-year-olds with and without friends of the opposite sex. They found that children whose primary friendships were with members of the opposite sex were perceived by peers as more aggressive and less helpful. These children also tended to be less popular with peers of both the same and the opposite sex. Moreover, teachers in the study sample rated children in the primary-opposites group lower for academic skills and for social competence. On the other hand, children with mostly opposite-sex friends had fewer stereotypes about gender roles than did children with mostly same-sex friends. They also tended to be better adjusted than children with no friends at all.

Children involved in cross-gender friendships often confront stereotyped gender role expectations in their relationships. Martin and Muthukrishna (2011) conducted an interesting interview study in South Africa in which they discovered the salience of these issues and the way children negotiate them. Girls often expressed the need to be 'normal' or to conform with traditional roles, whereas boys expressed the need for power.

Friendships between older and younger children

Epstein (1989, p. 168) suggested that the choice of a younger friend may indicate social problems; or it may be a healthy way to achieve balance. For instance, an older child who is physically smaller, cognitively slower, or less socially competent may benefit more from the friendship of a younger child, rather than that of an age-mate. Depressed, socially withdrawn, and learning-disabled children (Osman, 1982) frequently select younger friends. Friendships between older and younger children are more difficult to study than same-age friendships, due to the restrictions imposed by the age make-up of the classroom.

Having the wrong friends: friendship and the adjustment of children and adolescents with antisocial behavior patterns

It has often been emphasized that simply having friends may not serve positive functions, because one can have the wrong friends or troubled relationships with one's friends. Given the expectations that most children and adolescents have of their friends, one would expect aggressive youngsters to be systematically deprived of the benefits of friendship. It has long been known that many children with behavioral disorders tend to be disliked and rejected by their classmates (e.g. Cole and Carpentieri, 1990; Dishion, 1990; Gresham, 1982). In some recent studies, particular attention has been devoted to the sub-group of aggressive children who are chronically rejected by their peers over several years (Leflot *et al.*, 2011; Sturaro *et al.*, 2011). However, as discussed in Chapter 5, aggressive children may be considered generally popular and powerful and may be well liked in groups where antisocial behavior is the norm.

According to Sullivan (1953) and Selman (1980), a true friendship between children in middle childhood or later can emerge only when the relationship progresses to the point where the members are able to share intimate experiences. Many relationships involving aggressive children and adolescents may never reach that point because of the inability to resolve inevitable conflicts. According to most available research, these individuals are not proficient at generating appropriate solutions to problems or at seeing things from the perspective of another person (Richard and Dodge, 1982). The solutions they generate tend to be hostile and insensitive (Guerra and Slaby, 1989; Lochman and Dodge, 1994) and they tend to misinterpret the behavior of others as having hostile intent (Dodge and Frame, 1982). Conflict between friends during childhood has been found to lead to physical aggression later, especially for boys (Salvas *et al.*, 2014).

It has been demonstrated clearly that even the most aggressive children have friends (e.g. Dishion, Andrews and Crosby, 1995; Rys and Bear, 1997; Windle, 1994). Who are these friends? Consistent with the principle of homophily, according to which individuals form friendships with others who are similar to themselves (Berndt, 1982; Erwin, 1985), aggressive children tend to form friendships with other aggressive children. This has been confirmed many times, even for children as young as four years (Farver, 1996). In a study conducted with 886 boys from homes of low socioeconomic status in Montreal, Tessier, Tremblay and Bukowski (1994) found that boys formed friendships with peers who shared a similar level of aggressiveness. Similarly, homophily was found to be a factor in determining friendships between antisocial US boys with similar arrest records and levels of antisocial behavior in a study conducted by Dishion, Andrews and Crosby (1995). Kupersmidt, DeRosier and Patterson (1995) also found that aggressive and rejected third- and fourth-graders often became each other's friends. Further confirmation of the homophily effect for friendships among elementary school children was provided by Poulin and colleagues (1997), whose research featured multiple measures of different types of aggression in multiple settings.

Many studies also indicate the harm caused by mutual friendships between aggressive children and youth. Berndt and Keefe (1995) conducted a longitudinal study with adolescents in which it was determined that having friends who disrupted the class was associated with an increase in disruption later in the school year. In the Montreal study by Tessier, Tremblay and Bukowski (1994), aggressive boys who had aggressive friends displayed higher levels of delinquent behavior in their self-reports than aggressive boys whose friends were not aggressive. Moreover, researchers have noted increases in aggression over time among children who have relationships with aggressive peers (e.g. Boivin, Vitaro and Hodges, 1998; Poulin,

Dishion and Medici, 1998; Vitaro, Pedersen and Brendgen, 2007). The cultivation of friendships with aggressive peers is also a predictor of other negative outcomes, such as high school dropout (Véronneau *et al.*, 2008).

Much has been learned about the mechanisms by which aggressive friends exacerbate each other's problematic aggression. Cooper and colleagues (1994) speculated that one reason why delinquents sometimes seem to have close friendships may be because their good friendships are the result of lax parental supervision. They contended that lax supervision and the absence of parental monitoring may be the real risk factors, not the friendship itself. In a pioneering examination of conversation protocols, Dishion and colleagues (1997) found that deviant and violent talk was common in the conversations between aggressive male adolescents and their friends. In a study with elementary school-age participants, Grotpeter and Crick (1996) found that engaging together in aggressive acts is a prominent feature of the friendships of overtly aggressive children. Ettekal and Ladd (2015) proposed a causal model in which early aggression leads to peer rejection, which causes the aggressive child to cultivate friendships with deviant peers, leading to further rule-breaking in adolescence. Their longitudinal data indicated that all these factors do predict adolescent rule-breaking, but not necessarily in that sequence. Another causal pathway, involving dysfunctional parenting, was studied by van Ryzin and Dishion (2013). Their data indicated that dysfunctional parenting leads to 'coercive joining', i.e., dominant, hostile behavior during conflict between friends, which ends the conflict but which, in turn, leads to antisocial behavior.

Aggressive children and adolescents may also transmit their beliefs to each other. Children and youth may have to adopt the core attitudes and beliefs of friends or potential friends in order to remain a part of a particular social circle without experiencing high levels of cognitive dissonance. This may be especially true in the late elementary school grades, when students become quite concerned about their status among peers (e.g. Parker and Gottman, 1989). More information is needed about the effects of friends' interactions on thinking patterns and beliefs that may be related to aggression, particularly patterns of social problem-solving and maladaptive beliefs about aggressive behavior. Investigators have consistently found that aggressive children and adolescents are more likely than non-aggressive youngsters to attribute hostile intent to ambiguous social behaviors, to set social goals involving revenge and domination, to generate fewer non-aggressive solutions to social problems, to evaluate aggressive behaviors positively, and to lack confidence in their ability to implement non-aggressive strategies. Aggressive children and youth are also more likely than their non-aggressive peers to approve of aggressive behavior (Huesmann and Guerra, 1997).

Enemies

In the traditional sociometric literature, saying that you would not want to play with someone was considered the same as saying that the person nominated was your enemy (e.g. Shantz, 1985). This parallels the common practice in the literature of equating friendship with saying that you would choose to play or to work with someone. However, just as it is important to distinguish between a friend and a best friend, it is important to distinguish between levels of dislike. One can wish not to play or work with someone for a variety of reasons, as enumerated in Chapter 5. Not all of these reasons amount to the intense, extended loathing that characterizes hatred (Frude, 1993) and enemyship. Studying degrees of dislike is made difficult by the fact that children use the word 'hate' far too easily for their pronouncements of it to be taken seriously (Frude, 1993).

Just as friendship has distinct qualities above and beyond preferential choice of work or play companions, there are, at least in theory, certain special properties of relationships between enemies. These have been studied to a limited extent in the literature on adult interpersonal relationships. Wiseman and Duck (1995) summarized some of the distinct properties of 'enemyship' (a term they themselves had to coin). They make it clear that enemyship is not the same thing as rejecting a peer. It is, first of all, a relationship with a specific person, often one who has interfered with the attainment of one's goals. It is a fairly enduring relationship that often involves the conscious use of power against the enemy. Harsh feelings against enemies remain vivid after relatively long periods of time. In some but not all ways, enemyship is the opposite of friendship. People can rank their enemies as well as their friends – that is, speak of worst enemies and best friends. Enemies try to make each other feel uncomfortable, just as friends try to make each other feel at ease. Enemies also strive to give each other a negative self-image, whereas friends try to be rewarding to each other and to enhance each other's feelings of self-worth. In describing their enemies, adults speak primarily of malicious actions, not of personal qualities. Both friends and enemies are likely to be members of one's own sex. Only a small minority of adults report having no enemies.

Enemyship among children and adolescents has been studied much less frequently than friendship has. The few studies on the topic have mostly been conducted by a small group of dedicated, prolific researchers. In an early exploratory study designed to determine how early enemyship emerges in the developmental cycle, Hayes, Gershman and Bolin (1980) asked pre-schoolers to indicate 'Whom do you dislike more than anyone else?' More boys than girls were named as enemies by children of both genders. The researchers then asked the children to state the reasons for their dislike of their enemies. Aggressive behavior and breaking rules were the most frequent reasons. Hayes, Gershman and Halteman (1996) extended the early research by comparing the reasons for enemyship provided by males at four developmental levels – pre-school, primary school, early adolescence and young adulthood. Aggression and aberrant behavior (e.g. 'he talks too loud') were given as reasons for enemyship at all ages. There were also some age-specific findings: inappropriate play and breaking rules constituted a substantial basis for enemyship only during the pre-school years; early adolescents reported that their enemies were 'phony'; both early adolescents and especially young adult men also mentioned negative character traits (e.g. 'he is mean').

More research on enemyship has emerged since the turn of the century, although the phenomenon, given its prevalence and probable power, remains seriously understudied. Card (2010) was able to locate twenty-six studies for his influential meta-analysis of the topic, including seven conducted by himself. About half the studies in the meta-analysis were published; the remainder comprised conference papers and other unpublished documents. Unpublished studies are considered advantageous in a meta-analysis because they permit the inclusion of non-significant findings that may never have found their way into journals known to favor new and newsworthy content. On the other hand, unpublished studies may have flaws that would have been detected by journal reviewers. In any case, Card's meta-analysis, with data on studies involving over 23,000 participants, provides a very useful summary of what is known about enemyship among children and adolescents.

Card notes that the original researchers asked questions of varying intensity to determine enemyship status. Researchers have used descriptors of mild intensity (liked least among classmates), medium intensity (invoking the term 'dislike'), and very high intensity ('enemy'). If the question invokes minor intensity, such as when asking children to name the classmates they like least, the study may really be exploring peer rejection in the classic sense, rather than enemyship, with its intense feelings of dislike. Card's meta-analytic results showed that, across studies, children named fewer peers as enemies when the question asked invoked more intense feelings of dislike. Across studies, about one-third of the participants were found to have *mutual* enemies – peers that considered each other enemies. The figure would be twice as high if unilateral nominations for enemyship – situations in which one child named an enemy but the 'enemy' did not reciprocate – were tallied.

There were no significant differences in the rate of enemyship across the age range of the original samples. There was, however, an important gender difference: boys seem to have many more enemies than do girls. The meta-analytic results showed that having enemies is correlated with maladjustment, although most of the correlations were not large. The number of enemies was correlated in the direction predicted with virtually every measure of adjustment considered: aggression, anxiety, withdrawal, prosocial behavior, oppositional/defiant behavior, victimization by bullies and academic achievement. It is important to remember that the data are correlational in almost every case. Thus, the maladjustment could be either the cause or the result of having many enemies.

What purpose is served by having enemies? Some psychoanalytic writers have attempted to answer this question. However, their suggestions have yet to inspire systematic research even with adults, so there is little conclusive evidence regarding the function of enemies in children's social lives. In terms of basic instinctual needs, having enemies has been linked to stranger anxiety in infants, which typically emerges at about the eighth month of life (e.g. Volkan, 1988).

According to some speculations, stranger anxiety functions to help the infant learn the difference between close loved ones and everyone else, and to learn the difference between good and bad. Based on the psychoanalytic writings of Melanie Klein, Fornari (1966; see also Volkan, 1988) maintained that the stranger becomes the infant's first enemy, even though the stranger has never attacked the infant in any way. The infant senses the enemy as a 'bad presence' that the infant tries to eliminate.

Displacement is another source of enemyship in infancy, according to some psychoanalytic writings (Parens, 1979; Volkan, 1988). According to those sources, the infant develops a biologically based aggressive drive that surges for some reason at about nine months. Afraid that any aggression towards an individual in the immediate environment might lead to the loss of the mother's love, the infant displaces or channels the aggressive impulses and needs enemies to serve as targets.

Enemies also have functions in the play groups that emerge during the pre-school and school years. Opposition to a common enemy helps solidify a group that otherwise might be torn apart by disagreements within it. Second, people are thought to have a tendency to attribute their own shortcomings to their enemies: 'enemies in effect serve as receptacles of the protagonists' own assimilated garbage, what they cannot or will not acknowledge about themselves' (Aho, 1994, p. 87). Aho (1994, p. 117) also stated that well-adjusted individuals 'who have fully digested and assimilated their own garbage' might have no need for enemies and, therefore, might refrain from creating them. Unfortunately, very little is known about what types of children (or adults) tend to have the most enemies or hate them the most. There is also virtually no concrete knowledge about the effects enemies have on children.

A few studies suggest that children, like adults (see Wiseman and Duck, 1995), are very vigilant in the presence of their enemies. They seem to be constantly on the lookout for new offenses and seem to believe in advance that they will have to defend themselves against counterattack. Ray and Cohen (1997) conducted a study in which they read to a group of eleven-year-olds a series of stories about children in situations where they might have been provoked by other children. In some of the stories, it was clear that the other child's act was intentional; in others, the act was plainly an accident. The most interesting stories, however, were about situations in which the intention of the other child could not be determined from the information provided. In some of the stories, the children were described as friends, in others as enemies (i.e. children who disliked each other). The children participating in the research were asked whether the child in the story had provoked the other child accidentally or intentionally. They were much more likely to believe that the child's provocation was intentional in stories where the children were enemies. Enemies are often blamed for things that go wrong. This is exacerbated, at least among adults, by a tendency to attribute excessive blame to an enemy, which is seen as a way of compensating for one's own limited control over the environment and over one's own fate (Sullivan, Landau and Rothschild, 2010).

Enemyship also seems to affect children's use of language in everyday conversations. This was evident in an exploratory study by Bernicot and Mahrokhian (1988), who worked with Parisian children of five to eight years of age. The children were asked to complete a set of unfinished comic strips in which the hero (Mickey Mouse or Donald Duck) had to make a request for information or for some action from either a close friend or a 'mean enemy'. The requests made to enemies differed dramatically from those made to good friends, and they were phrased very carefully. They included elaborate reasons and justifications for the requests, as well as subtle but nasty innuendoes about the personalities of the enemies.

Enemyship may emerge when two individuals who align with different cliques come into contact with each other. This contact often involves dissimilarity between a member of a group representing the mainstream school culture and a member of a subculture that opposes the mainstream school culture. The 'opposite detracts' principle emerged in a study of Finnish fifteen-year-olds by Laursen and colleagues (2010).

There are many case-study reports indicating that an enemyship is often a friendship that has gone sour (Casper and Card, 2010), although this has yet to be demonstrated in longitudinal research in which friendships are tracked over time. Such research could determine whether the intense positive feelings that accompany a friendship convert into negative feelings that are at least as intense when the intimate bond of friendship is broken for some reason.

Enemyship in bully–victim interactions

Hafen, Laursen, Nurmi and Salmela-Aro (2013) articulate several reasons why bullies are particularly prone to having enemies. They may be disliked because they are perceived as hard and callous. They may attract enemies because they are socially inept. These researchers conducted a rigorous study to find out why bullies attract so many enemies. They were particularly interested in determining whether the high enemyship of bullies is manifest in mutual antipathy between particular pairs of friends or whether the antipathy is more generalized. The results indicated unambiguously that much of the antipathy is mutual, consisting of reciprocal antipathy nominations by two individuals.

This enemyship factor is not considered in anti-bullying programs in schools and communities, potent as it probably is. Indeed, the effects of mutual enemyship, which is probably a natural and inevitable process, may not be amenable to intervention by outsiders. Knowledge about exactly what causes the antipathy remains very limited. We can but hope that researchers will begin to redress the imbalance between what is known about friendship – a process that is intriguing because of its depth, consequences and beauty – and enemyship – a process that is intriguing because of its depth, consequences and ugliness.

8

PEER RELATIONS OF CHILDREN WITH ATYPICAL PATTERNS OF DEVELOPMENT

Developmental and behavior disorders, learning disabilities and giftedness are all known to affect children's interpersonal relations. Developmental psychopathologists emphasize the insight into the processes of human development that can be gained by studying atypical patterns of development, and vice versa. This chapter includes consideration of the mechanisms by which these atypical patterns of development influence peer relations.

As discussed in Chapter 1, the pioneers in peer-relations research during the 1920s and 1930s berated the psychoanalytic tradition for building its basic theories with insights gathered exclusively from the study of people who demonstrated atypical and problematic social behavior. Since that time, the call for more research on normal populations has been heeded. Ironically, many scholars are now engaged in eloquent appeals for more and better study of children with atypical development. Although research on children with atypical development has not declined since the 1920s (indeed, it has mushroomed), most of the research has been conducted with the certain purpose of understanding the atypical populations and finding better ways of educating them, not with the primary aim of acquiring knowledge about the human species that could contribute to developmental theory. One of the major challenges faced by contemporary scholars of child development is how to integrate data obtained from atypical and typical populations in formulating and refining coherent theories. One of the most comprehensive and readable writings on that problem is a chapter by Burack (1997), who offers a number of useful analogies to illustrate the importance of data from atypical samples. He notes that in physics, for example, scientists have discovered how to slow the motion of atoms almost to a standstill; and studying the atoms in that extreme and unusual situation has provided valuable insights into their essential nature. Similarly, studying persons who have had brain injuries has been a mainstay of research in the neurosciences.

Although many of the most influential early theorists in child development assigned little value to the study of exceptions to their general rules, a few scholars, led by Bronfenbrenner (Bronfenbrenner *et al.*, 1986), argued against this general world view that they regarded as too broad to capture the realities of children in their social worlds. They advocated, with some success, greater attention to individual, environmental and social differences. This chapter – along with Chapter 9 on cultural differences and the discussions on gender differences in Chapters 2 and 7 – describes only some of the work that has been conducted to understand individual differences in children's social relations.

Developmental and clinical psychology are usually seen as emphatically separate branches of the discipline. However, the emergence of the field of developmental psychopathology has clarified and strengthened the theoretical connections between knowledge about typical and atypical development. Among the core assumptions of developmental psychopathology is that studying abnormal development extends knowledge about normal development and that a knowledge of 'normal' development helps inform knowledge about the development of individuals who display atypical patterns. Developmental psychopathologists attempt to track the interplay of typical and atypical development across the lifespan. It is understood that the behavior and development of an individual can move in and out of the bounds of 'normal' development at several points during his or her lifetime. A traumatic life experience may trigger the display of atypical behavior but the 'trauma' is best understood as a trigger that usually brings to the surface a tendency toward atypical behavior (otherwise termed a 'risk factor' toward which the individual has been gravitating for some time). Developmental psychopathologists are very interested in understanding the processes that lead to individual gravitation away from normal, healthy development. They are particularly interested in learning about the processes of resiliency (protective factors) that propel an individual toward typical thinking and behavior despite the presence of an environmmental stressor that otherwise blows many individuals off course. Developmental psychologists believe that individuals are affected by life events that occur at any stage of development, not just early in childhood (Cicchetti, 2006; Perret and Faure, 2006; Rutter and Stevenson, 2010; Schneider, 2014; Sroufe *et al.*, 2000).

In addition to developmental psychology, the study of atypical child development has been informed by social psychology. Equity theory (e.g. Hatfield, Utne and Traupmann, 1979) is a cornerstone of the literature on friendship in social psychology. According to different versions of that theory, a relationship will survive if both partners believe that they derive equal benefit from it, or if they each perceive that they get out of the relationship as much as they put into it In friendships between children with atypical patterns of development and peers with disabilities, there is unlikely to be strict equity. One of the friends needs more help and is often incapable of providing as much reward as the other. Thus, the study of the peer relations tests the limits of equity theories. Can they be stretched to apply to equity in a *socialist* sense – where each relationship partner contributes as much as he or she can, and derives as much benefit as he or she needs?

The following pages provide an illustration of how children's peer relations are influenced by three atypical patterns of social interaction: those of children with developmental disorders (intellectual disability and autism spectrum disorder); learning disabilities; and giftedness. These three forms of exceptionality bring different features to interpersonal relationships. Intellectual disability and autism are often very visible disabilities because they may affect physical appearance. In the case of intellectual disability, and most often with autism spectrum disorder, it is obvious to classmates that children with these disabilities do poorly at most academic tasks, in many games, and in mastering the subtleties of interpersonal communication. Learning disabilities are more subtle because children with them are not recognizable by their physical appearance and because they may do well at certain tasks, while failing at others. Children with the potential for gifted behavior often make themselves apparent to others by their proficiencies and talents, which are positive attributes but none the less may distinguish them from most of their peers.

Bukowski and Adams (2005) provide a useful delineation of the ways in which peer relations may be linked to psychological disorder. They list five possible modalities of linkage.

- First of all, peer relations may be little more than a *marker* or sign that the disorder is present, but not the cause or result of the disorder.
- Peer relations may also function as a *moderator* that increases or decreases the effect of other processes that precipitate atypical behavior and development.
- Peer relations may function as a *mediator* in the chain that links a precipitating process with the outcome of atypical development. For example, children whose parents place excessive restrictions on their early social interaction may be rejected by peers as a result, causing, at least partially, socially withdrawn behavior, perhaps to the extent of diagnosable social anxiety disorder.
- Peer relations may also be a *mechanism* that leads to disorder, such as the deviant talk with friends and peers that often leads to delinquency and conduct disorder (Dishion, Piehler and Myers, 2008).
- Finally, peer relations may provide a framework for an individual to develop attributions regarding the *meaning* of his or her psychological disorder. A person might believe, for example, that one loses friends because of one's own mistakes. This thinking may lead to the person becoming lonely and depressed.

Friendships of children with intellectual disabilities

The friendships of children with disabilities test the limits of many of the theories discussed in Chapter 7. Similarity is a key characteristic of friendships between normally developing children. However, the classic finding embodied in the principle of homophily (see Chapter 7) that children select friends of the same gender, race, intellectual ability, social status and/or academic achievement (Berndt, 1982) may not extend to similarity in disability status (Dunbar, 2015). In fact, Cuksts (1988) found that, in integrated classrooms, adolescents with physical disabilities harbored negative feelings about having friends who also had disabilities. The usual reasons for becoming friends may not apply to children without intellectual disability who do befriend children with intellectual disability despite the fact that the friendships are not reciprocal, shared leisure activities may be difficult, and the friend with a disability may obtain much more support than the friend without a disability. In a friendship between a child with typical development and one with disabilities, the latter may have limited ability to partake in recreational activities and may not be able to 'give' as much as they 'receive'. This is documented by Cuksts (1988) finding that children with disabilities who were rejected by their peers did not report what they could contribute to a friendship, but did refer to their personal gains from friendship.

Some ground-breaking research illustrates the enormous benefits that accrue when children with intellectual disabilities are accepted by their peers. Fiasse and Nader-Grosbois (2012) studied the degree to which children with intellectual disabilities felt that they were accepted by their peers. These researchers hypothesized that children who displayed good 'theory of the mind skills' (i.e. those who were capable of understanding that other people have their own ways of understanding things) would be able to adjust well to their schools. Many children with intellectual disabilities do have such skills but develop them at later ages than other children do. Fiasse and Nader-Grosbois found that theory of mind skills are linked to school adjustment but that this depended on the children being accepted by their school peers.

Crystal, Watanabe and Chen (1999) suggested that culture should be an important moderator of children's acceptance of peers with disabilities. In their view, members of collectivistic cultures (see Chapter 9), where people have a heightened sense of obligation to fellow group members, should be more accepting of individuals with disabilities than members of individualistic societies, such as the United States, where higher value is placed on independence, self-reliance and competitiveness. These authors also proposed that concern and empathy for peers with disabilities increase over the course of development from early childhood through adolescence. This is because such complex cognitive processes as abstract thinking and perspective-taking – the ability to understand the perspective of other individuals in a social situation; see Selman (1980) – are needed in order to process the concept of equality and to think of other persons in a non-stereotyped manner. In addition to culture in the sense of nations or ethnic groups, the structure of the schooling experience may be an important moderator of peer acceptance: children with an intellectual disability appear to be better accepted in classrooms characterized by cooperation than they are in competitive settings (Piercy, Wilton and Townsend, 2002).

Sadly, there are very few indications that children of any age or culture accept peers with intellectual disability as readily as they accept others. Studies confirming the peer rejection of pupils with intellectual disability have mostly been conducted in the United States (Ballard *et al.*, 1977; Bender *et al.*, 1984; MacMillan and Morrison, 1980; Gresham and Reshley, 1987; O'Keefe, Saxon and Siperstein, 1991; Marlow, 1979; Morrison, Forness and MacMillan, 1983; Reese-Dukes and Stokes, 1978; Strichart and Gottlieb, 1975; Taylor, Asher and Williams, 1987). Peer rejection has also been reported in other countries (e.g. Nabuzoka and Ronning's (1997) study with schoolchildren in Zambia and Furnham and Gibbs' (1984) study in the United Kingdom). This rejection is, of course, a profound disappointment to those who hoped that integration of children with intellectual disability into regular neighborhood schools would end stigmatization. Perhaps that will occur with additional time as generations of children go through school and have contact with peers with disabilities. It should be noted that children with intellectual disability may be no more likely to have friends if they remain in a self-contained special class or school (Buysse, Goldman and Skinner, 2002; Cuckle and Wilson, 2002; Fryxell and Kennedy, 1995).

Only a few researchers studying the peer acceptance of children with intellectual disabilities have taken into account the social behavior of the children with intellectual disability. These studies suggest that children with intellectual disability may not be doomed to peer rejection solely because they have intellectual disability: they can achieve peer acceptance if their social behavior is perceived as competent (Gottlieb, Semmel and Veldman, 1978; Siperstein, Leffert and Widaman, 1996). Therefore, teaching socially competent behavior merits high priority by the teachers and parents of children with intellectual disability.

Special programming can facilitate acceptance but special programming does not necessarily mean segregation or institutionalization. Siperstein, Glick and Parker (2009) found that a special summer recreational camp in for children with and without intellectual disabilities was characterized by acceptance of the campers with disabilities. When asked which fellow campers they enjoyed hanging out with, the majority of children with disabilities were named by at least one of their fellow campers who had no disability. In an interview study with children in New Zealand, Townsend and Hassall (2007) found that children without disabilities welcomed the opportunity of joining in unified-sports programs of this type. Similarly, Italian researchers Nota, Ferrara and Soresi (2005) found that schoolchildren expressed – at least in principle – a willingness to help and befriend children with disabilities, depending on the nature of the potential friend's special needs. In another study conducted in Italy, Manetti, Schneider and Siperstein (2001) found that the attitudes of children without disabilities who had the opportunity to help children at their school in a special unit for children with very severe intellectual and physical disabilities displayed improved attitudes toward people with disability in general. Providing a 'peer buddy' for newly enrolled pupils with disability can also increase the likelihood of their being accepted in their new schools (Carter, Hughes, Guth and Copeland, 2005).

Autism spectrum disorder: a condition with social interaction problems at its core

Autism spectrum disorders are characterized by deficits in social communication and social interaction. Intellectual development ranges from considerably delayed to average. For reasons that are not well known, the population prevalence rate of autism spectrum disorder has been increasing for several decades. After the syndrome was first discovered in the 1940s, it was attributed to the harm caused by 'refrigerator mothers'; this has since been completely refuted. Also refuted is the contention that autism is linked to vaccinations received by children. Most authorities believe that there is a genetic basis to the disorder. Until the appearance of the latest edition of the *Diagnostic and Statistical Manual* in 2013, a separate label, Asperger's syndrome, was used to refer to individuals who display autistic symptoms but do not have intellectual disabilities. These people master language and engage in social interaction but in very atypical, idiosyncratic ways. They are now considered as falling within the autism spectrum; the common term is now 'higher-functioning autism' (Schneider, 2014).

Children with autism spectrum disorder are rejected by their peers far more often than children without any diagnosable disorder (e.g. Dean *et al.*, 2014). Reviewing twenty-four studies on the friendships of children with autism spectrum disorder, Petrina, Carter and Stephenson (2014) concluded that these children generally had fewer friends than other children. Moreover, the friendships they do have are lower in friendship quality and characterized by infrequent contact. Using a vignette method, Bottema-Beutel and Li (2015) interviewed adolescents about their reasons for excluding or not excluding hypothetical peers with autism spectrum disorder. The respondents varied considerably in their responses. Some students did feel that it was morally wrong to exclude fellow pupils with autism spectrum disorders on the basis of equity and fairness. Those who felt that it was acceptable to exclude believed that it was more justified to exclude fellow pupils with autism spectrum disorders from private spaces such as their homes than from public spaces such as schools. Their reasons included the contention that including the pupil with autism would prejudice the harmonious functioning of the social group. Others justified exclusion as an expression of a personal right to choose one's own associates.

Because social-interaction deficits are, by definition, a core component of autism spectrum disorder, social-skills training has been applied energetically with this population. The techniques used and their effectiveness are discussed in Chapter 12.

Children with learning disabilities and attention deficit/hyperactivity disorder

Although they are of average intelligence or higher, children with learning disabilities have specific deficits in some of their academic subject areas, or in processing information of some specific types (e.g. visual symbols or spoken language). These problems are thought to be associated with neurological dysfunctions, although it is not common to diagnose brain damage in each individual case. The nature and definition of learning disabilities have been debated extensively (see Polloway *et al.*, 1997). Wiener (1987) summarized the theories that have been proposed to account for the problems faced by children with learning disabilities in their relations with peers. One possibility is the *discrepancy hypothesis*, according to which children with learning disabilities are disliked because they lack abilities that are valued by their peers and that children without learning disabilities are more likely to possess. Depending on the peer group, such abilities could include proficiency in academic subjects, physical attractiveness, general intelligence, or athletic ability. In contrast, the *psychological processing deficit hypothesis* holds that the peer-relations problems of children with learning disabilities stem from the same basic perceptual, cognitive, and language-processing deficits that cause their difficulties in academic subjects. Those deficits may affect the ability to understand the intentions of others, to read other people's emotions, and to react to them in a manner that is appropriate to the situation. In a somewhat similar vein, the *strategic deficit hypothesis* holds that, just as children with learning disabilities lack the strategies needed to approach academic problems actively and competently, they lack the strategies that are needed to tackle and resolve social problems. Finally, the *differential treatment hypothesis* links the social problems of children with learning disabilities to differences in the way adults or peers interact with them. For example, teachers who are aware of the learning-disabled status of some of their pupils might treat them as they would children younger than the level of the classroom and peer group. San Miguel, Forness and Kavale (1996) proposed a *psychiatric comorbidity hypothesis*, according to which the peer-relations difficulties are attributable to the very high rates of depression and attention problems among children with learning disabilities. Both depression (e.g. Ederer, 1990; Oldehinkel *et al.*, 2007) and attention problems (see below) have been linked to the social rejection of children by their peers.

Most but not all studies indicate that children with learning disabilities are rejected by their peers (Bursuck, 1989; Garret and Crump, 1980; Horowitz, 1981; Johnson and Johnson, 1983; Juvonen and Bear, 1992; Lee, Yoo and Bok, 2003; Margalit, 1998; McMichael, 1980; Ochoa and Palmer, 1991; Prillaman, 1981; Stone and LaGreca, 1990; Vaughn *et al.*, 1992; Yu, Zhang and Yan, 2005). These studies were conducted in the United States, Canada, the United Kingdom, Israel, China and Korea. Of course, the results do not mean that every child with learning disabilities suffers rejection by peers. Wiener and Schneider (2002) found that children with learning disabilities have fewer friends than other children. The friendships they do have are of shorter duration and are characterized by high levels of conflict and deficiencies in conflict resolution and relationship-repair skills. Children with learning disabilities are also disproportionately victimized by school bullies (Luciano and Savage, 2007).

Children with both learning disabilities and attention deficit/hyperactivity disorder (ADHD) have been found to be even more rejected than children with learning disabilities alone (Kellner, Houghton and Douglas, 2003; McNamara, Willoughby and Chalmers, 2005). Peer-relations problems are so common among children with ADHD that peer problems are now considered a marker of the disorder, meaning that they are almost always present in children with the disorder, even though they are not a criterion for diagnosis. Pelham and Fabiano (2008) estimate that children with ADHD have two negative exchanges per minute with teachers or peers at school (based on data reported by Abikoff *et al.*, 1993) plus 0.7 per minute with peers outside of school (based on Pelham and Bender, 1982). Peers find them disruptive, obnoxious and socially awkward (e.g. Milich and Landau, 1982). Children brought together in play situations are known to dislike classmates with ADHD within hours of first meeting them (Greene *et al.*, 2001; Pelham and Bender, 1982). Normand and colleagues (2011) conducted an intensive observational study of the interactions of children with ADHD and their real-life close friends. The children with ADHD broke the rules of the game very frequently. In negotiating the sharing of an object, they were insensitive and enquired very infrequently about their friends' wishes. During the first wave of data collection, their friends reported that they were satisfied with the relationship; this was no longer the case at follow-up a year later (Normand *et al.*, 2013).

Children with special academic talent or exceptional creativity

Friendships between gifted children and their non-gifted peers are characterized by an inequality that is somewhat different in complexion from the relationships between children with and without disabilities. In some situations, gifted children can bring greater reward to their relationships with non-gifted peers than can their friends who do not share their special talents. This may occur to the extent that the 'Terman myth' is not a myth. Terman, an eminent American psychologist who conducted longitudinal studies of children with high IQs from the 1920s to the 1960s, believed that high IQ would enable children to be better than others at almost *everything* – school, sports, moral character, friendship, and, later, marriage. Accordingly, they should be better than their non-gifted friends at many of the activities that are valued in the peer group, which should make them popular. They should also be better at using their intellectual abilities to solve problems that arise within their relationships (Terman and Oden, 1959).

However, there are other situations in which the Terman myth may be less applicable to the peer relationships of gifted children. A lot depends on whom one regards as 'gifted'. If by this term one means children who fall in the top 2 or 3 percent of the distribution of IQ scores (i.e. IQ greater than 125 or so), in a primary school of four hundred pupils there would be ten or so gifted children. Those ten might share the interests of the group and be popular among them because of the things that they do well. However, if by 'gifted' one means a one-in-a-*thousand* genius, the situation could be quite different. That truly exceptional individual may be very different from his or her schoolmates. Like the gifted child in the top second or third percentile of IQ scores, the prodigious child displaying rarer levels of high ability is able to answer the teacher's questions very readily and do well in tests. However, that child's capacities and needs are far beyond the level of the regular academic program; their interests may be very different from those of most of their peers, who may have difficulty understanding them and may find them somewhat 'strange'; and the genius may be bored and/or alienated.

Similar ostracism may be the fate of the child whose giftedness is defined in terms of exceptional creativity rather than high IQ. By definition, creativity means the ability to see things in novel and often different ways; that novelty may be welcomed by peers in some cases, but the differences may not be valued. Furthermore, in order to translate their creative potential into an enduring contribution to science, the fine arts, or literature, creative children must withdraw for extended periods of time in order to develop their talents and produce their creative products. A musically precocious child cannot at the same time play football and compose a symphony or practice the violin. A budding writer cannot always afford to take the time away from the novel he or she is writing in order to join schoolmates who are listening to rock music, even if he or she shares that interest or would feign to in order to be better accepted. Going even further is the belief, widespread among artists and musicians, that truly creative persons must suffer in order to reach the pinnacle of their creative potential (Andreasen and Canter, 1975). Being rejected by one's peers is a sure way of suffering.

It has been traditional to study the lives of the gifted through historical records and biographical accounts. As noted in Chapter 1, such sources provide very limited information about social relations. This applies even more to biographies of eminent persons, because the biographers typically pay most attention to the early signs of greatness, eminence and creativity. Schneider (1987) surveyed autobiographies rather than biographies, based on the assumption that early peer relations have a far more enduring impression on a person writing his or her own life story than on a biographer chronicling the personal life of a famous person. He found clear, if brief, accounts of early relationships at the beginning of most autobiographies. The social competence depicted in them varied enormously by the discipline in which the individual achieved eminence. The childhoods of about half of the outstanding writers were marred by loneliness and/or peer rejection. The early histories of musicians and visual artists were quite similar to those of the writers. In contrast, scientists and political leaders apparently fared quite well in their relations with childhood friends.

The many studies on the peer reputations of children with high IQs leave no impression other than they are as talented in relating to others as they are in responding to intelligence tests (e.g. Bain and Bell, 2004; Cohen, Duncan and Cohen, 1994; Eccles, Bauman and Rosenberg, 1989; Lee, Olszewski-Kubilius and Thomson, 2012; Luftig and Nichols, 1991; Schneider *et al.*, 1989; Schneider and Daniels, 1992). Barber and Wasson (2015) found the same for adolescents participating in advanced-level coursework. It is worth noting that, in at least one major study, by Solano (1976), gifted boys were found to be popular, while gifted girls tended to be rejected. Nevertheless, in general, the Terman myth is not devoid of a substantial grain of truth. However, giftedness was defined in almost every study either by high IQ or by high academic achievement. This is partly because it is very difficult to measure creativity with similar precision. Furthermore, in order to achieve the sample size needed for the study, most researchers defined the top 1–3 percent of the population as gifted. As detailed by Schneider (1987), peer rejection would probably be much more common had the researchers focused on highly creative children rather than those with high IQs.

Peers' general acceptance of children with high levels of intellectual ability can be a mixed blessing. In some cases, bright children will deny their talents in order to become even more popular or refrain from cultivating their special talents in favor of the leisure activities that are more typical of their age groups (Cross and Swiatek, 2009; Schneider, 1987). This could lead to the unfortunate failure of some individuals to reach their true potential, which is too high a price to pay for popularity. Gifted children are also known to benefit from each other's intellectual stimulation (Lando and Schneider, 1997). Hopefully, their typical social success with non-gifted children does not drive them away from these learning opportunities.

Will the next generation be more accepting?

As more generations of children go through their school years in contact with children with exceptional patterns of social development, we can but hope that some of the stigma associated with disability will decline. This might occur because children may get used to seeing children with disabilities as peers who belong to the same group, with learning needs that are among the responsibilities of their own teachers. However, within the reality of schools as captured by most research, the examples of children with intellectual disability, learning disabilities, and gifted potential illustrate that children's friendships have difficulty overcoming the obstacles of dissimilarities between friends and inequalities in friends' abilities to provide rewarding relationships for each other. If the advantages intended by those who advocate educating children with exceptionalities in normal school settings are to be realized, much more will have to be done than is currently attempted in most places to help cement rewarding relationships between children with and without disabilities. Some practical ways of achieving this are discussed in Chapter 12.

9

CULTURAL DIFFERENCES IN PEER RELATIONS

Characteristics of cultures are thought to affect the relationships of individuals within them. The dichotomy between societal individualism and collectivism explains only part of the cross-cultural differences in both the place and nature of peer relationships. Research on children's peer relations outside of North America has burgeoned in recent years. Studies from China, in particular, are informing theory and research in unprecedented ways.

Cross-cultural comparisons of social behavior can help identify the origins of social competence. Research can attempt to link the characteristics of a society to the social behavior of its members. Such efforts have often been successful, as shown by some of the studies mentioned later in this chapter. However, cross-cultural research is also very revealing even if it emerges that a particular aspect of children's social relations is no different in different cultures. In this way, universal, species-wide aspects of social behavior are discovered. Results have indicated that there are a small number of 'scripts' for social interaction that are enacted by children of many different and distinct cultures (Whiting and Edwards, 1988). Children in all cultures appear to possess a desire to become capable individuals and to learn about themselves and social interactions (Edwards, 1986). Differences in culture can affect the ways in which children express their deep-seated need to become socially competent and the ages at which important milestones occur.

Research into the link between culture and children's peer relations draws on two main bodies of literature. The first compares features of one culture – such as its religion, economy or ideology – with the same features of other cultures; the cultures are regarded as separate and distinct. Effective use of this approach involves broad sampling of cultures that vary along a specific dimension. For example, one might wish to study cultures that vary in their levels of aggressive behavior in order to see whether the general aggressiveness of a culture translates into approval of aggression among children. However, there are many challenges in trying to conduct comprehensive cross-cultural comparisons, which require excellent communication between researchers in different places. Human and material resources must also be available at each data collection site. Comprehensive, cross-cultural sampling has been achieved more often in studies of adult interpersonal relations, although it is increasingly applied to research with children, too.

A second body of literature examines the relations between people from different subcultures coexisting within the same majority culture. Such interaction is common in many Western countries, which are the hosts of immigrants in unprecedented numbers. Throughout the twentieth century, individuals fleeing economic or political stress sought shelter in North America, Western Europe, Australia, and other Western societies. However, there is also increasing movement of populations across borders as the result of such political and economic unions as the European Union and the North American Free Trade Group. These social and political changes provide increasing opportunities to study such phenomena as inter-racial and inter-ethnic friendship, gauging the influence of culture on children's preferred relationship partners. There have been numerous studies on this topic, which may be due in part to the widespread media coverage of the events leading to the racial desegregation of American schools and of violence between young people of different cultural origins in Britain, France and Germany.

Individualism/collectivism

A fundamental distinction among cultures is whether they can be characterized as individualistic or collectivistic (Hofstede, 2003; Sun, 2014). Collectivistic cultures place importance on group identity over the individual autonomy associated with individualistic cultures. Individuals from collectivistic cultures also work toward a common goal and assume greater collective responsibility for the welfare of group members. This is often translated into the sharing of childcare responsibilities and collective child-rearing. The English-speaking countries of Canada, Great Britain, the United States, and Australia represent the most individualistic societies (Hofstede, 2003). Children in these nations are raised under a belief system that emphasizes personal autonomy and individuality to a far greater degree than almost all developing world cultures or even those of continental Europe. Because they rely less on common, shared opinions, people in individualistic cultures tend to hold more discrete, idiosyncratic beliefs about others. In an authoritative review of the theory and research, Oyserman and Lee (2008) establish, first of all, that the construct of individualism/collectivism is a very potent predictor of differences among cultures and people. They also point out that this predictive power is not unlimited.

Urban areas are usually more individualistic than rural locations in any given region (Madsen and Shapira, 1970). Immigration usually involves moving from a collectivistic society to one characterized by individualism (Triandis *et al.*, 1988). There may be enormous within-society variations in collectivism/individualism. For example, urban Koreans who are working toward industrialization in their collectivistic culture are also known to be highly individualistic (Cha, 1994). Indeed, it is common for societies to have both individualistic and collectivistic characteristics. For example, Indians living in India and abroad have been shown to have collectivistic ideals concerning family relations but an individualistic orientation toward interpersonal relationships and economic activity (Sinha and Tripathi, 1994). Some research indicates important differences among cultures that have often been lumped together as 'individualistic'. North Americans have been shown to value the pursuit of individual interest, whereas Western Europeans value egalitarianism and harmony, even though they also value individual autonomy (Schwartz and Ros, 1995, pp.111–12). In a discussion of the dynamic interplay between collectivistic and individualistic forces within cultures, Philipsen (1987) emphasized that cultures are in constant evolution and do not remain fixed in terms of their individualism or collectivism. He also insisted that, in order to understand a culture completely, the researcher must understand not only how collectivistic or individualistic it is but the forces within the culture that work to make it collectivistic or individualistic. Competing forces are at work in many societies, pulling them toward greater individualism or greater collectivism.

Personal identity is defined more extensively by membership of a cultural group when there is extensive contact between different cultural groups; this applies especially to multicultural societies (McGuire *et al.*, 1978), particularly among minority groups (e.g. Hewstone, Bond and Wan, 1983; Hofman, 1985). Research has explored the cultural identities of children in numerous cultures. Results from studies in which a collectivistic minority is surrounded by a majority culture indicate two opposite tendencies. One contention is that, if surrounded by a majority, minority parents will cling to their own cultural identity and protect their children from assimilation by infusing cultural values. However, a different outcome may occur, in which the parents teach their children the skills necessary to succeed in the majority culture (Ogbu, 1981). This may involve adopting different parenting styles in order to impart the competencies necessary to thrive in an individualistic society.

Individualism/collectivism is not the only dimension that influences social relationships in a society. For instance, Hall (1976) proposed another cultural distinction by differentiating between high-context and low-context cultures. In a low-context culture, such as English Canada, individuals openly communicate information about relationships to each other. In high-context cultures, such as China, Japan and Korea, this information is inferred from the context or situation. Thus, in a high-context society, a child may have to learn the skills necessary for this type of deduction. In order to be socially competent, the child must use intuition and knowledge of a situation instead of relying on direct messages used during social interaction. Although the skills necessary for social competence in high-context cultures emphasize interpretative ability, the ability to understand and interpret social situations remains essential even in a low-context culture (see, e.g., Argyle, Furnham and Graham, 1981; Brown, 2010).

The combination of individualism/collectivism and low/high context as cultural characteristics can influence the nature of interpersonal relationships (Gudykunst, 2003; Gudykunst and Ting-Toomey, 1988). There may be a need to preserve one's public image in individualistic, low-context cultures, whereas individuals living in collectivistic, high-context cultures may focus on the collective image of their group. Although maintaining an individual public image may also be a priority, individuals in a collectivistic society will try to ensure that their public image does not conflict with the norms and standards of their community. Research into this and other areas of social development should recognize the interplay between developmental and cultural differences, as culture may be more apparent in certain developmental stages. For example, adolescents are often depicted in the media as having far greater concern about their public images than either younger children or adults.

Tolerance of ambiguity and diversity

Cultures also differ in their levels of tolerance of ambiguity in relationships and diversity in behavior (Hofstede, 2003). In cultures where there is little tolerance of a departure from the norm, there is pressure on parents and children to conform and thus eliminate behavior which does not adhere to social norms. Moreover, a child may be encouraged not to associate with others who display atypical behavior, thus learning to reject non-conformists. Non-conformists may in turn encounter higher levels of stress and more emotional displays in their interpersonal relationships.

Cultures may also be characterized by the distance between individuals with high and low power. Hofstede (2003) adopted power distance as a cultural characteristic and found that individuals in certain cultures readily accept an unequal distribution of power. Children from these high-power-distance cultures may be more likely to value conformity, assume authoritarian beliefs, and obey adults without question.

Rules

Argyle (1983, p. 123) defined a social rule as 'a shared belief that certain things should or should not be done' within the confines of a particular setting. Social rules apply to all situations and the breaking of a rule most often leads to some form of repudiation by peers. Cultures may differ according to what rules apply to different situations. For example, Japanese adults are expected to restrict emotional display and defer to others far more than their British counterparts (Argyle *et al.*, 1986). Within a culture, different rules may apply to different settings; there may be fewer rules governing certain types of relationships than others. Rules also exist for relationships between children and adults.

Until the past few years, it was quite common to find articles in social-science journals that reported comparisons of the behaviors of children in different countries but did not explain the reasons for the comparison in any great detail. In recent years, however, there has been greater emphasis on research that is undertaken for a sound theoretical reason that is articulated very clearly in advance – for example, to study the effects of individualism or collectivism on the competitive behaviors of children. Not all interesting cross-cultural research can be reviewed in this chapter. The selection below represents the cross-cultural comparisons of children's peer relations that have been studied most extensively.

The peer relations of East Asian children

The most extensive database on the peer relations of children in non-Western countries is from East Asia, especially China. There are many reasons why data on Chinese children are particularly valuable, aside from the obvious fact that so many of the world's children live there. Chinese society is relatively homogeneous – there are few internal differences in ethnic or cultural origin. In contrast, many comparisons between different Western countries – for example, the United States and the United Kingdom – are complicated by the fact that the populations of both countries comprise citizens of many cultural origins and distinct social classes, each of which has differing values and priorities. Finally, the literary, philosophical and religious roots of Chinese people's expectations of others are documented very comprehensively and articulately (Chen *et al.*, 1999). Most importantly, data from China began to be collected in the 1990s and are still being collected today, providing an excellent opportunity to explore the effects of rapid urbanization, a market economy and a very competitive education system.

Traditional China differs greatly in terms of individualism/collectivism from the countries of North America and Western Europe, with traditional China occupying the collectivist end of the spectrum (Triandis, 1990). Despite the rapid urbanization of the country and the expansion of capitalism in the economy, the collectivism inherent in Chinese culture is seen as providing a structure for social behavior (Du, Li and Lin, 2015) in the domains of family life and interpersonal relationships, interaction among individuals accords with the needs and expectations of the group. According to Yang (1981), the Chinese anticipate the reactions of others and model their behavior accordingly. Related to this is Toupin's (1980) observation that Chinese society places great value on the rejection of verbal aggression, avoidance of direct expression of feelings, and avoidance of confrontation. Verbal conflict and direct confrontation run contrary to the Chinese notion of 'face' (Chiu, Tsang and Yang, 1988). The importance of conflict resolution through mediation and bargaining is reflected in China's non-adversarial or inquisitorial procedural model of community justice (Cloke, 1987; Leung, 1987).

Buddhism, Taoism and Confucianism make up the core of the traditional Chinese belief system. Emphasizing harmony, social obligations and interrelationships (Shenkar and Ronen, 1987), Buddhist, Taoist and Confucianist principles dominate and guide social relationships (Chao, 1983; Cryderman, 1992; Ryan, 1985). In Buddhism, the 'self' or ego is composed of social components that center on the immediate family, extended family, community and country (Ryan, 1985). Taoist principles promote the rejection of self-assertiveness and competitiveness (Ryan, 1985), and this may affect children's moral and ethical development by discouraging the fulfillment of their own goals at the expense of those of others. Confucianism asserts that there are four fundamental principles by which to live: self-cultivation, maintaining a harmonious relationship with the family, taking responsibility in community affairs, and serving the country (Kong, 1985). In particular, self-cultivation advocates the perfection of interpersonal skills and the fulfillment of the role and moral obligations one has in the community (Kong, 1985; Shenkar and Ronen, 1987). It fosters harmonious family relations and the avoidance of role conflict. There is clear role differentiation within the structure of the Chinese extended family (Tsui and Schultz, 1988). Chinese people believe that this well-defined family structure provides for continuity in society, because successive generations are linked with their ancestors and each individual possesses a role in history (Kong, 1985). For the most part, parents adopt an authoritarian parenting style and emphasize proper conduct, as prescribed by Confucian principles, in the socialization of their children. They emphasize obedience, control and academic achievement.

Shyness and peer acceptance in China

Well-planned studies have enabled scholars to trace parallels between the core principles of Chinese society and the patterns of peer relations among its children. Space permits description of only a few examples, focusing on changing perceptions of shyness in children and on the intimacy of friendship.

In a study conducted before years of social and economic change, Chen, Rubin and Li (1994) found that helpful prosocial behavior and aggression were correlated with social adjustment and social maladjustment, respectively; these results are analogous to findings with Western samples. However, the cultural meaning of shyness differed greatly, even though the behavior of shy children was very similar in Chinese and Western cultures (Rubin, 1998). In a Canadian study, shy and sensitive children, aged seven to nine, were found to be rejected by their peers. However, there was positive correlation between shyness-sensitivity and peer acceptance for Chinese children aged seven to ten (Chen, Rubin and Sun, 1992). This is probably the only research in any country in which shy children were shown to be popular. Chinese children who are shy tended at the time to be well liked by their peers because being soft-spoken, well mannered and academically inclined was considered virtuous in Chinese culture (Chen, Rubin and Li, 1994). Nevertheless, by the age of twelve, shyness and sensitivity in

Chinese children were associated with peer rejection, as in most other countries (Chen *et al.*, 1999). This finding may have occurred because there are different expectations in China once one reaches adolescence. High levels of academic pressure are evident during secondary school selection procedures (Dong, Yang and Ollendick, 1994). Pressure from within the school system may reflect the expectation that older children become more independent, responsible and self-controlling. For all these reasons, assertiveness and maturity regarding interpersonal relations may be prerequisites for successful social adjustment in older children in China, as elsewhere (Chen, Rubin and Li, 1994). Although these expectations are also found in Western cultures, age differences in the Chinese data pertaining to the shyness-sensitivity dimension raise the possibility that there is a later age for the developmental shift toward valuing assertiveness in the Chinese sample.

Even a few years later, shyness did not seem to be as valued by peers as it was in the early and mid-1990s (Hart *et al.*, 2000). Chen and his colleagues published an updated study in 2005 using much of the same methodology as in the first study. The 2005 paper contained reports on three cohorts of Chinese elementary school, with data collection in 1990 (the original study), 1998 and 2002. By 1998, there was no longer a significant correlation between shyness and peer acceptance. In the 2002 cohort, shyness was associated with active rejection by peers, school problems and depression. These longitudinal studies provide an incomparable picture of peer relations in eras of great social and economic change.

None of this means that Chinese children have become Machiavellian or mean. Chen and Chang (2012) studied the resource-acquisition strategies, social function, and social status of elementary school students in Shanghai. Based on responses to self-report questionnaires, the researchers divided the sample into five resource-acquisition strategies: bi-strategic controllers (Machiavellians); coercive controllers (who use power assertion); prosocial controllers; non-controllers; and others. The bi-strategic and coercive controllers were the most rejected by their school peers. Machiavellianism implies the clever use of deceit; it is about as far as one can travel from the traditional values of Confucianism, Taoism and Buddhism. Chinese children's culture does not seem to have changed to such an extreme extent, despite the rapid transformation of the surrounding society.

Peer-relations researchers have become very interested in continuing the exploration of the place of shyness and social withdrawal in a Chinese society that is undergoing remarkable change. Some of the more recent studies have focused on different forms of shyness/social withdrawal. Some shy, socially withdrawn children are fearful and anxious; they are afraid of social interactions and of being perceived negatively. Other socially withdrawn children do not display such wariness or anxiety; they simply dislike social interactions and appear not to want to be part of a social group. In Western society, these unsociable children are not as maladjusted as their shy peers who display marked distress in social situations (Coplan and Weeks, 2010). The reverse, however, applies to China, where unsociable children have been found to face marked adjustment problems (Liu *et al.*, 2015a). Being seen as not wanting to be part of a group can be understood as a distinct liability in a collectivistic society. Hence, Chinese collectivism may still be very present but may work in ways different from a generation ago. Interestingly, being perceived as not wanting to be part of a group was cited by Alvarez-Validivia *et al.* (2005) as a liability in Cuban children's groups. Cuba and China share the same communist political ideology, even though it is applied in somewhat different ways.

Intimacy in the friendships of East Asian children

The collectivism of East Asia provides a strong cultural context to the dyadic interactions that spawn close friendship. It is sometimes felt that the collectivist context is at the same time so strong and so supportive that there is little need for close friendships at the dyadic level. One's siblings, cousins and neighbors may be as supportive as friends. East Asia is an ideal place to study this issue. French, Lee and Pidada (2006) argue that the friendships of children in East Asia are not likely to be as stable or as close and intimate as those in capitalist, Western countries. This hypothesis was supported in data from Indonesia, which were compared to data from the United States (French, Pidada and Victor, 2005). However, some recent data suggest that the Indonesian data may not be typical of East Asian populations. Liu and colleagues (2015b) found that Indonesian adolescents reported less intimacy with their friends than the Chinese participants. Moreover, Indonesians felt lonely if they were not well liked in the larger peer group. In contrast, the Chinese children who reported low intimacy with friends also indicated that they were lonely.

Gummerum and Keller (2008) found that self-disclosure was less of an intrinsic feature of the reasoning of Chinese children about friendships in general than it was in the reasoning of children in several Western countries. In contrast, the qualitative observations of Japanese adolescent culture by Schneider, Lee and Alvarez-Valdivia (2011) indicate a very important function for closeness and self-disclosure. Sometimes Japanese adolescents may feel overwhelmed by the pressure to conform that is exerted in concert by parents, teachers and most members of the peer group. Interactions with close friends provide an opportunity to relax and be oneself.

The influence of the collectivistic context on children's interactions with close friends has been found to pervade intra-dyadic communication. Heyman, Genyue and Lee (2008) found that Chinese children wanted to disclose their performance to a third party if their performance was similar to that of their friends. A comparison group in the United States was very prepared to boast about their superior performance. Chinese children in that situation wanted their friends to understand their willingness to help the friend to do better.

Comparisons between Latin American children and children in the more individualistic Western societies

Studies of Latin American children constitute another substantial contribution to the cross-cultural literature on children's peer relations. Latin American society, like East Asian society, is highly collectivistic. As in East Asia, the extended family is a prominent feature of daily life and the prominent source of social support and guidance. However, comparisons between Latin American and North American or Western European children do not provide quite as clear a contrast as the East Asian studies, for several reasons. For the most part, Latin Americans share many of the religious beliefs of North Americans and Western Europeans as well as much of their cultural history. Most Latin American countries are not characterized by internal differences in cultural origin to the same degree as the United States or Canada, but many of them are more heterogeneous than China, Japan or Korea. Lower socioeconomic classes predominate in Latin America, though there are often drastic discrepancies in living conditions between the lower classes and the smaller middle-class and upper-class groups.

One of the earliest cross-cultural studies, by Kupersmidt and Trejos (1987), was motivated by the desire to find out whether, in spite of the collectivism of a society, individual children were still targets of rejection by their peer groups at school. Kupersmidt and Trejos investigated the peer relations of Costa Rican children. They administered a group sociometric interview to 328 primary schoolchildren divided into three different age groups. Because of its sixty-five-year history of political neutrality, non-violent changes of government, and lack of a formal standing army, Costa Rica presents researchers with an opportunity to study a level of collectivism that is unique among other collectivistic Latin American countries. Like the majority of Hispanic countries, Costa Rican culture places importance on traditional sex roles and on family relations over peer relations.

Kupersmidt and Trejos found that, on identical peer-nomination instruments, there was a similar proportion of popular children among Costa Rican and US samples (11 percent and 13 percent, respectively). There were also similar cross-cultural results for peer rejection, as 11 percent of Costa Rican children and 15 percent of US children were rejected by their peers. However, Kupersmidt and Trejos found that there were different specific behaviors affiliated with peer rejection. For example, in Costa Rica, peer rejection was often associated with withdrawal from group activity, but this was not indicated by US children. This difference may be connected to the distinction between collectivistic and individualistic societies, and it was also evident in some more recent studies conducted in China, as mentioned earlier in this chapter. Collectivism emphasizes the importance of the collective experience of society and therefore refusal to participate in a group event may be considered offensive to the group. In contrast, individualistic societies may regard non-participation as an individual's personal right; the group, therefore, does not take offense and reject the non-participant. Regardless of the greater commitment to the group, children from collectivistic cultures do still like and dislike particular individuals, as occurs in less collectivistic societies.

DeRosier (1989) examined Costa Rican children's attitudes toward their network of intimate relationships. She studied 148 Costa Rican primary schoolchildren, the majority of whom were from working-class and middle-class households. After administering Furman and Buhrmester's (1985) Network of Relationships Inventory to gauge children's perceptions of the people in their lives who provide social support, she compared the Costa Rican results with US data from Furman and Buhrmester's original study. Results indicated that Costa Rican children rated most people in their personal network (i.e. siblings, parents, best friends, teachers) more positively than did their US counterparts. Also, the Costa Rican children reported that their relationships were less conflictual. As suggested by DeRosier, these positive attitudes toward others are connected with the prosocial, cooperative nature of the surrounding Costa Rican culture. In terms of levels of intimacy in specific relationships, the Costa Rican children reported that they received the most companionship from their mothers and siblings. In contrast, US children felt that their best friends provided the most companionship. Both groups reported the lowest levels of companionship from teachers, who were also designated 'least affectionate' by US children. However, the Costa Rican children felt that their relationships with their best friends deserved the rating of 'least affectionate'. They also reported higher levels of conflict and lower levels of satisfaction within this relationship. Cultural ecology may thus determine the role of individuals within a supportive network, as well as the relative importance of peer relations.

The identical pattern of findings emerged in a cross-cultural study of support for academic achievement among adolescents in Canada, Cuba and Spain by Vitoroulis and colleagues (2012). Only among Canadian participants from the majority Anglo-European culture were friends an important source of support. It is useful to connect the findings from Costa Rica and Cuba with the Indonesian data discussed earlier in this chapter, which also indicate that relationships with friends are not very intimate in that collectivistic culture. Moreover, a number of studies on patterns of social support for children and youth in the Latino/Latina community in the United States show that families are by far the main source of social support for children and youth, with friends and other peers seen as relatively unimportant as supportive individuals (de Guzman, Jung and Do, 2012).

Intimacy in different cultural communities within the mosaic of Israeli society

Growing up on hakibbutz shehayah *(the kibbutz that once was)*

Kibbutzim today are very different from the kibbutzim built by the founders of the kibbutz movement. For the past two or three decades, children sleep with their parents, just as they do in the rest of Israel and almost everywhere else. The research done on children who were raised collectively in children's houses remains invaluable because this experience constitutes a unique social experiment that is not likely to be repeated. Long-term longitudinal data on people who were raised in this unusual setting are still being analyzed.

There have been copious studies on the psychological adaptation of children on Israeli kibbutzim. At the time of the upbringing in children's houses, and to a limited extent even now, individuals living in these collectivistic communities share their possessions and work responsibilities with each other and are permitted to leave whenever they wish. Kibbutzniks' group orientation does not lead to isolation, for they maintain contact with the surrounding – less collectivistic – Israeli society. Because membership is by choice, a kibbutz is an excellent setting to study collective ideology.

Schools on kibbutzim emphasize cooperation more than the European-style schools in surrounding Israeli cities. During the period in which most research was conducted, children were raised in a children's house but still maintained contact with their families. There are many possible implications of the structure of the kibbutz for children's social relations, especially in the old days of *hakibbutz shehayah*. Because children had more contact with caregivers than with parents in the collective environment, there may be an effect on the early formation of parental attachment relationships. This could in turn affect the children's formation of subsequent relationships.

How, then, is this collective upbringing reflected in children's behavior? There have been numerous observational studies of the social play of kibbutz and non-kibbutz pre-schoolers. Levy-Shiff and Hoffman (1985) compared the free-play of kibbutz and urban children. All participants were Israeli-born children of European descent. They found that kibbutz-raised children displayed more group interaction, less competition, and less emotional expression and affection than their non-kibbutz counterparts. The kibbutz children essentially replaced physical aggression with verbal confrontation. This type of behavior may be a predictor of future social adjustment patterns of children. Indeed, adult kibbutzniks are often characterized as group-oriented and emotionally detached.

Hertz-Lazarowitz and colleagues (1989) found that kibbutz children exhibited higher levels of social interaction than city children, in both traditional and more participation-oriented classrooms. There have also been indications that kibbutz children are more cooperative than non-kubbutznikim. Shapira and Madsen (1974) observed children's level of cooperation when attempting the marble-pull task. Participants were kibbutz and Tel Aviv city children aged four to eleven years. They found that, at all ages, kibbutz children exhibited less competitive behavior and more cooperation to achieve a common goal than the urban children. However, all children displayed increased levels of competition as they aged. This trend occurred at a slower pace in the kibbutz children, for, even at the age of eleven, they were still quite cooperative in a simulation (analog) task compared with the city children.

In Sharabany's (1982) study, kibbutz and Tel Aviv children were asked to share information about their social contacts. Results indicated that kibbutz youngsters had more social contacts than the city children. However, the kibbutz children also had less concern for peer group sanctions and identified less with their peer group than their city counterparts. In another study, similar structured self-report instruments indicated that anxiety about social relations or general, manifest anxiety appears to be no higher or lower among kibbutz children and pre-adolescents (Ginter *et al.*, 1989). Findings such as these illustrate the kibbutz youth's greater involvement with their peers, as well as their emotional distancing from peers.

From the beginnings of the kibbutz movement in the early twentieth century to the 1980s, most kibbutz children slept in children's houses, but they had contact with their parents for several hours during each day. This arrangement was instituted in order to promote self-reliance, equality of the sexes and commitment to collectivistic principles (Aviezer *et al.*, 1994). Some studies indicate that these communal sleeping arrangements may have had a negative effect on child–parent attachment. For instance, Sagi and colleagues (1982) found a large number of insecure attachment bonds (see discussion of attachment theory in Chapter 3) among children who slept in collective environments; they suggest that this may reflect the inconsistent nature of mothers' care. In collective sleeping arrangements, infants began at six weeks of age to sleep in children's houses and were monitored by unfamiliar, rotating caregivers at night. Some researchers suggest that the unavailability of a consistent, responsive, maternal caregiver at night conflicts with the availability of the mother during the day in influencing attachment patterns.

Later, Sagi and colleagues (1994) examined the impact of collective sleeping on mother–child attachment. They maintained that the social ecology of the communal sleeping environment creates obstacles for mothers and their children. Their study indicated that the attachment representations of children in collective sleeping arrangements did not relate to those of the mother, and concluded that the intergenerational transmission of attachment is greatly influenced by the context. They asserted that communal sleeping deviates from evolutionary adaptation. There was no difference in mother–infant interaction, infants' disposition, or other variables between the home-based and communal sleeping groups. However, among home-based infants, 80 percent were securely attached, whereas only 48 percent of communal-based infants were securely attached. The researchers maintained that mothers were continuously inaccessible during the night and that this conflicted with their availability during the day; this may have created a pattern of inconsistent interaction for the child.

Researchers also examined children's attachment to their primary caregivers, the *metapelet* in the communal children's houses. Oppenheim, Sagi and Lamb (1988) studied mother–child attachment in kibbutzim using the Strange Situation classification. Results indicated that future development of the children was unrelated to the attachment of infants to their mothers and fathers. However, there was a relationship between infant–metapelet attachment and future development, emphasizing the importance of these primary caregivers. For instance, Oppenheim, Sagi and Lamb reported that those infants who were securely attached to their metapelet were both more independent and more concerned about other people than were their counterparts with insecure attachments to their metapelet.

Friendships bonds of Jewish and Arab Israeli children

About one-fifth of Israel's current population is Arab; most of these Arabs are Muslims. Researchers have studied patterns of parenting and peer relations in Israel's Arab and Jewish communities. The Arab communities are considered highly collectivistic, family-oriented and somewhat traditional in their demands for respect of one's elders. The Jewish communities are known to be highly individualistic.

Sharabany, Eshel and Hakim (2008) studied parenting styles and friendship intimacy among adolescents enrolled in four Arab schools in Israel. Disconfirming the researchers' expectation that parenting in the Arab communities is based on strict discipline and demands for obedience, there was diversity in the reports of parenting style. Replicating results obtained in Western countries, sons and daughters of authoritative parents who enforce their demands with reasoning and display considerable affection to their children reported more intimacy in their friendships than children raised by strict, authoritarian parents. Despite the prohibition on relationships with the opposite sex among adolescents, many of the participants formed intimate friendships with members of the opposite sex at school. As in results from other countries, mothers' child-rearing style was linked to friendship intimacy of both male and female participants. Fathers' style was a significant predictor of the friendship intimacy only of boys.

Feldman, Masalha and Derdikman-Eiron (2010) conducted a comparative study of parenting and conflict resolution in Jewish and Palestinian communities. They worked with the parents who were recruited when their children were five months old. The study continued into the children's pre-school years. They found that similar styles of parenting predicted similar styles of conflict resolution in both cultures. In both the Jewish and Palestinian samples, marital hostility and discord and ineffective discipline predicted higher rates of aggression among the children. The more traditional nature of the Arab culture and its hierarchical social structure may be reflected in the patterns of conflict resolution among the children. Jewish children tended to resolve conflict by discussion and compromise, rather than by power assertion, in comparison to the children in the Palestinian sample.

Cultural dimensions of childhood aggression

Is children's aggression correlated with adult aggression?

The Zapotec communities in Oaxaca, Mexico, provide an interesting opportunity to examine the connection between adult aggression and children's aggressive behavior with peers. The Zapotec, who rely heavily on agriculture, are organized into small, separate communities. The rate of aggression varies widely between these communities. For example, in the 24 Zapotec communities studied so far, the annual homicide rate ranges from 4 to 123 per 100,000 people. It is not surprising, then, that attitudes toward violence vary, too. In the less aggressive communities, play fighting among children is looked upon with disfavor. However, the more violent communities are characterized by rough play even among adults as well as by corporal punishment of children.

Fry (1988) studied the behavior of twenty-four children, aged five to eight years, from two Zapotec communities with different levels of normative violence. Observations were restricted to incidences of serious fighting, play fighting and threats. Results indicated that there was twice the rate of play aggression in San Andres (a pseudonym) than in the less violent community of La Paz (6.9 incidents per hour versus 3.7 incidents per hour, respectively). Researchers observed lower rates of more serious aggression in both communities. Nevertheless, San Andres children still exhibited a higher rate than their La Paz counterparts (0.7 incidents per hour versus 0.39 incidents per hour, respectively). Older San Andres children engaged in serious play fighting more frequently than younger children, whereas the rate of serious play aggression in La Paz was lower for the older children than the younger children. Small correlations were found between serious fighting and play fighting, showing that children tend to engage in either one or the other, for the most part.

The results of this study imply that aggression, which does indeed occur across cultures and may have some evolutionary purpose, is significantly modified by cultural context. The findings also support Smith's (1989) contention that children prepare for their future adult roles within their communities by play fighting.

Subtle encouragement of aggression by boys in traditional Mediterranean culture

Italian studies are an excellent source of information about cultural differences in aggression, especially with regard to differential expectations for boys and girls (Schneider, 1971). As detailed below, traditional Italian society condoned aggression by males but not by females. Relevant data are available from major urban settings regarding the behavioral correlates of peer status in Italian pre-schools (Fonzi, Tomada and Ciucci, 1994) and Grade 2 classrooms (Attili, Vermigli and Schneider, 1997). These studies, which were conducted with large samples, used measures similar to those used in most US studies. The results indicate that both the pattern and strength of the behavioral correlates of peer acceptance in Italy are very similar to those of most other countries, with correlations every bit as strong as those found in studies conducted in North America with both pre-schoolers and elementary school-age children. There are some indications, though, that, unlike the results of studies conducted in central and northern Italy, youngsters in southern Italy perceive some forms of aggression as typical of peers they consider sociable (Casiglia, LoCoco and Zappulla, 1998).

In their study of aggression among children in small central Italian towns, Tomada and Schneider (1997) attempted to replicate Crick and Grotpeter's (1995) findings, which indicated that US boys displayed higher levels of overt aggression and lower levels of relational aggression than girls. As discussed in Chapter 3, overt aggression refers to physical and verbal expressions of hostility aimed directly at another person. Relational aggression, often referred to as 'covert aggression', involves displays of aggression involved in interpersonal relationships, such as spreading rumors or excluding another child from a play group (Crick and Grotpeter, 1995; Lagerspetz, Björkqvist and Peltonen, 1988). Overt aggression is common in Italian playgrounds: Genta and colleagues (1996) found there to be significantly more bullying among elementary schoolchildren in central Italy than in Norway, England, Spain and Japan. Thus, the display of aggression among Italian males may still be considered normal, just as it was even encouraged among adolescent boys in traditional Italian villages as a display of their sexual prowess and preparation for their future patriarchal roles. In contrast, overt aggression is discouraged among Italian girls (Maraspini,1968; Schneider, 1971). Tomada and Schneider (1997) analyzed peer nominations for aggressive and prosocial behavior provided by Italian elementary schoolteachers and students. They found that, contrary to their hypothesis, Italian girls did not have higher levels of relational aggression than boys; boys had higher levels of both relational and overt aggression than girls. However, the gender gap was narrower for levels of relational aggression. Therefore, despite the fact that Italian boys seem as relationally aggressive as Italian girls, it is still important to study relational aggression in Italy. That is because almost no girls were found to be physically aggressive. If relational aggression were not taken into account, one would arrive at the erroneous conclusion that aggression is relatively absent among females in Italy. Interestingly, recent data from six countries (Austria, Canada, Germany, Slovenia, Spain and Switzerland) indicate that boys in those societies display more relational aggression than do girls. The publication is appropriately entitled 'Rethinking indirect aggression: the end of the mean girl myth' (Artz, Kassis and Moldenhauer, 2013).

In cross-cultural studies of aggression, it is important to look not only at different rates of aggression but also at different antecedents of aggression in home and school life. Furthermore, there may be important cultural differences in the consequences of aggression for individual adjustment. For example, Kawabata and Crick (2013) found lower rates of relational aggression among Asian-American children than among European-American children. However, relational aggression is more likely to lead to adjustment problems, such as depression, among children of the Asian-American community. Similarly, Kawabata, Crick and Hamaguchi (2010) discovered that relational aggression is more strongly linked to various forms of maladjustment in Japan than in the United States.

Adult beliefs about aggression

Regarding the antecedents of aggression in different cultures, cross-cultural differences can affect the level of tolerance for atypical behavior, and these different thresholds may determine how adults react to aggressive behavior in children. Schneider and colleagues (1997) compared the beliefs of Italian and Canadian parents about aggression and social withdrawal. They hypothesized that Italian mothers would consider aggression to be more worrisome and that English-Canadian mothers would have stronger emotional responses to social withdrawal. They also studied ratings of mothers with children who were identified as withdrawn or aggressive. Results indicated that the Canadian mothers did indeed consider social withdrawal to be more problematic than did their Italian counterparts. However, both samples indicated that aggression was more worrisome than withdrawal. The researchers encountered some interesting gender differences, for the intensity of the Italian mothers' emotional reactions to withdrawal by girls were lower than their reactions to this behavior in boys; this gender difference was not found in the Canadian samples. A higher proportion of Italian mothers felt that problem behaviors in children were caused by stable, internal factors, such as personality traits. In contrast, Canadian mothers tended to believe that children's behavior could be easily changed. This difference may be connected to Italian villagers' belief in the role of fate and luck in children's future success (Maraspini, 1968). Behavior, therefore, may not be considered in traditional Italy as readily modifiable by parenting skills. In contrast, Canadian mothers seem to be more likely to believe that parental intervention and disciplinary style can modify the behavior of the child. This study provides insight into the way in which cultural characteristics can influence parents' attributions of their children's behavior, as well as their level of tolerance for social withdrawal and aggression.

Weisz and colleagues (1988) also studied tolerance thresholds for over-controlled (e.g. shy, withdrawn) behavior and under-controlled behavior (e.g. aggression) in research conducted in Thailand, Jamaica and the United States. The majority of Thais subscribe to Thai Buddhism's teaching that, although some degree of unhappiness is universal, this is not a permanent part or reflection of one's personality. The study involved Thai and US teachers and parents reading two vignettes, each of which provided an example of the behavior patterns studied. They were then asked to rate the seriousness of the behavior, as well as whether it was unusual. Additionally, the parents were asked to report the level of concern about the behavior they would experience if they were the protagonist's parent or teacher, the likelihood of a change in the behavior, what had caused the behavior, and what they should do about it. Results indicated that Thai participants rated over-controlled and under-controlled behavior less seriously than their US counterparts. In comparison to the US respondents, the Thai participants also rated these behavior patterns as less worrisome to a teacher or parent, less unusual, and more likely to improve on their own. Thai and

US psychologists reported equal levels of concern about the problem behaviors. The psychologists' level of concern was greater than those of Thai parents and teachers, but lower than that of all US subject groups. Thais attributed under-controlled and over-controlled behaviors to faulty child-rearing more often than Americans did; the latter tended to attribute these behaviors to environmental stressors, such as an unsettled day in the family and internal, personal conflicts. Participants in both cultures, however, felt that under-controlled behavior was more worrisome than over-controlled behavior.

Research has focused less on cross-cultural differences in the problem-behavior thresholds of teachers than of parents; the concept of 'threshold' refers to the level of disruptiveness or other atypical behavior that leads adults to conceive of the behavior as unacceptable or problematic. Walker and Lamon (1987) investigated such thresholds in their comparison of US and Australian primary schoolteachers' standards and expectations of children's behavior. Findings indicated that both samples rated similar behaviors as troublesome. US teachers were far less concerned about the children's problem behavior than about a lack of social skills; this gap was narrower for Australian teachers. Australian teachers placed more emphasis on the importance of classroom decorum. For example, they gave more negative ratings to children's extraneous comments during lessons and discussions. Both samples had similar and higher thresholds for atypical social behavior when working with pupils exhibiting behavioral disorders or those with disabilities. The results of Walker and Lamon's study are interesting, but a wider cross-cultural comparison of numerous nations would prove even more valuable.

Aggression in the peer culture

French, Setiono and Eddy (1999) studied aggression among childhood peers in Indonesia. Javanese society is extremely collectivistic (Hofstede, 1991) and emphasizes cooperation, conformity and harmony (Koentjaraningrat, 1985). Using the individualism/collectivism paradigm, these researchers hypothesized that aggression would be associated with high negative sociometric status in both the United States and Indonesia, but that this would be particularly pronounced in the latter country. They also predicted that social withdrawal would be associated with high social status for US children but not for their Indonesian counterparts. Results indicated the expected association of aggression with negative sociometric status. French, Setiono and Eddy suggested that this may reflect the characterization of aggression in childhood as an element of disorder in relationships (see Patterson, 1982), rather than an individual phenomenon. Results also suggested cross-cultural similarities in terms of the relationship between sociometric acceptance and reciprocal friendship. However, in US samples, those children who were aggressive did have peer groups and friends, whereas this was not found among Indonesian children. In Indonesia, aggressive children rarely had friends. The finding that there were fewer reciprocated friendships in Indonesian children may reflect the collectivistic ideology, for harmonious peer groups are commonly valued over a small number of close friendships (Noesjirwan, 1978).

Cultural features and peer-directed aggression around the world

In an effort to achieve a more global perspective on cross-cultural studies of aggression in peer groups, Bergeron and Schneider (2005) conducted a meta-analysis of data on peer-directed aggression in thirty-six studies. There were a total of 185 comparisons between different cultures in these studies. They compared the aggression data with scores for each country on Hofstede's dimensions of cultural variation, discussed earlier in this chapter. The results showed that there tends to be less aggression in more collectivistic cultures, cultures with high moral commitment, more egalitarian cultures, and cultures with less avoidance of uncertainty (i.e. where the cultural context makes the expectations of individuals highly explicit).

Cultural differences in the stability of aggression

One final dimension useful in the comparison of children's aggression in different cultures is that of the stability and continuity of aggression. Aggression is usually very stable across the development of individuals, but not uniformly so in different cultures. In an initial exploration of this issue, Kokko and colleagues (2014) found that aggression was stable at two measurement points – when the participants were eight years old and during their early adulthood – in the United States but not in Finland. The highest stability rate was among US participants of non-professional backgrounds. Of course, stability needs to be investigated in many more societies. The widespread assumption that aggressive behavior is highly stable is based mostly on US data, which may not generalize cross-culturally.

The challenges in conducting cross-cultural comparisons

Perhaps the most important advance in knowledge about children's peer relations over the past thirty years has been the rapid expansion of the database around the world. The studies discussed in this chapter bear witness to the talents of researchers in overcoming the many obstacles inherent in comparing data from different societies. Scanning the results makes it look deceptively simple to compare the peer relations of children in different countries. To begin with, such research requires in-depth knowledge of each of the countries to be compared. Such in-depth knowledge may reveal, first, that the issue to be studied is of greater importance to only some of the societies to be targeted. In almost every country, there are internal distinctions – such as in ethnicity, socioeconomic status, or gender – that may turn out to explain more differences in core values and social behavior than the contrast to another country. An added complication is the near impossibility of translating questions without losing some of the original meaning. Furthermore, participants in different countries may feel differently about participating in research. Some may see this as a source of novelty and honor; others may regard it as an intrusion into their privacy. Researchers and their students in different societies also differ in research training.

None of the existing studies on cultural differences in children's peer relations has overcome all of these problems. Nevertheless, the growing research base does indicate some important and logical differences in peer relations between differing societies in such key areas as the peer acceptance of shy children and the extent of competition between children. Other studies serve the other purpose of cross-cultural research: to show how children are the same in different societies. The overall peer rejection of children who display impulsive aggression is an example of the latter.

Despite the increasing research activity on peer relations in different parts of the world, there is still very little translational research on how this knowledge can be used in interventions to enhance peer relations. We can but hope that such work will be undertaken, but in a manner that is respectful of the values of the cultures in which the children will come to benefit from an increase in such applied work.

10

CULTURAL IMPRINTS ON CHILDREN'S FRIENDSHIPS

This chapter provides a review of theory and research linking features of culture to features of children's friendships. The extent and significance of inter-cultural friendship in multicultural societies are also discussed. Children in different societies differ in the extent to which they depend on close friends for social support. In cultures where extended family ties are strong, children may be able to depend on cousins and other relatives for assistance and companionship in times of stress. Some theorists and some but not all research results suggest that children in collectivistic societies may not have to negotiate individual friendships as much as children in many Western countries do, although friendships appear to be important in all cultures. In some very collectivistic societies, friendship may provide a respite from pressures to conform to group norms. In the current era of mass immigration to many Western countries, only some children form friendships with members of other cultures. This is sometimes – but not always – considered an indication of welcome to the new society.

As detailed in the previous chapter, people in collectivistic societies derive much of their sense of personal identity from their membership of a larger collective unit, such as their communities, extended families, or nations. Despite the possibilities that the functions of friends are not identical in all societies, and that children's behavior with friends differs across cultures, enough data exist to indicate, at the most fundamental level, that children around the world regard friendship as an intimate relationship based on reciprocal personal commitment. Explorations of children's basic concepts of friendship have been conducted not only in the United States (e.g. Berndt, Hawkins and Hoyle, 1986) but in Canada and Scotland (Bigelow and La Gaipa, 1975), Iceland (Keller and Edelstein, 1990), Germany (Hofer *et al.*, 1990, cited in Krappmann, 1996), China (Keller, Schuster and Edelstein, 1990, cited in Krappmann, 1996), and Cuba (Santana-Gonzalez, Silot-Moreno and Schneider, 2004). These studies, which are based on interviews and written essays about friendship, reveal very few important differences between cultures in children's basic conceptions of friendship. Moreover, children's thinking about friendships seems to progress developmentally in much the same way in different cultures. Young children emphasize tangible gains to themselves. As development progresses, children emphasize companionship, mutual understanding, closeness and support. The fact that there are few cultural differences in the basic concept of friendship does not at all mean that children in all cultures reach the same levels of maturity in their understanding of friendship at exactly the same ages, however. Children raised in collectivistic cultures have been found to display more mature friendship reasoning at earlier stages than children in other countries. This may be attributable to collectivistic values or to the emphasis on obligations to the social group in some collectivistic, socialist countries, such as China (Gummerum and Keller, 2008).

There may be cultural differences in people's expectations of their friends. Not surprisingly, in certain collectivistic cultures, the extended family may provide much of the supportive role that friendship assumes in North America, as in DeRosier's (1989) study of the social networks of Costa Rican children, or in Westen's (1995) study of Canadian children of East Asian origin. In some societies, friends may tend to provide more tangible, practical help than anything else; in others, they may provide more emotional support and guidance (Cohen, 1966; Krappmann, 1996).

Krappmann (1996) offers some interesting speculations about the possible constraints on children's friendships in collectivistic cultures. One of the most important issues is the leeway for voluntariness of interpersonal affiliation in a culture, because the voluntary nature of friendships lies at the heart of many concepts of friendship. The social organization of some societies restricts the number of individuals with whom a child or adult has regular contact, thus restricting the possibility of forming friendships. This is especially the case in isolated fishing or agricultural villages (documented, for example, by Edelstein (1983) in Iceland). In some cultures, the basic social structure and patterns of economic activity dictate the identities of the peers one encounters in everyday life; it is not always possible to arrange more extensive companionship with a peer with whom one wishes to cultivate a friendship.

Aside from the general structure of social and economic life in a society, it is important to consider the interplay of family life and social life with peers. Although families are important to children everywhere, the extended family unit is a far more prominent element in people's daily lives and thinking in most of Southern Europe, Asia, Africa and Latin America than it is in North America or Northern Europe (Stanton, 1995). In the more family-oriented societies, members of extended families, including grandparents, aunts, uncles and cousins, provide a great deal of emotional support, practical assistance and advice. One might suspect that people need friends much less in those societies than in places where individuals must form voluntary relationships with friends in order to receive the social support they need in moments of stress.

Only a few of the studies on the topic indicate that friendship is any weaker or less important in collectivistic societies or societies with rich family life than in more individualistic cultures. Cultural artifacts, such as artwork and literature, as well as the writings of philosophers, usually extol the value of friendship but there are a few exceptions. The extreme example is that of some writings from Ghana, captured most graphically in a well-known Ghanaian poem entitled *No Time to Die* (Kyei and Schreckenbach, 1975). The poet warns readers to 'beware of friends', some of whom are 'snakes under grass' and intensely jealous inside despite the compliments they lavish. In an attempt to make sense of this dark and puzzling poem, Heine (2012) proposes that it is the low relationship mobility and not the collectivism of Ghana that underlies the poet's warnings. In other words, Ghanaians tend to remain in the same communities and social circles, with the same few 'friends', for much longer than, for example, Americans. This may occur not only because people tend to live in the same places for most of their lives in many non-Western countries. The lack of mobility may be imbedded in the understanding of friendship as a long-term bond rather than a relationship that one seeks and develops based on feelings and needs experienced at a given point in time. These long-term 'friendships' become stale and sour despite the overt trappings of friendship that are displayed to keep up appearances in the small, stable social circle.

Some – but certainly not all – empirical comparisons of children's friendships in collectivistic and individualistic cultures corroborate the contention that societal collectivism may attenuate the benefits of friendship at the dyadic level. As mentioned in the previous chapter, French, Lee and Pidada (2006) invoke collectivism to explain their finding that Indonesian children's friendships are, on the whole, less close than those of children the same age in the United States. Scharf and Hertz-Lazarowitz (2003) found that Jewish Israeli participants reported higher levels of security and friendship, and lower levels of conflict, with their friends than did the Arab Israeli participants. They attributed these findings to the difference between the collectivism of the Arab Israeli culture and the individualism of the Jewish Israeli culture. In their study comparing the expectations of friends among Cuban and Canadian early adolescents, Santana-Gonzalez, Sigot-Moreno and Schneider (2004) found that in Cuba – a highly collectivistic society where practical assistance is needed on a daily basis by most people – concrete help constituted a larger part of participants' expectations of their friends compared to a Canadian sample of the same age. The latter group emphasized the closeness and security of their friendships. The Canadians also underscored the companionship a friendship provides, which may be less salient in Cuba, where almost all children spend extended periods of time in the company of their school and neighborhood peers.

Rich family life as a training ground for rich friendships

However, a society characterized by rich family life does not have to be a society characterized by impoverished social life with peers. It could also be argued that strong bonds with kin do not preclude high-quality relationships with others

(Kirchler, Pombeni and Palmonari, 1991), and that the high-quality interaction style learned in relating with one's kin might even be generalized to other close relationships. This could explain the ode to friendship by Jose Marti, the statesman and author who is regarded as the founding father of the Republic of Cuba, who describes a friend as a trusted haven, a comfortable cushion, a source of hope, richer than the owner of a sumptuous garden, gold and grain (Marti, 1997, p. 115).

Even in highly collectivistic cultures, parents have been found to recognize the distinct benefits that friendships may have for their children. Aukrust and her colleagues (2003) surveyed parents in Norway, the United States, Turkey and Korea about the importance of friendships for their children. They found that parents in all of these countries regarded friendship as very important for their children, but parents in Korea and Norway placed significantly higher value on these friendships than parents in the United States, who in turn valued their children's friendships higher than parents in Turkey. As Korea is probably the most collectivistic country in the sample, at least with regard to social relationships, the results obtained in this study show that children's friendships may be very important to parents in collectivistic societies. However, it should be noted that these findings, like many discussed in this chapter, do not suggest a clear correlation between individualism/collectivism and friendship. It is important to consider other features of cultures.

Close family bonds often occur in collectivistic cultures. It is possible that family orientation in a culture is linked with rich friendships outside the family. This is implicit in attachment theory, as detailed in Chapter 3. The core of attachment theory is that a child explores interpersonal relationships outside the family based on the security obtained in close, intimate bonds with a caregiver. Close family bonds could be one of the reasons why Schneider and colleagues (1997) found that the friendships among eight-year-old girls in Italy – a very family-oriented country that is also quite individualistic – were significantly more stable than those of their counterparts in Ontario, Canada (there were no parallel findings for boys). They also found that, for both genders, there was less discrepancy in the Italian sample between the two friends' ratings of the quality of their relationship. This suggests that the communication between friends is of higher quality in Italy.

Using direct observation, Schneider and colleagues (2000) subsequently compared the behaviors of Italian and English-Canadian eight-year-olds in situations of potential conflict with their friends. While playing the car-race – a fast-paced, competitive game – with their friends, the Canadian children committed significantly more infractions of the rules. Italian friends were also found to be more involved in the race. Schneider and his colleagues (2000) also videotaped the Italian and Canadian friends in a simulated negotiation sequence. The friends were shown a Kinder egg – a chocolate egg with a toy hidden inside – and were asked to discuss how they would share it. In discussing how they might share the single egg, the Italian youngsters made fewer proposals in total, but they were still able to achieve a greater discrepancy between initial and final negotiating positions, suggesting superior skill at negotiation and compromise. The authors speculated that the differences between the Italian and Canadian children's performances might be attributed to the Italian children's exposure to compromise within relationships as a result of their more extensive contact with extended family members. These differences might also be attributable to the emphasis in northern Italian schools on teaching children how different people have different perspectives on social situations and problems.

Another interesting comparison of children's friendships in different cultures comes from research conducted in East and West Berlin shortly before and shortly after the reunification of Germany. An important follow-up study was conducted fifteen years later (Gummerum and Keller, 2012). Children's daily lives were very different in these two parts of the city during the period when the initial research was conducted, including important differences in many aspects of schooling and family life that seem to have affected both children's opportunities to befriend each other and the nature of their friendships with other children. In East Berlin at the time, children spent most of the day, including the afternoon hours after the regular school day, under adult supervision in schools or day-care centers. An explicit norm of cooperation was emphasized by the adults who provided the supervision. In implementing this ideology, the adults praised whatever cooperative behavior they saw, criticized any conflictual behavior as immature, and resolved disagreements between the children. In contrast, parents in West Berlin had the primary responsibility for structuring their children's social lives in the afternoons after school. The school authorities of West Berlin shared the goal of promoting mutual helpfulness, but the school personnel did not promote a fixed ideology or monitor pupils' social behavior with anything approaching the vigor of their colleagues in the eastern zone (Oswald and Krappmann, 1995).

Perhaps because they were provided with so much emphatic discussion about the responsibilities of peers, primary schoolchildren in East Berlin displayed more mature concepts of friendship than children of the same age in West Berlin (Krappmann, Uhlendorff and Oswald, 1995). There were both similarities and differences between the two cultures with regard to actual friendships as opposed to abstract concepts of friendship, as described in detail by Little and colleagues (1999). Despite the more mature concepts of friendship among the young East Berliners, friends in both East and West Berlin often disagreed with each other about the quality of their friendships. Furthermore, children in East Berlin reported greater conflict with friends than children in West Berlin, perhaps because the former had become keenly aware of conflict after hearing it discussed and criticized so extensively but remained unskilled in resolving conflict, which adults did on their behalf. Children in East Berlin also reported having less fun with their friends, perhaps because the active monitoring of their play inhibited horseplay and joking. Nevertheless, there were no differences between the two cultures in the closeness perceived in the relationships with friends.

As mentioned, some of the East German participants in the original studies were interviewed again fifteen years after the initial data collection (Gummerum and Keller, 2012). Their reasoning about friendship had matured in many ways over those years. For instance, there was less concern about achieving individual personal gain from the friendship. Much more empathy for the friends and altruism were also in evidence. Although the shift in the surrounding society from collectivism and individualism may have had something to do with these changes, the authors speculated that the economic challenges faced by former East Germans may have left them with greater need for friends to provide practical help. Of course, social relationships had become more personalized and more voluntary, with less emphasis on the broader peer group that had formal and official status during the communist years.

In addition to the lessons to be learned about the effects of culture on children's friendships, the Berlin research is useful in illustrating the apparently universal importance of closeness in friendship. It also demonstrates that – in friendships as in many other aspects of children's lives – abstract concepts often fail to correspond to observable behavior.

Using a very different method to study cultural differences in children's ideas about friendship, Pinto, Bombi and Cordioli (1997) studied children's pictorial representations of similarity in friendship. The participants in the study were children from five different parts of the world that were known to differ in terms of the individualism/collectivism of adults, peace/war, and ethnic homogeneity/heterogeneity: Rome; Villafranca (a smaller town in Italy); the Bolivian town of Camiri; the Bolivian forest village of Ipitacito del Monte; and Beirut, Lebanon. Pinto, Bombi and Cordioli hypothesized that friendships in collectivistic cultures would emphasize sharing and mutual affinity, whereas those in individualistic cultures would place importance on maintaining a personal sense of uniqueness. They predicted that, according to this paradigm, children from Ipitacito del Monte, a highly collectivistic culture, should create more similar pictorial representations of themselves and their friends. The authors also suggested that people living in environments characterized by war may display radical judgements about strangers and may develop defensive attitudes. Accordingly, they predicted that children from Beirut would draw two friends as very similar. They asserted that multi-ethnicity can have positive or negative outcomes in terms of tolerance levels, and speculated that children from Camiri, where integration has been positive, would not feel as much of a need to represent similarity as an aspect of friendship as would their counterparts in Beirut, where there is religious division.

Results indicated that children from Ipitacito del Monte exhibited the greatest overall degree of similarity in their pictorial representations of themselves and their friends; this was especially true for the younger children. Pinto, Bombi and Cordioli concluded that dimensions of individualism/collectivism are the only ones among those they studied that affect similarity between friends. It is interesting to note that in the Lebanese samples the children tended to differentiate between themselves and their friends using dimensions in space, emphasizing a hierarchical nature of their friendships. This suggests that, in an area marked by war, the ability to protect may be more important than similarities in age or other personal characteristics.

Intensive observations by Corsaro (1985) of the interactions of pre-schoolers in the United States and Italy indicate that children in both countries use very similar strategies to protect the exclusiveness of their friendships and the private, shared play spaces of friends.

Before concluding this section, it is important to mention the many important and instructive studies in which no significant differences were found in the closeness or intimacy of the friendships of children from collectivistic and individualistic cultures. This research includes an important longitudinal study of friends in China and the United States (Gupta *et al.*, 2013), a now-classic comparison of friendships in the United States and Costa Rica (DeRosier and Kupersmidt, 1991), a comparison of best-friend closeness in China and Canada (Chen *et al.*, 2004), a comparison of friendship in Taiwan and Canada (Benjamin *et al.*, 2001), and a comparison of friendship ratings by early adolescents in Zimbabwe and the United States (Harrison *et al.*, 1995). It should be remembered that the lack of differences in the closeness of friendship does not mean that friendship is identical or serves the same functions in all places. It is still possible to have – and/or want – a very close friendship in a society where companionship, help and support are parts of a larger bond with extended family, community or clan.

Friendship as a refuge from the ubiquity of pressures to conform

Schneider, Lee and Alvarez-Valdivia (2011) discuss the possibility that close friendship provides a respite from the pressures of collective living in some very collectivistic societies. They base their observations on cultural artifacts such as films and novels from Cuba and Japan. In both of these societies, parents, teachers and even neighbors are active agents of socialization who are expected to guide the child toward the responsibilities of citizenship and toward behavior that is seen as consistent with the goals and well-being of the group. In many cases, these adults are in close contact with each other. Despite the love, encouragement and support provided by all of these agents of socialization, this interconnected network of adult authority figures often has little leeway for thoughts and impulses that the larger society may deprecate. In both countries, though with different nuances in each, a close friend may provide a comfortable refuge in which children and adolescents may 'be themselves' without fear of rebuke or retribution.

Conflict and conflict resolution between friends

Probably more cultural differences have been found in the extent of conflict between child and adolescent friends than in the closeness of the relationships. In many ways, the conflict within the friendship dyad mirrors the permissiveness or restriction in the surrounding society on the expression of conflict. Overt expression of negative emotion is particularly discouraged in many East Asian societies (e.g. Argyle, 1978). This has been mirrored in several cross-cultural studies in which East Asian children and adolescents have reported lower levels of conflict with their friends than have children in other societies. These studies include comparisons between Canada and Taiwan (Benjamin *et al.*, 2001), Indonesia and the United States (French *et al.*, 2005) and Indonesia and Germany (Haar and Krahé, 1999).

Competition does not always entail conflict but hostile, hypercompetitive forms of competition are indeed conflictual. *Hypercompetitiveness* refers to a hard-driven form of competition in which the competitor competes to win at any cost and to prove himself/herself superior to others. Non-hostile social comparison, in contrast, refers to competition motivated by the need to become better at the particular activity that is the locus of the competition. Sullivan (1953) decried competition in general but felt that innocent, non-hostile comparison of achievements was not harmful, especially in male friendships.

Schneider, Woodburn, Soteras-de Toro and Udvari (2005) used a short-term longitudinal design in their comparison of children's friendships in Canada, Cuba and Costa Rica. Their study featured a distinction between these forms of competition. The researchers found that Canadian participants were tolerant of hypercompetitiveness in their friendship bonds. However, hostile competition predicted the dissolution of friendships in the two samples from collectivistic societies, Cuba and Costa Rica.

Schneider and his colleagues found important cultural differences in the implications of competition for friendship. Non-hostile social comparison was generally linked with closeness in friendship, especially in Cuba, a country where education and achievement are valued highly. This form of relating was associated with closeness in friendship in both Latin American samples among male participants only. This suggests that friendly competition may be a way in which males bond with their friends, as suggested by Sullivan. In contrast, hypercompetitiveness was linked with the termination of friendship in Cuba and Costa Rica, and among Canadian females. Canadian males, however, did not seem to take their friends' hypercompetitiveness into account when making decisions about a friendship.

This study indicates that the dyadic interactions between friends reflect some of the values of the surrounding culture. The results also suggest that researchers should take both gender and culture into account when conducting their studies and analyzing their findings.

Inter-ethnic and inter-racial friendship

The enrollment of immigrants in urban schools in North America, Western Europe and Australia has given researchers an opportunity to study the relations between different racial and ethnic groups. Surmounting the obstacles that are often inherent in choosing a friend from a member of a different ethnic group has been seen as a clear indication of multicultural respect (Raabe and Beelmann, 2011). Cross-ethnic friendship has also been seen as a facilitator of social competence and emotional adjustment (Eisenberg *et al.*, 2009).

Prejudice is a major barrier to inter-ethnic friendship. *Social reflection theories* maintain that children become prejudiced because they learn that society values different ethnic groups differently; they may also become prejudiced due to their parents instilling prejudicial attitudes in them. Psychodynamic explanations assert that children become prejudiced because their parents punish expressions of hostility. Children therefore displace this hostility onto lower-status minority ethnic groups. Cognitive-developmental theories maintain that prejudice reflects the young child's egocentrism (Aboud and Doyle, 1995).

Children encounter others who may differ from them in many respects – such as race/ethnicity, gender and age – and such variables are often used by them when choosing or rejecting friends. Because similarity is often an important prerequisite for interpersonal attraction, many conjecture that children will often choose friends who are of the same ethnic or racial group. Many studies have found this to be the case (Alvarez-Valdivia, Schneider and Villalobos, in press; Bellmore *et al.*, 2007; Clark and Ayers, 1992; Denscombe *et al.*, 1986; De Souza Briggs, 2007; Lease and Blake, 2005; Howes and Wu, 1990). Furthermore, there are methodological limitations to many reports that may mean that the rate of inter-ethnic friendship has been systematically *overestimated*. Importantly, many studies feature unidirectional friendship nominations in which participating children are asked to name their close friends. Unless the researchers also find out whether the child who is named reciprocates the friendship nomination, the data may be inaccurate (Echols and Graham, 2013). Theoretically, he principle of *propinquity* – forming friends with people who are physically close and therefore available (see Chapter 7) – should operate to facilitate cross-ethnic friendships. However, it has been remarked that inter-group friendship also depends on *network propinquity* – having a mutual friend among the larger social group – without which friendship will not emerge even if members of different groups are in close physical proximity for extended periods of time (Mouw and Entwistle, 2006). Awareness of the role of network propinquity has inspired important new studies on *indirect friends* – or friends of friends. In an innovative longitudinal study conducted in Montreal, Aboud, Friedmann and Smith (2015) found that having an indirect friend of another ethnic group increased the probability over time of having a direct friend who is a member of an outgroup.

Weinreich (1983) maintains that friendships play a fundamental role in the process of redefinition of the personal and social identities of adolescent immigrants. In their attempts to resolve the inevitable discrepancies between the cultural values of their families and those of their school culture, they often turn to friends for guidance, support and validation (Shih, 1998). Adolescent immigrants undergo the typical growing pains of the teenage years in counterpoint with the challenges of moving to a new and unfamiliar culture. Several aspects of friendship are related to the well-being of immigrants, especially social support in times of need (Vitoroulis *et al.*, 2012). Communication with friends seems to be an integral part of acculturation to the school experience (Tong, 2014).

The cultural background of a pupil's friends may mediate the extent and nature of their influence. Studies conducted in the United States have shown some benefits in terms of successful acculturation for having friends both inside and outside one's own cultural group (Chan and Birman, 2009; Hamm, Brown and Heck, 2005). In a short-term longitudinal study of German and Turkish pre-adolescents in Germany, Jugert, Noack and Rutland (2011) found that positive classroom identification was linked to an increase in inter-ethnic friendship. Adding an important individual characteristic to research on inter-ethnic friendship, Echols and Graham (2013) found in a study of early adolescents in Los Angeles that it was the more respected, socially competent participants who tended to reach out to members of other ethnic groups as friends. Although inter-ethnic friendship is studied most often in the context of immigration to multicultural Western societies, there are also many African and Asian countries in which members of different ethnic groups study together in school. Eisenberg and her colleagues (2009) found that Indonesian middle-school students who had close friends of another religion displayed higher social competence and more prosocial behavior than their classmates whose best friends were of the same religion.

Unfortunately, the positive influences of cross-ethnic friendships may sometimes be limited by the fact that they are often not as stable or satisfying as co-ethnic friendships (Jugert, Noack and Rutland, 2011; Schneider, Udvari and Dixon, 2007). Cross-ethnic friendships may also be characterized by greater conflict than inter-ethnic friendships (Schneider, Udvari and Dixon, 2007). This conflict may lead to dissolution of friendship, as reflected, perhaps, in the short half-lives often found for inter-ethnic friendships. Most authorities on friendship regard conflict between friends as inevitable and not necessarily unhealthy. However, they highlight the adaptive importance of the conflict-resolution abilities that enable a good friendship to continue and grow (Schneider, 2000). Akhtar (2009) observes that having friends of one's own culture typically helps counteract the profound feeling of being alone that he sees as integral to the lives of immigrants. Encountering other members of their cultures of origin provides immigrants with a feeling of belonging and kinship. Perhaps for this reason, most available data indicate that adolescents tend to choose friends from among members of the same ethnic group (e.g. Smith and Schneider, 2000; Verkuyten and Thijs, 2002; Verkuyten and Martinovic, 2006). In some situations, friends of the same cultural group who identify positively with the experience of schooling exert an important positive influence. This has been found among Mexican-Americans (Azmitia, 2010) and in the Comoran community of Marseille. The Comorans are a Muslim group who traditionally place very high value on education. Transmission of that value to the new generation depends very heavily on friendship within the Comoran community rather than with neighboring communities that often do not share this value (Allès-Jardel, Schneider and Boutry, 2002).

Allport (1954, p. 281), in his classic theory about prejudice, maintained that 'equal-status contact between majority and minority groups in the pursuit of common goals' is a condition for mutual acceptance. The theory proceeds to emphasize not just contact among the groups but specifically *positive* contact. Slavin (1979) examined the effects of cooperative learning groups on cross-ethnic/cross-racial friendship selection. (Cooperative learning was discussed in Chapter 4.) The cooperative learning groups in Slavin's study were composed of students of different ethnic/racial groups and differing scholastic capabilities. Students were assigned the responsibilities of tutoring and quizzing their peers, and the group was rewarded for the achievement of its members. Every student in the group was given an equal opportunity to add points to the group's score by improving his or her previous performance. The results of Slavin's study indicated a statistically significant effect for the cooperative learning context on the number and proportion of cross-race friends selected. Similarly, Zigler (1981) found that more casual cross-ethnic friendships were formed in the cooperative learning group than in the regularly instructed control group. Only until ten weeks after the experiment ended was there a treatment effect on close inter-racial friendship. Nevertheless, cooperative groups did have positive effects on students' interaction with peers of a different race.

Kawabata and Crick (2015) added an important longitudinal perspective to research on cross-ethnic and same-ethnic friendships. They conducted their study with a large sample of nine–ten-year-old participants in the United States using a short-term longitudinal design. Information was obtained from students, teachers and peers at the beginning and end of a single school year. The results showed that children involved in cross-ethnic friendships experienced more positive peer experiences by the end of the school year, including a significant reduction in non-verbal, relational forms of bullying.

Should society or schools be disturbed by the findings that children tend to choose friends of their own cultural or racial group? This depends on how one views race and ethnic relations. Lundberg and Dickson (1952, p. 34) asserted that 'a certain amount of ethnocentrism is a normal and necessary ingredient of all group life' and it is, 'therefore, not in itself necessarily to be regarded as a problem'. However, there are ample data indicating the benefits of cross-ethnic friendship. For example, Bagci and his colleagues in London found that East Asian children in the city's schools who had friendships of good quality with fellow students of other ethnic groups tended to be less affected by perceived racial discrimination than East Asian children whose friends were mostly other East Asians (Bagci *et al.*, 2014).

Expanding knowledge about children's friendships around the planet

As in research about most other aspects of children's peer relations, the studies discussed in this chapter demonstrate both important differences and equally important similarities in children's friendships in different cultures. There is little doubt that friendship is important in most cultures, although the database does not clearly indicate why. In many important studies published recently, researchers have attempted to link some known characteristic of the cultures studied to multiple aspects of children's friendships, instead of merely measuring children's friendships in different countries without a clear reason to justify the cross-cultural comparisons. Theory-driven research is of course better than casual cross-cultural comparisons that have no theoretical justification. Based on the current state of knowledge, however, it appears impossible to draw a line between any known feature of cultures and important dimensions of child and adolescent friendships. Most researchers mention the very well-known distinction between individualism and collectivism, but the data do not indicate in any convincing way that friendship is linked clearly to either pole of that continuum. Cultural familism – the psychological importance of family ties – has also been invoked, but it is not clear whether this is associated with depth or superficiality in friendship.

It is probably more profitable to understand the specific role of friendship in each culture against the backdrop of many dimensions of that culture – individualism/collectivism, familism, the school experience, the nature of parental workplaces, the leeway for expressing emotions, and many more. It is also possible that the inconsistent research findings have more to do with the different research methods used rather than with any true cultural differences. Indeed, methodology has been very eclectic – ranging from questionnaires to observations, and interviews about hypothetical friends and real ones, to name only a few. Despite the pesky inconsistencies it may generate, this eclecticism is surely invaluable, given the need for in-depth understanding of how friendship is articulated and negotiated in different cultures.

11

ELECTRONIC COMMUNICATION AND PEER RELATIONSHIPS

Barry H. Schneider and Yair Amichai-Hamburger

Electronic communication has become a prominent feature of the interpersonal relationships of children and youth. When this technology first appeared, it was feared that interpersonal relationships would suffer, leading to widespread loneliness. Although such fears have not subsided completely, some research has shown how electronic communication can in fact enhance interpersonal relationships for individuals who are both proficient and deficient in relating face to face. In this chapter the unique properties of the virtual environment are considered in terms of their utility in relationship formation and maintenance. The electronic medium functions simultaneously as a tool used by the rich (i.e. those who already have a strong relational network) to get richer, by the poor to get richer, and, in some cases, by perpetrators of cyber-aggression, who try to further impoverish their victims.

In a creative study conducted in a laboratory, Clayton, Leshner and Almond (2015) discovered that young people experience marked psychological distress when denied the possibility of using their iPhones for just a few minutes. Of course, it could be argued that the participants in the study are not attached to their iPhones at all, only to the people they contact on them. That would mean that the iPhone is nothing more than a relationship tool that has replaced the landline telephone, love letters sent through the mail (post), or confessions of true love sent by messengers, as in the plays of Shakespeare. The intermediary role of the messenger becomes very much a part of the plot. In many cases, the writer makes the deliberate decision to communicate 'his' feelings (they are usually those of a man) without direct communication with the woman he loves. A classic example is in *Twelfth Night*: Orsino uses Cesario to express his feelings about Olivia to her. As noted by Professor Cyrus Mulready, Orsino probably made this choice of medium because he knew that Olivia was not interested in Cesario (https://newpaltzshakespeare.wordpress.com/2014/09/15/love-letters-and-messengers/, retrieved January 22, 2015). Face-to-face contact would have been very awkward. Some contemporary victims of unrequited love may resort to electronic communication for the very same reason.

However, Clayton, Leshner and Almond's research into attachment to the iPhone is based on the premise that young people may become attached to the *medium itself*, not only to the people it is used to contact. Harkin (2003) remarks that mobile phones often become comfort objects that shield the user from the hostile nature of the outside world. He invokes the image of an umbilical cord. An addicted user may experience anxiety about missing some important event or topic in their interpersonal networks (called 'FOMO' – fear of missing out) or about missing the latest developments in smartphone technology (King *et al.*, 2013). The phone itself becomes an extension of the user's physical self, as articulated in Belk's (2013) *extended self theory*. Belk proposes that an individual's possessions become an integral and important part of his or her personal identity. The crowds of young people waiting to purchase each new version of the iPhone can thus be seen as young people in search of themselves. It is unlikely that many of these young people are thinking about the relationships that begin or continue over the iPhone as they contemplate the features of the new model.

Electronic communication is now available to the vast majority of children and adolescents in most developed countries. It is also increasingly accessible in developing nations. In the United States, the number of children between the ages of twelve and seventeen going online reached 95 percent in 2013, with substantial numbers of young people accessing the internet from personal devices, such as smartphones. Children and youth of minority cultural background are not as connected as other US teens, but access rates now exceed 85 percent for all cultural and economic groups included in a Pew Institute (2013) survey.

Burgeoning access to electronic media is by no means limited to the United States. Young people in Europe and the Far East may have even greater access than Americans. In recent years, media access has expanded not only geographically but also to children much younger than the adolescents whose media addiction is the subject of much debate and lament. Finnish researcher Sirkku Kotilainen has traced an interesting development progression of media use over the course of child development based on her observational and interview study of media use in 743 Finnish homes with children. Some awareness of media is evident even among toddlers. However, a dramatic shift occurs around age seven–eight years, when there is a substantial increase in the use of both internet and mobile phone (Ólafsson, Livingstone and Haddon, 2013). Internet cafés have mushroomed in much of the developing world, compensating – to some extent – for the fact that relatively few people in these countries have connections at home. Ybarra and colleagues (2006) found that 48 percent of the adolescents surveyed in the town of Mbarara, Uganda, accessed the internet regularly. The researchers suggested that internet access in towns like Mbarara is greater than in smaller villages but not as common as it is in large Ugandan cities.

Much of the time spent on the internet involves social interaction: after homework, email and electronic messaging are adolescents' most common online activities, with 85 percent of online teens use electronic messaging and emails to communicate (Pew Institute, 2013). Although Facebook's terms and conditions of use indicate a restriction of service to individuals no younger than thirteen years, authoritative data reported in the magazine *Consumer Reports* in 2011 indicated that at least 7.5 million children under that age had Facebook accounts (www.consumerreports.org/cro/magazine-archive/2011/june/electronics-computers/state-of-the-net/facebook-concerns/index.htm, retrieved March 3, 2015).

The most eloquent speculations about the effects of electronic communication on human relationships are those of Harvard communications professor Sherry Turkle, mentioned in Chapter 1. Her treatise is summarized in a book that is aptly entitled *Alone together: why we expect more from technology and less from each other* (2011). The book begins with a review of research from past decades about scientists' attempts to construct robots that can mimic human relationships. The robots have come close but their human relationship partners have always had to reduce their relationship expectations to match what the robots can provide. On the basis of interviews with several hundred adolescents (not sampled in any systematic fashion), Turkle concludes that young people are similarly reducing their expectations in order to accommodate to the most convenient use of the new technology. Relationships are becoming superficial, emotionally flat, and largely devoid of intimacy. Turkle has observed mothers looking after their email exchanges at dinner rather than attending to their children and families. She has attended memorial services for departed relatives during which the mourners spend the hour sending text messages rather than taking leave of the departed loved one. She reminds readers that adolescence is a period during which young people have to explore their identities and often experience considerable angst as they do so. The internet causes additional anxiety by forcing adolescents to play with their identities to the point of creating online identities that have little to do with their real selves; rather, they focus on creating impressions for those with whom they connect electronically. It is possible to bring the image of a friend or loved one to the screen but, according to Turkle, most users find these images more intense than they would like them to be and switch to another screen after a brief glance. Users become too lazy to explore the gamut of emotions that arise in close relationships. The potential risk inherent in intensifying the friendship experience is avoided by creating 'friendships' in which there is little enduring intimate exchange. Facebook has cheapened the notion of friendship and reduced its scope to a few parameters that can be tabulated and posted without serious contemplation. The book concludes with an earnest plea for all users of new technology to discipline themselves enough to turn off their devices when it is time to relate on a face-to-face basis.

Below, we consider theories in the literature about the implications of relating to others through interpersonal communication. First, we study the implications of electronic communication for the general population of children. Theories about individual differences in the benefit or harm engendered by electronic communication follow. The next section is devoted to selected longitudinal studies on the possible implications of electronic communication on the children's and adolescents' relationships. The concluding remarks include a discussion of the 'dark side' of online relationships – cyber-aggression.

Theoretical vantage points: the internet seen as generally good, generally bad and essentially neutral

Several theorists espousing the *reduction hypothesis* insist that electronic communication destroys close interpersonal ties. Many of these ideas emerged in the years after electronic communication first became widespread. The reduction hypothesis and a few studies supporting it were reported prominently in the mass media in the 1990s. The essence of the hypothesis is that the internet is basically used to establish superficial, ephemeral, interpersonal contacts that cannot really be considered friendships of good quality. The excessive time spent on these superficial online 'friendships' detracts from the time needed to cultivate rewarding, high-quality friendships in real life (Locke, 1998; Baiocco *et al.*, 2011a). Kraut and colleagues (1998) expressed many people's greatest fear regarding the internet, when he argued that it is an isolated environment that has a negative impact on our 'real world'.

There are many ways, however, in which electronic communication may help children and young people to befriend each other. The internet creates a unique psychological environment for its users. McKenna, Green and Gleason (2002) suggested four major factors that differentiate between internet and face-to-face interactions: greater anonymity; the decreased importance of physical appearance; greater control; and finding similar others.

- *Greater anonymity.* Many websites allow surfers to move around freely without disclosing any personal information. In fact, even when people do divulge personal information on the internet, they still subjectively feel relatively anonymous (McKenna and Bargh, 2000; McKenna, Green and Gleason, 2002). The *online disinhibition effect* – the loosening or complete elimination of the social constraints and restrictions that would be evident in face-to-face interactions – results in a sense of anonymity that frees people from social norms in their physical environment and reduces personal inhibitions (Joinson, 2007; Suler, 2004a). Potier (2007) contends that this disinhibition effect may go as far as encouraging narcissism.
- *Decreased importance of physical appearance.* Physical appearance significantly influences the ways in which a person is perceived and judged by others. One factor in their judgment is as a result of the *halo effect* (Asch, 1946), a phenomenon whereby one positive characteristic of a person leads observers to believe that other positive characteristics are present (e.g. an attractive person may be perceived as possessing superior personality traits), whereas

people who are physically unappealing are frequently judged unfavorably on unrelated issues. Online social interactions are typically text-based; consequently, participants' physical characteristics remain unknown. This may appeal to people with unattractive physical characteristics or visible disabilities, who are likely to suffer from prejudice and discrimination in face-to-face interactions. Online, they have an opportunity to present themselves in any way they choose (Suler, 2004b). In some cases this may lead to deception.

- *Greater control.* One of the unique features of internet communication is that participants can explore the world and meet exotic strangers from the safety and comfort of their own homes. Internet users feel in greater control of their social interactions as they can easily escape from an interaction, remain unidentified and experience a subjective sense of privacy (Madell and Muncer, 2007).
- *Finding similar others.* The need to 'belong' is one of the significant needs in Maslow's (1971) hierarchy. For individuals, being a member of a group that shares goals and interests is likely to enhance self-esteem (Tajfel and Turner, 1986), which in turn is an important factor in overall well-being (Branden, 1969). The internet is an extremely effective tool for discovering like-minded others due to the vast numbers of people online and the efficient search facilities. This is particularly relevant to people who belong to stigmatized or minority groups, since they frequently experience difficulties both in locating similar others offline and finding opportunities to interact with them face to face. Both of these challenges are made easier in cyberspace. Indeed, as McKenna and colleagues (2002) pointed out, once similar others have been found, group identification frequently develops faster online than it does offline.

Perhaps the internet helps shy, withdrawn individuals connect with each other, share, and overcome their difficulties in interacting with others. Together, these different features form a highly protected environment for the surfer. In other words, users may well feel freed from their usual undeviating offline persona and believe that they are able to express aspects of themselves online that they are unable to articulate in face-to-face interactions. This may result in their displaying a huge variety of behaviors on the internet: for example, an individual may develop social skills that he or she was unable – possibly through shyness – to utilize offline. On the other hand, an individual may exhibit extreme uninhibited aggressive behavior within the internet environment.

Other theorists have suggested several additional properties of electronic communication that explain its appeal as a relationship-building tool.

- *Accessible anytime, anywhere.* The electronic medium may intensify relationships because the relationship partners can interact as often as they wish.
- *Fun.* Many young people find the online experience pleasant and enjoy the task of mastering the technology that is used to relate.

- *Equity.* Social networks provide the user with the ability to have a voice on any and every topic. People who previously may have felt inadequate and powerless may unite with ease to seek change (Amichai-Hambuger, 2013).
- *Safety and warmth.* Turkle (2004) believes that the internet provides an individual with space, warmth, safety and understanding. Psychotherapy provides something similar – a safe environment in which to rework elements from the past and try out different alternatives for the present and the future. In addition, the internet provides an environment that helps to create a 'time out' for the individual, so it can serve as a moratorium, as was recommended by Erickson for adolescents in offline society.
- *Anonymity.* The anonymity of the internet and the feelings of safety it brings provide opportunities for people to discuss topics that may be awkward or even taboo to discuss offline. Magid (1998) found that older children are much more likely than younger children to use chat rooms and online forums to discuss relationships and sexual activity. Stern (2002) believes that the internet provides a forum for teenage girls to express themselves as they undergo social and sexual changes in their lives. As well as providing a forum for such discussions, the internet constitutes a place where teenagers sought advice, information and support when discussing socially taboo topics (Subrahmanyam *et al.*, 2004; Suzuki and Calzo, 2004; Gray *et al.*, 2005).

Online chat consists of online instantaneous transmission of text messages from one sender to many receivers. Anonymous chat users have a tendency to be closed and rather introverted. Anolli, Villani and Riva (2005) conclude that these internet users view the chat environment as an appropriate forum in which to generate and develop personal relationships. The researchers point out the similarities between their findings and those of Amichai-Hamburger, Wainapel and Fox (2002) with respect to the behavior of introverts who choose the internet, rather than the offline world, as the preferred environment for their interactions. In this case, the chat room can be seen as a forum in which introverts may express themselves. Anolli, Villani and Riva point out that participants in chat rooms appear to be people who need support and approval, and this forum provides them with these benefits.

A blog is a net diary, usually personal and updated frequently. Blogs aim to build a community of people around them who comment on the posts and create a dialogue on the topic of the blog. The blog's content is often expressive and includes links and comments regarding other websites and blogs, news, ideas, photos, poetry, project updates, and stories (Riva, 2002). New technology allows a direct uploading of text, photos and links without users needing a high level of technological understanding, allowing the blog to be read at any time and in any situation where there is an internet connection. Blog owners can allow their readers to write comments after each post (Huffaker, 2004). Blogs are often written as a series of continuous comments on a specific agenda. This type of format enables a permanent and continuous information update, it provides convenient tools for use, and it is offered for free to everyone (Lawson-Borders and Kirk, 2005). In addition, the blogosphere allows the creation of intimate communities of communication (Ó Baoill, 2004). Herring and colleagues (2005) believe that the importance of the blog as an intimate form of self-expression is underestimated.

The blog format, which allows users to maintain their anonymity, would seem to be an ideal setting for people with social inhibitions, since their involvement in the blog would allow them to feel totally protected and so enable them to recreate themselves and express themselves freely. However, Guadagno, Okdie and Eno (2008) found that the personality characteristics that are related to blogging are openness to new experiences and neuroticism; moreover, perhaps surprisingly, they found no relationship between introversion and blogging.

The situation is actually more complex than this, though, as Guadagno and her colleagues did not focus on blogs where authors maintain their anonymity. Cyberspace contains many different types of blog with varying degrees of anonymity – from completely anonymous to easily identifiable. Guadagno and her colleagues report that many bloggers provide identifying information such as their name, and they suggest that an identified blog does not provide a protective environment for any surfer with social inhibitions; in fact, it does the opposite. It is therefore suggested that future studies should examine the relationship between introversion and blogging on *unidentified* blogs. We predict that such a study would find that introverts see such blogs as protective environments that help them to express themselves freely, and therefore that a strong link between introversion and anonymous blogging may well exist.

Forming friendships online

For many people, the internet is an excellent medium through which to meet people and in some cases start relationships that may eventually develop into face-to-face meetings. Friendship and intimate relationships evolve through the development of disclosure and mutual trust (Jourard, 1971). Offline, this gradual revelation may develop over a long period, with the exception being those who meet as strangers with no intention of forming a relationship or even meeting again (Rubin, 1975). The process of meeting in cyberspace may be seen as much more akin to the 'strangers-on-a-train' phenomenon than the usual gradual emergence of intimacy seen in the face-to-face world. This is due to the cyberspace environment, with its opportunities to 'disappear off the train' and into oblivion, coupled with the protection it offers that allows for anonymity. This results in speedier self-disclosure than is found in the offline world (McKenna *et al.*, 2002; Ben-Ze'ev, 2005). Indeed, accelerated and increased self-disclosure is typical in virtual interpersonal relationships (e.g. Joinson and Paine, 2007). This self-disclosure tends to be reciprocated (Barak and Gluck-Ofri, 2007).

Simulation experiments have been used successfully to understand the differences between online and offline communication among adults; we are aware of no similar studies with children or adolescents. McKenna and colleagues (2002, study 3) assigned undergraduates randomly in cross-sex pairs. The pairs were to meet initially either face to face or in an internet chat room. After the meeting, those who had met online reported feeling that they knew the other person better and they liked that person more, when compared to the reports of those participants who had met face to face. This effect continued when participants met their original dating partner on two further occasions, once over the internet and once face to face. It is important to add that participants were unaware that they were meeting with the same partner face to face and online.

Individual differences in the implications of electronic communication on relationships

As should be evident by this point, any harm or benefit to close relationships probably depends heavily on how the electronic medium is used and who is using it. This section includes some information on studies conducted with adults, because individual differences have not been explored as comprehensively in studies conducted with children and adolescents.

Shy, anxious and introverted people

Individual differences in disposition and self-efficacy beliefs may determine reasons for internet usage and its effects (LaRose, Eastin and Gregg, 2001). The *rich-get-richer hypothesis* (Kraut *et al.*, 1998) predicts that the internet is used primarily by extroverts to expand their network of contacts. In contrast, the *social compensation hypothesis* (e.g. Hamburger and Ben-Artzi, 2000) maintains that introverts, lonely, depressed and socially anxious people are drawn to the internet to compensate for their anxieties during offline social interaction. In turn, their preference for virtual communication may exacerbate their personal problems. People who are socially anxious report that they find forging and maintaining relationships with others easier online than in person (McKenna and Bargh, 1998). The anonymity of online relationships, especially in their early stages, may reduce inhibition because online communicators may feel that they are shielded from the consequences of disclosing personal information (McKenna and Bargh, 1998). This anonymity allows individuals to manipulate their self-presentations with ease, often to the point of online identity 'experimentation' (e.g. Valkenburg *et al.*, 2005). The shy adolescents interviewed by Henderson and colleagues (1999) indicated that they preferred to talk about personal and emotional issues online to a greater degree than do non-shy students. Maczewski (2002) proposed that ineffectual, powerless youth can use the internet to their benefit to assume a more powerful stance in their interpersonal interactions. Thus, electronic communication can make it easy to avoid intimacy if that is what one wants to do. However, if one's goal is to pursue a relationship to a stage of heightened intimacy, the internet can permit the necessary relational communication even if geography and circumstances make face-to-face contact difficult.

Peter, Valkenburg and Schouten (2005) proposed a model to explain how introverted people, presumably including shy, withdrawn children and adolescents, form friendships online. Included in their model are several links established in previous research: introverted people self-disclose online more than others and use electronic communication more often than others. Introverts are also motivated to turn to online communication in order to compensate for social-communication deficits they encounter in face-to-face interactions. This social compensation motive also leads to greater online self-disclosure regardless of one's introversion. The researchers found empirical support for the path model in a study conducted with 600 Dutch participants between nine and eighteen years of age. Their data also confirmed that girls self-disclose more than boys online. Older adolescents communicated more online than the younger participants in the study, but younger participants formed more friendships online.

According to the well-known homophily process in friendships, people of all ages tend to select others who are similar to themselves as friends. The electronic medium may make it easy for young people to locate potential friends who are similar to themselves in some salient way. This is an important consideration, especially in the study of the friendships of socially withdrawn children and adolescents. Although these children and youth do indeed have friendships that are not totally devoid of rewarding qualities, many of the friends they have are themselves socially withdrawn, at least to a certain degree (Rubin *et al.*, 2006; Schneider, 1999).

Although, in theory, electronic communication may facilitate contact between people who are similar in some important way, there is reason to believe that homophily is less important for friendships formed online than for those formed face to face, especially in schools. The greater willingness to befriend peers who are somewhat dissimilar may stem from the absence of cues online that would indicate many aspects of similarity. In a study featuring home interviews with almost 1,000 Israeli adolescents, Mesch and Talmud (2007) found that homophily was far less evident in online than in offline relationships. Thus, electronic communication may be helpful to socially anxious, withdrawn children and youth in two opposite ways: forming friends with other socially anxious children and youth (due to the facilitation of contact with similar others, discussed earlier); and forming friends with others who are more socially competent (due to the decreased importance of physical indicators of homophily).

In many situations in the offline world, physical impressions are crucial (e.g. Fiske and Taylor, 1991). This puts individuals who belong to stigmatized social groups – for example, those with physical disabilities – at a major disadvantage. Such people may find it easier to meet others in an environment where they can control how they wish to be portrayed. The internet provides such an environment, where interaction is text-based, physical cues are limited, and individuals are free to choose with whom they wish to interact and when (e.g. Ben-Ze'ev, 2005; McKenna *et al.*, 2002).

Gender and cultural differences

The specific possibilities the internet offers shy, withdrawn people must be understood in light of broader gender and cultural differences. Suler (2004a) argues that women, in particular, benefit from being able to reframe their identities and self-definition online, especially in patriarchal societies where they would have difficulty doing so using other media. Boneva, Kraut and Frohlich (2001) observed that men and women in Western societies tend to use the internet in different ways. Women and girls express emotions more extensively online and generally use email more often. Men and boys use electronic communication in more instrumental ways, such as setting times for contacts with friends and associates or gathering information related to recreational pursuits. In many cultures with strong gender-role distinctions, parents and peers may provide greater support to boys in learning to use technology than to girls. Vekiri and Chronaki (2008), working in Greece, found that female elementary school pupils perceived less parental and peer support than did boys for becoming proficient with electronic technology.

Electronic communication also provides unique opportunities for self-expression in societies where direct expression of emotion is discouraged. Kamibeppu and Sugiura (2005) conducted a questionnaire study with Japanese early adolescents. Socially effective students used the internet or cell phones to expand and consolidate existing relationships with others in close proximity. This phenomenon may apply more strongly in Japan than elsewhere. Kamibeppu and Sugiura describe many cases of pathological internet addiction among Japanese youths. They also describe the use of electronic communication as a criterion for inclusion in the circle of popular peers: groups of popular children exclude potential group members who do not have cell phones or access to the internet.

Many other cultural differences in the relationship implications of electronic communication remain to be explored. It is possible that electronic communication may have some effect on the core features of some societies. For example, in cultures where there is little tolerance for diversity, the internet may become a vehicle for members of minority groups to contact each other and achieve greater social success and satisfaction. As is known by totalitarian regimes that block access to certain websites, the internet can make it more difficult for authority figures to exercise absolute control over society. This could change the nature of societies in which authority figures are highly revered – termed cultures that are high in 'power distance' in Hofstede's (1983) schema. Finally, since children and adolescents may acquire electronic communication skills faster than adults, electronic communication may promote the development of more distinct children's or adolescents' cultures in societies where the extended family has previously been the most important social unit.

Empirical studies of electronic communication and the friendships of children and adolescents: challenges in studying the implications of electronic communication

The researcher's perspective

It is not likely that a researcher will be in a position to observe directly an individual's interaction with electronic communication tools or even monitor these behaviors electronically. Even in the very rare instance in which this might be possible, the effects of the observer on the behavior of the participants in a study would likely be considerable. Observer effects might be particularly problematic in this situation because many individuals engage in interactions via electronic communication because of its perceived privacy and relative anonymity, as discussed earlier. Therefore, questionnaire and survey methods – whether completed on paper or online – have become the mainstays of research in this area. Self-reporting in this area of inquiry is a logical method: the respondent knows best about his or her online communication. However, the problems inherent in questionnaire research are the same as when using paper-and-pencil methods to study any other relationship phenomenon. First of all, the respondent may wish to convey to the researcher impressions that are socially desirable. Second, the study participant who completes a questionnaire at a specific moment in time may not accurately remember or accurately portray the events occurring over a longer period of time. His or her responses may be affected by his or her mood at the moment, which may be particularly troublesome in studies of participants' loneliness or anxiety.

In the vast majority of studies conducted to date, questionnaire responses are used in correlational analyses of data obtained at a single moment in time. Despite the problems inherent in this strategy, it is by no means easy for researchers to improve on it. The newspaper headlines in 1998 proclaiming to the world that the internet was causing people to be lonely were based on a one-shot correlational study by Kraut and colleagues (1998). Even the journalists who commented on that contention a few days later were aware that, as is made clear in any basic textbook on research methods, correlations cannot indicate the direction of causation: any correlation between internet use and loneliness, for example, may indicate *either* that internet use causes loneliness *or* that people who are already lonely are more likely than others to use the internet (see Amichai-Hamburger and Ben-Artzi, 2003). Furthermore, it is possible that some other variable might explain the connection, if any, between loneliness and internet use. Along these lines, Caplan (2007) argued, with supporting data obtained from university students, that the correlation between internet use and loneliness is spurious because social anxiety probably explains *both* loneliness and internet use.

Era effects

The half-life of a research report in this area is very short. Many studies were published in the late 1990s, meaning they pertain to an era when access to the internet was expanding rapidly but still not widespread. At the time, people with specific needs to connect to others may have been among the first to go online. The correlational studies of the time, such as the well-known study by Kraut and colleagues (1998), were interpreted as meaning that the internet increased loneliness. Widespread as this belief may have become, it is equally possible that lonely people were among the first to seek internet access. These results may be out of date in an era when most people have access, including many who now access the internet with portable personal devices that they carry with them.

Developmental differences

Developmental issues are essentially ignored by researchers studying the relationship implications of electronic communication. As time goes on, electronic communication is being used by younger children and adolescents. It was estimated in 2010 that about one-quarter of children aged three to five years were using the internet at home, compared with about half of the population of six to eleven-year-olds and over three-quarters of twelve–seventeen-year-olds (www.childtrends.org/?indicators=home-computer-access#sthash.SAXSn7VK.dpuf, retrieved April 15, 2015).

The visual appearance of web pages is being increasingly adapted to the tastes of younger users. It is commonly perceived that children and adolescents use electronic communication far more extensively than adults to form and maintain relationships. This is not an illogical contention, because electronic communication was available to today's younger generation during the developmental phases in which they learn to relate with others. Nevertheless, there has been little speculation or research about possible age differences in the extent or ways that electronic communication is used to relate. Much more data are available about adults' electronic communication than that of children or adolescents. As in any other area of inquiry, there are many problems in extrapolating the results of research conducted with adults to form conclusions about the social behavior of children and adolescents.

Three major longitudinal studies

The literature contains a substantial number of recent correlational studies in which the use of electronic communication is linked with various indices of friendship. These studies are of interest for heuristic purposes, although they are very difficult to interpret: electronic communication might cause good or bad friendships, but good or bad friendships could equally lead to electronic communication. For that reason, the few longitudinal studies in the literature are emphasized here. Longitudinal studies involving correlations among the same variables at different points of time can be useful in suggesting the likely direction of causality, although they cannot provide conclusive evidence of causality.

One of the first longitudinal studies on the use of computers in friendship-making was conducted by Desjarlais and Willoughby (2010) with over 1,000 Canadian adolescents. The study began during early adolescence, with follow-up data collected two and three years after the original data collection. The participants provided reports on their internet use, especially with regard to chat rooms, their friendship quality, participation in group sports, and social anxiety. These results indicated that early use of the internet in friendship formation was linked to subsequent friendship quality. Among male (but not female) participants, this depended on the initial level of social anxiety. Socially anxious boys who used the internet as a compensatory mechanism tended to have better friendships later than socially anxious boys who did not.

Another interesting longitudinal study was conducted by Mikami and her colleagues (2010) with ninety-two young people in Virginia. The participants were first assessed when they were thirteen to fourteen years old, then followed up at age twenty-two to twenty-four years. Youth who used social-networking websites during their adolescence had friendships of better quality during their adolescence and as adults. Furthermore, they had become better adjusted adults in general. This study is remarkable because of the length of the follow-up, even though it is limited by the small sample size.

Koutamanis and colleagues (2013) conducted a three-wave longitudinal study with 690 young Dutch people ranging in age from ten to seventeen years. The results provide incontrovertible evidence that instant messaging leads to enhanced ability to initiate not only offline friendships in general but specifically friendships with members of different age and ethnic groups.

These three longitudinal studies indicate, most importantly, that Kraut and colleagues' (1998) idea that electronic friendship leads to friendlessness and loneliness does not apply to adolescents fifteen to twenty years after his data were collected. Although the results of all three support the contention that electronic communication tends to be a useful and positive relationship-building tool, the data also contain evidence that individuals experiencing difficulties in their interpersonal relationships use electronic communication to compensate for these deficiencies.

Individual differences in introversion/extroversion, shyness and relationship studies have been targeted most frequently by researchers interested in corroborating a possible compensatory mechanism, which, again, does not necessarily invalidate the rich-get-richer hypothesis, even if the 'poor' get richer, too. In some of their earlier work in the Netherlands, Valkenburg and her colleagues (e.g. Peter, Valkenburg and Schouten, 2005) demonstrated that extroverts benefit more than introverts, probably because they learn how to self-disclose judiciously with online relationship partners. Similar results emerged from cross-sectional studies by a team of Italian and Canadian researchers who focused on the use of electronic communication by shy, withdrawn early adolescents (Laghi *et al.*, 2013). These researchers found that shy, withdrawn adolescents inappropriately used the online modality to disclose strong, negative emotions, such as anger. In contrast, other participants who were not shy had learned that it is better to express such emotions in face-to face encounters.

Selfhout and his colleagues (2009) conducted a longitudinal study with adolescents in the Netherlands to determine the possible effects of electronic communication on depressed feelings among participants who reported that they did not have friendships that were of high quality. They found that in this group of participating adolescents with low friendship quality, those who used the internet extensively for communication tended to feel less depressed than other participants.

Other dimensions of individual differences have been studied to a limited extent. Possible gender differences were the specific focus of a one-shot correlational study conducted in Australia by Donchi and Moore (2004). They found that electronic communication enhanced the friendships of boys much more than those of girls. Regardless of gender, participants who valued their online friendships very highly were lonelier than others and had lower self-esteem. Thus, there is some support here for the poor-get-richer hypothesis, especially for adolescent boys.

Clearly, more systematic research on gender differences is needed. New studies on gender differences should go beyond reporting any differences between boys and girls in terms of the final outcome to include possible mediating variables that might explain whatever differences are found. These variables might include needs for intimacy, self-disclosure and the social goals of the participants.

Disability status

Sharabi and Margalit (2011) studied friendship-making online among Israeli adolescents with and without learning disabilities. They found that the students with learning disabilities were lonelier than others. Regardless of learning-disability status, participants who communicated electronically with existing friends whom they met offline were less lonely than those who communicated with their friends in person only. In contrast, the relatively small number of participants who communicated with virtual friends were found to be quite lonely.

Minority sexual orientation

As discussed earlier in this chapter, electronic communication is often a vehicle used by members of various minority groups to make contact with people who are similar to them. This applies particularly to LGBT adolescents. In a qualitative study featuring online focus groups of adolescents of both majority and minority sexual orientation, Hillier, Mitchell and Ybarra (2012) found that LGBT adolescents used the internet far more than non-LGBT participants to make friends. The LGBT participants went on to meet their virtual friends in person very frequently, whereas other participants emphasized the inherent danger in doing so.

Culture

Although online friendship-making among children and adolescents has been studied in a number of different cultures, few, if any, of these studies permit systematic, sound cross-cultural comparisons. Unfortunately, the limited sample of children involved in the pan-European Kids Online study (1,000 participants in total) is unsuitable for comparisons of countries. However, in one of the analyses of the data, Barbovschi (2013) did report one interesting preliminary finding that could be subject to better scrutiny in future studies: relatively few of the participants overall arranged face-to-face meetings with people they met online. The percentage doing so, however, ranged widely: from under 4 percent in Italy, Turkey and Ireland to about 25 percent in Estonia and Lithuania.

Cross-cultural comparisons including countries in East Asia are particularly needed in light of the prohibitions in many East Asian cultures on the expression of emotion in personal encounters. There has been one interesting study on the consequences of positive self-presentation in Facebook on the network of Facebook friends among university-age students in South Korea and the United States (Lee-Won *et al.*, 2014). The Korean participants engaged in more positive self-presentation than did the Americans, probably because of self-consciousness.

Interpersonal violence migrates into cyberspace

Sadly, electronic communication has become a weapon used in interpersonal aggression by children and youth as well as a tool that is useful in forming positive relationship bonds. Sugarman and Willoughby (2013) point out that this phenomenon is best described by the term 'cyber-aggression' rather than the more common term 'cyber-bullying' (see Ybarra and colleagues (2012) for fuller discussion of definitional issues). Cyber-aggression may be more insidious than offline aggression because the aggressive act is repeated every time a bystander accesses the website in which the victim is insulted. Bullying implies the use of force by a powerful individual against a weaker peer. It is, of course, difficult to assess the relative power of the children and youth involved in online aggression. Power imbalance in cyber-aggression may depend more on the technical skills of the individuals involved than their physical strength or self-confidence. In most cases, cyber-aggression reflects conflict between individuals who know each other to some extent (Dooley, Pyzalski and Cross, 2009). Although the experiences of online and offline victimization are qualitatively different in many ways, they are correlated empirically. Most studies indicate that a substantial number – if not the majority – of children and youth who report being victims of online aggression also report being victims of offline aggression (Ybarra and Mitchell, 2004).

Preventing and reducing cyber-aggression is a daunting task because the boundaries of cyberspace are difficult to delimit. Schools and parents may be able to reduce physical aggression and bullying by setting and enforcing limits on behavior at school and in the neighborhood. Scrutinizing electronic communication in the age of the iPhone is much more challenging.

Relating online: concluding remarks

The fragmented research conducted on the possible effects of relating to friends online does not corroborate the contention that the new electronic technology is making young people lonely. The research, for the most part, confirms possible benefits of electronic communication for individuals in need of closer friends and those who already enjoy such relationships. If the interpersonal relationships of children and adolescents are indeed becoming more superficial than in previous eras – which has not been proven – it is by no means clear that the new technology is at fault. Many other changes in Western society could be the culprits if there is indeed a crime, including urbanization, increased competition for resources, and larger public spaces, including schools (Goodwin, 2009), as mentioned in Chapter 1.

There has been considerable research with adult and adolescent populations alike on the benefits of electronic communication for introverts and extroverts. Much less is known, unfortunately, about other dimensions of individual difference. Given the rapid increase in internet access among younger children, studies with younger participants are probably the most needed at this point to complement the studies conducted with adolescents. In addition, given the world-wide proliferation of internet access, systematic cross-cultural comparison would be very interesting.

Although the research to date appears to indicate more benefit than harm in establishing and maintaining friendships online, some disadvantages must be recognized. Cyber-aggression tends to involve people in enemy relationships. Moreover, it has been found that friendship-making online is related to internet addiction among adolescents, although this does not necessarily mean that the friendship-making caused the addiction (Smahel, Brown and Binka, 2012).

Children learn how to use the internet and how to relate online by doing and by imitating others. Relating competently online is a vital twenty-first-century social skill. Perhaps some effort should be made to facilitate this social skill in a twenty-first-century version of social-skills training.

12

FACILITATING CHILDREN'S PEER RELATIONS

This chapter contains descriptions of the various techniques developed to enhance peer relationships both for entire child populations and for children with intellectual and behavioral exceptionalities. The evidence for their effectiveness is reviewed. Traditional social-skills training is considered, as are more recent interventions designed to facilitate friendships at the dyadic level, including recent parent-mediated interventions. Many of the existing techniques are based on the highly debatable assumption that children experiencing difficulties in their interpersonal relationships can benefit from increased rational planning in their social exchange. However, the techniques have been found to be somewhat successful. The chapter closes with a discussion of the added value of multi-pronged interventions that involve individuals as well as their peers, families and schools.

As discussed in Chapter 1, researchers studying children's peer relations have always considered it part of their mission to apply what they learn to the prevention and correction of peer-relations problems. As early as the 1930s brief, focused efforts were made to improve the acceptance of rejected children. Some of the early interventions went no further than teaching young children the proper rules of games, and such skills as assembling designs with colored blocks, learning stories that popular children enjoyed, and assembling picture puzzles. Unsophisticated as it sounds, such intervention did succeed in persuading peers to increase their acceptance of children whom they had previously rejected. At the same time, Moreno's psychodrama became a standard feature of care in psychiatric facilities and institutions for delinquent youth.

However, most of the techniques in current use originated later in the century, during the heyday of behavioral psychology in North America in the 1960s and 1970s. In its purest form, behaviorism defines overt behavior – and overt behavior only – as the subject matter of psychology (Wolman, 1973). Some behaviorally oriented practitioners began applying the basic principles and procedures of behavior modification to interpersonal skills and behaviors. Stated very simply, these procedures entail creating an environment where behaving appropriately leads to more rewards than behaving inappropriately does. The basic idea of reinforcing children for behaving properly has been found acceptable to most parents and most members of the general public (e.g. Diller, Brown and Patros, 2013), although some practical and philosophical objections have been raised (Filcheck and McNeil, 2004).

Social-skills training was developed mostly by psychologists trained within the behavioral model who participated in several fundamental transformations of classic behavior theory. One of these new slants on behavioral theory was the introduction of the notion of 'skill', as chronicled by the theorist E. Lakin Phillips (1979), who proposed that social skills form a nexus between the individual and the environment (the word 'nexus' means connection or link). Classical behaviorists had no need for a concept other than reinforcement to link individuals to their environments. Struggling to insert the notions of nexus and skill into a behavioral model that he did not wish to destroy, Phillips insisted that social skills were largely understandable by means of observable behavior, although by 'skills' he meant capacities that could be inferred from behaviors, not behaviors themselves. Examples of the social skills he emphasized were the 'skills in managing oneself, in dealing with others, in aligning situations so as to reduce friction and optimize problem solving' (Phillips, 1979, p. xii). Importantly, social-skills training was to be considered successful only if it led to an appreciable improvement in observable behavior, which is probably the majority position to the present day. None the less, in order to do anything substantial with the notion of 'skill', at least a change in the emphasis or spirit of classical behaviorism was needed. Although Phillips insisted that social skills were modifiable by changing the reinforcement patterns in individuals' environments, the direct regulation of reinforcement is quite peripheral in many of the techniques he promoted with great vehemence, including teaching children systematic ways of solving problems (discussed later in this chapter) and of coping with frustration.

Not all parents and teachers want to control the contingencies of reinforcement so carefully, and not all have the capacity to do so. Therefore, without abandoning the principles of the behavioral movement, and certainly without discarding its research tradition, many scientists and practitioners were ready for some alternative modes of intervention. Bandura's (1978) reciprocal determinism brought substantial changes to the behavioral tradition, which had previously wanted to consider little or none of any processes that might occur between the environment and the learning it engenders. Several elements of Bandura's model inspired many of the major contemporary techniques of social-skills training in current use with children. One of these elements is observational learning – the process in which children can learn things by watching and imitating others. Observational learning often occurs in the absence of any tangible reinforcement at the moment of observation, but it is enhanced if the person being observed appears to be reinforced for the behavior he or she is modeling.

Cognitive abilities and beliefs also form important parts of Bandura's model of reciprocal determinism. As illustrated below, many techniques in children's social-skills training deal with such cognitions and beliefs as children's understanding of other people and their intentions, children's beliefs about what is right or wrong in a social situation, their abilities to plan their social behavior, their satisfaction with what they have done, and their beliefs in their own effectiveness in social situations. All of these derive directly from Bandura's social-learning approach, and, although they have been adopted by many who were trained in the pure behavioral model, the techniques could not have emerged from Skinner's behavioral (stimulus-response) theories.

Social-skills training can be implemented for primary prevention (i.e. before any problems have been observed) in whole classrooms or in small groups for secondary prevention – with children who already are beginning to show signs of maladaptive patterns of relating to peers. The whole-class format avoids stigmatizing any individuals by assigning them to special groups. The small-group format provides for more individualized attention, just as individualized remediation is often provided to children who have difficulties with their schoolwork. In some cases, especially with adolescents, bringing aggressive children together in groups can backfire because the members of the group encourage each other's maladaptive behavior (Dishion, McCord and Poulin, 1999). Despite the caution indicated by the results obtained by these researchers, it should be emphasized that at least one important attempt at replicating the original study by Dishion, McCord and Poulin revealed that aggregating adolescent peers in intervention groups was actually quite beneficial (Mager *et al.*, 2005). If there is indeed any unintended harmful effect of aggregation, there is no reason to believe that this occurs any more or less in social-skills training groups than in any other form of group counseling or therapy. Some success in overcoming this problem has been reported by including children with both competent and incompetent social behavior in the training groups (Bierman and Furman, 1984).

Basic methods

Structured learning

The basic steps in implementing structured learning are described in detail by Cartledge and Milburn (1995) and by Glick and Gibbs (2011). As recalled by Cartledge and Milburn, observational learning, according to Bandura's social-learning theory, does not occur to any appreciable extent as a result of casual exposure to a model. Rather, optimal imitation of models happens when the observer pays attention to the model, understands the salient features that are to be imitated, encodes those features for future reference, and is convinced that there is some incentive for imitating the model. Therefore, the elements of structured learning are designed around these conditions.

The first step is to provide a rationale in order to motivate the trainees. This can be done by using stories, folktales or anecdotes that illustrate how children are better off if they behave in a socially skilled manner. It is important to select skills in which the trainees are deficient and will be important to them to succeed socially in their daily lives. These skills are taught one by one. First, the skill must be presented in sufficient detail for the trainees to appreciate the important elements. Often this is taught by breaking the skills down into 'skill steps'. For example, the skill steps used to teach the skills of introducing oneself in Glick and Gibbs' (2011) structured learning model are:

1. Decide if you want to meet the person.
2. Decide if it is a good time.
3. Walk up to the person.
4. Introduce yourself.
5. Wait for the person to tell you his/her name. If he/she doesn't tell you, ask.

Once the skill has been explained, it must be modeled (Glick and Gibbs, 2011). Puppets, videotapes, adult demonstrations and live demonstrations by peers or older children have all been used successfully as models. Sometimes, both a positive and a negative modeling display (i.e. depicting correct and incorrect performance) are provided to ensure that the trainees understand the important points of the skill, although there is always some chance that some children will imitate the negative model. It is important for the trainees to rehearse performance of the skills they have been shown by the model. This is often done through role-playing, which can be videotaped. The videotapes can be played back to the trainees, who can then be given feedback by the other children or by the adult leader regarding how close their performance approximates the model (Ladd, 1981; Nash and Schaefer, 2011; Schneider and Byrne, 1987). Guided imagery can also be used in rehearsal; the trainees are instructed to imagine themselves implementing the skill properly, followed by a pleasant outcome (Cartledge and Milburn, 1995). Appropriate imitation of the skills must be reinforced (e.g. Glick and Gibbs, 2011). In some cases, verbal praise is all that is needed. In other situations, especially in groups of children with behavioral disorders, tangible reinforcers are used, to reinforce both imitation of the model and cooperation with the smooth running of the group. The reinforcers may be points that can be redeemed for a special privilege, favored activity, or small gift.

Social problem-solving

Problem-solving interventions represent a major application of the cognitive-behavioral approach to intervention, which is arguably the best-developed modality of therapeutic intervention for children and adults with various forms of psychological disorder. Social problem-solving techniques have been used extensively in primary prevention programs designed for whole schools. These techniques are also in widespread use in the treatment of psychological disorders as diverse as social anxiety disorder (Mueser, Gottlieb and Gingerich, 2013), attention deficit/hyperactivity disorder (Aberson, Shure and Goldstein, 2007), depression (Stark *et al.*, 2012) and conduct disorder (Lochman *et al.*, 2012). Elaborate curricula, including stories, games and teaching materials, have been developed to make it easier for teachers to implement this form of intervention (Elias and Butler, 2005). Problem-solving techniques evolved from research into the problem-solving styles of aggressive children. Such youngsters have been found to believe that they have few alternatives to aggression in dealing with provocations. This is made all the worse by their tendency to be on the lookout for provocation and to interpret as provocations behaviors that other children would not interpret as containing hostile intent (e.g. Dodge and Tomlin, 1987). Aggressive children are also more likely than others to believe that an aggressive solution is perfectly legitimate in response to such provocation.

The problem-solving sequence that is typically taught is depicted in Figure 12.1. The problem-solving process is very similar to rational decision-making or rational planning processes used in organizations and in urban planning (e.g. Koehler and Harvey, 2007). The first step in implementing problem-solving training is to get the trainees to recognize that they have a problem (Shure, 2001). Through guided discussions, the children learn to recognize problems either in vignettes or in

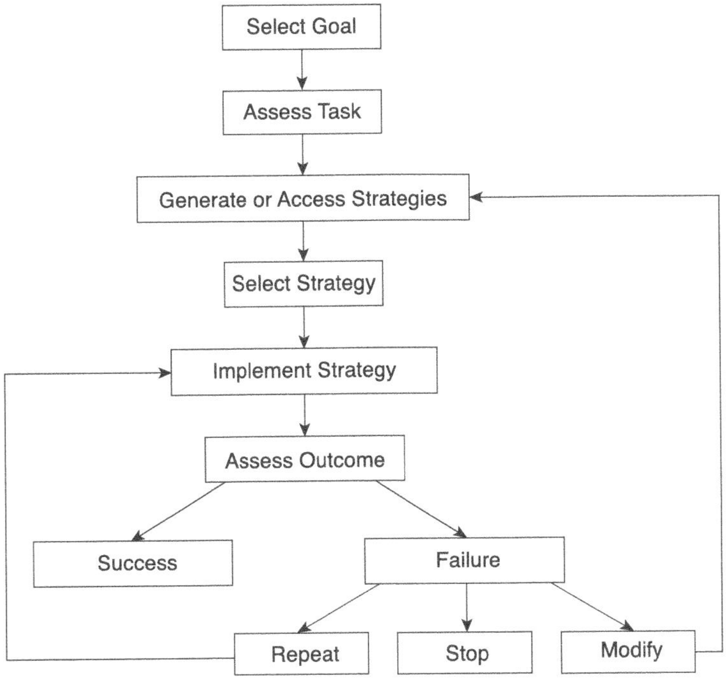

FIGURE 12.1 Social problem-solving model (Source: Rubin and Rose-Krasner, 1986)

situations drawn from their daily experiences. The next step is brainstorming – having the children enumerate all their alternatives in solving the problem.

The next part of the program is the promotion of consequential thinking – having the child recognize what would happen if each of the solutions contemplated were carried out. In guided discussions, the group learns to recognize that hitting the other child could result in injury and sanctions by the school authorities, while walking away could either defuse the situation or lead to more teasing, and so on. Once the children have learned to evaluate the alternatives in this way, they are assisted in planning, step by step, how to go about implementing the solution that has the highest likelihood of leading to a satisfactory outcome.

Self-control interventions

Self-control interventions are another product of the 'cognitive revolution', one that reflects in particular the work of the Russian psychologists Luria and Vygotsky, who studied the ways in which language influences behavior. Vygotsky demonstrated that the internalization of verbal commands is necessary in order to control one's behavior (Kendall and Braswell, 1985). Self-control approaches are best known for their applications in helping children who display problems in controlling their impulsive reactions and anger. Like other forms of social-skills training, self-control can be taught to whole classes in small groups (the usual format for anger-control interventions) or with individuals (Luczynski and Hanley, 2013; Reddy, 2012).

The crux of self-control therapy is getting impulsive children to 'stop and think' (Kendall and Braswell, 1982, p. 8). An important first step is to help the children become aware of the problem behaviors by teaching them to observe their own behavior carefully and record it objectively. A variety of gimmicks has been used to help children slow down, observe and reflect, rather than automatically revert to the familiar trigger reactions that have led to difficulties in the past. For example, they can be taught to visualize a traffic 'Stop' sign, or to count backwards from ten to one. Once they are aware of the situations in which behavioral improvement is needed, the children can use language to redirect their behavior away from maladaptive behaviors that are all too familiar. They are taught to use self-statements whose content suggests self-control. Typically, the teacher or leader begins by providing a self-statement that the children can repeat out loud, such as 'I am being teased, but I can stay in charge of things.' Gradually, the self-statements are relegated to whispers, then to private speech. It is considered vital that the children monitor their use of the self-statements in their daily lives outside the training sessions, and learn to evaluate their own behavior objectively (Ervin, Bankert and DuPaul, 1996). Paralleling this use of the construct of self-verbalization in working with aggressive children and youth are assessment and intervention techniques focusing on the negative self-statements of children with anxiety and depression (Cummings, Caporino and Kendall, 2014). These young people may not have to stop and think, because that is what they do to excess. What they need to do is explore in a more objective way the empirical basis of their self-deprecation, which can infiltrate their interactions with peers.

Harnessing the help of peers represents an important alternative to adults training an individual child in social skills and relying on that child to implement what he or she has learned. Enhanced peer involvement probably represents the most viable way of increasing the effectiveness of current peer-relations interventions. Cartledge and Milburn (1995, p. 324) maintain that peers have an enormous influence on each other's behavior. That influence can undermine what adults try to teach, as when the peer group rewards the aggressive behaviors that adult social-skills trainers try to eliminate. Peers have participated in several ways. One of these ways, mentioned earlier, is by involving them in social-skills training groups. By including prosocial peers, the groups are not dominated by antisocial children, which results in the mutual encouragement of aggression. Peers have also been taught to monitor each other's behavior, and reinforce the use of positive social skills (Fowler, 1988). Peers have been trained as mediators who help reduce conflict in schools by assisting other pupils to negotiate peaceful solutions to disagreements that could lead to violence (see review of research by Johnson and Johnson (1996)). Finally, in comprehensive anti-bullying campaigns, peers can be enlisted to provide support to victims or potential victims of bullies. This would help make bullying less rewarding to the bullies. It could also make victims less vulnerable. Under typical conditions, victims tend to be outsiders who do not really belong to any cohesive social group in the school (Salmivalli, Huttenen and Lagerspetz, 1997). If victims could be integrated into the peer network, bullies might be less prone to attack them, because the victims would have friends who might rally to their defense.

Social-skills training as part of multi-modal interventions

Multi-modal programs to combat aggression and bullying

The most recent thinking in dealing with the problems of children who display the most serious and pervasive problems in their peer relations is to intervene simultaneously in a number of ways in several parts of the children's social worlds. Kazdin, Siegel and Bass (1992) conducted an influential study illustrating that, in work with children displaying behavioral problems severe enough to warrant clinical treatment, it might be best to provide both social-skills training for the child and training for the parents in managing their children's behavior, rather than debate about which treatment route to choose. They assigned ninety-seven children referred to a clinic because of severe behavioral problems to one of three conditions: social-skills training only; parent-management training only; or both treatments simultaneously. The children in either of the two conditions involving only one form of treatment improved somewhat. However, both at the end of treatment and at one-year follow-up, the children who had received the combined treatment improved much more. Similar results emerged in a more recent study of structured family therapy and social problem-solving training for depressed adolescents (Dietz, Marshal, Burton, Bridge, Birmaher, Kolko, Duffy and Brent, 2014).

The largest and best-known multi-pronged intervention in the peer-relations field was known as Project FAST Track ('FAST' is an acronym for Families And Schools Together). It was an intensive intervention conducted in the early 1990s at four sites in the United States to determine whether intensive, simultaneous intervention in schools, homes, communities and families can prevent youngsters already showing signs of aggressive behavior from following the familiar path to lives of school failure, violence and delinquency. Children and families participating in Project FAST Track received individual social-skills training and supervised play experiences in 'friendship groups' that met on Saturday mornings when school was closed. Class-wide lessons on social skills were provided to their schools. Their parents received intensive instruction in parenting skills. Assistance was provided in arranging summer camp and after-school recreational activities for the participating children. Transportation was offered to families who would not otherwise be able to bring their children to the activities of the program (Bierman and Greenberg, 1996).

The evaluation of FAST Track is comprehensive: reports are still appearing in the literature years after the intervention, which itself continued for ten years. Initial findings after a few years of intervention do indicate some success. Importantly, children in the treatment group who were at the highest risk for long-term maladjustment ended up with far lower rates of diagnosed psychological disorder than high-risk members of the control group (Conduct Problems Prevention Research Group, 2011). There were some improvements at school, especially for boys, in terms of reduced aggression and increased prosocial behavior (Bierman *et al.*, 2010). Unfortunately, though, there was no effect on long-term school outcomes (Bierman *et al.*, 2013). At age nineteen, participants in the program had lower rates of juvenile arrests than the controls (Conduct Problems Prevention Research Group, 2010). There was, however, no effect on early substance abuse or early sexual activity (Conduct Problems Prevention Research Group, 2014).

Some methodologists have criticized evaluations of FAST Track because excessive attention has been devoted to the variables on which improvement was achieved, while little attention has been paid to many other variables included in the evaluation (Foster, 2010). Interestingly, some of the more recent analyses have focused on gene × environment interaction. Albert and his colleagues (2015) discovered that the success of the intervention depended in part on whether the child carried copies of the A allele of the single nucleotide polymorphism rs10482672. Presence of this allele predicted better response to the intervention, whereas members of the control group who carried copies of this allele displayed very negative outcomes. Testosterone reactivity has also emerged as a mediator of the effect of the intervention on aggressive behavior (Carré *et al.*, 2014).

FAST Track was intended as a demonstration project. It is doubtful that many communities that would like to repeat the experiment will have the resources to mount something similar. Nevertheless, the data from the project are invaluable, because it is important to establish how successful intervention can be with children in high-risk situations, given the best intervention attempt that current knowledge can offer.

Multi-pronged interventions have also become the norm in dealing with the exasperating problem of bullying in schools. The best-known program designed to reduce bullying in schools was implemented by Olweus (1993) in Norway. The unifying thread of the program is changing the opportunity and reward structure for bullying – that is, reducing the opportunities for bullying to occur and making bullying a less rewarding behavior. The core components include a public campaign to sensitize adults about the problem, better training of teachers in recognizing bullying as a serious problem, closer supervision of play periods, clear classroom rules enforced consistently and conferences with the parents of bullies and victims. This 'restructuring of the social environment' of bullying (Olweus, 1999, p. 41) has resulted in a very marked drop in incidents of bullying in Norwegian schools.

Olweus' intervention was certainly facilitated by the Scandinavian traditions of strong national policies on social problems and of heavy investment in matters of social well-being. However, similar interventions have been successful in other countries as well, although with effects that are not as clear or consistent. Meta-analyses of this literature are as inconsistent as the original studies, with some indicating that the programs are quite successful (Ttofi and Farrington, 2012) whereas others report very small effects (e.g. Merrell *et al.*, 2008; Smith *et al.*, 2004). In a recent review of the latest studies (2009–13), Evans, Fraser and Cotter (2014) found that about half the published evaluations indicate significant post-interventions in bullying perpetration. They note that few researchers have measured bullying with instruments that are methodologically valid. Yeager and his colleagues (2015) conducted a meta-analysis of age effects. They reported that the programs were quite effective among younger pupils but not with older adolescents. Smith, Salmivalli and Cowie (2012), all leading researchers in the field, commented that the issues in reviewing the research on anti-bullying programs are complex. They insist that it is too early to use the results of these reviews in long-range policy decisions.

There have been some attempts to tailor the programs to the desires and characteristics of individual schools. For example, in Sheffield, England, Smith and Sharp (1994) adapted a multi-modal approach to the varying resources, interests and motivation in different schools. Some elements were considered core components of the intervention to be implemented in all schools: consciousness raising; consultation with teaching and non-teaching staff, parents and pupils; and clear school policies about bullying, in order to leave no doubt that pupils may communicate their concerns about bullies and to provide guidelines for teachers, pupils and parents regarding the handling of bullying incidents. Schools could choose from among the optional components of the program depending on their own interests, needs and resources. Those components included the incorporation of anti-bullying content in the school curriculum, using videos, books, or drama; enhanced playground supervision; assertiveness training for victims; and counseling by peer helpers. Evaluations of the project clearly indicate a reduction in incidents of bullying in Sheffield's schools.

Student-mediated conflict resolution is gaining in popularity as an intervention that capitalizes on the peer perspective. As noted by Cunningham and colleagues (1998), most conflicts at school occur in the playground, often outside of the awareness of adults. Therefore, sanctions by adults are often ineffectual in dealing with bullying. Cunningham and his colleagues provided fifteen hours of training in conflict resolution to selected students at two Canadian primary schools, using a detailed training manual and providing ongoing teacher support and direction. At a school assembly, the trainees were introduced to their fellow students as mediators who could be approached to solve conflicts on the playground. Direct observations of recess play suggested that the program resulted in a reduction in aggressive incidents by at least 50 percent.

The most important recent innovation in school-based anti-bullying programs is the KiVa program, developed by Finnish researcher Christina Salmivalli and her colleagues. The program includes not only direct content related to bullying but considerable emphasis on the role of peers, especially bystanders, in bully–victim problems. Inasmuch as peers have the power to stop a bully, encourage a bully, or do nothing, it is imperative to include their role in interventions (Saarento, Boulton and Salmivalli, 2015). Evaluations of the KiVa program reveal reductions in the number of students identified as victims of bullies and as perpetrators of bullying. Importantly, there is a significant reduction in the number of pupils identified as being *both* bullies and victims, depending on the time and the circumstances. This common phenomenon is associated with long-term risk of maladjustment (Yang and Salmivalli, 2015). Further evaluation of the KiVa program, especially by researchers in different countries who are not members of the KiVa research group, is needed, and will surely emerge over the next few years.

A multi-modal intervention to help socially withdrawn pre-schoolers

Multi-modal interventions to combat problematic aggression are better known than multi-modal interventions designed to assist children and youth who are shy, withdrawn and/or depressed. Although socially withdrawn and anxious youth do respond well to interventions based on a single intervention modality, the multi-modal approach may enhance treatment effectiveness. The Turtle program is a recent intervention for extremely shy and anxious pre-school children. It involves social-skills training and play activities in small groups together with an intervention for parents. The parents learn the benefits of moderation in managing their children's social activities, aiming at age-appropriate granting of autonomy rather than overprotection or excessive control. They also learn to encourage their children to express themselves. In comparison to a control group, children who participated in the program with their parents became less anxious and less inhibited, with results generalizing to the school setting (Chronis-Tuscano *et al.*, 2015).

Does social-skills training work?

Promoting generalization and maintenance: social-skills training travels uphill

As discussed in Chapter 1, scholars interested in children's peer relations have always been – perhaps not entirely coincidentally – very active researchers or avid readers of the research literature. For that reason, the effects of children's social-skills training have been studied very thoroughly. Research and practice related to children's peer relations are very closely linked. This is not the case for other modalities in the prevention and treatment of children's emotional and behavioral problems, such as many forms of child psychotherapy.

It was probably naive on the part of social-skills trainers in the 1970s to expect that a brief, verbal intervention would permanently change the course of ingrained patterns of maladaptive social behavior patterns that may be partly genetic in origin. Nevertheless, and perhaps paradoxically, these brief, focused interventions *do* have a track record of some degree of success, as will be discussed in greater detail later in this chapter. As evidenced in statistical summaries of the literature by Schneider (1992) and Beelmann, Pfingsten and Loesel (1994), many (but certainly not all) of the published studies on children's social-skills training demonstrate positive effects when effectiveness is measured immediately after treatment. Until recently, there were very few long-term follow-up studies. This has become ever more problematic over the years, as experts insist that treatment evaluation must include long-term follow-up (e.g. Foxx, 2013).

What has long been criticized as 'train and hope' (Stokes and Baer, 1977) social-skills training no longer represents the state of the art. At the height of the cognitive revolution in psychology, Meichenbaum (1977), one of the early revolutionaries, introduced the distinction between cognitive-behavior modification and cognitive-HYPHEN-behavior modification. Cognitive-behavior modification means working on cognition with the intent of affecting behavior via the route of cognitive change. Cognitive-HYPHEN-behavior modification means intervening to correct maladaptive cognitive processes *and* also working on the behavioral level to help consolidate and promote the use of what is learned. Thus, only in cognitive-HYPHEN-behavior modification is any specific attempt made to facilitate the transfer between cognitive change during training and behavioral change in the trainee's natural environment. This transfer can be implemented in several ways, which are emphasized increasingly in recent social-skills training manuals, as summarized by Cartledge and Milburn (1995) and by Kamps (2010).

Some of the ways of promoting generalization and maintenance involve making the training setting as similar as possible to the setting in which the skills are supposed to be used. If videotapes are used for modeling, the settings depicted in the videos might be several places within a typical school. The actors should resemble the trainees and the people in their immediate social worlds, such as the teachers at the school. The groups themselves can be led by several different adults, so that the learning is not specific to a specific group leader. 'Homework' can be assigned, in which trainees are required to chart their use of the skills they have learned during the school week (e.g. Sasso, Melloy and Kavale, 1990).

Thus, some aspects of the training sessions can be adapted in order to promote generalization and maintenance of the skills. By far the most promising means of promoting generalization and maintenance is to enlist the cooperation of other children, teachers and parents to monitor, prompt and reinforce the trainees' use of the skills learned in the training session outside the training sessions. This reality may come as something of a disappointment to some enthusiastic proponents of social-skills training who expect the training itself to be so effective that it changes the child's response repertoire sufficiently for the responses to be evoked spontaneously by the child in his or her natural environment without any change on the part of the people in that environment. To no one is that disappointment more acute than to some 'reformed' behaviorists who fleetingly harbored the belief that they could permanently improve the peer relations of seriously maladjusted children by working only with the children. True to their earlier behavioral training, they discovered that the child's social environment has to be reengineered for change, though perhaps not exactly in accordance with Skinner's *Walden Two* fantasy.

Emblematic of the benefits of incorporating specific techniques to foster generalization are studies showing the long-term effects of social-skills training with children displaying several forms of psychological disorder. Beidel, Turner and Young (2006) demonstrated that the gains of an enhanced social-skills training for children experiencing social anxiety remained strong even five years after the intervention. O'Callaghan and colleagues (2003) showed that social-skills training for children with attention deficit/hyperactivity disorder (ADHD) generalizes to other settings when specific generalization techniques are incorporated. Unfortunately, not all studies have shown such benefits of generalization and maintenance add-ons to social-skills training (Schneider, 1992).

The 'bottom line'

As social-skills training expanded and enthusiasm for it grew, it became apparent that its success was not unlimited. The limits of social-skills training would probably never have been discovered had it not been for the strong research tradition in the study of peer relations. Careful assessment of the success of an intervention includes finding out whether it works in different settings, whether the improvement it generates will be maintained over time, and whether it can work with individuals who chronically display dysfunctional social behavior. Children's social-skills training measured up only partially to this very demanding yardstick. As aptly expressed by Beelmann, Pfingsten and Loesel (1994), it is not that social-skills training is any less effective than it once was, only that researchers are asking it to do more.

Over three decades after the sobering reminder that not all social-skills training 'sticks' as well as the trainers would like, most experts believe that it is still worth doing, even if it is not a panacea. There have been ten review papers and meta-analyses of the effects of social-skills training (Ang and Hughes, 2001; Beelmann, Pfingsen and Lösel, 1994; Chenier *et al.*, 2011; Cook *et al.*, 2008; Godbold *et al.*, 2010; January, Casey and Paulson, 2011; Lösel and Beelmann, 2003; Quinn *et al.*, 1999; Schneider, 1992; Schneider and Byrne, 1985). Gresham (2011; Gresham and Elliot, 2014) has concluded that social-skills training for children with behavioral and emotional problems appears to be effective on average for about 65 percent of children who participate in it, compared with about 35 percent of children randomly assigned to control groups. Importantly, this effect size is based on studies of high methodological quality, including random assignment to treatment and control groups (Godbold *et al.*, 2010). However, both the reviews themselves and the studies within them indicate highly variable rates of success. There are some discernible patterns in the findings among results that otherwise fluctuate enormously. First of all, young children – around the beginning of the primary school years – seem to respond better than older children. Second, interventions in which there is active interaction between the group leader and the participants are typically more effective than didactic instruction alone (January, Casey and Paulson, 2011; Schneider, 1992; Schneider and Byrne, 1985).

Interventions with a focus on friendship

Paralleling the burgeoning interest in studying children's relationships at the dyadic rather than the group level is the emergence of interventions designed specifically to foster children's friendships. Murphy and Schneider (1994) implemented an intervention focusing on friendship with twelve-year-olds who were rejected by their classroom peers according to sociometric choice nominations. The researchers decided to concentrate on friendship based on their speculation that it might be easier to help rejected children find one close friend than to reverse the history of rejection by substantial numbers of their schoolmates.

Murphy and Schneider conducted the intervention in a private, counseling format, for no more than ten sessions. The participants were asked to select a classmate with whom they wished to form or enhance a friendship. The adult counselors guided the rejected children through a series of steps designed to indicate to the intended friend the friendly intentions of the child receiving counseling. The counselors supported the children in case the overtures were rebuffed, and helped them direct friendly overtures to other potential friends where necessary. At the end of the intervention, both the children receiving counseling and the targeted friends indicated significantly greater liking for each other. There was no change in the friendship ratings given and received by children in the control group, who were on a waiting list to receive the counseling after the first experimental group had completed the study. This approach was replaced by pair therapy (described below) several years ago at the University of Ottawa Social Development and Mental Health laboratory directed by Barry Schneider. However, given the complicated logistics of pair therapy and the limited research base, Schneider later returned to the friendship coaching approach he developed with Murphy.

Pair therapy is a modality of intervention in which an adult therapist works to facilitate the relationship between two children who have the potential to become friends. The technique evolved from Robert Selman and his colleagues' intensive friendship research at Harvard University (Selman, Watts and Schultz, 1997). In pair therapy, the hope is that children develop skills that are useful in close relationships in general, irrespective of whether the two children who participate directly decide to become and stay friends. The children are brought together as pairs for a specified reason that requires considerable forethought, and implies that the two members would benefit from a deeper understanding of each other. In some cases, it is a bully and a victim; in others, the pair consists of two aggressive children of different cultural or racial origins.

Pair therapy is not as structured as other forms of social-skills training, such as modeling, coaching or problem-solving. The children select a 'baseline activity' – something they would like to do together, but which does not absorb all of their attention – leaving some room for conversation and sharing. Often they decide to play chess or checkers or assemble a model. Inevitably, conflict arises. The task of the therapist is to help resolve the conflict, help the children understand each other's perspectives, and help them reflect on their friendships and the problems within it. Often, pair therapy continues for months or even years. Observations of the interactions of the pairs and of their understanding of interpersonal relationships indicate the potential of this method to enhance children's understanding of the concept of friendship (Selman, Watts and Schultz, 1997).

More systematic research, featuring long-term follow-up, is needed to confirm that this rich, intriguing form of therapy achieves its aim of fostering friendship. However, it will not be easy for researchers to garner the evidence needed to validate pair therapy to the level that corresponds to the requisites for empirically validated treatment in the current era of accountability. It probably would not be sufficient to demonstrate that pair therapy enhances understanding of friendship, as some existing studies already do (Selman, Watts and Schultz, 1997). To justify an intervention as intensive as pair therapy, researchers would have to gain access to the real-life future friendships of the participating children. These future friendships should benefit from what has been learned in therapy. Schneider returned to the Murphy and Schneider technique of counseling individuals regarding ways of enhancing their friendships (see above) after finding it difficult to recruit needy children in pairs for pair therapy. Curtis (2014) has developed a more structured version of pair therapy for children with ADHD that is conducted with dyads but contains clearer goals, benchmarks for progress, and closely prescribed techniques for redirecting maladaptive behavior. His method has yet to be subjected to formal evaluation. It is to be hoped that these approaches will permit the dyadic pair modality to remain a locus of intervention, one supported by data indicating that it does indeed enhance friendship.

Despite the evident intrinsic value of working on specific friendships with one or both real-life members of a friendship dyad, there has been some success with didactic classroom instruction on friendship in secondary schools. In an important and well-designed study conducted in Sydney, Australia, Rose, Hawes and Hunt (2014) demonstrated that adding sessions about friendship to a standard cognitive-behavioral program designed to prevent depression enhanced effectiveness.

Social-skills training for children with autism spectrum disorders: a new lease of life?

As discussed in Chapter 8, the population of people with autism spectrum disorders is increasing rapidly for reasons that are not well understood. Impaired social communication and impaired peer relationships are central features of this disorder. It is therefore unsurprising that social-skills training has been attempted with this population, both in its traditional forms and with techniques and content modified to fit the nature of the disorder. As the database on social-skills training with children and youth with autism spectrum disorders has expanded, comprehensive review articles and meta-analyses have gauged the success. For the most part, social-skills training seems to be no more successful with this population than with children with other emotional and behavioral problems, who constitute the largest and best-studied group of participants in social-skills training. A meta-analysis by Bellini and colleagues (2007) indicated only low-to-moderate effectiveness. The gains that were made tended to persist over time but not to generalize to settings in the children's lives in which no intervention took place.

There have been some recent attempts to modify social-skills training to either the individual needs of children with autism spectrum disorders or to the general nature of this disorder. A few of the initial results are promising. One approach entails using social stories to help high-functioning children with autism understand the subtleties of social interaction. The stories depict ways of being friendly and helpful. Although the social-story method has attracted a strong following among practitioners working in this field, a meta-analysis by Kokina and Kern (2010) indicated results for the social-narrative approach that were no greater than those of other forms of social-skills training with this population.

More promising results have emanated from controlled trials of *naturalistic intervention* and *pivotal response training*. In both of these approaches, intervention is custom tailored to the personal interests, skills, daily activities and social settings of each participating child (Otero *et al.*, 2015). French psychiatrist Amalia Baghdadli and her colleagues (2013) reported good results of an intervention containing much more content pertaining to recognizing emotions in facial expressions than would usually be included in a social-skills program. Many children with autism spectrum disorder are known to be deficient in this particular skill. The French study is important because it compared the social-skills intervention to an active alternative treatment focused on leisure skills. This is methodologically stronger and more ethical than a no-treatment control because the expectancy effects inherent in receiving attention are controlled.

Having the intervention mediated by classroom peers has been found to be successful in social-skills training for children with autism spectrum disorder (Strain, Schwartz and Bovey, 2008). Importantly, it has been shown that both the peer mediators and the children for whom the intervention is intended benefit. There has also been some work on parent-mediated social-skills training for children with autism spectrum disorders, although much more research is needed. In their evaluation of a parent-assisted group intervention, Laugeson and colleagues (2011) demonstrated impressive gains in several important areas of social competence and cooperation as well as reduction in autistic mannerisms. Importantly, the changes were evident in ratings by teachers not involved in the intervention. Nearly all of the gains were evident at fourteen-week follow-up. Unfortunately, there was no control condition.

The appeal of the internet for many high-functioning children with autism spectrum disorders (many of whom would previously be diagnosed as having Asperger's syndrome, a term that was dropped from the Diagnostic and Statistical Manual (DSM) system in 2013) has prompted several successful applications of new technologies in prompting social skills, especially conversational skills. Research on computer-assisted intervention for this population was reviewed by Ramdoss and colleagues (2012), who documented a number of successful trials.

Working with and through parent, teacher and peer mediators

Moving beyond enlisting the support of parents and teachers to help with the generalization and maintenance of social-skills training are a number of interventions in which parents, teachers and peers are recruited to *conduct* the social-skills training or another form of peer-relations intervention. The Check in/Check out program is an outstanding example of a research-based teacher- and parent-mediated program for children of school age who display problematic patterns of internalizing behavior such as shyness and depressed feelings. This approach is better established with aggressive acting-out students. Early in the school day, the student checks in with an adult mentor who reminds him/her of his/her behavioral goals for the day. The student and the mentor set a daily points target. The student asks his/her teacher to rate his/her progress toward that goal at several points during the day. At the end of the day, the student 'checks out' with the mentor, receives the reward that corresponds with the teachers' ratings, and delivers the report form to his/her parents (Hunter, Chenier and Gresham, 2014).

Conclusion

The euphoric enthusiasm of the early pioneers of social-skills training has left contemporary researchers with an armamentarium of techniques that do not work miracles but are helpful, even in small ways, to many children. The challenge facing their contemporary descendants is to interpret the knowledge that has accrued about peer-relationship interventions in ways that lead to the greatest degree of improvement possible, while maintaining realistic expectations. More important is the challenge of continuing to refine the techniques that have some success. At the time of writing, the most promising improvements appear to be based on harnessing the cooperation of important persons in the children's social settings as mediators; adapting the content of the intervention to the setting and characteristics in which the practitioner works; and combining social-skills training with other effective techniques, including, but not limited to, parental training in managing the problem behaviors of their children. In eight decades of trial and error, it has become evident that facilitating children's peer relations depends not only on how to help the child directly but on how to help the people in the child's environment to help that child.

Most of the children who need help because of peer-relations problems are not rational beings to the extent that they can learn a problem-solving process or the steps in a social skill, internalize the learning, recognize when the skill or process is needed, bring it to consciousness, and implement what they have been taught. The rational decision-making model in organizational psychology, a close cousin of the social problem-solving model on which much of social-skills training is based, has similarly come under fire within its own discipline because of its presumption of rationality as an inherent human characteristic and its inattention to the context in which the planning or problem-solving must occur (e.g. Suchman, 2007). This means that the classic methods of modeling→role-play→feedback and social problem-solving may not bring gains as sweeping as was once hoped. Some contemporary social-skills trainers have combined the classic techniques, which are still useful, with such methods as motivational interviewing in an attempt to adapt social-skills training to a population that may not be prone to solving problems in rational ways, such as adolescents struggling with problems of substance abuse (Wagner and Austin, 2009).

Many of the techniques are suitable for use in online therapies. Online versions of social-skills training do exist (Zao, Zhang and Yu, 2011; www.socialskillscentral.com, retrieved May 22, 2015), but little is known about their effectiveness. Other than these recent developments, social-skills training is still based almost entirely on classical methods that have been in use for four decades. These techniques may be used separately but they are often combined in multi-modal interventions. In most cases, the evaluation results do not indicate the relative benefits of each of these components. An important exception is a recent school-based multi-pronged intervention in Spain. Espada and colleagues (2012) found that the combination of social problem-solving and structured training of behavioral social skills is superior to either component by itself or to no treatment.

Moreno, the founding father of peer-relations research (see Chapter 1) emphasized the social context in his radical theory. He believed that broader social change around the world could be engendered by changes at the level of the dyad. The world could be improved relationship by relationship. Environmental reengineering is the core of behavioral approaches. Few contemporary theorists or practitioners are ready to advocate environmental change in as radical a way as was contemplated by Moreno or Skinner, grandfather of the behavioral movement. Hence, the field is still striving to find an optimal balance between working directly with the child and indirect approaches involving important people in the child's social world, with a number of promising new ideas for intervention currently being perfected and evaluated.

Some recent research suggests that more intensive and more extensive interventions – involving families, schools and communities – may be needed to achieve long-term improvement for those children who need it most. Thus, despite their failure to agree on a common definition of social competence, despite the fact that different measures of peer relations often tell different tales about the social lives of individual children, and despite the fact that social-skills interventions have not yet proved as successful as the need indicates, contemporary scholars studying children's peer relations have not totally abandoned Moreno's dream (see Chapter 1) of changing a troubled world by changing the interpersonal relationships in it one by one.

REFERENCES

Aberson, B., Shure, M.B. and Goldstein, S. 2007: Social problem-solving intervention can help children with ADHD. *Journal of Attention Disorders* **11**, 4–7.

Abikoff, H., Courtney, M., Pelham, W.E. and Koplewicz, H.S. 1993: Teachers' ratings of disruptive behaviors: the influence of halo effects. *Journal of Abnormal Child Psychology* **21**, 519–33.

Aboud, F.E. 1993: The developmental psychology of racial prejudice. *Transcultural Psychiatric Research Review* **30**, 229–42.

Aboud, F.E. and Doyle, A. 1995: The development of in-group pride in black Canadians. *Journal of Cross-Cultural Psychology* **26**, 243–54.

Aboud, F.E., Friedmann, J. and Smith, S. 2015: Direct and indirect friends in cross-ethnolinguistic peer relations. *Canadian Journal of Behavioural Science* **47**, 68–79.

Abramovitch, R., Corter, C., Pepler, D.J. and Stanhope, L. 1986: Sibling and peer interaction: a final follow-up and a comparison. *Child Development* **57**, 217–29.

Achenbach, T.M. and Edelbrock, C.S. 1986: *Child behavior checklist and youth self-report*. Burlington, VT: University of Vermont Department of Psychiatry.

Ackerman, R.A., Donnellan, M., Kashy, D.A. and Conger, R.D. 2012: Dyadic data analyses in a developmental context. In Laursen, B., Little, T.D. and Card, N.A. (Eds.), *Handbook of developmental research methods*. New York: Guilford, 537–56.

Adams, G.P. and Roopnarine, J.L. 1994: Physical attractiveness, social skills, and same-sex peer popularity. *Journal of Group Psychotherapy, Psychodrama and Sociometry* **47**, 15–35.

Adler, J.C., Mueller, R.J. and Ary, D. 1987: Non-gifted elementary and middle school children's sociometric choices of gifted versus non-gifted helpers. Paper presented at the annual meeting of the American Educational Research Association, Washington, DC, April.

Adler, P.A. and Adler, P. 1998: *Peer power: preadolescent culture and identity*. New Brunswick, NJ: Rutgers University Press.

Aho, J.S. 1994: *This thing of darkness: a sociology of the enemy*. Seattle, WA: University of Washington Press.

Ainsworth, M.D.S., Blehar, M.C., Waters, E. and Wall, S. 1978: *Patterns of attachment: a psychological study of the strange situation*. Hillsdale, NJ: Erlbaum.

Ainsworth, M.D.S. and Marvin, R.S. 1995: On the shaping of attachment theory and research: an interview with Mary D.S. Ainsworth Fall 1994. *Monographs of the Society for Research in Child Development* **60**, 3–21.

Ainsworth, M.D.S. and Whittig, B.A. 1969: Attachment and exploratory behaviour of one-year-olds in a strange situation. In Foss, B.M. (Ed.), *Determinants of infant behaviour.* London: Methuen, vol. 4, 113–36.

Akhtar, A. 2009: Friendship, socialization and the immigrant experience. *Psychoanalysis, Culture and Society* **14**, 253–72.

Albee, G.W. 1959: *Mental health manpower trends.* New York: Basic Books.

Albee, G.W. and Gullotta, T.P. 1997: *Primary prevention works.* Thousand Oaks, CA: Sage.

Alexandrovna, D.N. 1999: Gender differences in aggression by young children. Paper presented at the ninth European Conference on Developmental Psychology, Spetses, Greece, September.

Albert, D., Belsky D.W., Crowley D.M., Bates J.E., Pettit G.S., Lansford J.E., Dick D. and Dodge K.A. 2015: Developmental mediation of genetic variation in response to the Fast Track prevention program. *Development and Psychopathology* **27**, 81–95.

Allès-Jardel, M., Schneider, B.H. and Boutry, V. 2002: Friendship and attitudes toward school among children of two Muslim communities in Marseille. *Early Education and Development* **13**, 153–66.

Allport, G.W. 1954: *The nature of prejudice.* Cambridge, MA: Addison-Wesley.

Alsaker, F.D. and Gutzwiller-Helfenfinger, E. 2010: Social behavior and peer relationships of victims, bully-victims and bullies in kindergarten. In Jimerson, S.R., Swearer, S.M. and Espelage, D.L. (Eds.), *Handbook of bullying in schools.* Mahwah, NJ: Erlbaum, 87–100.

Altermatt, E.R. and Pomerantz, E.M. 2003: The development of competence-related and motivational beliefs: an investigation of similarity and influence among friends. *Journal of Educational Psychology* **95**, 111–23.

Altman, I. and Taylor, D.A. 1973: *Social penetration: the development of interpersonal relationships.* New York: Holt, Rinehart and Winston.

Alvarez-Valdivia, I., Schneider, B.H., Lorenzo Chavez, K. and Chen, X. 2005: Social withdrawal and maladjustment in a very group-oriented society. *International Journal of Behavioral Development* **29**, 219–28.

Alvarez-Valdivia, I.M., Schneider, B.H. and Villalobos, C. In press: School adjustment and friendship quality of first- and second-generation adolescent immigrants to Spain as a function of acculturation. *Journal of Adolescent Research.*

American Psychiatric Association 2013: *Diagnostic and statistical manual of mental disorders.* 5th Edition. Washington, DC: American Psychiatric Association.

Amichai-Hamburger, Y. 2013: *The social net: understanding our on-line behavior.* 2nd Edition. Oxford: Oxford University Press.

Amichai-Hamburger, Y. and Ben-Artzi, E. 2003: Loneliness and internet use. *Computers in Human Behavior* **19**, 71–80.

Amichai-Hamburger, Y., Wainapel, G. and Fox, S. 2002: On the internet no one knows I'm an introvert: extroversion, neuroticism, and internet interaction. *Cyberpsychology and Behavior* **5**, 125–8.

Analitis, F., Velderman, M.K., Ravens-Sieberer, U., Detmar, S., Erhart, M., Herdman, M., Berra, S., Alonso, J. and Rajmil, L. 2009: Being bullied: associated factors in children and adolescents 8 to 18 years old in 11 European countries. *Pediatrics* **123**, 569–77.

Anderson, S. and Messick, S. 1974: Social competency in young children. *Developmental Psychology* **10**, 282–93.

Andreasen, N.C. and Canter, A. 1975: Genius and insanity revisted: psychiatric symptoms and family history in creative writers. In Wirt, R., Winokur, G. and Roff, M. (Eds.), *Life history research in psychopathology*. Minneapolis, MN: University of Minnesota Press, 187–210.

Ang, R. and Hughes, J.N. 2001: Differential benefits of skills training with antisocial youth based on group composition: a meta-analytic investigation. *School Psychology Review* **31**, 164–85.

Anolli, L., Villani, D. and Riva, G. 2005: Personality of people using chat: an on-line research. *Cyberpsychology and Behavior* **8**, 89–94.

Antia, S.D. and Kreimeyer, K.H. 1997: The generalization and maintenance of the peer social behaviours of young children who are deaf or hard of hearing. *Language, Speech and Hearing Services in the Schools* **28**, 59–69.

Arbeau, K.A., Coplan, J. and Weeks, M. 2010: Shyness, teacher–child relationships, and socio-emotional adjustment in grade 1. *International Journal of Behavioral Development* **34**, 259–69.

Argyle, M. 1978: Non-verbal communication and mental disorder. *Psychological Medicine* **8**, 551–4.

Argyle, M. 1983: *The psychology of interpersonal behaviour*. New York: Pergamon.

Argyle, M. 1991: *Cooperation: the basis of sociability*. London: Routledge.

Argyle, M. 1992: *The social psychology of everyday life*. London: Routledge.

Argyle, M., Furnham, A. and Graham, J.A. 1981: *Social situations*. Cambridge: Cambridge University Press.

Argyle, M., Henderson, M., Bond, M., Iizuka, Y. and Contarello, A. 1986: Cross-cultural variations in relationship rules. *International Journal of Psychology* **21**, 287–315.

Argyle, M. and Lu, L. 1990: Happiness and social skills. *Personality and Individual Differences* **11**, 1255–61.

Artz, S., Kassis, W. and Moldenhauer, S. 2013: Rethinking indirect aggression: the end of the mean girl myth. *Victims and Offenders* **8**, 308–28.

Asch, S. 1946: Forming impressions of personality. *Journal of Abnormal and Social Psychology* **41**, 258–90.

Asendorpf, J.B. 1986: Shyness in middle and late childhood. In Jones, W.H., Cheek, J.M. and Briggs, S.R. (Eds.), *Shyness: perspectives on research and treatment*. New York: Plenum Press, 91–103.

Asendorpf, J.B. and van Aken, M.A.G. 1994: Traits and relationship status: stranger versus peer group inhibition and test intelligence versus peer group competence as early predictors of later self-esteem. *Child Development* **65**, 1786–98.

Asher, S. 1985: An evolving paradigm in social skills training research with children. In Schneider, B.H., Rubin, K.H. and Ledingham, J.E. (Eds.), *Children's peer relations: issues in assessment and intervention*. New York: Springer-Verlag, 151–71.

Asher, S.R. and Coie, J.D. (Eds.) 1990: *Peer rejection in childhood*. New York: Cambridge University Press.

Asher, S.R. and Dodge, K.A. 1986: Identifying children who are rejected by their peers. *Developmental Psychology* **22**, 444–9.

Asher, S.R. and Hymel, S. 1981: Children's social competence in peer relations: sociometric and behavioural assessment. In Wine, J.D. and Smye, M.D. (Eds.), *Social competence*. New York: Guilford Press, 52–77.

Asher, S.R., Hymel, S. and Renshaw, P.D. 1984: Loneliness in children. *Child Development* **55**, 1456–64.

Asher, S.R., MacEvoy, J.P. and McDonald, K.L. 2008: Children's peer relations, social competence, and school adjustment: a social tasks and social goals perspective.

In Maehr, M.L., Karabenick, S. and Urdan, T. (Eds.), *Advances in achievement and motivation*, vol. 15: *Social psychological perspectives*. Bingley: Emerald, 357–90.

Asher, S.R. and McDonald, K.L. 2009: The behavioral basis of acceptance, rejection and perceived popularity. In Rubin, K.H., Bukowski, W.M. and B. Laursen (Eds.), *Handbook of peer interactions, relationships and groups*. New York: Guilford, 232–48.

Asher, S.R. and Taylor, A.R. 1981: Social outcomes of mainstreaming: sociometric assessment and beyond. *Exceptional Education Quarterly* **1**, 13–30.

Asher, S.R. and Wheeler, V.A. 1985: Children's loneliness: a comparison of rejected and neglected peer status. *Journal of Consulting and Clinical Psychology* **53**, 500–5.

Ashman, A.F. and Gillies, R.M. 1997: Children's cooperative behavior and interactions in trained and untrained workgroups in regular classrooms. *Journal of School Psychology* **35**, 261–79.

Attili, G., Vermigli, P. and Schneider, B.H. 1997: Peer acceptance and friendship patterns among Italian elementary-school children within a cross-cultural perspective. *International Journal of Behavioural Development* **21**, 277–98.

Auerbach-Major, S.T. 1997: Contributors to early childhood social competence: the direct and interactive effects of parent disciplinary style and child temperament [CD-ROM]. Abstract from: *ProQuest File: Dissertation Abstracts* Item: 9735204.

Aukrust, V.G., Edwards, C.P., Kumru, A., Knoche, L. and Kim, M. 2003: Young children's close relationships outside the family: parental ethnotheories in four communities in Norway, United States, Turkey and Korea. *International Journal of Behavioral Development* **27**, 481–94.

Austin, A.B. and Lindauer, S.K. 1990: Parent–child conversation of more-liked and less-liked children. *Journal of Genetic Psychology* **151**, 5–23.

Aviezer, O., van IJzendoorn, M.H., Sagi, A. and Schuengel, C. 1994: 'Children of the dream' revisited: 70 years of collective early child care in Israeli kibbutzim. *Psychological Bulletin* **116**, 99–116.

Ayer, M.E. and Bernreuter, R. 1936: A study of the relationship between discipline and personality traits in little children. *Journal of Genetic Psychology* **50**, 165–70.

Ayjan, H. and Isiksal, S. 2004: Memory recall errors in retrospective surveys: a reverse record check study. *Quality and Quantity: International Journal of Methodology* **38**, 475–93.

Azeredo, C.M., Rinaldi, A.E.M., de Moraes, C.L., Levy, R.B. and Menezes, P.R. 2015: School bullying: a systematic review of contextual-level risk factors in observational studies. *Aggression and Violent Behavior* **15**, 65–76.

Azmitia, M. 1988: Peer interaction and problem solving: when are two heads better than one? *Child Development* **59**, 87–96.

Azmitia, M. 2010: Families, peers, and Mexican-heritage adolescents' negotiation of school transitions. In Cabrera, N., Villarruel, F. and Fitzgerald, H.E. (Eds.), *Latina and Latino children and mental health*, vol: 1: *Development in Context*. New York: Praeger, 217–42.

Azmitia, M. and Hesser, J. 1993: Why siblings are important agents of cognitive development: a comparison of siblings and peers. *Child Development* **64**, 430–44.

Azmitia, M. and Perlmutter, M. 1989: Social influences in children's social cognition. In Reese, H. (Ed.), *Advances in child development and behaviour*. New York: Academic Press, vol. 22, 89–144.

Babcock, B., Marks, P.E.L., Crick, N.R. and Cillessen, A.H.N. 2014: Limited nomination reliability using single- and multiple-item measures. *Social Development* **23**, 518–36.

Bagci, S.C., Rutland, M., Kumashiro, M., Smith, P.K. and Blumberg, H. 2014: Are minority status children's cross-ethnic friendships beneficial in a multiethnic context? *British Journal of Developmental Psychology* **32**, 107–15.

Baghdadli, A., Brisot, J., Henry, V., Michelon, C., Soussana, M., Rattaz, C. and Picot, M.C. 2013: Social skills improvement in children with high-functioning autism: a pilot randomized controlled trial. *European Child and Adolescent Psychiatry* **22**, 433–42.

Bagwell, C.L. and Schmidt, M.E. 2011: *Friendships in childhood and adolescence.* New York: Guilford.

Bain, S.K. and Bell, S.M. 2004: Social self-concept, social attributions, and peer relationships in fourth, fifth, and sixth graders who are gifted compared to high achievers. *Gifted Child Quarterly* **48**, 167–78.

Baiocco, R., Laghi, F., Carotenuto, M. and Del Miglio, C. 2011a: On-line friendship: is it a stimulation or a social disengagement? *Psicologia Clinica dello Sviluppo* **15**, 335–52.

Baiocco, R., Laghi, F., Schneider, B.H., d'Alessio, M., Amichai-Hamburger, Y., Coplan, R.J., Koszcyki, D. and Flament, M. 2011b: Daily patterns of on-line and off-line communication between early adolescents and their friends. *Cyberpsychology, Human Behavior and Social Networking* **14**, 467–71.

Bakeman, R.R. and Gottman, J.M. 1997: *Observing interaction: an introduction to sequential analysis.* New York: Cambridge University Press.

Baldwin, A.L. 1948: Socialization and the parent–child relationship. *Child Development* **19**, 127–36.

Ballard, M., Corman, L., Gottlieb, J. and Kaufman, M.J. 1977: Improving the social status of mainstreamed retarded children. *Journal of Educational Psychology* **69**, 605–11.

Bandura, A. 1978: The self-system in reciprocal determinism. *American Psychologist* **33**, 344–58.

Bandura, A. and Walters, R.H. 1963: *Social learning and personality development.* New York: Holt, Rinehart and Winston.

Barak, A. and Gluck-Ofri, O. 2007: Degree and reciprocity of self-disclosure in online forums. *CyberPsychology and Behavior* **10**, 407–17.

Barber, C. and Wasson, J.W. 2015: A comparison of adolescents' friendship networks by advanced coursework participation status. *Gifted Child Quarterly* **59**, 23–37.

Barbovschi, M. 2013: Children's meetings offline with people met online: a pan-European study of their characteristics and differences. *Journal of Children and Media* **7**, 28–43.

Barnett, L.A. and Fiscella, J. 1985: A child by any other name . . . a comparison of the playfulness of gifted and non-gifted children. *Gifted Child Quarterly* **29**, 61–6.

Barr, D. 1997: Friendship and belonging. In Selman, R.S., Watts, C.L. and Schultz, L.H. (Eds.), *Fostering friendship for treatment and prevention.* New York: de Gruyter, 19–30.

Barton, E.J. and Ascione, F.R. 1984: Direct observation. In Ollendick, T.H. and Herson, M. (Eds.), *Child behavioural assessment: principles and procedures.* New York: Pergamon, 164–94.

Bash, M.A. and Camp, B.W. 1985: *Think aloud: increasing social and cognitive skills.* Champaign, IL: Research Press.

Baumeister, R.F. and Leary, M.R. 1995: The need to belong: desire for interpersonal attachments as a fundamental human motivaton. *Psychological Bulletin* **117**, 497–529.

Baumrind, D. 1989: Rearing competent children. In Damon, W. (Ed.), *Child development today and tomorrow.* San Francisco, CA: Jossey-Bass, 349–78.

Baumrind, D. 1996: The discipline controversy revisited: family relations. *Journal of Applied Family and Child Studies* **45**, 405–14.

Baumrind, D. and Black, A.E. 1967: Socialization practices associated with dimensions of competence in preschool boys and girls. *Child Development* **38**, 291–327.

Baumrind, D., Larzelere, R.E. and Owens, E.B. 2010: Effects of preschool parents' power assertive patterns and practices on adolescent development. *Parenting: Science and Practice* **10**, 157–201.

Bear, G.G., Juvonen, J. and McInerney, F. 1993: Self-perceptions and peer relations of boys with and boys without learning disabilities in an integrated setting: a longitudinal study. *Learning Disability Quarterly* **16**, 127–36.

Bearison, D.J., Magzamen, S. and Filardo, E.K. 1986: Cognitive conflict and cognitive growth in young children. *Merrill-Palmer Quarterly* **32**, 51–72.

Becker, W.C., Peterson, D.R., Hellmer, L.A., Shoemaker, D.J. and Quay, H.S. 1959: Factors in parental behaviour and personality as related to problem behavior in children. *Journal of Consulting Psychology* **3**, 107–18.

Becker, W.C., Peterson, D.R., Luria, Z., Shoemaker, D.J. and Hellmer, L.A. 1962: Relations of factors derived from parent-interview ratings to behavior problems of five-year olds. *Child Development* **33**, 509–35.

Beelmann, A., Pfingsten, U. and Lösel, F. 1994: Effects of training social competence in children: a meta-analysis of recent evaluation studies. *Journal of Clinical Child Psychology* **23**, 260–71.

Beidel, D.C., Turner, S.M. and Young, B.J. 2006: Social effectiveness therapy for children: five years later. *Behavior Therapy* **37**, 416–25.

Belk, R. 2013: Extended self in a digital world. *Journal of Consumer Research* **40**, 477–500.

Bellack, A.S. and Hersen, M. 1979: *Behaviour modification: an introductory textbook*. Baltimore, MD: Williams and Wilkins.

Bell-Dolan, D.J., Foster, S.L. and Christopher, J.S. 1992: Children's reactions to participating in a peer relations study: an example of cost-effective assessment. *Child Study Journal* **22**, 137–55.

Bell-Dolan, D.J., Foster, S.L. and Sikora, D.M. 1989: Effects of sociometric testing on children's behavior and loneliness in school. *Developmental Psychology* **25**, 306–11.

Bell-Dolan, D.J., Foster, S.L. and Tishelman, A.C. 1989: An alternative to negative nomination sociometric measures. *Journal of Clinical Child Psychology* **18**,153–7.

Bell-Dolan, D.J. and Wessler, A.E. 1994: Ethical administration of sociometric measures: procedures in use and suggestions for improvement. *Professional Psychology: Research and Practice* **25**, 23–32.

Bellini, S., Peters, J., Benner, L. and Hopf, A. 2007: A meta-analysis of school-based social skill interventions for children with autism spectrum disorders. *Remedial and Special Education* **28**, 153–62.

Bellmore, A.D., Nishina, A., Witkow, M.R., Graham, S. and Juvonen, J. 2007: The influence of classroom ethnic composition on same- and other-ethnicity peer nominations in middle school. *Social Development* **16**, 720–40.

Belsky, J. and Cassidy, J. 1995: Attachment theory and evidence. In Rutter, M. and Hay, D. (Eds.), *Development through life*. London: Blackwell, 373–402.

Bender, W.N., Wyne, M.D., Stuck, G.B. and Bailey, D.B. Jr. 1984: Relative peer status of learning disabled, educable mentally retarded, mentally handicapped, low achieving and normally achieving children. *Child Study Journal* **13**, 209–16.

Benenson, J.F. and Alavi, K. 2004: Sex differences in children's investment in same-sex peers. *Evolution and Human Behavior* **25**, 258–66.

Benenson, J.F. and Schinazi, J. 2004: Sex differences in reactions to outperforming same-sex friends. *British Journal of Developmental Psychology* **22**, 317–33.

Benjamin, W.J., Schneider, B.H., Greenman, P.S. and Hum, M. 2001: Conflict and childhood friendship in Taiwan and Canada. *Canadian Journal of Behavioural Science* **33**, 203–11.

Ben-Ze'ev, A. 2005: 'Detachment': the unique nature of online romantic relationships. In Amichai-Hamburger, Y. (Ed.), *The social net: the social psychology of the internet*. Oxford: Oxford University Press, 115–38.

Bergeron, N. and Schneider, B.H. 2005: Explaining cross-national differences in peer-directed aggression: a quantitative synthesis. *Aggressive Behavior* **31**, 116–37.

Berndt, T.J. 1981: Age changes and changes over time in prosocial intentions and behavior between friends. *Developmental Psychology* **17**, 408–16.

Berndt, T.J. 1982: The features and effects of friendship in early adolescence. *Child Development* **53**, 1447–60.

Berndt, T.J. 1996: Transitions in friendship and friends' influence. In Garber, J.A. and Brooks-Gunn, J. (Eds.), *Transitions through adolescence: interpersonal domainsand context.* Mahwah, NJ: Lawrence Erlbaum Associates, 57–84.

Berndt, T.J. and Hanna, N.A. 1995: Intimacy and self-disclosure in friendships. In Rotenberg, K.J. (Ed.), *Disclosure processes in children and adolescents.* Cambridge studies in social and emotional development. New York: Cambridge University Press, 57–77.

Berndt, T.J., Hawkins, J.A. and Hoyle, S.G. 1986: Changes in friendships during a school year: effects on children's and adolescents' impressions of friendships and sharing with friends. *Child Development* **57**, 1284–97.

Berndt, T.J., Hawkins, J.A. and Jiao, Z. 1999: Influences of friends and friendships on adjustment to junior high school. *Merrill-Palmer Quarterly* **45**, 13–41.

Berndt, T.J. and Keefe, K. 1992: Friends' influence on adolescents' perceptions of themselves in school. In Schunk, D.H. and Meece, J.L. (Eds.), *Students' perceptions in the classroom.* Hillsdale, NJ: Erlbaum, 51–73.

Berndt, T.J. and Keefe, K. 1995: Friends' influence on adolescents' adjustment to school. *Child Development* **66**, 1312–29.

Berndt, T.J. and Perry, T.B. 1986: Children's perceptions of friendships as supportive relationships. *Developmental Psychology* **22**, 640–8.

Berndt, T.J., Perry, T.B. and Miller, K.E. 1988: Friends' and classmates' interactions on academic tasks. *Journal of Educational Psychology* **80**, 506–13.

Bernicot, J. and Mahrokhian, A. 1988: La production de demandes par les enfants: le rôle de la nature de la demande et du statut de l'interlocuteur [Production of requests by children: the effects of the nature of the request and the status of the interlocutor]. *Revue Internationale de Psychologie Sociale* **1**, 389–407.

Berscheid, E. and Walster, E.H. 1978: *Interpersonal attraction.* 2nd Edition. Reading, MA: Addison-Wesley.

Besnard, T., Verlaan, P., Davidson, M., Vitaro, F., Poulin, F. and Capuano, F. 2013: Bidirectional influences between maternal and paternal parenting and children's disruptive behaviour from kindergarten to grade 2. *Early Child Development and Care* **183**, 515–33.

Betts, L.R. and Rotenberg, K.J. 2008: A social relations analysis of children's trust in their peers across the early years of school. *Social Development* **17**, 1039–55.

Bierman, K L., Coie, J.D., Dodge, K.A., Greenberg, M.T., Lochman, J.E., McMahon, R.J. and Pinderhughes, E. 2010: The effects of a multiyear universal social-emotional learning program: the role of student and school characteristics. *Journal of Consulting and Clinical Psychology* **78**, 156–68.

Bierman, K.L., Coie, J., Dodge, K., Greenberg, M., Lochman, J., McMahan, R. and Pinderhughes, E. 2013: School outcomes of aggressive-disruptive children: prediction from kindergarten risk factors and impact of the Fast Track prevention program. *Aggressive Behavior* **39**, 114–30.

Bierman, K.L. and Furman, W. 1984: The effects of social skills training and peer involvement in the social adjustment of preadolescents. *Child Development* **57**, 230–40.

Bierman, K.L. and Greenberg, M.T. 1996: Social skills training in the Fast Track program. In Peters, R.D. and McMahon, R.J. (Eds.), *Preventing childhood disorders, substance abuse, and delinquency.* Thousand Oaks, CA: Sage, 65–89.
Bigelow, B.J. 1977: Children's friendship expectations: a cognitive-developmental study. *Child Development* **48**, 246–53.
Bigelow, B.J. and La Gaipa, J.J. 1975: Children's written descriptions of friendship: a multidimensional analysis. *Developmental Psychology* **11**, 857–8.
Björkqvist, K., Lagerspetz, K.M.J. and Osterman, K. 1992: *The direct and indirect aggression scales.* Vasa: Abo Akademi University, Department of Social Sciences.
Björkqvist, K. and Osterman, K. 1999: Finland. In Smith, P.K., Morita, Y., JungerTas, J., Olweus, D., Catalano, R. and Slee, P. (Eds.), *The nature of school bullying: a cross-national perspective.* London: Routledge, 56–67.
Björkqvist, K., Osterman, K. and Kaukiainen, A. 1992: The development of direct and indirect aggressive strategies in males and females. In Björkqvist, K. and Niemela, P. (Eds.), *Of mice and women: aspects of female aggression.* San Diego, CA: Academic Press, 125–57.
Black, B. and Logan, A. 1995: Links between communication patterns in mother–child, father–child, and child–peer interactions and children's social status. *Child Development* **66**, 255–71.
Blatz, W.E. 1944: *Understanding the young child.* Toronto: Clarke, Irwin and Company.
Bloom, B.S. 1977: Affective outcomes of school learning. *Phi Delta Kappan* **59**, 193–8.
Blos, P. 1967: The second individuation process of adolescence. *Psychoanalytic Study of the Child* **22**, 162–86.
Blyth, D.A, Hill, J.P. and Thiel, K.S. 1982: Early adolescents' significant others: grade and gender differences in perceived relationships with familial and nonfamilial adults and young people. *Journal of Youth and Adolescence* **11**, 425–50.
Boivin, M. and Begin, G. 1989: Peer status and self-perception among early elementary school children: the case of the rejected children. *Child Development* **60**, 591–6.
Boivin, M., Dodge, K.A and Coie, J.D. 1995: Individual-group behavioral similarity and peer status in experimental play groups of boys: the social misfit revisited. *Journal of Social and Personality Psychology* **69**, 269–79.
Boivin, M., Vitaro, F. and Hodges, E. 1998: Proactive and reactive aggression among preadolescent boys: the cumulative experience of affiliating with other aggressive boys and the moderating role of negative peer status. Poster session presented at the biennial meeting of the International Society for the Study of Behavioural Development, Berne, Switzerland, July.
Bokhorst, C.L., Sumter, S.R. and Westenberg, P.M. 2010: Social support from parents, friends, classmates, and teachers in children and adolescents aged 9 to 18 years: who is perceived as most supportive? *Social Development* **19**, 417–26.
Boneva, B., Kraut, R. and Frohlich, D. 2001: Using e-mail for personal relationships: the difference gender makes. *American Behavioral Scientist* **45**, 530–49.
Bonn, M. and Kruger, P. 1996: Popularity and rejection in children's peer groups: a South African perspective. *Early Child Development and Care* **125**, 1–14.
Bott, H. 1928: Observation of play activities of three-year-old children. *Genetic Psychology Monographs* **4**, 44–88.
Bottema-Beutel, K. and Li, Z. 2015: Adolescent judgments and reasoning about the failure to include peers with social disabilities. *Journal of Autism and Developmental Disorders* **45**, 1873–86.
Boulton, M.J. and Smith, P.K. 1994: Bully/victim problems among middle school children. *British Journal of Developmental Psychology* **12**, 315–29.

Bowlby, J. 1969: *Attachment and loss.* New York: Basic Books.

Bowlby, J. 1978: *Attachement et perte* [Attachment and loss]. Paris: Presses Universitaires de France.

Bowlby, J. 1980: *Attachment and loss*, vol. 3. New York: Basic Books.

Bowlby, J. 1990: The study and reduction of group tensions in the family. In Trist, E. and Murray, H. (Eds.), *The social engagement of social science: a Tavistock anthology*, vol. 1: *The socio-psychological perspective.* Philadelphia: University of Pennsylvania Press, 291–8.

Bowman-Perrott, L., Davis, H., Vannest, K., Williams, L., Greenwood, C. and Parker, R. 2013: Academic benefits of peer tutoring: a meta-analytic review of single-case research. *School Psychology Review* **42**, 39–55.

Boyum, L.A. and Parke, R.D. 1995: The role of emotional expressiveness in the development of children's social competence. *Journal of Marriage and the Family* **57**, 593–608.

Boyd, J.H. 2008: Have we found the holy grail? Theory of mind as a unifying construct. *Journal of Religion and Health* **47**, 366–85.

Brand, J.L. 1966: The United States: a historical perspective. In Williams, R.H. and Ozarin, L.D. (Eds.), *Community mental health.* San Francisco, CA: Jossey-Bass, 18–43.

Branden, N. 1969: *The psychology of self-esteem.* New York: Bantam.

Brans, K., van Mechelen, I., Rimé, B. and Verduyn, P. 2013: The relation between social sharing and the duration of emotional experience. *Cognition and Emotion* **27**, 1023–41.

Brendgen, M. 2012: Genetics and peer relations: a review. *Journal of Research on Adolescence* **22**, 419–37.

Brendgen, M., Lamarche, V., Wanner, B. and Vitaro, F. 2010: Links between friendship relations and early adolescents' trajectories of depressed mood. *Development and Psychopathology* **46**, 491–501.

Bretherton, I., Lambert, J.D. and Golby, B. 2005: Involved fathers of preschool children as seen by themselves and their wives: accounts of attachment, socialization, and companionship. *Attachment and Human Development* **7**, 229–51.

Brighi, A., Mazzanti, C., Guarini, A. and Sansavini, A. 2015: Young children's cliques: a study on processes of peer acceptance and cliques' aggregation. *International Journal of Emotional Education* **7**, 69–83.

Bronfenbrenner, U., Kessel, F., Kessen, W. and White, S. 1986: Toward a critical social history of developmental psychology. *American Psychologist* **41**, 1218–30.

Brook, J.S., Whiteman, M.M. and Finch, S. 1992: Childhood aggression, adolescent delinquency, and drug use: a longitudinal study. *Journal of Genetic Psychology* **153**, 369–83.

Brook, J.S., Whiteman, M., Finch, S. and Cohen, P. 1995: Aggression, intrapsychic distress, and drug use: antecedent and intervening processes. *Journal of the American Academy of Child and Adolescent Psychiatry* **34**, 1076–84.

Brook, J.S., Whiteman, M.M., Finch, S.J. and Cohen, P. 1996: Young adult drug use and delinquency: childhood antecedents and adolescent mediators. *Journal of the American Academy of Child and Adolescent Psychiatry* **35**, 1584–92.

Brooks-Gunn, J. and Duncan Johnson, A. 2006: G. Stanley Hall's contribution to science, practice and policy: the child study, parent education, and child welfare movements. *History of Psychology* **9**, 247–58.

Brown, S. 2010: Students as cultural beings. In Fallon, M.A. and Brown, S.C. (Eds.), *Teaching inclusively in higher education.* Charlotte, NC: IAP Information Age Publishing, 17–37.

Brownell, C.A. and Brown, E. 1992: Peers and play in infants and toddlers. In Van Hasselt, V.B. and Hersen, M. (Eds.), *Handbook of social development: a lifespan perspective.* New York: Plenum Press, 183–200.

Brownell, C.A. and Carriger, M.S. 1990: Changes in cooperation and self-other differentiation during the second year. *Child Development* **61**, 1164–74.

Buchanan, H.T., Blankenbaker, J. and Cotton, D. 1976: Academic and athletic abiity as popularity factors in elementary school children. *Research Quarterly* **47**, 320–5.

Buhrmester, D. 1996: Need fulfillment, interpersonal competence, and the developmental contexts of early adolescent friendship. In Bukowski, W.M., Newcomb, A.F. and Hartup, W.W. (Eds.), *The company they keep: friendship in childhood and adolescence.* New York: Cambridge University Press, 158–85.

Buhs, E.S., Rudasill, K., Kalutskaya, I.N. and Griese, E. R. 2015: Shyness and engagement: contributions of peer rejection and teacher sensitivity. *Early Childhood Research Quarterly* **30**, 12–19.

Bukowski, W.M. and Adams, R. 2005: Peer relationships and psychopathology: markers, moderators, mediators, mechanisms, and meanings. *Journal of Clinical Child and Adolescent Psychology* **34**, 3–10.

Bukowski, W.M., Boivin, M. and Hoza, B. 1994: Measuring friendship quality during pre- and early adolescence: the development and psychometric properties of the Friendship Qualities Scale. *Journal of Social and Personal Relationships* **11**, 471–84.

Bukowski, W.M., Gauze, C., Hoza, B. and Newcomb, A.F. 1993a: Differences and consistency between same-sex and other-sex peer relationships during early adolescence. *Developmental Psychology* **29**, 255–63.

Bukowski, W.M. and Hoza, B. 1989: Popularity and friendships: issues in theory, measurement, and outcome. In Berndt, T.J and Ladds, G.W. (Eds.), *Peer relations in child development.* New York: Wiley, 15–45.

Bukowski, W.M. and Kramer, T.L. 1986: Judgements of the features of friendship among early adolescent boys and girls. *Journal of Early Adolescence* **6**, 331–8.

Bukowski, W.M., Laursen, B. and Hoza, B. 2010: The snowball effect: friendship moderates escalations in depressed affect among avoidant and excluded children. *Development and Psychopathology* **22**, 749–57.

Bukowski, W.M. and Newcomb, A.F. 1984: Stability and determinants of sociometric status and friendship choice: a longitudinal perspective. *Developmental Psychology* **20**, 941–52.

Bukowski, W.M., Newcomb, A.F. and Hoza, B. 1987: Friendship conceptions among early adolescents: a longitudinal study of stability and change. *Journal of Early Adolescence* **7**, 143–52.

Bukowski, W.M., Sippola, L., Gauze, C., Hoza, B. and Newcomb, A.F. 1993b: Differences in the processes, properties, and perceptions of friendship among boys and girls. Paper presented at the Society for Research in Child Development, New Orleans, LA, March.

Bulotsky-Shearer, E.R.J., Bell, R., Romero, S.L. and Carter. T.M. 2012: Preschool interactive peer play mediates problem behavior and learning for low-income children. *Journal of Applied Developmental Psychology* **33**, 53–65.

Burack, J. 1997: The study of atypical and typical populations in developmental psychology: the quest for a common science. In Luthar, S.S., Burack, J.A., Cicchetti, D. and Weisz, J.R. (Eds.), *Developmental psychology: perspectives on adjustment, risk, and disorder.* Cambridge: Cambridge University Press, 36–65.

Burghardt, G.M., Bartmess-LeVasseur, J.N., Browning, S.A. *et al.* 2012: Perspectives: minimizing observer bias in behavioral studies: a review and recommendations. *Ethology* **118**, 511–17.

Burkhardt, R.W. Jr. 2014: Tribute to Tinbergen: putting Niko Tinbergen's 'four questions' in historical context. *Ethology* **120**, 215–23.

Burks, V.S., Dodge, K.A. and Price, J.M. 1995: Models of internalizing outcomes of early rejection. *Development and Psychopathology* **7**, 683–96.

Burleson, B.R., Applegate, J.L., Burke, J.A., Clark, R.A., Delia, J.G. and Kline, S.L. 1986: Communicative correlates of peer acceptance in childhood. *Communicative Education* **35**, 349–61.

Burleson, B.R., Delia, J.G. and Applegate, J.L. 1992: Effects of maternal communication and children's social-cognitive and communication skills on children's acceptance by the peer group. *Family Relations* **41**, 264–72.

Burlingham, D. and Freud, A. 1942: *Young children in wartime in a residential nursery school*. London: Allen and Unwin.

Bursuck, W.D. 1983: Sociometric status, behaviour ratings and social knowledge of learning disabled and low achieving students. *Learning Disability Quarterly* **6**, 329–38.

Bursuck, W.D. 1989: A comparison of students with learning disabilities to low achieving and higher achieving students on 3 dimensions of social competence. *Journal of Learning Disabilities* **22**, 188–94.

Buss, A.H. 1985: Two kinds of shyness. In Schwarzer, R. (Ed.), *Self-related cognitions in anxiety and motivation*. Hillsdale, NJ: Erlbaum, 65–75.

Buss, A.H. and Plomin, R. 1975: *A temperament theory of personality development*. New York: Wiley-Interscience.

Buss, A.H. and Plomin, R. 1984: *Temperament: early developing personality traits*. Hillsdale, NJ: Erlbaum.

Buysse, V., Goldman, B.D. and Skinner, M.L. 2002: Setting effects on friendship formation among young children with and without disabilities. *Exceptional Children* **6**, 503–17.

Buzzelli, C.A. 1988: The development of trust in children's relations with peers. *Child Study Journal* **18**, 22–46.

Byrne, B. and Schneider, B.H. 1986: Student–teacher concordance on dimensions of student social competence: a multitrait–multimethod analysis. *Journal of Psychopathology and Behavioural Assessment* **8**, 263–79.

Cairns, R.B. and Cairns, B.D. 1994: *Lifelines and risks: pathways of youth in our time*. Cambridge: Cambridge University Press.

Cairns, R.B. and Cairns, B.D. 2006: The making of developmental psychology. In Lerner, R.M. and Damon, W. (Eds.), *Handbook of child psychology*, vol. 1: *Theoretical models of human development*. 6th Edition. Hoboken, NJ: Wiley, 89–165.

Cairns, R.B., Cairns, B.D., Neckerman, H.J., Gest, S.D. and Gariépy, N. 1988: Social networks and aggressive behavior: peer support or peer rejection? *Developmental Psychology* **24**, 815–23.

Campbell, P.T. and Fiske, D.W. 1959: Convergent and discriminant validation by the multitrait–multimethod matrix. *Psychological Bulletin* **56**, 81–105.

Cantor, N. and Harlow, R.E. 1994: Social intelligence and personality: flexible life task pursuit. In Sternberg, R.J. and Ruzgis, P. (Eds.), *Personality and intelligence*. New York: Cambridge University Press, 137–68.

Cantrell, V.L. and Prinz, R.J. 1985: Multiple perspectives of rejected, neglected, and accepted children: relation between sociometric status and behavioral characteristics. *Journal of Consulting and Clinical Psychology* **53**, 884–9.

Caplan, S.E. 2007: Relations among loneliness, social anxiety, and problematic internet use. *CyberPsychology and Behavior* **10**, 234–41.

Card, N. 2010: Antipathetic relationships in child and adolescent development: a meta-analytic review and recommendations for an emerging area of study. *Developmental Psychology* **46**, 516–29.

Carlson, C.L., Lahey, B.B. and Neeper, R. 1984: Peer assessment of the social behavior of accepted, rejected, and neglected children. *Journal of Abnormal Child Psychology* **12**, 187–98.

Carré, J.M, Iselin, A.M., Welker, K.M., Hariri, A.R. and Dodge, K. 2014: Testosterone reactivity to provocation mediates the effect of early intervention on aggressive behavior. *Psychological Science* **25**, 1140–6.

Carter, E.W., Hughes, C., Guth, C.B. and Copeland, S.R. 2005: Factors influencing social interaction among high school students with intellectual disabilities and their general education peers. *American Journal on Mental Retardation* **110**, 366–77.

Carter, K.A. and Kuechenmeister, M.A. 1986: Evaluating the consequences of participating in a gifted pull-out program. *Journal for the Education of the Gifted* **9**, 265–75.

Cartledge, G.C. and Milburn, J.F. 1995: *Teaching social skills to children and youth: innovative approaches.* 3rd Edition. Needham Heights, MA: Allyn and Bacon.

Casiglia, A.C., LoCoco, A. and Zappulla, C. 1998: Aspects of social reputation and peer relationships in Italian children: a cross-cultural perspective. *Developmental Psychology* **34**, 723–30.

Casper, D.M. and Card, N.A. 2010: We were best friends, but . . . two studies of antipathetic relationships emerging from broken friendships. *Journal of Adolescent Research* **25**, 499–526.

Caspi, A. 1998: Personality development across the life course. In Damon, W. and Eisenberg, N. (Eds.), *Handbook of child psychology*, vol. 3: *Social, emotional, and personality development.* 5th Edition. New York: Wiley, 311–88.

Caspi, A., Elder, G.H. Jr. and Bem, D.J. 1988: Moving away from the world: life-course patterns of shy children. *Developmental Psychology* **24**, 824–31.

Cha, J.H. 1994: Aspects of individualism and collectivism in Korea. In Kim, U., Triandis, H.C., Kagitcibasi, C., Choi, S. and Yoon, G. (Eds.), *Individualism and collectivism: theory, methods, and applications.* Thousand Oaks, CA: Sage, 157–74.

Chan, W. and Birman, D. 2009: Cross- and same-race friendships of Vietnamese immigrant adolescents: a focus on acculturation and school diversity. *International Journal of Intercultural Relations* **33**, 313–24.

Chang, L. 2004: The role of classroom norms in contextualizing the relations of children's social behaviors to peer acceptance. *Developmental Psychology* **40**, 691–702.

Chao, P. 1983: *Chinese kinship.* London: Kegan Paul.

Charlton, J.J.V. and Law, J. 2014: 'The story in a box': measuring the online communication behaviours of children identified as having emotional and behavioural difficulties using LENA and Noldus OBSERVER. *Emotional and Behavioural Difficulties* **19**, 41–58.

Chen, B. and Chang, L. 2012: Are 'Machiavellian' Chinese children well-adapted in the peer group? The relationship between resource acquisition strategies and social functioning and status. *Asian Journal of Social Psychology* **15**, 122–31.

Chen, X., Cen, G., Li, D. and He, Y. 2005: Social functioning and adjustment in Chinese children: the imprint of historical time. *Child Development* **76**, 182–95.

Chen, X., Hastings, P.D., Rubin, K.H., Chen, H., Cen, G. and Stewart, S.L. 1998: Child-rearing attitudes and behavioural inhibition in Chinese and Canadian toddlers: a cross-cultural study. *Developmental Psychology* **34**, 667–86.

Chen, X., Kaspar, V., Zhang, Y., Wang, L. and Zheng, S. 2004: Peer relationships among Chinese and North American boys: a cross-cultural perspective. In Way, N. and Chu, J. (Eds.), *Adolescent boys in context.* New York: New York University Press, 197–218.

Chen, X., Rubin, K.H. and Li, B. 1995: Social and school adjustment of shy and aggressive children in China. *Developmental Psychopathology* **7**, 337–49.

Chen, X., Rubin, K.H., Li, B. and Li, D. 1999: Adolescent outcomes and social functioning in Chinese children. *International Journal of Behavioural Developmental* **23**, 199–223.

Chen, X., Rubin, K.H. and Li, D. 1997: Relation between academic achievement and social adjustment: evidence from Chinese children. *Developmental Psychology* **33**, 518–25.

Chen, X., Rubin, K.H. and Li, Z.Y. 1994: Social functioning and adjustment in Chinese children: a longitudinal study. Paper presented at the meeting of the International Society for the Study of Behavioural Development, Amsterdam, The Netherlands, July.

Chen, X., Rubin, K.H. and Sun, Y. 1992: Social reputation and peer relationships in Chinese and Canadian children: a cross-cultural study. *Child Development* **63**, 1336–43.

Chen, X. and Tse, H. 2008: Social functioning and adjustment in Canadian-born children with Chinese and European backgrounds. *Developmental Psychology* **44**, 1184–9.

Chenier, J.A.J., Fischer, K., Hunter, E.P.L., Libster, M.A., O'Leary, K., York, H. and Robichaux, N. 2011: What works regarding social skills interventions using single subject designs? Paper presented to the National Association of School Psychologists, Baton Rouge, LA, February.

Cherng, H.S., Turney, K. and Kao, G. 2014: Less socially engaged? Participation in friendship and extracurricular activities among racial/ethnic minority and immigrant adolescents. *Teachers College Record* **116**, 226–34.

Chess, S. and Thomas, A. 1996: *Temperament: theory and practice*, vol. 12. New York: Brunner-Mazel.

Child, S. and Nind, M. 2013: Sociometric methods and difference: a force for good – or yet more harm. *Disability and Society* **28**, 1012–23.

Chiu, C.Y., Tsang, S.C. and Yang, C.F. 1988: The role of face situation and attitudinal antecedents in Chinese consumer complaint behavior. *Journal of Social Psychology* **128**, 173–80.

Christie, D., Warden, D., Fitzpatrick, H. and Reid, K. 1999: Assessing and promoting children's social competence. Paper presented at the ninth European Conference on Developmental Psychology, Spetses, Greece, September.

Chronis-Tuscano, A., Rubin, K.H., O'Brien, K.A., Coplan, R.J., Thomas, S.R., Dougherty, L.R., Cheah, C.S.L., Watts, K., Heverly-Fitt, S., Huggins, S.L., Menzer, M., Begle, A.S. and Wimsatt, M. 2015: Preliminary evaluation of a multimodal early intervention program for behaviorally inhibited preschoolers. *Journal of Consulting and Clinical Psychology* **83**, 534–40.

Chu, L. 1979: The sensitivity of Chinese and American children to social influences. *Journal of Social Psychology* **109**, 175–86.

Cicchetti, D. 2006: Development and psychopathology. In Cicchetti, D. and Cohen, D.J. (Eds.), *Developmental psychopathology*. Hoboken, NJ: John Wiley and Sons, vol. 1, 1–23.

Cillessen, A.H.N. 2011: Integration. In Cilleseen, A.N.H., Schwartz, D. and Mayeux, L. (Eds.), *Popularity in the peer system*. New York: Guilford, 273–99.

Cillessen, A.H.N. and Bellmore, A. 2011: Social skills and social competence in interactions with peers. In Smith, P.K. and Hart, C.H. (Eds.), *The Wiley-Blackwell handbook of childhood social development*. 2nd Edition. Malden, MA: Blackwell, 393–412.

Cillessen, A.H.N. and Borch, C. 2008: Analyzing social networks in adolescence. In Card, N.A., Selig, J.P. and Little, T.D. (Eds.), *Modeling dyadic and interdependent data in the developmental and behavioral sciences*. New York: Routledge/Taylor and Francis Group, 61–85.

Cillessen, A.H.N., van IJzendoorn, H.W., van Lieshout, C.F.M. and Hartup, W.W. 1992: Heterogeneity among peer-rejected boys: subtypes and stabilities. *Child Development* **63**, 893–905.

Cillessen, A.H.N. and Mayeux, L. 2004: From censure to reinforcement: developmental changes in the association between aggression and social status. *Child Development* **75**, 147–63.

Cillessen, A.H.N., Mayeux, L., Ha, T., de Bruyn, E. and Lafontana, K.M. 2014: Aggressive effects of prioritizing popularity in early adolescence. *Aggressive Behavior* **40**, 204–13.

Clark, M.L. and Ayers, M. 1992: Friendship similarity during early adolescence: gender and racial patterns. *Journal of Psychology* **126**, 393–405.

Clark, M.L. and Drewry, D.L. 1985: Similarity and reciprocity in the friendships of elementary school children. *Child Study Journal* **15**, 251–64.

Clayton, R.B., Leshner, G. and Almond, A. 2015: The extended iSelf: the impact of iPhone separation on cognition, emotion and physiology. *Journal of Computer-Mediated Communication*. http://onlinelibrary.wiley.com/doi/10.1111/jcc4.12109/full, retrieved May 2, 2015.

Cloke, K. 1987: Politics and values in mediation: the Chinese experience. *Mediation Quarterly* **17**, 69–82.

Cohen, R., Duncan, M. and Cohen, S. 1994: Classroom peer relations of children participating in a pull-out enrichment program. *Gifted Child Quarterly* **38**, 33–7.

Cohen, Y.A. 1966: Forms of friendship. In Cohen, Y.A. (Ed.), *Social structure and personality*. New York: Holt, Rinehart and Winston, 351–86.

Coie, J. 1985: Fitting social skills training to the target group. In Schneider, B.H., Rubin, K.H. and Ledingham, J. (Eds.), *Children's peer relations: issues in assessment and intervention*. New York: Springer-Verlag, 141–74.

Coie, J.D. and Dodge, K.A. 1988: Multiple sources of data on social behavior and social status in the school: a cross-age comparison. *Child Development* **59**, 815–29.

Coie, J.D., Dodge, K.A. and Coppotelli, H. 1982: Dimensions and types of social status: a five-year longitudinal study. *Developmental Psychology* **18**, 557–70.

Coie, J.D., Dodge, K.A. and Kupersmidt, J. 1990: Peer group behavior and social status. In Asher, S.R. and Coie, J.D. (Eds.), *Peer rejection in childhood*. Cambridge: Cambridge University Press, 17–59.

Coie, J.D. and Krehbiel, G. 1984: Effects of academic tutoring on the social status of low-achieving, socially rejected children. *Child Development* **55**, 1465–78.

Coie, J.D. and Kupersmidt, J.B. 1983: A behavioral analysis of emerging social status in boys' groups. *Child Development* **54**, 1400–16.

Coie, J.D., Terry, R., Lenox, K., Lochman, J. and Hyman, C. 1995a: Childhood peer rejection and aggression as predictors of stable patterns of adolescent disorder. *Development and Psychopathology* **7**, 697–714.

Coie, J.D., Terry, R., Zabriski, A. and Lochman, J. 1995b: Early adolescent social influences on delinquent behavior. In McCord, J. (Ed.), *Coercion and punishment in long-term perspective*. New York: Cambridge University Press, 229–44.

Cole, D.A. and Carpentieri, S. 1990: Social status and the comorbidity of child depression and conduct disorder. *Journal of Consulting and Clinical Psychology* **58**, 748–57.

Coleman, J.S. 1961: *The adolescent society*. New York: Free Press of Glencoe.

Collins. W.A., Maccoby. E.E., Steinberg, L., Hetherington, E.M. and Bornstein, M.H. 2000: Contemporary research on parenting: the case for nature and nurture. *American Psychologist* **55**, 218–32.

Conduct Problems Prevention Research Group 2010: Fast Track intervention effects on youth arrests and delinquency. *Journal of Experimental Criminology* **6**, 131–15.

Conduct Problems Prevention Research Group 2011: The effects of the Fast Track preventive intervention on the development of conduct disorder across childhood. *Child Development* **82**, 331–45.

Conduct Problems Prevention Research Group 2014: Trajectories of risk for early sexual activity and early substance use in the Fast Track prevention program. *Prevention Science* **15** (Suppl. 1), S33–S46.

Conrad, M. and Hammen, C. 1993: Protective and resource factors in high-risk and low-risk children: a comparison of children with unipolar, bipolar medically ill, and normal mothers. *Development and Psychopathology* **5**, 593–607.

Conrad, R. 1998: Darwin's baby and baby's Darwin: mutual recognition in observational research. *Human Development* **41**, 47–64.

Contarello, A. and Volpata, C. 1991: Images of friendship: literary depictions through the ages. *Journal of Social and Personal Relationship* **8**, 49–75.

Cook, C.R., Williams, K.R., Guerra, N.G. and Kim, T.E. 2010: Variability in the prevalence of bullying and victimization. In Jimerson, S.R., Swearer, S.M. and Espelage, D.L. (Eds.), *The handbook of bullying in schools: an international perspective*. New York: Routledge, 347–62.

Cook, C.R., Williams, K.R., Guerra, N.G. and Cook, H. 1992: Matrilocality and female aggression in Margeriteno society. In Björkqvist, K. and Nimela, P. (Eds.), *Of mice and women: aspects of female aggression*. San Diego, CA: Academic Press, 149–62.

Cook, C.R., Gresham, F.M., Kern, L., Barreras, R.B. and Crews, S.D. 2008: Social skills training for secondary EBD students: a review and analysis of the meta-analytic literature. *Journal of Emotional Behavioral Disorders* **6**, 33–4.

Cooper, C.R., Marquis, A. and Edward, D. 1986: Four perspectives on peer learning among elementary school children. In Mueller, E.C. and Cooper, C.R. (Eds.), *Process and outcome in peer relations*. New York: Academic Press, 269–99.

Cooper, J.E., Brooks, A.J., LeCroy, C.W. and Ashford, J.B. 1994: Adolescent friendship patterns: mediators of risky behaviours. Paper presented at the Society for Research in Adolescence, San Diego, CA, February.

Coplan, R.J., DeBow, A., Schneider, B.H. and Graham, A. 2009: The social behaviours of inhibited children 'in' and 'out' of preschool. *British Journal of Developmental Psychology* **27**, 891–905.

Coplan, R.J., Girardi, A., Findlay, L.C. and Frohlick, S.L. 2007: Understanding solitude: young children's attitudes and responses towards hypothetical socially withdrawn peers. *Social Development* **16**, 390–409.

Coplan, R.J. and Rubin, K.H. 2010: Social withdrawal and shyness in childhood: history, theories, definitions, and assessments. In Rubin, K.H. and Coplan, R.J. (Eds.), *The development of shyness and social withdrawal*. New York: Guilford, 2–20.

Coplan, R.J. and Weeks, M. 2010: Unsociability in middle childhood: conceptualization, assessment, and associations with socio-emotional functioning. *Merrill–Palmer Quarterly* **56**, 105–30.

Corsaro, W.A. 1981: Friendship in the nursery school: social organization in a peer environment. In Asher, R. and Gottman, J.M. (Eds.), *The development of children's friendships*. New York: Cambridge University Press, 207–44.

Corsaro, W.A. 1985: *Friendship and peer culture in the early years*. Norwood, NJ: Ablex.

Corsaro, W.A. 1988: Routines in the peer culture of American and Italian nursery school children. *Sociology of Education* **61**, 1–14.

Corsaro, W.A. 2003: *We're friends, right? Inside kids' culture*. Washington, DC: Joseph Henry Press.

Corsaro, W.A. and Rizzo, T.A. 2008: Discussione and friendship in Italian peer culture. In LeVine, R.A. and New, R.S. (Eds.), *Anthropology and child development: a cross-cultural reader*. Malden: Blackwell, 227–43.

Cowen, E.L., Pedersen, A., Babigian, H., Izzo, L.D. and Trost, M.A. 1973: Long-term follow-up of early-detected vulnerable children. *Journal of Consulting and Clinical Psychology* **41**, 438–46.

Craig, M. 1922: Some aspects of education and training in relation to mental disorder. *Journal of Mental Science* **68**, 209–28.

Craig, W.M. and Pepler, D.J. 1997: Observations of bullying and victimization in the school yard. *Canadian Journal of School Psychology* **13**, 41–57.

Craik, K. 1943: *The nature of explanation*. Cambridge: Cambridge University Press.

Crick, N.R., Bigbee, M.A. and Howes, C. 1996: Gender differences in children's normative beliefs about aggression: how do I hurt thee? Let me count the ways. *Child Development* **67**, 1003–14.

Crick, N.R., Casas, J.F. and Mosher, M. 1997: Relational and overt aggression in preschool. *Developmental Psychology* **33**, 579–88.

Crick, N.R. and Dodge, K.A. 1994: A review and reformulation of social information-processing mechanisms in children's social adjustment. *Psychological Bulletin* **115**, 74–101.

Crick, N.R. and Dodge, K.A. 1996: Social information-processing mechanisms in reactive and proactive aggression. *Child Development* **67**, 993–1002.

Crick, N.R. and Dodge, K.A 1999: Superiority is in the eye of the beholder: a comment on Sutton, Smith and Swettenham. *Social Development* **8**, 128–31.

Crick, N.R. and Grotpeter, J.K. 1995: Relational aggression, gender, and social-psychological adjustment. *Child Development* **66**, 710–22.

Cross, T.L. and Swiatek, M.A. 2009: Social coping among academically gifted adolescents in a residential setting: a longitudinal study. *Gifted Child Quarterly* **53**, 25–33.

Cryderman, B.K. 1992: Chinese. In Cryderman, B.K. and Fleras, A. (Eds.), *Police, race, and ethnicity: a guide for police ser vices*. Toronto: Butterworths, 191–208.

Crystal, D.S., Watanabe, H. and Chen, R. 1999: Children's reactions to physical disability: a cross-national and developmental study. *International Journal of Behavioural Development* **23**, 91–111.

Csikszentmihalyi, M. and Larson, R. 1987: The experience sampling method. *Journal of Nervous and Mental Disease* **175**, 537–44.

Cuckle, P. and Wilson, J. 2001: Social relationships and friendships among young people with Down's syndrome in secondary schools. *British Journal of Special Education* **29**, 66–71.

Cuksts, B. 1988: Peer acceptance, friendships, and attitudes towards academically integrated physically disabled adolescents. Unpublished master's thesis, Ontario Institute for Studies in Education, Ontario, Canada.

Cummings, C.M., Caporino, N.E. and Kendall, P.C. 2014: Comorbidity of anxiety and depression in children and adolescents: 20 years after. *Psychological Bulletin* **140**, 816–45.

Cunningham, C.E., Cunningham, L.J., Martorelli, V., Tran, A., Young, J. and Zacharias, R. 1998: The effects of primary division, student-mediated conflict resolution programs on playground aggression. *Journal of Child Psychology and Psychiatry and Allied Disciplines* **39**, 653–62.

Curtis, D.F. 2014: Structured dyadic behavior therapy processes for ADHD intervention. *Psychotherapy* **51**, 110–16.

Daniels E. and Leaper, C. 2006: A longitudinal investigation of sport participation, peer acceptance, and self-esteem among adolescent girls and boys. *Sex Roles* **55**, 878–80.

Dean, M., Kasari, C., Shih, W., Frankel, F., Whitney, R., Landa, R., Lord, C., Orlich, F., King, B. and Harwood, R. 2014: The peer relationships of girls with ASD at school: comparison to boys and girls with and without ASD. *Journal of Child Psychology and Psychiatry* **55**, 1218–25.

De Bruyn, E.H. and Cillessen, A.H.N. 2006: Popularity in early adolescence: prosocial and antisocial subtypes. *Journal of Adolescent Research* **21**, 607–27.

De Bruyn, E.H., Cillessen, A.H.N. and Wissink, I.B. 2010: Associations of peer acceptance and peer popularity with bullying and victimization in early adolescence. *Journal of Early Adolescence* **30**, 543–66.

Deci, E.L. and Ryan, R.M. 2012: Self-determination theory. In Van Lange, P.A.M., Kruglanski, A.W. and Higgins, E.T. (Eds.), *Handbook of theories of social psychology*. Thousand Oaks, CA: Sage, vol. 1, 416–37.

DeFries, J.C., Plomin, R. and Fulker, D.W. (Eds.) 1994: *Nature and nurture during middle childhood*. Oxford: Blackwell.

De Goede, I.H.A., Branje, S.J.T. and Meeus W.H.T. 2009: Developmental changes in adolescents' perceptions of relationships with their parents. *Journal of Youth and Adolescence* **38**, 75–88.

de Guzman, M.R.T., Jung, E. and Do, K.T. 2012: Perceived social support networks and prosocial outcomes among Latino/a youth in the United States. *Revista Interamericana de Psicologia* **46**, 413–24.

Dekovic, M. and Gerris, J.R.M. 1994: Developmental analysis of social cognitive and behavioral differences between popular and rejected children. *Journal of Applied Developmental Psychology* **15**, 367–86.

Dekovic, M. and Janssens, J.M. 1992: Parents' child-rearing style and child's sociometric status. *Developmental Psychology* **28**, 925–32.

DeLay, D., Hartl, A.C., Laursen, B., Denner, J., Werner, L., Campe, S. and Ortiz, E. 2014: Learning from friends: measuring influence in a dyadic computer instructional setting. *International Journal of Research Methods in Education* **37**, 190–205.

Denham, S.A. 2006: Social-emotional competence as support for school readiness: what is it and how do we assess it? *Early Education and Development* **17**, 57–89.

Denscombe, M. 1983: Ethnic group and friendship choice in the primary school. *Educational Research* **5**, 184–90.

Denscombe, M., Szulc, H., Patrick, C. and Wood, A. 1986: Ethnicity and friendship: the contrast between sociometric research and fieldwork observation in primary school classrooms. *British Educational Research Journal* **12**, 221–35.

DeRosier, M. 1989: Costa Rican children's perceptions of their social networks. Paper presented at the biennial meeting of the Society for Research in Child Development, Kansas City, MO, April.

DeRosier, M.E. and Kupersmidt, J.B. 1991: Costa Rican children's perceptions of their social networks. *Developmental Psychology* **27**, 656–62.

DeRosier, M., Kupersmidt, J. and Patterson, C. 1994: Children's academic and behavioural adjustment as a function of the chronicity and proximity of peer rejection. *Child Development* **65**, 1799–1813.

DeRosier, M.E. and Mercer, S.H. 2009: Perceived behavioral atypicality as a predictor of social rejection and peer victimization: implications for emotional adjustment and academic achievement. *Psychology in the Schools* **46**, 375–87.

Desjarlais, M. and Willoughby, T. 2010: A longitudinal study of the relation between adolescent boys and girls' computer use with friends and friendship quality: support for the social compensation or the rich-get-richer hypothesis? *Computers in Human Behavior* **26**, 896–905.

De Souza Briggs, X. 2007: 'Some of my best friends are . . .': interracial friendships, class, and segregation in america. *City and Community* **6**, 263–90.

Deutz, M.H.F, Lansu, T.A.M. and Cillessen, A.H.N. 2015: Children's observed interactions with best friends: associations with friendship jealousy and satisfaction. *Social Development* **24**, 39–56.

Dewey, J. 1900: *The school and society*. Chicago, IL: University of Chicago Press.

Diehl, D.S., Lemerise, E.A., Caverly, S.L., Ramsay, S. and Roberts, J. 1998: Peer relations and school adjustment in ungraded primary children. *Journal of Educational Psychology* **90**, 506–15.

Dietz, L.J., Marshal, M.P., Burton, C.M., Bridge, J.A., Birmaher, B., Kolko, D., Duffy, J.N. and Brent, D.A. 2014: Social problem solving among depressed adolescents is enhanced by structured psychotherapies. *Journal of Consulting and Clinical Psychology* **82**, 202–11.

Dijkstra, J., Lindenberg, S. and Veenstra, R. 2008: Beyond the class norm: bullying behavior of popular adolescents and its relation to peer acceptance and rejection. *Journal of Abnormal Child Psychology* **36**, 1289–99.

DiLalla, L.F. and John, S. F. 2014: Genetic and behavioral influences on received aggression during observed play among unfamiliar preschool-aged peers. *Merrill-Palmer Quarterly* **60**, 168–92.

Diller, J.W., Brown, R.M. and Patros, C.H.G. 2013: Revisiting Kazdin (1980): contemporary treatment acceptability for problem behavior in children. *International Journal of Psychology and Psychological Therapy* **13**, 233–42.

Dion, K.K. and Berscheid, E. 1974: Physical attractiveness and peer perception among children. *Sociometry* **37**, 1–12.

Dishion, T.J. 1990: The ecology of boys' peer relations in middle childhood. *Child Development* **61**, 874–92.

Dishion, T.J., Andrews, D.W. and Crosby, L. 1995: Antisocial boys and their friends in early adolescence: relationship characteristics, quality, and interactional process. *Child Development* **65**, 139–51.

Dishion, T.J., Eddy, M., Haas, E., Li, F. and Spracklen, S. 1997: Friendships and violent behaviour during adolescence. *Social Development* **6**, 207–23.

Dishion, T.J., McCord, J. and Poulin, F. 1999: When interventions harm: peer groups and problem behavior. *American Psychologist* **54**, 755–64.

Dishion, T.J., Piehler, T.F. and Myers, M.W. 2008: Dynamics and ecology of adolescent peer contagion. In Prinstein, M.J. and Dodge, K.A. (Eds.), *Understanding peer influence in children and adolescents*. New York: Guilford, 72–93.

Dodge, K.A. 1983: Behavioural antecedents of peer social status. *Child Development* **54**, 1386–99.

Dodge, K.A. 1985: Attributional bias in aggressive children. In Phillips, P.C. (Ed.), *Advances in cognitive-behavioural research and therapy.* Vol. 4: *Advances in cognitive-behavioral research and therapy.* Orlando, FL: Academic Press, 73–110.

Dodge, K.A. and Coie, J.D. 1987: Social-information-processing factors in reactive and proactive aggression in children's peer groups. *Journal of Personality and Social Psychology* **53**, 1146–58.

Dodge, K.A., Coie, J.D. and Brakke, N.P. 1982: Behaviour patterns of socially rejected and neglected preadolescents: the roles of social approach and aggression. *Journal of Abnormal Child Psychology* **10**, 389–410.

Dodge, K.A., Coie, J.D., Pettit, G.S. and Price, J.M. 1990: Peer status and aggression in boys' groups: developmental and contextual analyses. *Child Development* **55**, 163–73.
Dodge, K.A. and Frame, C.L. 1982: Social cognitive biases and deficits in aggressive boys. *Child Development* **53**, 620–35.
Dodge, K.A., Schlundt, D.C., Schocken, I. and Delugach, J.D. 1983: Social competence and children's sociometric status: the role of peer group entry strategies. *Merrill-Palmer Quarterly* **29**, 309–36.
Dodge, K.A. and Tomlin, A.M. 1987: Utilization of self-schemas as a mechanism of interpretational bias in aggressive children. *Social Cognition* **5**, 280–300.
Doey, L., Coplan, R.J. and Kingsbury, M. 2014: Bashful boys and coy girls: a review of gender differences in childhood shyness. *Sex Roles* **70**, 255–66.
Doise, W. and Mugny, G. 1984: *The social development of the intellect*. Oxford: Pergamon.
Doise, W., Mugny, G. and Perret-Clermont, A. 1975: Social interaction and the development of cognitive operations. *European Journal of Social Psychology* **5**, 367–83.
Donchi, L. and Moore, S. 2004: It'a a boy thing: the role of the internet in young people's psychological wellbeing. *Behaviour Change* **21**, 76–89.
Dong, Q., Yang, B. and Ollendick, T.I. 1994: Fears in Chinese children and adolescents and their relations to anxiety and depression. *Journal of Child Psychology and Psychiatry* **35**, 351–63.
Donnelly, M. 1992: *The politics of mental health in Italy*. New York: Tavistock/Routledge.
Dooley, J.J., Pyzalski, J. and Cross, D. 2009: Cyberbullying versus face-to-face bullying: a theoretical and conceptual review. *Zeitschrift für Psychologie/Journal of Psychology* **217**, 182–8.
Dosen, A. 1994: The European scene. In Bourras, N. (Ed.), *Mental health in mental retardation*. Cambridge: Cambridge University Press, 375–8.
Doyle, A.B. and Aboud, F.E. 1995: A longitudinal study of white children's racial prejudice as a social-cognitive development. *Merrill-Palmer Quarterly* **41**, 209–28.
Du, H., Li, X. and Lin, D. 2015: Individualism and sociocultural adaptation: discrimination and social capital as moderators among rural-to-urban migrants in China. *Asian Journal of Social Psychology* **18**, 176–81.
Dubow, E.F. and Cappas, C.L. 1988: Peer social status and reports of children's adjustment by their teachers, by their peers, and by their self-ratings. *Journal of School Psychology* **26**, 69–75.
Duck, S. 1991: Diaries and logs. In Montgomery, B.M. and Duck, S. (Eds.), *Studying interpersonal interaction*. New York: Plenum Press, 141–61.
Duck, S.W., Miell, D.K. and Gaebler, H.C. 1980: Attraction and communication in children's interactions. In Foot, H.C., Chapman, A.J. and Smith, R.J. (Eds.), *Friendship and social relations in children*. New York: Wiley, 89–115.
Dumas, J.E. and LaFrenière, P.J. 1993: Mother–child relationships as sources of support or stress: a comparison of competent, average, aggressive, and anxious dyads. *Child Development* **64**, 1732–54.
Dunbar, R. 2015: Social networks and their implications for community living for people with a learning disability. *International Journal of Developmental Disabilities* **61**, 101–6.
Dunifon, R. 2013: The influence of grandparents on the lives of children and adolescents. *Child Development Perspectives* **7**, 55–60.
Dunn, J. 1993: *Young children's close relationships: beyond attachment*. London: Sage.
Dijkstra, J.K., Lindenberg, S. and Veenstra, R. 2008: Beyond the class norm: bullying behavior of popular adolescents and its relation to peer acceptance and rejection. *Journal of Abnormal Child Psychology* **36**, 1289–99.

East, P.L. and Rook, K.S. 1992: Compensatory patterns of support among children's peer elationships: a test using school friends, nonschool friends, and siblings. *Developmental Psychology* **28**, 163–72.

Eccles, A.L., Bauman, E. and Rotenberg, K.J. 1989: Peer acceptance and self-esteem in gifted children. *Journal of Social Behaviour and Personality* **4**, 401–9.

Echols, L. and Graham, S. 2013: Birds of a *different* feather: how do cross-ethnic friends flock together? *Merrill-Palmer Quarterly* **59**, 461–88.

Edelstein, L.N. 1983: Maternal bereavement: coping with the unexpected death of a child. *Dissertation Abstracts International* **43**(10–b), 3356–7.

Eder, D. and Hallinan, M.T. 1978: Sex differences in children's friendships. *American Sociological Review* **43**, 237–50.

Ederer, E. 1990: Peer relations and depressed mood in children and early adolescents: a critical review of recent reviews. In Zapatoczeky, H.G. and Wenzel, T. (Eds.), *The scientific dialogue: from basic research to clinical intervention.* Annual series on European research in behaviour therapy. Amsterdam: Swets and Zeitlinger, vol. 5, 55–63.

Edwards, C.P. 1986: *Promoting social and moral development in young children: creative approaches for the classroom.* New York: Teachers College Press.

Edwards, C.P., de Guzman, M.R., Brown, J. and Kumru, A. 2006: Children's social behaviors and peer interactions in diverse cultures. In Chen, X., French, D. and Schneider, B. (Eds.), *Peer relationships in cultural context.* Cambridge, MA: Cambridge University Press, 23–51.

Eggum-Wilkens, N.D., Lemery-Chalfant, K., Aksan, N. and Goldsmith, H.H. 2015: Self-conscious shyness: growth during toddlerhood, strong role of genetics, and no prediction from fearful shyness. *Infancy* **20**, 160–88.

Eibl-Eibesfeldt, I. 1989: *Human ethology.* New York: Aldine de Gruyter.

Eisenberg, L. 1958: School phobia: a study in the communication of anxiety. *American Journal of Psychiatry* **114**, 712–18.

Eisenberg, M. 2008: The peer assumption: a review of *The Nurture Assumption. Journal of the Learning Sciences* **17**, 588–94.

Eisenberg, N., Fabes, R.A. and Murphy, B. 1996: Parents' reactions to children's negative emotions: relations to children's social competence and comforting behavior. *Child Development* **67**, 2227–4.

Eisenberg, N., Vaughan, J., French, D.C., Purwono, U. and Suryanti, T. 2009: The relations of majority/minority group status and having an other-religion friend to Indonesian youths' socioemotional functioning. *Developmental Psychology* **45**, 248–59.

Eisenberger, N.I. 2013: Why rejection hurts: the neuroscience of social pain. In DeWall, C.N. (Ed.), *The Oxford handbook of social exclusion.* New York: Oxford University Press, 152–62.

Elias, M. and Butler, L.B.B. 2005: *Social decision making/social problem solving: a curriculum for academic, social and emotional learning: Grades 2–3.* Champaign, IL: Research Press.

Elias, M.J., Zins, J.E., Weissberg, R.P., Frey, K.S., Greenberg, M.T., Haynes, N.M., Kessler, R., Schwab-Stone, M.E. and Shriver, T.P. 1997: *Promoting social and emotional learning: guidelines for educators.* Alexandria, VA: Association for Supervision and Curriculum Development.

Endedijk, H.M. and Cillessen, A.H.N. 2015: Computerized sociometric assessment for preschool children. *International Journal of Behavioral Development* **39**, 383–8.

Engfer, A. 1993: Antecedents and consequences of shyness in boys and girls: a 6-year longitudinal study. In Rubin, K.H. and Asendorf, J.B. (Eds.), *Social withdrawal, inhibition, and shyness in childhood*. Hillsdale, NJ: Lawrence Erlbaum Associates, 49–79.

Enright, D.J. and Rawlinson, D. (Eds.) 1992: *The Oxford book of friendship*. Oxford: Oxford University Press.

Entralgo, P.L. 1985: *Sobre la amistad* [About friendship]. Madrid: Austral.

Epley, N. and Schroeder, J. 2014: Mistakenly seeking solitude. *Journal of Experimental Psychology* **14**, 1980–9.

Epstein, J.L. 1989: The selection of friends: changes across the grades and in different classroom environments. In Berndt, T.J. and Ladd, G.W. (Eds.), *Peer relationships in child development*. New York: Wiley, 158–87.

Erdley, C.A., Nangle, D.W., Carpenter, M.E., Grover, R. and Newman, J.E. 1999: Children's friendship experiences as buffers to loneliness and depression. Paper presented at the biennial meeting of the Society for Research in Child Development, Albuquerque, NM, April.

Erdley, C.A., Nangle, D.W. and Gold, J.A. 1998: Operationalizing the construct of friendship among children: a psychometric comparison of sociometric-based definitional methodologies. *Social Development* **7**, 62–71.

Eron, L.D. and Huesmann, L.R. 1987: The stability of aggressive behaviour in cross-national comparisons. In Kagitcibasi, C. (Ed.), *Growth and progress in cross-cultural psychology*. Lisse: Swets, 207–18.

Eron, L.D., Walder, L.O., Toigo, R. and Lefkowitz, M.M. 1963: Social class, parental punishment for aggression, and child aggression. *Child Development* **34**, 849–67.

Ervin, R.A., Bankert, C.L. and DuPaul, G.J. 1996: Treatment of attention-deficit/hyperactivity disorder. In Reinecke, M.A., Dattilio, F.M. and Freeman, A. (Eds.), *Cognitive therapy with children and adolescents*. New York: Guilford, 38–61.

Erwin, P.G. 1985: Similarity of attitudes and constructs in children's friendships. *Journal of Experimental Child Psychology* **40**, 470–85.

Erwin, P.G. 1994: Social problem solving, social behaviour, and children's peer popularity. *Journal of Psychology* **128**, 299–306.

Espada, J.P., Griffin, K.W., Pereira, J.R., Orgiles, M. and Garcia-Fernandez, J.M. 2012: Component analysis of a school-based substance use prevention program in Spain: contributions of problem solving and social skills training content. *Prevention Science* **13**, 86–95.

Ettekal, I. and Ladd, G.W. 2015: Developmental pathways from childhood aggression: disruptiveness, chronic peer rejection, and deviant friendships to early-adolescent rule breaking. *Child Development* **86**, 614–31.

Evans, C.B.R., Fraser, M.W. and Cotter, K.L. 2014: The effectiveness of school-based bullying prevention programs: a systematic review. *Aggression and Violent Behavior* **19**, 532–44.

Farmer, T.W. and Farmer, E.M.Z. 1996: Social relationships of students with exceptionalities in mainstream classrooms: social networks and homophily. *Exceptional Children* **62**, 431–50.

Farmer, T.W., Hall, C.M., Leung, M.C., Estell, D. and Brooks, D. 2011: Social prominence and the heterogeneity of rejected status in late elementary school. *School Psychology Quarterly* **26**, 260–74.

Farver, J.M. 1996: Aggressive behaviour in preschoolers' social networks: do birds of a feather flock together? *Early Childhood Research Quarterly* **11**, 333–50.

Farver, J.M., Welles-Nyström, B., Frosch, D.L., Wibarti, S. and Hoppe-Graff, S. 1997: Toy stories: aggression in children's narratives in the United States, Sweden, Germany and Indonesia. *Journal of Cross-Cultural Psychology* **28**, 393–420.

Fehr, B. 1996: *Adult friendships*. Thousand Oaks, CA: Sage.

Feldman, E. and Dodge, K.A. 1987: Social information processing and sociometric status: sex, age, and situational effects. *Journal of Abnormal Child Psychology* **15**, 211–27.

Feldman, R., Masalha, S. and Derdikman-Eiron, R. 2010: Conflict resolution in the parent–child, marital, and peer contexts and children's aggression in the peer group: a process-oriented cultural perspective. *Developmental Psychology* **46**, 310–25.

Feldman, S.S., Rubenstein, J.L. and Rubin, C. 1988: Depressive affect and restraint in early adolescents: relationships with family structure, family process and friendship support. *Journal of Early Adolescence* **8**, 279–96.

Feldman, S.S. and Wentzel, K.R. 1990: The relationship between parenting styles, sons' self-restraint, and peer relations in early adolescence. *Journal of Applied Developmental Psychology* **12**, 205–18.

Felson, R.B. and Russo, N. 1988: Parental punishment and sibling aggression. *Social Psychology Quarterly* **51**, 11–18.

Fenzel, M.L. and Blyth, D.A. 1986: Individual adjustment to school transition: an exploration of the role of supportive peer relations. *Journal of Early Adolescence* **6**, 315–29.

Ferrans, S.D. and Selman, R.L. 2014: How students' perceptions of the school climate influence their choice to upstand, bystand, or join perpetrators of bullying. *Harvard Educational Review* **84**, 162–87.

Fiasse, C. and Nader-Grosbois, N. 2012: Perceived social acceptance, theory of mind and social adjustment in children with intellectual disabilities. *Research in Developmental Disabilities* **33**, 1871–80.

Filcheck, H.A. and McNeil, C.B. 2004: The use of token economies in preschool classrooms: practical and philosophical concerns. *Journal of Early and Intensive Behavior Intervention* **1**, 94–104.

Finnie, V. and Russell, A. 1988: Preschool children's social status and their mothers' behavior and knowledge in the supervisory role. *Developmental Psychology* **24**, 789–801.

Fiske, S.T. and Taylor, S.E. 1991: *Social cognition*. New York: McGraw-Hill.

Fite, P.J., Raine, A., Stouthamer-Loeber, M., Loeber, R. and Pardini, D.A. 2010: Reactive and proactive aggression in adolescent males. *Criminal Justice and Behavior* **37**, 141–57.

Flanagan, K.S., Vanden Hoek, K.K., Ranter, J.M. and Reich, H.A. 2012: The potential of forgiveness as a response for coping with negative peer experiences. *Journal of Adolescence* **35**, 1215–23.

Flashman, J. and Gambetta, D. 2014: Thick as thieves: homophily and trust among deviants. *Rationality and Society* **26**, 3–45.

Fletcher, G., Simpson, J.A., Campbell, L. and Overall, A. 2013: *The science of intimate relationships*. Hoboken, NJ: Wiley-Blackwell.

Flicek, M. and Landau, S. 1985: Social status problems of learning disabled and hyperactive/learning disabled boys. *Journal of Clinical Child Psychology* **14**, 340–4.

Fontaine, N., Carbonneau, R., Barker, E.D., Vitaro, F., Hebert, M., Cote, S.M., Nagin, D.S., Zoccolillo, M. and Tremblay, R.E. 2008: Girls' hyperactivity and physical aggression during childhood and adjustment problems in early adulthood: a 15-year longitudinal study. *Archives of General Psychiatry* **65**, 320–8.

Fonzi, A., Tomada, G. and Ciucci, E. 1994: Uso di indici informativi nell'interazione tra bambini del nido [Use of informative indexes in the interaction among crèche children]. *Eta Evolutiva* **47**, 5–13.

Fonzi, A.F., Genta, M.L., Menesini, E., Bacchini, D., Bonino, S. and Costabile, A. 1999: Italy. In Smith, P.K., Morita, Y., Junger-Tas, J., Olweus, D., Catalano, R. and Slee, P. (Eds.), *The nature of school bullying: a cross-national perspective.* New York: Routledge, 140–56.

Fonzi, A.F., Schneider, B.H., Tani, F. and Tomada, G. 1997: Predicting the continuation of children's friendship from their behavior in structured situations of potential conflict. *Child Development* **68**, 496–506.

Ford, M.E. 1982: Social cognition and social competence in adolescence. *Developmental Psychology* **18**, 323–40.

Forgatch, M.S. and Patterson, G.R. 1998: Behavioral family therapy. In Dattilio, F.M. (Ed.), *Case studies in couple and family therapy: systemic and cognitive perspectives.* The Guilford family therapy series. New York: Guilford Press, 85–107.

Fornari, G. 1966: *Psicanalisi della guerra* [Psychoanalysis of war]. Milan: Feltrinelli.

Foster, E.M. 2010: Costs and effectiveness of the Fast Track intervention for antisocial behavior. *Journal of Mental Health Policy and Economics* **13**, 101–19.

Foster, S.L., Bell-Dolan, D. and Berler, E.S. 1986: Methodological issues in the use of sociometrics for selecting children for social skills training. *Advances in the Behavioural Assessment of Children and Families* **2**, 227–48.

Foster, S.L. and Ritchey, W. 1979: Issues in the assessment of social competence in children. *Journal of Applied Behaviour Analysis* **12**, 625–38.

Fowler, J.H., Settle, J.E. and Christakis, N.A. 2011: Correlated genotypes in friendship networks. *PNAS Proceedings of the National Academy of Sciences of the United States of America* **108**, 1993–7.

Fowler, S. 1988: The effects of peer-mediated interventions on establishing, maintaining, and generalizing children's behaviour changes. In Horner, R., Dunlop, G. and Koegel, R. (Eds.), *Generalization and maintenance.* Baltimore, MD: Paul H. Brookes, 143–70.

Fox, N.A., Calkins, S.D. and Stewart, S.L. 1994: Being alone, playing alone, and acting alone: distinguishing among reticence, and passive, and active solitude in young children. *Child Development* **65**, 129–37.

Foxx, R.M. 2013: The maintenance of behavioral change: the case for long-term follow-ups. *American Psychologist* **68**, 728–36.

Franz, D.Z. and Gross, A.M. 1996: Parental correlates of socially neglected, rejected and average children: a laboratory study. *Behavior Modification* **20**, 170–82.

Frazee, H.E. 1953: Children who later became schizophrenic. *Smith College Studies in Social Work* **23**, 125–49.

Frazier, S.L., Atkins, M.S., Hess Olson, L. and Lyon, A.R. 2009: Same-sex and other-sex peer reports: unique contributors to understanding children's school adjustment. *Journal of Psychopathology and Behavioral Assessment* **31**, 152–8.

Frederickson, N.L. and Furnham, A.F. 1998: Sociometric classification methods in school peer groups: a comparative investigation. *Journal of Child Psychology and Psychiatry and Allied Disciplines* **39**, 921–33.

Freeman, H., Newland, L.A. and Coyl, D.D. 2010: New directions in father attachment. *Early Child Development and Care* **180**, 1–8.

French, D.C. 1988: Heterogeneity of peer-rejected boys: aggressive and nonaggressive subtypes. *Child Development* **59**, 976–85.

French, D.C. 1990: Heterogeneity of peer-rejected girls. *Child Development* **61**, 2028–31.

French, D.C., Lee, O. and Pidada, S.U. 2006: Friendships of Indonesian, South Korean, and US youth: exclusivity, intimacy, enhancement of worth, and conflict. In Chen, X., French, D. and Schneider, B.H. (Eds.), *Peer relationships in cultural context.* New York: Cambridge University Press, 379–402.

French, D.C., Pidada, S., Denoma, J., McDonald, K. and Lawton, A. 2005: Reported peer conflicts of children in the United States and Indonesia. *Social Development* **14**, 458–72.

French, D.C., Pidada, S. and Victor, A. 2005: Friendships of Indonesian and United States youth. *International Journal of Behavioral Development* **29**, 304–13.

French, D.C., Setiono, K. and Eddy, J.M. 1999: Bootstrapping through the cultural comparison minefield: childhood social status and friendship in the United States and Indonesia. In Collins, W.A. and Laursen, B. (Eds.), *Relationships as developmental contexts: the Minnesota symposia on child psychology*. Mahwah, NJ: Lawrence Erlbaum Associates, vol. 30, 109–31.

Freud, S. 1920: *A general introduction to psychoanalysis*. New York: Boni and Liveright.

Frones, I. 1995: *Among peers: on the meaning of peers in the process of socialization*. Cambridge, MA: Scandinavian Universities Press.

Frude, N. 1993: Hatred between children. In Varma, V. (Ed.), *How and why children hate*. London: Kingsley, 72–93.

Fry, D.P. 1988: Intercommunity differences in aggression among Zapotec children. *Child Development* **59**, 1008–19.

Fryxell, D. and Kennedy, C.H. 1995: Placement along the continuum of services and its impact on students' social relationships. *Journal of the Association for Persons with Severe Handicaps* **20**, 259–69.

Furfey, P.H. 1928: *The gang age: a study of the preadolescent boy and his recreational needs*. New York: Macmillan.

Furman, W. 1996: The measurement of friendship perceptions: conceptual and methodological issues. In Bukowski, W.M., Newcomb, A.F. and Hartup, W.W. (Eds.), *The company they keep: friendship in childhood and adolescence*. Cambridge: Cambridge University Press, 41–65.

Furman, W. and Bierman, K.L. 1983: Developmental changes in young children's conceptions of friendship. *Child Development* **54**, 549–56.

Furman, W. and Buhrmester, D. 1985: Children's perceptions of the personal relationships in their social networks. *Developmental Psychology* **21**, 1016–24.

Furnam, W. and Robbins, P. 1985: What's the point? Issues in the selection of treatment objectives. In Schneider, B.H., Rubin, K. and Ledingham, J.E. (Eds.), *Children's peer relations: issues in assessment and intervention*. New York: Springer-Verlag, 141–54.

Furnham, A. and Gibbs, M. 1984: School children's attitudes towards the handicapped. *Journal of Adolescence* **7**, 99–117.

Galdston, I. 1965: Community psychiatry: its social and historic derivations. *Journal of the Canadian Psychiatric Association* **10**, 461–73.

Gallagher, E., Huth-Bocks, A. and Schmitt, T. 2015: The impact of mothers' relationship quality and parenting on children's peer relationships. *Journal of Family Issue* **36**, 421–42.

Galloway, B. and Porath, M. 1997: Parent and teacher views of gifted children's social abilities. *Roeper Review* **20**, 118–21.

García, C., Rivera, N. and Greenfield. P.N. 2015: The decline of cooperation, the rise of competition: developmental effects of long-term social change in Mexico. *International Journal of Psychology* **50**, 6–11.

Garmezy, N. 1989: The role of competence in the study of children and adolescents under stress. In Schneider, B.H., Attili, G., Nadel, J. and Weissberg, R.D. (Eds.), *Social competence in developmental perspective*. NATO Science Institutes series. Series D: Behavioural and social sciences. Dordrecht: Kluwer Academic Publishers, vol. 51, 25–39.

Garandeau, C.F., Wilson, T. and Rodkin, P.C. 2010: The popularity of elementary school bullies in gender and racial context. In Jimerson, S.R., Swearer, S.M. and Espelage, D.L. (Eds.), *The handbook of bullying in schools: an international perspective*. New York: Routledge, 119–36.

Garret, M.K. and Crump, W.D. 1980: Peer acceptance, teacher preference and self-appraisal of social status among learning disabled students. *Learning Disability Quarterly* **3**, 42–8.

Gazelle, H. 2008: Behavioral profiles of anxious solitary children and heterogeneity in peer relations. *Developmental Psychology* **44**, 1604–24.

Gazelle, H. 2013: Is social anxiety in the child or in the anxiety-provoking nature of the child's interpersonal environment? *Child Development Perspectives* **7**, 221–6.

Gazelle, H., Faldowski, R.A. and Peter, D. 2015: Using peer sociometrics and behavioral nominations with young children. In Saracho, O.N. (Ed.), *Handbook of research methods in early childhood education: review of research methodologies*. Charlotte, NC: IAP Information Age Publishing, vol. 1, 27–69.

Gazelle, H., Putallaz, M., Li, Y., Grimes, C.L., Kupersmidt, J. and Coie, J.D. 2005: Anxious solitude across contexts: girls' interactions with familiar and unfamiliar peers. *Child Development* **76**, 227–46.

Gelb, R. and Jacobson, J.L. 1988: Popular and unpopular children's interactions during cooperative and competitive peer group activities. *Journal of Abnormal Child Psychology* **16**, 247–61.

Genta, M.L., Menesini, E., Fonzi, A., Constable, A. and Smith, P.K. 1996: Bullies and victims in schools in central and southern Italy. *European Journal of Psychology of Education* **11**, 97–110.

Georgas, J., Christakopoulou, S., Poortinga, Y.H., Angleitner, A., Goodwin, R. and Charalambous, N. 1997: The relationship of family bonds to family structure and function across cultures. *Journal of Cross-Cultural Psychology* **28**, 303–20.

Gesell, A. and Ilg, F.L. 1943: *Infant and child in the culture of today*. New York: Harper.

Gest, S.D. 1997: Behavioural inhibitions: stability and associations with adaptation from childhood to early adulthood. *Journal of Personality and Social Psychology* **72**, 467–75.

Ginsberg, D., Gottman, J.M. and Parker, J.G. 1986: The importance of friendship. In Gottman, J.M. and Parker, J.G. (Eds.), *Conversations of friends: speculations on affective development*. Cambridge: Cambridge University Press, 3–48.

Ginter, E.J., Lufi, D., Trotzky, A.S. and Richmond, B.O. 1989: Anxiety among children in Israel. *Psychological Reports* **65**, 803–9.

Girard, M. and Mullet, E. 2012: Development of the forgiveness schema in adolescence. *Universitas Psychologica* **11**, 1235–44.

Glick, B. and Gibbs, J.C. 2011: *Aggression replacement training*. 3rd Edition. Champaign, IL: Research Press.

Godbold, E., Vance, M., Chenier, J. *et al.* 2010: Evidence-based social skills interventions: what really works. Symposium presented at the annual meeting of the National Association of School Psychologists, Chicago, February.

Godleski, S.A., Kamper, K.E., Ostrov, J.M., Hart, E.J. and Blakely-McClure, S.J. 2015: Peer victimization and peer rejection during early childhood. *Journal of Clinical Child and Adolescent Psychology* **44**, 380–92.

Goldbeck, L. 1998: Die familiäre Bewältigung einer Krebserkrankung im Kindes- und Jugendalter. Möglichkeiten der standardisierten Erfassung mit Selbstbeurteilungsverfahren: Ergebnisse einer empirischen Vorstudie [Families coping with cancer during childhood and adolescence: practicability of standardized self-assessment methods]. *Praxis der Kinderpsychologie und Kinderpsychiatrie* **47**, 552–73.

Gomez, R. 2014: Correlated trait-correlated method minus one analysis of the convergent and discriminant validities of the Strengths and Difficulties Questionnaire. *Assessment* **21**, 372–82.

Gommans, R. and Cillessen, A.H.N. 2015: Nominating under constraints: a systematic comparison of unlimited and limited peer nomination methodologies in elementary school. *International Journal of Behavioral Development* **39**, 77–86.

Goodlad, S. and Hirst, B. (Eds.) 1990: *Explorations in peer tutoring*. Oxford: Blackwell.

Goodwin, R. 2009: *Changing relations: achieving intimacy in a time of social transition*. New York: Cambridge University Press.

Goodwin, S. 1990: *Community care and the future of mental-health service provision*. Aldershot: Avebury.

Gordon, J.E. and Smith, E. 1965: Children's aggression, parental attitudes, and the effects of an affiliation-arousing story. *Journal of Personality and Social Psychology* **1**, 654–9.

Gottlieb, B.W., Gottlieb, J., Berkell, D. and Levy, L. 1986: Sociometric status and solitary play of learning disabled boys and girls. *Journal of Learning Disabilities* **19**, 619–22.

Gottlieb, J., Semmel, M.I. and Veldman, D.J. 1978: Correlates of social status among mainstreamed mentally retarded children. *Journal of Educational Psychology* **70**, 396–405.

Gottman, J.M. 1983: How children become friends. *Monographs of the Society for Research in Child Development* **48**, Serial No. 201.

Goudena, P. and Sánchez, J.A. 1996: Peer interaction in Andalusia and Holland: a comparative study. *Infancia y Aprentizaje* **75**, 49–58.

Gray, N.J., Klein, J.D., Noyce, P.R., Sessellberg, T.S. and Cantrill, J.A. 2005: Health information-seeking behaviour in adolescence: the place of the internet. *SocialScience and Medicine* **60**, 1467–78.

Grayling, A.C. 2013: *Friendship*. New Haven, CT: Yale University Press.

Green, K.D., Vosk, B. and Beck, S. 1981: An examination of differences among psychometrically identified accepted, rejected, and neglected children. *Child Study Journal* **11**, 117–24.

Greenspan, S.I. 1981: *Psychopathology and adaptation in infancy and early childhood*. New York: International University Press.

Greenwood, C., Carta, J. and Kamps, D. 1990: Teacher-mediated versus peer-mediated instruction: a review of educational advantages and disadvantages. In Foot, H.C., Morgan, M.J. and Shute, R.H. (Eds.), *Children helping children*. New York: John Wiley and Sons, 177–205.

Greene, R.W., Biederman, J., Faraone, S.V., Monuteaux, M.C., Mick, E., DuPre, E.P., Fine, C.S. and Goring, J.G. 2001: Social impairment in girls with ADHD: patterns, gender comparisons, and correlates. *Journal of the American Academy of Child and Adolescent Psychiatry* **40**, 704–10.

Gresham, F.M. 1981: Assessment of children's social skills. *Journal of School Psychology* **19**, 120–33.

Gresham, F.M. 1982: Misguided mainstreaming: the case for social skills training with handicapped children. *Exceptional Children* **48**, 422–33.

Gresham, F.M. 1986: Conceptual and definitional issues in the assessment of children's social skills: implications for classification and training. *Journal of Clinical Child Psychology* **15**, 3–15.

Gresham, F.M. 2011: Social behavior assessment and intervention: observations and impressions. *School Psychology Review* **40**, 275–83.

Gresham, F.M. and Elliott, S.N. 2014: Social skills assessment and intervention in emotional and behavioral disorders. In Walker, H.M. and Gresham, F.M. (Eds.), *Handbook of evidence based practices for addressing school related behavioral disorders.* New York: Guilford, 152–72.

Gresham, F.M., Elliott, S.N., Vance, M.J. and Cook, C.R. 2011: Comparability of the social skills rating system to the social skills improvement system: content and psychometric comparisons across elementary and secondary age levels. *School Psychology Quarterly* **26**, 27–44.

Gresham, F.M. and Reschly, D.J. 1986: Social skills deficits and low peer acceptance of mainstreamed learning disabled children. *Learning Disability Quarterly* **9**, 23–32.

Gresham, F.M. and Reschly, D.J. 1987: Differences between mildly handicapped and nonhandicapped black and white children. *Journal of Educational Psychology* **79**, 195–7.

Gresham, F.M., Vance, M.J. and Chenier, J. 2013: Improving academic achievement with social skills. In Hattie, J. and Anderman, E.M. (Eds.), *International guide to student achievement.* New York: Routledge/Taylor and Francis, 327–8.

Grotpeter, J.K. and Crick, N.R. 1996: Relational aggression, overt aggression, and friendship. *Child Development* **67**, 2328–38.

Grusec, J.E. and Lytton, H. 1988: *Social development: history, theory, and research.* New York: Springer-Verlag.

Guadagno, R.E., Okdie, B.M. and Eno, C.A. 2008: Who blogs? Personality predictors of blogging. *Computers in Human Behavior* **24**, 441–9.

Gudykunst, W.B. 2003: Intercultural communication theories. In: Gudykunst, W.B. (Ed.), *Cross-cultural and intercultural communication.* Thousand Oaks, CA: Sage, 167–89.

Gudykunst, W.B. and Ting-Toomey, S. 1988: *Culture and interpersonal communication.* Newbury Park, CA: Sage.

Guerra, N.C. and Slaby, R.C. 1989: Evaluative factors in problem solving by aggressive boys. *Journal of Abnormal Child Psychology* **17**, 277–89.

Gummerum, M. and Keller, M. 2008: Affection, virtue, pleasure and profit: developing an understanding of friendship closeness and intimacy in Western and Asian societies. *International Journal of Behavioral Development* **32**, 218–31.

Gummerum, M. and Keller, M. 2012: East German children's and adolescents' moral reasoning before and after German reunification. *Journal of Genetic Psychology* **17**, 440–62.

Gumpel, T. and Frank, R. 1999: An expansion of the peer paradigm: cross-age peer tutoring of social skills among socially rejected boys. *Journal of Applied Behavior Analysis* **32**, 115–18.

Gupta, T., Way, N., McGill, R.K., Hughes, D., Santos, C., Jia, Y., Yoshikawa, H., Chen, X. and Deng, H. 2013: Gender-typed behaviors in friendships and well-being: a cross-cultural study of Chinese and American boys. *Journal of Research on Adolescence* **23**, 57–68.

Haar, B.F. and Krahé, B. 1999: Strategies for resolving interpersonal conflicts in adolescence: a German–Indonesian comparison. *Journal of Cross-Cultural Psychology* **30**, 667–83.

Hafen, C.A., Allen, J.P., Schad, M.M. and Hessel, E.T. 2015: Conflict with friends, relationship blindness, and the pathway to adult disagreeableness. *Personality and Individual Differences* **81**, 7–12.

Hafen, C.A., Laursen, B., Burk, W.J., Kerr, M. and Stattin, H. 2013: Homophily in stable and unstable adolescent friendships: similarity breeds constancy. *Personality and Individual Differences* **51**, 607–12.

Hafen, C.A., Laursen, B., Nurmi, J. and Salmela-Aro, K. 2013: Bullies, victims, and antipathy: the feeling is mutual. *Journal of Abnormal Child Psychology* **41**, 801–9.

Hagekull, B. and Bohlin, G. 1998: Preschool temperament and environmental factors related to the five-factor model of personality in middle childhood. *Merrill-Palmer Quarterly* **44**, 194–215.

Halberstadt, A.G., Denham, S.A. and Dunsmore, J.C. 2001: Affective social competence. *Social Development* **10**: 79–119.

Hall, E.T. 1976: *Beyond culture*. New York: Doubleday.

Hall, J.A. 2011: Sex differences in friendship expectations: a meta-analysis. *Journal of Social and Personal Relationships* **28**, 723–47.

Hallinan, M.T. and Smith, S.S. 1985: The effects of classroom racial composition on students' interracial friendliness. *Social Psychology Quarterly* **48**, 3–16.

Hallinan, M.T. and Williams, R.A. 1987: The stability of students' interracial friendships. *American Sociological Review* **52**, 653–64.

Hamburger, Y.A. and Ben-Artzi, E. 2000: The relationship between extraversion andneuroticism and the different uses of the internet. *Computers in Human Behaviour* **16**, 441–9.

Hamm, J.V., Brown, B.B. and Heck, D.J. 2005: Bridging the ethnic divide: student and school characteristics in African American, Asian American, European American, and Latino adolescents' cross-ethnic friend nomination. *Journal of Research on Adolescence* **15**, 21–46.

Han, H.S. and Kemple, K.M. 2006: Components of social competence and strategies of social support: considering what to teach and how. *Early Childhood Education Journal* **34**, 241–6.

Han, P., Song, P. and Wang, L. 2015: Achieving semiparametric efficiency bound in longitudinal data analysis with dropouts. *Journal of Multivariate Analysis* **135**, 59–70.

Hare, A.P. and Hare, J.R. 1996: *J.L. Moreno*. London: Sage Publications.

Hareven, T.K. 1989: Historical changes in children's networks in the family and community. In Belle, D. (Ed.), *Children's social networks and social supports*. New York: Wiley, 15–36.

Hargreaves, D. 1967: *Social relations in a secondary school*. London: Routledge.

Hari, R., Himberg, T., Nummenmaa, L., Hamalainen, M. and Parkkonen, L. 2013: Synchrony of brains and bodies during implicit interpersonal interaction. *Trends in Cognitive Sciences* **17**, 105–6.

Harkin, J. 2003: *Mobilisation: the growing public interest in mobile technology*. London: Demos.

Harralson, T.L. and Lawler, K.A. 1992: The relationship of parenting styles and social competency to Type A behaviour in children. *Journal of PsychosomaticResearch* **36**, 625–34.

Harris, J.R. 1998: *The nurture assumption: why children turn out the way they do*. New York: Free Press.

Harrison, A.O., Stewart, R.B., Myambo, K. and Teveraishe, C. 1995: Perceptions of social networks among adolescents from Zimbabwe and the United States. *Journal of Black Psychology* **21**, 382–407.

Harrist, A.W. 1992: Synchronous and nonsynchronous parent–child interaction: relations with children's later competence with peers [CD-ROM]. Abstract from: ProQuest File: *Dissertation Abstracts* Item: 9212750.

Hart, C.H., DeWolf, M. and Burts, D.C. 1993: Parental disciplinary strategies and preschoolers' play behavior in playground settings. In Hart, C.H. (Ed.), *Children on playgrounds: research perspectives and applications*. Albany, NY: State University of New York Press, 271–313.

Hart, C.H., DeWolf, D.M., Wozniak, P. and Burts, D.C. 1992: Maternal and paternal disciplinary styles: relations with preschoolers' playground behavioral orientations and peer status. *Child Development* **63**, 872–92.

Hart, C.H., Ladd, G.W. and Burleson, B.R. 1990: Children's expectations of the outcomes of social strategies: relations with sociometric status and maternal disciplinary styles. *Child Development* **61**, 127–37.

Hart, C.H., Nelson, D.A., Robinson, C.C., Olsen, S.F. and McNeilly-Choque, M.K. 1998a: Overt and relational aggression in Russian nursery-school-age children: parenting style and marital linkages. *Developmental Psychology* **34**, 687–97.

Hart, C.H., Robinson, C.C., Nelson, D.A., Porter, C. and Nelson, L.J. 1998b: Subtypes of aggression and victimization in Russian preschoolers: linkages with parenting and family processes. Paper presented at the International Society for the Study of Behavioral Development, Berne, Switzerland, July.

Hart, C.H., Yang, C., Nelson, L.J., Robinson, C.C., Olsen, J.A. and Nelson, D.A. 2000: Peer acceptance in early childhood and subtypes of socially withdrawn behavior in China, Russia and the United States. *International Journal of Behavioral Development* **24**, 73–81.

Hart, C.H., Young, C., Nelson, D.A., Jin, S., Bazarskaya, N., Nelson, L., Wu, X. and Wu, P. 1999: Peer contact patterns, parenting practices, and preschoolers' social competence in China, Russia, and the United States. In Slee, P.T. and Rigby, K. (Eds.), *Children's peer relations.* London: Routledge, 3–30.

Hartshorne, H. and May, M. 1928: *Studies in deceit.* New York: Macmillan.

Hartup, W.W. 1989: Behavioural manifestations of children's friendships. In Berndt, T.J. and Ladd, G.W. (Eds.), *Peer relationships in child development.* New York: Wiley, 46–70.

Hartup, W.W. 1992: Conflict and friendship relations. In Shantz, C.U. and Hartup, W.W. (Eds.), *Conflict in child and adolescent development.* Cambridge studies in social and emotional development. New York: Cambridge University Press, 186–215.

Hartup, W.W. 1995: The three faces of friendship. *Journal of Social and Personal Relationships* **12**, 569–74.

Hartup, W.W. 1996: The company they keep: friendships and their developmental significance. *Child Development* **67**, 1–13.

Hartup, W.W., French, D.C., Laursen, B., Johnston, M.K. and Ogawa, J.R. 1993: Conflict and friendship relations in a closed-field situation. *Child Development* **64**, 445–54.

Hartup, W.W. and Stevens, N. 1997: Friendships and adaptation in the life course. *Psychological Bulletin* **121**, 355–70.

Hatfield, E., Utne, M.K. and Traupmann, J. 1979: Equity theory and intimate relationships. In Burgess, R.L. and Huston, T.L. (Eds.), *Social exchange in developing relationships.* New York: Academic Press, 99–133.

Hawley, P. 2003: Strategies of control, aggression, and morality in preschoolers: an evolutionary perspective. *Journal of Experimental Child Psychology* **85**, 213–35.

Hawkins, J.D., Catalano, R.F., Morrison, D.M., O'Donnell, J., Abbott, R.D. and Day, L.E. 1992: The Seattle Social Development Project: effects of the first four years on protective factors and problem behaviors. In McCord, J. and Tremblay, R. (Eds.), *The prevention of antisocial behavior in children.* New York: Guilford, 139–61.

Hayat, Z. and Amichai-Hamburger, Y. 2013: Kids in the fast lane: achieving well-being through on-line support. In Costabile, A. and Spears, B. (Eds.), *The impact of technology on relationships in educational settings.* New York: Routledge, 102–16.

Hayes, D.S., Gershman, E. and Bolin, L.J. 1980: Friends and enemies: cognitive bases for preschool children's unilateral and reciprocal relationships. *Child Development* **51**, 1276–9.

Hayes, D.S., Gershman, E.S. and Halteman, W. 1996: Enmity in males at four developmental levels: cognitive bases for disliking peers. *Journal of Genetic Psychology* **157**, 153–60.

Haynie, D.L., Doogan, N.J. and Soller, B. 2014: Gender, friendship networks, and delinquency: a dynamic network approach. *Criminology* **52**, 688–722.

Hayvren, M. and Hymel, S. 1984: Ethical issues in sociometric testing: impact of sociometric measures on interaction behavior. *Developmental Psychology* **20**, 844–9.

Hazen, N.L., McFarland, L., Jacobvitz, D. and Boyd-Soisson, E. 2010: Fathers' frightening behaviours and sensitivity with infants: relations with fathers' attachment representations, father–infant attachment, and children's later outcomes. *Early Child Development and Care* **180**, 51–69.

Healy, K., Sanders, M. and Iyer, A. 2015: Parenting practices, children's peer relationships and being bullied at school. *Journal of Child and Family Studies* **24**, 127–40.

Heflin, A.H. 1989: An exploration of links between parental nurturance and control and children's sociometric status [CD-ROM]. Abstract from: ProQuest File: *Dissertation Abstracts* Item: 8823429.

Heine, S.J. 2012: *Cultural psychology*. 2nd Edition. New York: Norton.

Hektner, J., Schmidt, J. and Csikszentmihalyi, M. 2007: *Experience sampling method: measuring the quality of everyday life*. Thousand Oaks, CA: Sage.

Henderson, L., Zimbardo, P., Smith, C. and Buell, S. 1999: *Shyness and technology use in high school students*. Palo Alto, CA: Psychology Department, Stanford University.

Henggeler, S.W., Edwards, J.J., Cohen, R. and Summerville, M.B. 1991: Predicting changes in children's popularity: the role of family relations. *Journal of Applied Developmental Psychology* **12**, 205–18.

Herring, S.C., Scheidt, L.A., Wright, E. and Bonus, S. 2005: Weblogs as a bridging genre. *Information, Technology and People* **18**, 142–71.

Hertz-Lazarowitz, R. 1995: Understanding interactive behaviours: looking at six mirrors of the classroom. In Hertz-Lazarovitz, R. and Miller, N. (Eds.), *Interaction in cooperative groups: the theoretical anatomy of group learning*. New York: Cambridge University Press, 71–101.

Hertz-Lazarowitz, R., Fuchs, I., Sharabany, R. and Eisenberg, N. 1989: Students' interactive and noninteractive behaviours in the classroom: a comparison between two types of classrooms in the city and the kibbutz in Israel. *Contemporary Educational Psychology* **14**, 22–32.

Hewitt, J.P. 1998: *The myth of self-esteem*. New York: St. Martin's Press.

Hewstone, M., Bond, M.H. and Wan, K. 1983: Social facts and social attributions: the explanation of intergroup differences in Hong Kong. *Social Cognition* **2**,142–57.

Heyman, G.D., Genyue, F. and Lee, K. 2008: Reasoning about the disclosure of success and failure to friends among children in the United States and China. *Developmental Psychology* **44**, 908–18.

Hillier, L., Mitchell, K.J. and Ybarra, M.L. 2012: The internet as a safety net: findings from a series of online focus groups with LGB and non-LGB young people in the United States. *Journal of LGBT Youth* **9**, 225–46.

Hinde, R.A. 1979: *Towards understanding relationships*. London: Academic Press.

Hinde, R.A. 1988: Continuities and discontinuities: conceptual issues and methodological considerations. In Rutter, M. (Ed.), *Studies of psychosocial risk: the power of longitudinal data*. Cambridge: Cambridge University Press, 367–83.

Hirshfeld, D.R., Rosenbaum, J.F., Biederman, J., Bolduc, E.A., Faraone, S.V., Snidman, N., Reznick, J.S. and Kagan, J. 1992: Stable behavioural inhibition and its association with anxiety disorder. *Journal of American Academic Child Adolescent Psychiatry* **31**, 103–11.

Hodge, R.L. 1989: *A myriad of values: a brief history*. ERIC Document Reproduction Service No. ED 307 218.

Hodgens, J.B. and McCoy, J.F. 1989: Distinctions among rejected children on the basis of peer-nominated aggression. *Journal of Clinical Child Psychology* **18**, 121–8.

Hofman, P. 1985: Aperçus de la prise en charge educative [General survey on educational handling]. *Neuropsychiatrie de l'Enfance et de l'Adolescence* **33**, 37–42.

Hofstede, G. 1979: Value systems in forty countries. In Eckensberger, L., Lonner, W. and Poortinga, Y. (Eds.), *Cross-cultural contributions to psychology*. Lisse: Swets and Zeitlinger, 398–407.

Hofstede, G. 1980: *Culture's consequences: international differences in work-related values*. Beverly-Hills, CA: Sage.

Hofstede, G. 1983: Dimensions of national cultures in fifty countries and three regions. In Deregowski, J., Dzuirawiec, S. and Annis, R. (Eds.), *Explications in cross-cultural psychology*. Lisse: Swets and Zeitlinger, 335–55.

Hofstede, G. 1984: The cultural relativity of the quality of life concept. *Academy of Management Review* **9**, 389–98.

Hofstede, G. 1991: *Cultures and organization: software on the mind*. London: McGraw-Hill.

Hofstede, G. 2003: *Culture's consequences: comparing values, behaviors, institutions and organization across nations*. 2nd Edition. Thousand Oaks, CA: Sage Publications.

Hogan, S. and Prater, M.A. 1998: The effects of peer tutoring and self-management on on-task, academic, and disruptive behaviours. *Behavioral Disorders* **18**, 118–28.

Hollander, E. 1958: Conformity, status, and idiosyncrasy credit. *Psychological Review* **65**, 117–27.

Holly, A.F. and McNeil, C.B. 2004: The use of token economies in preschool classrooms: practical and philosophical concerns. *Journal of Early and Intensive Behavioral Intervention* **1**, 91–104.

Hops, H., Davis, B. and Longoria, N. 1995: Methodological issues in direct observation: illustrations with the living in familial environments (LIFE) coding system. *Journal of Clinical Child Psychology* **24**, 193–203.

Horowitz, E.C. 1981: Popularity, decentering ability and role-taking skills in learning disabled and normal children. *Learning Disability Quarterly* **4**, 23–30.

Hortaçsu, N. 1994: Parents' education level, popularity, individual cognitions, and academic performance: an investigation with Turkish children. *Journal of Genetic Psychology* **155**, 179–89.

Howes, C. 1983: Patterns of friendship. *Child Development* **54**, 1041–53.

Howes, C. 1988: *Peer interaction of young children*. Monographs of the Society for Research in Young Children, 53 Serial No. 217.

Howes, C. 1996: The earliest friendships. In Bukowski, W.M., Newcomb, A.F. and Hartup, W.W. (Eds.), *The company they keep: friendship in childhood and adolescence*. New York: Cambridge University Press, 66–86.

Howes, C. 2009: Friendship in early childhood. In Rubin, K.H., Bukowski, W.M. and Laursen, B. (Eds.), *Handbook of peer interactions, relationships, and groups*. New York: Guilford, 180–94.

Howes, C. and Farver, J. 1987: Toddlers' responses to the distress of their peers. *Journal of Applied Developmental Psychology* **8**, 441–52.

Howes, C. and Phillipsen, L.C. 1992: Gender and friendship: relations within peer groups of young children. *Social Development* **1**, 231–42.

Howes, C. and Wu, F. 1990: Peer interactions and friendships in an ethnically diverse school setting. *Child Development* **61**, 537–41.

Hoyle, S.G. and Serafica, F.C. 1988: Peer status of children with and without learning disabilities: a multimethod study. *Learning Disability Quarterly* **11**, 322–32.

Hoza, B., Molina, B.S.G., Bukowski, W.M. and Sippola, L.K. 1995: Peer variables as predictors of later childhood adjustment. *Development and Psychopathology* **7**, 787–802.

Hubbard, J.A., Parker, E.H., Ramsden, S.R. *et al.* 2004: The relations among observational, physiological, and self-report measures of children's anger. *Social Development* **13**, 14–39.

Huesmann, L.R., Eron, L.D. and Warnick Yarmel, P. 1987: Intellectual functioning and aggression. *Journal of Personality and Social Psychology* **53**, 232–40.

Huesmann, L.R. and Guerra, N.G. 1997: Children's normative beliefs about aggression and aggressive behaviour. *Journal of Personality and Social Psychology* **72**, 408–19.

Huesmann, L.R., Lagerspetz, K. and Eron, L.D. 1984: Intervening variables in the TV violence–aggression relation: evidence from two countries. *Developmental Psychology* **20**, 746–75.

Huffaker, D. 2004: The educated blogger: using weblogs to promote literacy in the classroom. *First Monday* **9**. www.firstmonday.dk/issues/issue9_6/huffaker/index.html, retrieved January 4, 2012.

Hundert, J. and Houghton, A. 1992: Promoting social interaction of children with disabilities in integrated preschools: a failure to generalize. *Exceptional Children* **58**, 311–20.

Hunter, K.K., Chenier, J.S. and Gresham, F.M. 2014: Evaluation of Check in/Check out for students with internalizing behavior problems. *Journal of Emotional and Behavioral Disorders* **22**, 135–48.

Hwang, J.M., Cheong, P.H. and Feeley, T.H. 2009: Being young and feeling blue in Taiwan: examining adolescent depressive mood and offline activities. *New Media and Society* **11**, 1101–21.

Hymel, S. and Rubin, K.H. 1985: Children with peer relationship and social skills problems: conceptual, methodological, and developmental issues. In Whitehurst, G.J. (Ed.), *Annals of child development*. Greenwich, CT: JAI Press, vol. 2, 254–97.

Hymel, S., Rubin, K.H., Rowden, L. and LeMare, L. 1990: Children's peer relationships: longitudinal predictions of internalizing and externalizing problems from middle to late childhood. *Child Development* **61**, 2004–21.

Hymel, S., Wagner, E. and Butler, L. 1990: Reputational bias: view from the peer group. In Asher, S.R. and Coie, J. (Eds.), *Peer rejection in childhood*. Cambridge: Cambridge University Press, 156–86.

Isaacs, S. 1933: *Social development in young children: a study of beginnings*. London: Routledge.

Isherwood, G.B. and Ahola, J.A. 1981: School life: a conceptual model, or where you stand depends on where you sit. In Epstein, J.L. (Ed.), *The quality of school life*. Lexington, MA: Lexington Books, 173–7.

Jack, L.M. 1934: *An experimental study of ascendant behavior in pre-school children*. Des Moines, IA: University of Iowa Press.

Jackson, J. 2000: What ought psychology to do? *American Psychologist* **55**, 328–30.

January, A.M., Casey, R.J. and Paulson, D. 2011: A meta-analysis of classroom-wide interventions to build social skills: do they work? *School Psychology Review* **40**, 242–56.

Jiang, X. and Cillessen, A. 2005: Stability of continuous measures of sociometric status: a meta-analysis. *Developmental Review* **25**, 1–25.

Jimerson, S.R., Swearer, S.M. and Espelage, D.L. 2010: International scholarship advances science and practice addressing school bullying. In Jimerson, S.R., Swearer, S.M. and Espelage, D.L. (Eds.), *Handbook of bullying in schools: an international perspective*. New York: Routledge/Taylor and Francis Group, 1–6.

Johnson, D.W. and Johnson, R. 1989: *Co-operation and competition: theory and research*. Edina, MN: Interaction.

Johnson, D.W. and Johnson, R.T. 1996: Conflict resolution and peer mediation programs in elementary and secondary schools: a review of the research. *Review of Educational Research* **66**, 459–506.

Johnson, R. 1989: Thatcherism and English education: breaking the mould, or confirming the pattern? *History of Education* **18**, 91–121.
Johnson, R.T. and Johnson, D.W. 1983: Effects of co-operative, competitive and individualistic learning experiences on social development. *Exceptional Children* **49**, 323–30.
Johnstone, B., Frame, C. and Bouman, D. 1992: Physical attractiveness and athletic and academic ability in controversial-aggressive and rejected-aggressive children. *Journal of Social and Clinical Psychology* **11**, 71–9.
Joinson, A.N. 2007: Disinhibition and the internet. In Gackenbach, J. (Ed.), *Psychology and the internet: intrapersonal, interpersonal and transpersonal implications*. 2nd Edition. San Diego, CA: Elsevier, 76–92.
Joinson, A.N. and Paine, C.B. 2007: Self-disclosure, privacy and the Internet. In Joinson, A.N., McKenna, K.Y.A., Postmes, T. and Reips, U.-D. (Eds.), *Oxford handbook of internet psychology*. Oxford: Oxford University Press, 237–52.
Jones, D.C. 1985: Persuasive appeals and responses to appeals among friends and acquaintances. *Child Development* **56**, 757–63.
Jordan, D.W. and Le Métais, J. 1997: Social skills through co-operative learning. *Educational Research* **39**, 3–21.
Jourard, S.M. 1971. *Self-disclosure: an experimental analysis of the transparent self*. New York: Wiley.
Joussemet, M., Vitaro, F., Barker, E.D., Côté, S., Nagin, D.S., Zoccolillo, M. and Tremblay, R.E. 2008: Controlling parenting and physical aggression during elementary school. *Child Development* **79**, 411–25.
Jugert, P., Noack, P. and Rutland, A. 2011: Friendship preferences among German and Turkish preadolescents. *Child Development* **82**, 812–29.
Juvonen, J. and Bear, G. 1992: Social adjustment of children with and without learning disabilities in integrated classrooms. *Journal of Educational Psychology* **84**, 322–30.
Juvonen, J., Graham, S. and Schuster, M.A. 2003: Bullying among young adolescents: the strong, the weak, and the troubled. *Pediatrics* **112**, 1231–7.
Kagan, J. 1998: The nature of nurture: parents or peers? Interview with Microsoft Network Slate, November 21.
Kagan, S. and Madsen, M.C. 1971: Co-operation and competition of Mexican, Mexican-American, and Anglo-American children of two ages under four instructional sets. *Developmental Psychology* **5**, 32–9.
Kagan, S. and Madsen, M.C. 1972: Experimental analysis of cooperation and competition of Anglo-American and Mexican children. *Developmental Psychology* **6**, 49–59.
Kamibeppu, K. and Sugiura, H. 2005: Impact of the mobile phone on junior high-school students' friendships in the Tokyo metropolitan area. *CyberPsychology and Behavior* **8**, 121–30.
Kamps, D. 2010: Social skills instruction and generalization strategies. In Algozzine, B., Daunic, A.P. and Smith, S.W. (Eds.), *Preventing problem behaviors: schoolwide programs and classroom practices*. 2nd Edition. Thousand Oaks, CA: Corwin Press, 71–111.
Kawabata, Y. and Crick, N.R. 2011: The significance of cross-racial/ethnic friendships: associations with peer victimization, peer support, sociometric status and classroom diversity. *Developmental Psychology* **47**, 1763–75.
Kawabata, Y. and Crick, N.R. 2013: Relational and physical aggression, peer victimization, and adjustment problems in Asian American and European American children. *Asian American Journal of Psychology* **4**, 211–16.
Kawabata, Y. and Crick, N.R. 2015: Direct and interactive links between cross-ethnic friendships and peer rejection, internalizing symptoms, and academic engagement

among ethnically diverse children. *Cultural Diversity and Ethnic Minority Psychology* **21**, 191–200.

Kawabata, Y., Crick, N.R. and Hamaguchi, Y. 2010: The role of culture in relational aggression: associations with social-psychological adjustment problems in Japanese and US school-aged children. *International Journal of Behavioral Development* **34**, 354–62.

Kawabata, Y., Tseng, W. and Crick, N.R. 2014: Adaptive, maladaptive, mediational, and bidirectional processes of relational and physical aggression, relational and physical victimization, and peer liking. *Aggressive Behavior* **40**, 273–87.

Kazdin, A.E., Esveldt-Dawson, K., French, N.K. and Unis, A.S. 1987: Effects of parent management training and problem-solving skills training combined in the treatment of antisocial child behavior. *Journal of the American Academy of Child and Adolescent Psychiatry* **26**, 416–24.

Kazdin, A.E., Siegel, T.C. and Bass, D. 1992: Cognitive problem-solving skills training and parent management training in the treatment of antisocial behavior in children. *Journal of Consulting and Clinical Psychology* **60**, 733–47.

Keller, M. and Edelstein, W. 1990: The emergence of morality in personal relationships. In Wren, T. (Ed.), *The moral domain*. Cambridge, MA: MIT Press, 255–82.

Kellner, R., Houghton, S. and Douglas, G. 2003: Peer-related personal experiences of children with attention-deficit/hyperactivity disorder with and without comorbid learning disabilities. *International Journal of Disability, Development and Education* **50**, 119–36.

Kendall, P.C. and Braswell, L. 1982: Cognitive-behavioural self-control therapy for children: a components analysis. *Journal of Consulting and Clinical Psychology* **50**, 672–89.

Kendall, P.C. and Braswell, L. 1985: *Cognitive-behavioral therapy for impulsive children*. New York: Guilford.

Kendrick K., Jutengren G. and Stattin H. 2012: The protective role of supportive friends against bullying perpetration and victimization. *Journal of Adolescence* **35**, 1069–80.

Kennedy, J.H. 1992: Relationship of maternal beliefs and childbearing strategies to social competence in preschool children. *Child Study Journal* **22**, 39–60.

Kennedy, M. 1990: Controlled evaluation of peer tutoring on the tutors: are the 'learning by teaching' theories viable? In Goodlad, S. and Hirst, B. (Eds.), *Explorations in peer tutoring*. Oxford: Blackwell, 58–72.

Kerns, K.A. 1996: Individual differences in friendship quality: links to child–mother attachment. In Bukowski, W.M., Newcomb, A.F. and Hartup, W.W. (Eds.), *The company they keep: friendship in childhood and adolescence*. New York: Cambridge University Press, 137–57.

Kerns, K.A., Klepac, L. and Cole, A. 1996: Peer relationship and preadolescents' perceptions of security in the mother–child relationship. *Developmental Psychology* **32**, 457–66.

Kerr, M., Lambert, W.W. and Bem, D.J. 1996: Life course sequelae of childhood shyness in Sweden: comparison with the United States. *Developmental Psychology* **32**, 1100–5.

Keysers, C. and Gazzola, V. 2014: Dissociating the ability and propensity for empathy. In Mikulincer, M. and Shaver, P.R. (Eds.), *Mechanisms of social connection: from brain to group*. Washington, DC: American Psychological Association, 71–88.

Kidd, J.W. 1951: An analysis of social rejection in a college men's residence hall. *Sociometry* **14**, 226–34.

Kiesner, J., Kerr, M. and Stattin, H. 2004: Very Important Persons in adolescence: going beyond in-school, single friendships in the study of peer homophily. *Journal of Adolescence* **27**, 545–60.

Kindermann, T.A. and Gest, S.D. 2009: Assessment of the peer group: identifying social networks in natural settings and measuring their influences. In Rubin, K.H., Bukowski, W.

and Laursen, B. (Eds.), *Handbook of peer interactions, relationships, and groups*. New York: Guilford, 100–17.

King, G.A., Specht, J.A., Schultz, I., Warr-Leeper, G., Redekop, L. and Risebrough, C. 1997: Social skills training for withdrawn unpopular children with physical disabilities: a preliminary evaluation. *Rehabilitation Psychology* **42**, 47–60.

King, A.L.S., Valença, A.M., Silva, A.C.O., Baczynski, T., Carvalho, M.R. and Nardi, A.E. 2013: Nomophobia: dependency on virtual environments or social phobia? *Computers in Human Behavior* **29**, 140–4.

Kirchler, E., Pombeni, M.L. and Palmonari, A. 1991: Sweet sixteen: adolescents' problems and the peer group as social support. *European Journal of the Psychology of Education* **6**, 393–410.

Kim, B.S. and Darling, L.F. 2009: Monet, Malaguzzi, and the constructive conversations of preschoolers in a Reggio-inspired classroom. *Early Childhood Education Journal* **37**, 137–45.

Kingery, J.N., Erdley, C.A. and Marshall, K.C. 2011: Peer acceptance and friendship as predictors of early adolescents' adjustment across the middle school transition. *Merrill-Palmer Quarterly* **57**, 215–43.

Kistner, J.A. and Gatlin, D. 1989: Correlates of peer rejection among children with learning disabilities. *Learning Disability Quarterly* **12**, 133–40.

Klinger, J.K. and Vaughn, S. 1996: Reciprocal teaching of reading comprehension strategies for students with learning disabilities who use English as a second language. *Elementary School Journal* **96**, 275–93.

Klinger, J.K., Vaughn, S. and Schumm, J.S. 1998: Collaborative strategic reading during social studies and heterogeneous fourth-grade classrooms. *Elementary School Journal* **99**, 3–22.

Knack, J.M., Tsar, V., Vaillancourt, T., Hymel, S. and McDougall, P. 2012: What protects rejected adolescents from also being bullied by their peers? The moderating role of peer-valued characteristics. *Journal of Research on Adolescence* **22**, 467–79.

Koentjaraningrat, R.M. 1985: *Javanese culture*. New York: Oxford University Press.

Koehler, D.J. and Harvey, N. 2007: *Blackwell handbook of judgment and decision making*. New York: Blackwell.

Kohlberg, L., LaCrosse, J. and Ricks, D. 1972: The predictability of adult mental health from childhood behaviour. In Wolman, B.B. (Ed.), *Manual of child psychopathology*. New York: McGraw-Hill, 1217–84.

Kokina, A. and Kern, L. 2010: Social story interventions for students with autism spectrum disorders: a meta-analysis. *Journal of Autism and Developmental Disorders* **40**, 812–26.

Kokko, K., Simonton, S., Dubow, E., Lansford, J.E., Olson, S.L., Huesmann, L.R., Boxer, P., Pulkkinen, L., Bates, J.E., Dodge, K.A. and Pettit, G.S. 2014: Country, sex, and parent occupational status: moderators of the continuity of aggression from childhood to adulthood. *Aggressive Behavior* **40**, 552–67.

Kong, S.L. 1985: Counselling Chinese immigrants: issues and answers. In Samnite, R.J. and Wolfgang, A. (Eds.), *Intercultural counselling and assessment: global perspectives*, Lewiston: C.J. Hogrefe, 181–9.

Kosir, K. and Pecjak, S. 2005: Sociometry as a method for investigating peer relationships: what does it actually measure? *Educational Research* **47**, 127–44.

Koutamanis, M., Vossen, H.G.M., Peter, J. and Valkenberg, P.M. 2013: Practice makes perfect: the longitudinal effect of adolescents' instant messaging on their ability to initiate offline friendships. *Computers in Human Behavior* **29**, 2265–72.

Kovacks, M. 1981: Rating scales to assess depression in school-aged children. *Acta Paedopsychiatrica* **46**, 305–15.

Kovacs, D.M., Parker, J.G. and Hoffman, L.W. 1996: Behavioural, affective, and social correlates of involvement in cross-sex friendship in elementary school. *Child Development* **67**, 2269–86.

Krantz, M. 1987: Physical attractiveness and popularity: a predictive study. *Psychological Reports* **60**, 723–6.

Krappmann, L. 1989: Family relationships and peer relationships in middle childhood: an exploratory study of the associations between children's integration into the social network of peers and family development. In Kreppner, K. and Lerner, R.M. (Eds.), *Family systems and life-span development.* Hillsdale, NJ: Erlbaum, 93–104.

Krappmann, L. 1996: Amicitia, drujba, shin-yu, philia, freundschaft, friendship: on the diversity of a human relationship. In Bukowski, W.M., Newcomb, A.F. and Hartup, W.W. (Eds.), *The company they keep: friendship in childhood and adolescence.* Cambridge: Cambridge University Press, 19–40.

Krappmann, L., Uhlendorff, H. and Oswald, H. 1995: Existence and effects of close relationships in childhood and preadolescence. Paper presented at the meeting of the European Conference of Developmental Psychology, Krakow, Poland, August.

Kraut, R., Lundmark,V., Patterson, M., Kiesler, S., Mukopadhyay,T. and Scherlis,W. 1998: Internet paradox: a social technology that reduces social involvement and psychological well-being. *American Psychologist* **53**, 1017–31.

Kupersmidt, J.B. and Coie, J.D. 1990: Preadolescent peer status, aggression and school adjustment as predictors of externalizing problems in adolescence. *Child Development* **61**, 1350–62.

Kupersmidt, J.B., DeRosier, M.E. and Patterson, C.P. 1995: Similarity as the basis for children's friendships: the roles of sociometric status, aggressive and withdrawn behaviour, academic achievement and demographic characteristics. *Journal of Social and Personal Relationships* **12**, 439–52.

Kupersmidt,J.B. and Patterson, C.J. 1991: Childhood peer rejection, aggression, withdrawal, and perceived competence as predictors of self-reported behavior problems in preadolescence. *Journal of Abnormal Child Psychology* **19**, 427–49.

Kupersmidt, J.B. and Trejos, L. 1987: Behavioural correlates of sociometric status among Costa Rican children. Paper presented at the biennial meeting of the Society for Research in Child Development, Baltimore, MD, April.

Kushner, T. 1993: *Angels in America: a gay fantasia on national themes.* New York: Theatre Communications.

Kyei, K.G. and Schreckenbach, H. 1975: *No time to die.* Accra: Catholic Press.

Kyriakides, L., Creemers, B.P.M., Papastylianou, D. and Papadatou-Pastou, M. 2014: Improving the school learning environment to reduce bullying: an experimental study. *Scandinavian Journal of Educational Research* **5**, 453–78.

Ladd, G.W. 1981: Effectiveness of a social learning method for enhancing children's social interactions and peer acceptance. *Child Development* **52**, 171–8.

Ladd, G.W. 1983: Social network of popular, average and rejected children in school settings. *Merrill-Palmer Quarterly* **29**, 283–307.

Ladd, G.W. 1990: Having friends, keeping friends, making friends, and being liked by peers in the classroom: predictors of children's early school adjustment? *Child Development* **61**, 1081–1100.

Ladd, G.W. 2005: *Children's peer relations and social competence: a century of progress.* New Haven, CT: Yale University Press.

Ladd, G.W. and Emerson, E.S. 1984: Shared knowledge in children's friendships. *Developmental Psychology* **20**, 932–40.

Ladd, G.W. and Golter, B.S. 1988: Parents' management of preschoolers' peer relations: is it related to children's social competence? *Developmental Psychology* **24**, 109–17.

Ladd, G.W. and Hart, C.H. 1992: Creating informal play opportunities: are parents' and preschoolers' initiations related to children's competence with peers? *Developmental Psychology* **28**, 1179–87.

Ladd, G.W., Hart, C.H., Wadsworth, E.M. and Golter, B.S. 1988: Preschoolers' peer networks in nonschool settings: relationship to family characteristics and school adjustment. In Salzinger, S., Antrobus, J. and Hammer, M. (Eds.), *Social networks of children, adolescents and college students.* Hillsdale, NJ: Erlbaum, 61–92.

Ladd, G.W., Kochenderfer, B.J. and Coleman, C.C. 1996: Friendship quality as a predictor of young children's early school adjustment. *Child Development* **67**, 1103–18.

Ladd, G.W., Kochenderfer-Ladd, B., Visconti, K.J., Ettekal, I., Sechler, C.M. and Cortes, K.I. 2014: Grade-school children's social collaborative skills: links with partner preference and achievement. *American Educational Research Journal* **5**, 152–83.

Ladd, G.W. and Price, J.M. 1987: Predicting children's social and school adjustment following the transition from preschool to kindergarten. *Child Development* **58**, 1168–89.

Lagerspetz, K.M., Björkqvist, K. and Peltonen, T. 1988: Is indirect aggression typical of females? Gender differences in aggressiveness in 11- to 12-year-old children. *Aggressive Behaviour* **14**, 403–14.

Laghi, F., Schneider, B.H., Vitoroulis, R.J., Coplan, R J. and Baiocco, R. 2013: Knowing when not to use the internet: shyness and adolescents' on-line and off-line interactions with friends. *Computers in Human Behavior* **29**, 51–7.

Laird, R.D., Pettit, G.S., Mize, J., Brown, E.G. and Lindsey, E. 1994: Mother–child conversations about peers: contributions to competence. *Family Relations* **43**, 425–32.

Landau, S. and Moore, L.A. 1991: Social skill deficits in children with attention deficit-hyperactivity. *School Psychology Review* **20**, 235–51.

Lando, B.Z. and Schneider, B.H. 1997. Intellectual contributions and mutual support among developmentally advanced children in homogeneous and heterogeneous work/discussion groups. *Gifted Child Quarterly* **41**, 44–57.

Lansford, J.E., Putallaz, M., Grimes, C.L, Schiro-Osman, K.A., Kupersmidt, J.B. and Coie, J.D. 2006: Perceptions of friendship quality and observed behaviors with friends: how do sociometrically rejected, average, and popular girls differ? *Merrill-Palmer Quarterly* **52**, 694–720.

Lansu, T.A.M., Cillessen, A.H.N. and Karremans, J.C. 2014: Adolescents' selective visual attention for high-status peers: the role of perceiver status and gender. *Child Development* **85**, 421–8.

Larkin, S. 2009: Socially mediated metacognition and learning to write. *Thinking Skills and Creativity* **4**, 149–59.

Larson, R.W. 2014: Studying experience: pursuing the 'something more'. In Lerner, R.M., Petersen, A.C., Silbereisen, R.K. and Brooks-Gunn, J. (Eds.), *The developmental science of adolescence: history through autobiography*. New York: Psychology Press, 267–76.

Larzelere, R.E. 1986: Moderate spanking: model or deterrent of children's aggression in the family? *Journal of Family Violence* **1**, 27–36.

Laugeson, E.A, Frankel, F., Gantman, A., Dillon, A.R. and Mogil, C. 2011: Evidence-based social skills training for adolescents with autism spectrum disorders: the UCLA peers program. *Journal of Autism and Developmental Disorders* **42**, 1025–36.

Laursen, B., Bukowski, W.M., Nurmi, J.E., Marion, D., Salmela-Aro, K. and Kiuru, N. 2010: Opposites detract: middle school peer group antipathies. *Journal of Experimental Child Psychology* **106**, 240–56.

Laursen, B., Denissen, J. and Bjorklund, D. 2012: Event frequency measurement. In Laursen, B., Little, T.S. and Card, N.A. (Eds.), *Handbook of developmental research methods*. New York: Guilford, 65–81.

Laursen, B., Furman, W. and Mooney, K.S. 2006: Predicting interpersonal competence and self-worth from adolescent relationships and relationship networks: variable-centered and person-centered perspectives. *Merrill-Palmer Quarterly* **52**, 572–600.

Laursen, B. and Hartup, W.W. 2002: The origins of reciprocity and social exchange in friendships. In Laursen, B. and Graziano, W.G. (Eds.), *Social exchange in development*. San Francisco: Jossey-Bass, 27–40.

Laursen, B. and Pursell, G. 2009: Conflict in peer relationships. In Rubin, K.H., Bukowski, W.M. and Laursen, B. (Eds.), *Handbook of peer interactions, relationships, and groups*. New York: Guilford, 267–86.

Lavallee, K.L. and Parker, J.G. 2009: The role of inflexible friendship beliefs, rumination, and low self-worth in early adolescents' friendship jealousy and adjustment. *Journal of Abnormal Child Psychology* **37**, 873–85.

Lawson-Borders, G. and Kirk, R. 2005: Blogs in campaign communication. *American Behavioral Scientist* **49**, 548–59.

Leadbeater, B.J. 2006: *Ethical issues in community-based research with children and youth*. Toronto: University of Toronto Press.

Lease, A.M. and Blake, J.J. 2005: A comparison of minority-race children with and without a minority-race friend. *Social Development* **14**, 20–41.

Ledingham, J.E. 1999: Children and adolescents with oppositional defiant disorder and conduct disorder in the community: experiences at school and with peers. In Quay, H.C. and Hogan, A.E. (Eds.), *Handbook of disruptive behaviour disorders*. New York: Kluwer-Plenum, 353–70.

Ledingham, J.E. and Schwartzman, A.E. 1984: A 3-year follow-up of aggressive and withdrawn behaviour in childhood: preliminary findings. *Journal of Abnormal Child Psychology* **12**, 157–68.

Lee, S.H., Yoo, S.Y. and Bok, S.H. 2003: Characteristics of friendships between children with and without mild disabilities. *Education and Training in Developmental Disabilities* **38**, 157–66.

Lee, S.Y., Olszewski-Kubilius, P. and Thomson, D.T. 2012: Academically gifted students' perceived interpersonal competence and peer relationships. *Gifted Child Quarterly* **56**, 90–104.

Lee-Won, R.J., Shim, M., Joo, Y.K.K. and Park, S.G. 2014: Who puts the best 'face' forward on Facebook? Positive self-presentation in online social networking and the role of self-consciousness, actual-to-total friends ratio, and culture. *Computers in Human Behavior* **39**, 413–23.

Leflot, G., van Lier, P.A., Verschueren, K., Onghena, P. and Colpin, H. 2011: Transactional associations among teacher support, peer social preference, and child externalizing behavior: a four-wave longitudinal study. *Journal of Clinical Child and Adolescent Psychology* **40**, 87–99.

Lehman, H.C. 1926: The play activities of persons of different ages, and growth stages in play behavior. *Pedagogical Seminary* **33**, 250–72.

Lerner, R.M. and Lerner, J.V. 1977: Effects of age, sex, and physical attractiveness on child–peer relations, academic performance, and elementary school adjustment. *Developmental Psychology* **13**, 585–90.

Lesser, G.R. 1957: The relationship between overt and fantasy aggression as a function of maternal response to aggression. *Journal of Abnormal and Social Psychology* **55**, 218–21.

Leung, K. 1987: Some determinants of reactions to procedural models for conflict resolution: a cross-national study. *Journal of Personality and Social Psychology* **53**, 898–908.

Leve L.D., Winebarger, A.A., Fagot, B.I., Reid, J.B. and Goldsmith, H.H. 1998: Environmental and genetic variance in children's observed and reported maladaptive behaviour. *Child Development* **69**, 1286–98.

Levine, F.M., Fasnacht, G., Funabiki, D. and Burkart, M.R. 1979: Methodological considerations regarding the evaluation of maintenance of gains due to token programs. *Psychology in the Schools* **16**, 568–75.

Levinger, G. 1980: Toward the analysis of close relationships. *Journal of Experimental Social Psychology* **16**, 510–44.

Levy D.M. 1966: *Maternal overprotection*. New York: Norton.

Levy L. and Gottlieb, J. 1984: Learning disabled and non-learning disabled children at play. *Remedial and Special Education* **5**, 43–50.

Levy-Shiff, R. and Hoffman, M.A. 1985: Social behavior of urban and kibbutz preschool children in Israel. *Developmental Psychology* **21**, 1204–5.

Lewis, M. and Feiring, C. 1989: Infant, mother, and mother–infant interaction behaviour and subsequent attachment. *Child Development* **60**, 831–7.

Lewis, C., Freeman, N.H., Kyriakidou, C., Maridaki-Kassotaki, K. and Berridge, D.K. 1996: Social influences on false belief access: specific sibling influences or general apprenticeship? *Child Development* **67**, 2930–47.

Li, Y., Lynch, A.D., Kalvin, C., Liu, J. and Lerner, R.M. 2011: Peer relationships as a context for the development of school engagement during early adolescence. *International Journal of Behavioral Development* **35**, 329–42.

Libet, J.M. and Lewinsohn, P.M. 1973: Concept of social skills with special reference to the behavior of depressed persons. *Journal of Consulting and Clinical Psychology* **40**, 304–12.

Light, P. and Glachan, M. 1985: Facilitation of individual problem solving through peer interaction. *Educational Psychology* **5**, 217–25.

Lin, T.J., Anderson, R.C., Hummel, J.E., Jadallah, M., Miller, B.W., Nguyen-Jahiel, K., Morris, J.A., Kuo, L.J., Kim, I.H., Wu, X. and Dong, T. 2012: Children's use of analogy during collaborative reasoning. *Child Development* **83**, 1429–43.

Lindsey, E.W., Mize, J. and Pettit, G.S. 1997: Mutuality in parent–child play: consequences for children's peer competence. *Journal of Social and Personal Relationships* **14**, 523–38.

Little, T.D., Brendgen, M., Wanner, B. and Krappmann, L. 1999: Children's reciprocal perceptions of friendship quality in the sociocultural contexts of East and West Berlin. *International Journal of Behavioural Development* **23**, 63–89.

Litwinski, L. 1950: Constitutional shyness: its active and passive forms. *Journal of General Psychology* **42**, 299–311.

Liu, J., Coplan, R.J., Ooi, L.L., Chen, X. and Li, D. 2015a: Examining the implications of social anxiety in a community sample of mainland Chinese children. *Journal of Clinical Psychology* **71**, 979–93.

Liu, J., Li, D., Purwono, U., Chen, X. and French, D.C. 2015b: Loneliness of Indonesian and Chinese adolescents as predicted by relationships with friends and parents. *Merrill-Palmer Quarterly* **61**, 362–82.

Lloyd, J.W., Crowley, E.P., Kohler, F.W. and Strain, P.S. 1988: Redefining the applied research agenda: co-operative learning, preferral, teacher consultation, and peer-mediated interventions. *Journal of Learning Disabilities* **21**, 43–52.

Lochman, J.E., Coie, J.D., Underwood, M.K. and Terry, R. 1993: Effectiveness of a social relations intervention program for aggressive and nonaggressive, rejected children. *Journal of Consulting and Clinical Psychology* **61**, 1053–8.

Lochman, J.E. and Dodge, K.A. 1994: Social-cognitive processes of severely violent, moderately aggressive and nonaggressive boys. *Journal of Consulting and Clinical Psychology* **62**, 366–74.

Lochman, J.E., Powell, N.R., Whidby, J.M. and FitzGerald, D.P. 2012: Aggression in children. In Kendall, P.C. (Ed.), *Child and adolescent therapy: cognitive-behavioral procedures*. 4th Edition. New York: Guilford, 27–60.

Locke, J.L. 1998: *The de-voicing of society: why we don't talk to each other anymore?* New York: Simon and Schuster.

Loeber, R., Green, S.M., Keenan, K. and Lahey, B.B. 1995: Which boys will fare worse? Early predictors of the onset of conduct disorder in a six-year longitudinal study. *Journal of the American Academy of Child and Adolescent Psychiatry* **34**, 499–509.

Loehlin, J.C. 1989: Models of behaviour and the behaviour of models. *International Journal of Behavioural Development* **12**, 403–6.

Lonigro, A., Schneider, B.H., Laghi, F., Baiocco, R., Pallini, S. and Brunner, T. 2015: Is cyberbullying related to trait or state anger? *Child Psychiatry and Human Development* **46**, 445–54.

Lopata, H.Z. 1981: Friendship: historical and theoretical introduction. *Research in the Interweave of Social Roles* **2**, 1–19.

López, E.J., Ehly, S. and García-Vázquez, E. 2002: Acculturation, social support and academic achievement of Mexican and Mexican-American high school students: an exploratory study. *Psychology in the Schools* **39**, 245–57.

Lorion, R.P., Cowen, E.L., Kraus, R.M. and Milling, L.S. 1977: Family background characteristics and school adjustment problems. *Journal of Community Psychology* **5**, 142–8.

Lösel, F. and Beelmann, A. 2003: Effects of child skills training in preventing antisocial behavior: a systematic review of randomized evaluations. *Annals of the American Academy of Political and Social Science* **587**, 84–109.

Lowenstein, P. and Svendsen, M. 1938: Experimental modification of the behavior of a selected group of shy and withdrawn children. *American Journal of Orthopsychiatry* **8**, 639–54.

Lucassen, N., Tharner, A., Van IJzendoorn, M.H., Bakermans-Kranenburg, M.J., Volling, B.L., Verhulst, F.C., Lambregtse-Van den Berg, M.P. and Tiemeier, H. 2011: The association between paternal sensitivity and infant–father attachment security: a meta-analysis of three decades of research. *Journal of Family Psychology* **25**, 986–92.

Luciano, S. and Savage, R.S. 2007: Bullying risk in children with learning difficulties in inclusive educational settings. *Canadian Journal of School Psychology* **22**, 14–31.

Luczynski, K.C. and Hanley, G.P. 2013: Prevention of problem behavior by teaching functional communication and self-control skills to preschoolers. *Journal of Applied Behavioral Analysis* **46**, 355–68.

Luftig, R.L. and Nichols, M.L. 1991: An assessment of the social status and perceived personality and school traits of gifted students by nongifted peers. *Roeper Review* **13**, 148–53.

Lundberg, G.A. and Dickson, L. 1952: Selective association among ethnic groups in a high school population. *American Sociological Review* **17**, 23–35.

Lupkowski, A.E. 1989: Social behaviours of gifted and typical preschool children in laboratory school programs. *Roeper Review* **11**, 124–7.

Maccoby, E. 1988: Gender as a social category. *Developmental Psychology* **24**, 755–65.

Maccoby, E. 1990: Gender and relationships: a developmental account. *American Psychologist* **45**, 513–20.

MacDonald, K. 1987: Parent–child physical play with rejected, neglected, and popular boys. *Developmental Psychology* **23**, 705–11.

MacDonald, K. and Parke, R.D. 1984: Bridging the gap: parent–child play interaction and peer interactive competence. *Child Development* **55**, 1265–77.
MacDonald, M.A. and Sherman, P.D. 1987: Stuck for words: combining social skills training with a token economy system for adolescents. *Journal of Child Care* **3**, 51–8.
MacEvoy, J.P. and Asher, S.R. 2012: When friends disappoint: boys' and girls' responses to transgressions of friendship expectations. *Child Development* **83**, 104–19.
MacLaren Chorney, J., McMurtry, C.M., Chambers, C.T. and Bakeman, R. 2015: Developing and modifying behavioral coding schemes in pediatric psychology: a practical guide. *Journal of Pediatric Psychology* **40**, 154–64.
MacMillan, D.L. and Morrison, G.M. 1980: Correlates of social status among mildly handicapped learners in self-contained special cases. *Journal of Educational Psychology* **72**, 437–44.
Maczewski, M. 2002: Exploring identities through the internet: youth experiences online. *Child and Youth Care Forum* **31**, 111–29.
Maddox, S.J. and Prinz R.J. 2003: School bonding in children and adolescents: conceptualization, assessment, and associated variables. *Clinical Child and Family Psychology Review* **6**, 31–49.
Maddux, C.D., Scheiber, L.M. and Bass, J. 1982: Self-concept and social distance in gifted children. *Gifted Child Quarterly* **26**, 77–81.
Madell, D.E. and Muncer, S.J. 2007: Control over social interactions: an important reason for young people's use of the internet and mobile phones for communication. *CyberPsychology and Behavior* **10**, 137–40.
Madsen, M.C. 1971: Developmental and cross-cultural differences in the cooperative and competitive behaviour of young children. *Journal of Cross-Cultural Psychology* **2**, 365–71.
Madsen, M.C. and Shapira, A. 1970: Co-operative and competitive behavior of urban Afro-American, Anglo-American, Mexican-American, and Mexican village children. *Developmental Psychology* **3**, 16–20.
Mager, W., Milich, R., Harris, M.J. and Howard, A. 2005: Intervention groups for adolescents with conduct problems: is aggregation harmful or helpful? *Journal of Abnormal Child Psychology* **33**, 349–62.
Magid, L.J. 1998: Child safety on the information highway. National Center for Missing and Exploited Children. www.safekids.com/child_safety.htm, retrieved November 18, 2015.
Manetti, M., Schneider, B.H. and Siperstein, G. 2001: Social acceptance on developmentally challenged children: testing the contact hypothesis with an Italian sample. *International Journal of Behavioral Development* **25**, 279–86.
Mannarino, A.P. 1978: The interactional process in preadolescent friendships. *Psychiatry* **41**, 308–12.
Manning, B.H. 1990: A categorical analysis of children's self-talk during independent school assignments. *Journal of Instructional Psychology* **17**, 208–17.
Maraspini, A.J. 1968: *The study of an Italian village.* Paris: Mouton.
Margalit, M. 1998: Loneliness and coherence among preschool children with learning disabilities. *Journal of Learning Disabilities* **31**, 173–80.
Marion, D., Laursen, B., Zettergren, P. and Bergman, L.R. 2013: Predicting life satisfaction during middle adulthood from peer relationships during mid-adolescence. *Journal of Youth and Adolescence* **42**, 1299–1307.
Marlowe, M. 1979: The games analysis intervention: a procedure to increase the peer acceptance and social adjustment of a retarded child. *Education and Training of the Mentally Retarded* **14**, 262–8.

Marotz Ray, B. 1985: Measuring the social position of the mainstreamed handicapped child. *Exceptional Children* **52**, 57–62.

Marti, J. 1997: *Versos sencillos/Simple verses.* Translated by Manual A. Tellechea. Houston, TX: Arte Público Press.

Martin, M. and Muthukrishna, N. 2011: Desconstructing discourses of gender equality in cross-gender friendships: Grade seven boys and girls in an inner-city school. *Gender and Behaviour* **9**, 3798–816.

Martin-Storey, A., Serbin, L.A., Stack, D.M., Ledingham, J.E. and Schwartzman A.E. 2011: Self and peer perceptions of childhood aggression, social withdrawal and likeability predict adult substance abuse and dependence in men and women: a 30-year prospective longitudinal study. *Addictive Behaviors* **36**, 1267–74.

Marvin, R., Cooper, G., Hoffman, K. and Powell, B. 2002: The Circle of Security project: attachment-based intervention with caregiver–pre-school child dyads. *Attachment and Human Development* **4**, 107–24.

Maslow, A. 1971: *The farther reaches of human nature.* New York: Viking Press.

Masten, A.S., Morrison, P. and Pellegrini, D.S. 1985: A revised class play method of peer assessment. *Developmental Psychology* **21**, 523–33.

Masten, C.L., Eisenberger, N.I., Pfeifer, J.H. and Dapretto, M. 2010: Neural responses to witnessing peer rejection after being socially excluded: fMRI as a window into adolescents' emotional processing. *Developmental Science* **165**, 743–59.

Mathieson, L.C and Crick, N.R. 2010: Reactive and proactive subtypes of relational and physical aggression in middle childhood: links to concurrent and longitudinal adjustment. *School Psychology Review* **39**, 601–11.

Mayeux, L., Underwood, M.K. and Risser, S.D. 2007: Perspectives on the ethics of sociometric research with children: how children, peers, and teachers help to inform the debate. *Merrill-Palmer Quarterly* **53**, 53–78.

McCord, W., McCord, J. and Howard, A. 1961: Familial correlates of aggression in nondelinquent male children. *Journal of Abnormal and Social Psychology* **62**, 79–93.

McCoy, S. and Banks, J. 2012: Simply academic? Why children with special educational needs don't like school. *European Journal of Special Needs Education* **27**, 81–97.

McDonald, K.L, Dashiell-Aje, E., Menzer, M.M., Rubin, K.H., Oh, W. and Bowker, J.C. 2013: Contributions of racial and sociobehavioral homophily to friendship stability and quality among same-race and cross-race friends. *Journal of Early Adolescence* **33**, 897–919.

McDougall, P. and Hymel, S. 1998: Moving into middle school: individual differences in the transition experience. *Canadian Journal of Behavioural Science* **30**, 108–20.

McFall, R.M. 1982: A review and reformulation of the concept of social skills. *Behavioral Assessment* **4**, 1–33.

McGuire, K.D. and Weisz, J.R. 1982: Social cognition and behavior correlates of preadolescent chumship. *Child Development* **53**, 1478–84.

McGuire, W.J., McGuire, C.V., Child, P. and Fujioka, T. 1978: Salience of ethnicity in the spontaneous self-concept as a function of one's ethnic distinctiveness in the social environment. *Journal of Personality and Social Psychology* **36**, 511–20.

McKenna, K.Y.A., Green, A.S. and Gleason, M.J. 2002: Relationship formation on the internet: what's the big attraction? *Journal of Social Issues* **58**, 9–32.

McKenna, K.Y.A. and Bargh, J.A. 1998: Coming out in the age of the internet: identity 'demarginalization' through virtual group participation. *Journal of Personality and Social Psychology* **75**, 681–94.

McMichael, P. 1980: Reading difficulties, behaviour and social status. *Journal of Educational Psychology* **72**, 76–86.

McNamara, J.K., Willoughby, T. and Chalmers, H. 2005: Psychosocial status of adolescents with learning disabilities with and without comorbid attention deficit hyperactivity disorder. *Learning Disabilities Research and Practice* **20**, 234–44.

Mehl, M.R and Robbins, M.L. 2012: Naturalistic observation sampling: the Electronically Activated Recorder (EAR). In Mehl, M.R. and Conner, T.S. (Eds.), *Handbook of research methods for studying daily life*. New York: Guilford, 176–92.

Meichenbaum, D. 1975: Enhancing creativity by modifying what subjects say to themselves. *American Educational Research Journal* **12**, 129–45.

Meichenbaum, D. 1977: *Cognitive-behaviour modification: an integrative approach*. New York: Plenum Press.

Mendelson, M.J., Aboud, F.E. and Lanthier, R.P. 1994: Personality predictors of friendship and popularity in kindergarten. *Journal of Applied Developmental Psychology* **15**, 413–35.

Menesini, E., Berdondini, L., Ciucci, E. and Almeida, A. 1999: Emotion attributions and feelings in bully/victim relationships. Paper presented at the ninth European Conference on Developmental Psychology, Spetses, Greece, September.

Merrell, K.W. and Gimpel, G.A. 1998: *Social skills of children and adolescents: conceptualization, assessment, and treatment*. Mahwah, NJ: Erlbaum.

Merrell, K.W., Gueldner, B.A., Ross, S.W. and Isava, D.M. 2008: How effective are school bullying intervention programs? A meta-analysis of intervention research. *School Psychology Quarterly* **23**, 26–42.

Mesch, G.S. and Talmud, I. 2007: Similarity and the quality of online and offline social relationships among adolescents in Israel. *Journal of Research in Adolescence* **17**, 455–66.

Meunier, J.C., Bisceglia, R. and Jenkins, J.M. 2012: Differential parenting and children's behavioral problems: curvilinear associations and mother-father combined effects. *Developmental Psychology* **48**, 987–1002.

Mikami, A.Y., Szwedo, D.E., Allen, J.P., Evans, M.A. and Hare, A.L. 2010: Adolescent peer relationships and behavior problems predict young adults' communication on social-networking websites. *Developmental Psychology* **46**, 46–56.

Milich, R. and Landau, S. 1982: Socialization and peer relations in hyperactive children. *Advances in Learning and Behavioral Disabilities* **1**, 283–339.

Miller, S.R., Brody, G.H. and Murry, V.M. 2010: Mothers' and fathers' responsive problem solving with early adolescents: do gender, shyness, and social acceptance make a difference? *Journal of Child and Family Studies* **19**, 298–307.

Miller-Johnson, S., Coie, J.D., Maumary-Gremaud, A., Bierman, K.L. and Conduct Problems Prevention Research Group 2002: Peer rejection and aggression and early starter models of conduct disorder. *Journal of Abnormal Child Psychology* **30**, 217–30.

Mills, R.S.L. and Rubin, K.H. 1993: Socialization factors in the development of social withdrawal. In Rubin, K.H. and Asendorf, J.B. (Eds.), *Social withdrawal, inhibition, and shyness in childhood*. Hillsdale, NJ: Lawrence Erlbaum, 117–48.

Mischel, W. 1983: Alternatives in the pursuit of the predictability and consistency of persons: stable data that yield unstable interpretations. *Journal of Personality* **51**, 578–604.

Mize, J. and Pettit, G.S. 1997: Mother's social coaching, mother–child relationship style, and children's peer competence: is the medium the message? *Child Development* **68**, 312–32.

Moffitt, T.E. and Caspi, A. 2001: Childhood predictors differentiate life-course persistent and adolescence-limited antisocial pathways among males and females. *Development and Psychopathology* **13**, 355–75.

Moreno, J.L. 1953: *Who shall survive? Foundations of sociometry, group psychotherapy and sociodrama*. Beacon, NY: Beacon House.

Moreno, J.L. (Ed.) 1960: *The sociometry reader*. Glencoe, IL: Free Press.

Moreno, J.L. 1972: *Psychological drama*, vol. 1. Beacon, NY: Beacon House.

Morgan, W.R. and Sawyer, J. 1967: Bargaining, expectations, and the preference for equality over equity. *Journal of Personality and Social Psychology* **6**, 139–49.

Morrison, G.M., Forness, S.R. and MacMillan, D.L. 1983: Influences on the sociometric ratings of mildly handicapped children: a path analysis. *Journal of Educational Psychology* **75**, 63–74.

Moskowitz, D.S. and Schwartzman, A.E. 1989: Painting group portraits: studying life outcomes for aggressive and withdrawn children. *Journal of Personality* **57**, 723–46.

Mounts, N.S. 2011: Parental management of peer relationships and early adolescents' social skills. *Journal of Youth and Adolescence* **40**, 416–27.

Mouw, T. and Entwistle, B. 2006: Residential segregation and interracial friendship in schools. *American Journal of Sociology* **112**, 394–41.

Mueser, K.T., Gottlieb, J.D. and Gingerich, S. 2013: Social skills and problem solving training. In Hoffman, S.G., Dozois, D., Smits, J.A.J. and Rief, W. (Eds.), *Cognitive behavioral therapy: a complete reference guide*, vol. 1: *CBT general strategies*. New York: Wiley-Blackwell, 243–72.

Mugny, G., Giroud, J. and Doise, W. 1979: Conflict of centration and cognitive progress, II: New experimental illustrations. *Bulletin de Psychologie* **32**, 979–85.

Murphy, K. and Schneider, B.H. 1994: Coaching socially rejected early adolescents regarding behaviours used by peers to infer liking: a dyad-specific intervention. *Journal of Early Adolescence* **14**, 83–95.

Murray, B. 1999: Boys to men: emotional miseducation. *APA Monitor* July/August, 1–39.

Murray, C. and Greenberg, M. 2001: Relationships with teachers and bonds with school: social emotional adjustment correlates for children with and without disabilities. *Psychology in the Schools* **38**, 25–41.

Murray-Harvey, R. and Slee, P.T. 2010: Comparative and cross-cultural research on school bullying. In Jimerson, S.R., Swearer, S.M. and Espelage, D.L. (Eds.), *Handbook of bullying in schools*. Mahwah, NJ: Lawrence Erlbaum Associates, 35–47.

Nabuzoka, D. and Ronning, J.A. 1997: Social acceptance of children with intellectual disabilities in an integrated school setting in Zambia: a pilot study. *International Journal of Disability, Development and Education* **44**, 105–15.

Nabuzoka, D. and Smith, P.K. 1993: Sociometric status and social behaviour of children with and without learning difficulties. *Journal of Child Psychology and Psychiatry and Allied Disciplines* **34**, 1435–48.

Nadel, J. and Butterworth, G. 1999: *Imitation in infancy*. New York: Cambridge University Press.

Nadel, J. and Tremblay-Leveau, H. 1999: Dyadic and triadic paradigms: early perception of social contingencies and interpersonal intentionality. In Rochat, P. (Ed.), *Early social cognition understanding others in the first months of life*. Mahwah, NJ: Erlbaum, 189–212.

Nangle, D.W., Grover, R.L., Cassano, M., Holleb, L. and Fales, J. 2010: Defining competence and identifying target skills. In Nangle, D.W., Hansen, D.J., Erdley, C.A. and Norton, P.J. (Eds.), *Practitioner's guide to empirically based measures of social skills*. New York: Springer, 3–19.

Nangle, D.W., Grover, R.L. and Fales, J. 2011: On the situational variability of social competence and the stability of traitlike conceptions. *Behavior Therapist* **34**, 40–6.

Nash, J.B. and Schaefer, C.E. 2011: Social skills play groups for children with disruptive behavior disorders: integrating play and group therapy approaches. In Drewes, A.A., Bratton, S.C. and Schaefer, C.E. (Eds.), *Integrative play therapy*. Hoboken, NJ: Wiley, 95–104.

Neal, J.W., Neal, Z.P. and Cappella, E. 2014: I know who my friends are, but do you? Predictors of self-reported and peer-inferred relationships. *Child Development* **85**, 1366–72.

Neel, R.S., Cheney, D., Meadows, N.B. and Gelhar, S. 1992: *Interviewing middle school students to determine problematic social tasks in school settings*. Monograph in Behavioral Disorders: Severe Behavior Disorders of Children and Youth. 15th Edition. Reston, VA: Council for Children with Behavioral Disorders.

Neiderheiser, J.N. and McGuire, S. 1994: Competence during middle childhood. In DeFries, J.C., Plomin. R. and Fulker, D.W. (Eds.), *Nature and nurture during middle childhood*. Oxford: Blackwell, 141–51.

Nelson, J. and Aboud, F.E. 1985: The resolution of social conflict between friends. *Child Development* **56**, 1009–17.

Newcomb, A.F. and Bagwell, C.L. 1996: The developmental significance of children's friendship relations. In Bukowski, W.M., Newcomb. A.F. and Hartup, W.W. (Eds.), *The company they keep: friendship in childhood and adolescence*. New York: Cambridge University Press, 289–321.

Newcomb, A.F. and Brady, J.E. 1982: Mutuality in boys' friendship relations. *Child Development* **53**, 392–5.

Newcomb, A.F., Brady, J.E. and Hartup, W. 1979: Friendship and incentive condition as determinants of children's task-oriented social behaviour. *Child Development* **50**, 878–81.

Newcomb, A.F. and Bukowski, W.M. 1983: Social impact and social preference as determinants of children's peer group status. *Developmental Psychology* **19**, 856–67.

Newland, L.A. and Coyl, D.D. 2010: Fathers' role as attachment figures: an interview with Sir Richard Bowlby. *Early Child Development and Care* **180**, 25–32.

Nietzel, M.T., Guthrie, P.R. and Susman, D.T. 1991: Utilization of community and social support resources. In Kanfer, F.H. and Goldstein, A.P. (Eds.), *Helping people change: a textbook of methods*. 4th Edition. New York: Pergamon, 396–421.

Noesjirwan, J. 1978: A rule-based analysis of cultural differences in social behavior: Indonesia and Australia. *International Journal of Psychology* **13**, 305–16.

Normand, S., Schneider, B.H., Lee, M.D., Maisonneuve, M.F., Chupetlovska, A., Kuehn, S. and Robaey, P. 2013: Continuities and changes in the friendships of children with and without ADHD: a longitudinal, observational study. *Journal of Abnormal Child Psychology* **41**, 1161–75.

Normand, S., Schneider, B.H., Lee, M.D., Maisonneuve, M.F., Kuehn, S. and Robaey, P. 2011: How do children with ADHD (mis)manage their real-life dyadic friendships? A multi-method investigation. *Journal of Abnormal Child Psychology* **39**, 293–305.

Northway, M. 1952: *A primer of sociometry*. Toronto: University of Toronto Press.

Northway, M. 1956: *Well children: a progress report*. Toronto: University of Toronto Press.

Northway, M. 1967: *A primer of sociometry*. 2nd Edition. Toronto: University of Toronto Press.

Nota, L., Ferrari, L. and Soresi, S. 2005: Elementary school children's willingness to help and be friends with disabled peers. *International Journal on Disability and Human Development* **4**, 131–7.

Nowicki, S. and Duke, M.P. 1992: The association of children's nonverbal decoding abilities with their popularity, locus of control, and academic achievement. *Journal of Genetic Psychology* **153**, 385–93.

Ó Baoill, A. 2004: Conceptualizing the weblog: understanding what it is in order to imagine what it can be. *Interfacings: Journal of Contemporary Media Studies*. http://blog.lib. umn.edu/blogosphere, retrieved April 12, 2015.

O'Callaghan, P.M., Reitman, D., Northup, J., Hupp, S.D.A. and Murphy, M.A. 2003: Promoting social skills generalization with ADHD-diagnosed children in a sports setting. *Behavior Therapy* **34**, 313–30.

Ochoa, S.H. and Palmer, D.J. 1991: A sociometric analysis of between-group differences and within group status variability of Hispanic learning disabled and non-handicapped pupils in academic and play contexts. *Learning Disability Quarterly* **14**, 208–18.

Oden, S. and Asher, S.R. 1977: Coaching children in social skills for friendship making. *Child Development* **48**, 495–506.

Ogbu, J.U. 1981: Origins of human competence: a cultural-ecological perspective. *Child Development* **52**, 413–29.

Ojanen, T., Stratman, A., Card, N.A. and Little, T.D. 2013: Motivation and perceived control in early adolescent friendships: relations with self-, friend-, and peer-reported adjustment. *Journal of Early Adolescence* **33**, 552–77.

O'Keefe, P.J., Saxon, SE. and Siperstein, G.N. 1991: Relationship between social status and peer assessment of social behaviour among mentally retarded and non-retarded children. Paper presented at the biennial meeting of the Society for Research in Child Development, Seattle, WA, March.

Ólafsson, K., Livingstone, S. and Haddon, L. 2013: *Children's use of online technologies in Europe: a review of the European evidence base.* London: EU Kids Online.

Oldehinkel, A.J., Rosmalen, J.G.M., Veenstra, R., Dijkstra, J.K. and Ormel, J. 2007: Being admired or being liked: classroom social status and depressive problems in early adolescent girls and boys. *Journal of Abnormal Child Psychology* **35**, 417–27.

Oldenburg, B., van Duijn, M., Sentse, M., Huitsing, G., van der Ploeg, R., Salmivalli, C. and Veenstra, R. 2015: Teacher characteristics and peer victimization in elementary schools: a classroom-level perspective. *Journal of Abnormal Child Psychology* **43**, 33–44.

Oldenburg, C.M. and Kerns, K.A. 1997: Associations between peer relationships and depressive symptoms: testing moderator effects of gender and age. *Journal of Early Adolescence* **17**, 319–37.

Olson, S.L., Lopez-Duran, N., Lunkenheimer, E.S., Chang, H. and Sameroff, A.J. 2011: Individual differences in the development of early peer aggression: integrating contributions of self-regulation, theory of mind, and parenting. *Development and Psychopathology* **23**, 253–66.

Olthof, T. and Goossens, F.A. 2008: Bullying and the need to belong: early adolescents' bullying-related behavior and the acceptance they desire and receive from particular classmate *Social Development* **17**, 24–46.

Olweus, D. 1980: Familial and temperamental determinants of aggressive behavior in adolescent boys: a causal analysis. *Developmental Psychology* **16**, 644–60.

Olweus, D. 1993: *Bullying at school: what we know and what we can do*. Oxford: Blackwell.

Olweus, D. 1999: Norway. In Smith, P.K., Morita, Y., Junger-Tas, J., Olweus, D., Catalono, R. and Slee, P. (Eds.), *The nature of school bullying.* London: Blackwell, 28–48.

Olweus, D. 2010: Understanding and researching bullying: some critical issues. In Jimerson, S.R., Swearer, S.M and Espelage, D.L. (Eds.), *Handbook of bullying in schools: an international perspective.* New York: Routledge, 9–33.

Oppenheim, D., Sagi, A. and Lamb, M.E. 1988: Infant–adult attachments on the kibbutz and their relation to socioemotional development four years later. *Developmental Psychology* **24**, 427–33.

Orlick, T., Zhou, Q.Y. and Partington, J. 1990: Co-operation and conflict within Chinese and Canadian kindergarten settings. *Canadian Journal of Behavioural Science* **22**, 20–5.

Osguthorpe, R.T. and Scruggs, T.E. 1990: Special education students as tutors: review and analysis. In Goodlad, S. and Hirst, B. (Eds.), *Explorations in peer tutoring*. Oxford: Blackwell, 76–93.

Osman, B.B. 1982: *No-one to play with: the social life of learning disabilities*. New York: Warner Books.

Osterman, K., Björkqvist, K., Lagerspetz, K.M.J., Kaukiainen, A., Huesmann, L.R. and Fraczek, A. 1994: Peer and self-estimated aggression and victimization in 8-year-old children from 5 ethnic groups. *Aggressive Behaviour* **20**, 411–28.

Ostrov, J., Hubbard, J., Prinstein, M. and Rose, A. 2015: Advances and future directions in the study of peer relations across development: key questions in theory and translation. Paper presented to the Society for Research in Child Development, Philadelphia, PA, March.

Oswald, H. and Krappmann, L. 1995: Social life of children in a former bipartite city. In Noack, P., Hofer, M. and Youniss, J. (Eds.), *Psychological responses to social change: human development in changing environments*. Berlin: de Gruyter, 163–85.

Otero, T.L., Schatz, R.B., Merrill, A.C. and Bellini, S. 2013: Social skills training for youth with autism spectrum disorders: a follow-up. *Child and Adolescent Psychiatric Clinics of North America* **24**, 99–115.

Oyserman, D. and Lee, S.W.S. 2008: Does culture influence what and how we think? Effects of priming individualism and collectivism. *Psychological Bulletin* **134**, 311–42.

Pakaslahti, L., Spoof, I., Asplund-Peltola, R. and Keltikangas-Jaevinen, L. 1998: Parents' social problem-solving strategies in families with aggressive and non-aggressive girls. *Aggressive Behaviour* **24**, 37–51.

Palinscar, A.S. and Brown, A.L. 1984: The reciprocal teaching of comprehension-fostering and comprehension-monitoring activities. *Cognition and Instruction* **1**, 117–75.

Pallini, S., Schneider, B.H., Baiocco, R., Madigan, S. and Atkinson, L. 2014: Early child–parent attachment and peer relations: a meta-analysis of recent research. *Journal of Family Psychology* **28**, 118–23.

Paquette, D. and Bigras, M. 2010: The risky situation: a procedure for assessing the father–child activation relationship. *Early Child Development and Care* **180**, 33–50.

Parens, H. 1979: *The development of aggression in early childhood*. London: Jason Aronson.

Park, J.H., Enright, R.D., Essex, M.J., Zahn-Waxler, C. and Klatt, J.S. 2013: Forgiveness intervention for female South Korean adolescent aggressive victims. *Journal of Applied Developmental Psychology* **34**, 268–76.

Park, Y.O. and Enright, R.D. 1997: The development of forgiveness in the context of adolescent friendship conflict in Korea. *Journal of Adolescence* **20**, 393–402.

Parke, R.D., O'Neil, R., Spitzer, S., Isley, S., Welsh, M., Wang, S., Lee, J., Strand, C. and Cupp, R. 1997: A longitudinal assessment of sociometric stability and the behavioural correlates of children's social acceptance. *Merrill-Palmer Quarterly* **43**, 635–62.

Parker, J.G. 1986: Becoming friends: conversation skills for friendship formation in young children. In Gottman, J.M. and Parker, J.G. (Eds.), *Conversations of friends: speculations on affective development*. Cambridge: Cambridge University Press, 103–38.

Parker, J.G. and Asher, S.R. 1987: Peer acceptance and later personal adjustment: are low-accepted children at risk? *Psychological Bulletin* **102**, 357–89.

Parker, J.G. and Asher, S.R. 1993a: Beyond group acceptance: friendship and friendship quality as distinct dimensions of children's peer adjustment. In Perlman, D. and Jones, W. (Eds.), *Advances in personal relationships*. London: Kingsley, vol. 4, 261–94.

Parker, J.G. and Asher, S.R. 1993b: Friendship and friendship quality in middle childhood: links with peer group acceptance and feelings of loneliness and social dissatisfaction. *Developmental Psychology* **29**, 611–21.

Parker, J.G. and Gottman, J.M. 1989: Social and emotional development in a relational context: friendship interaction from early childhood to adolescence. In Berndt, T.J. and Ladd, G.W. (Eds.), *Peer relationships in child development*. New York: John Wiley, 95–131.

Parker, J.G., Kruse, S.A. and Aikins, J.W. 2010: When friends have other friends: friendship jealousy in childhood and early adolescence. In Hart, S.L. and Legerstee, M. (Eds.), *Handbook of jealousy: theory, research, and multidisciplinary approaches*. New York: Wiley-Blackwell, 516–46.

Parkhurst, J.T. and Asher, S.R. 1992: Peer rejection in middle school: subgroup differences in behaviour, loneliness and interpersonal concerns. *Developmental Psychology* **28**, 231–41.

Parkhurst, J.T. and Hopmeyer, A. 1998: Sociometric popularity and peer-perceived popularity: two distinct dimensions of peer status. *Journal of Early Adolescence* **18**, 125–44.

Parks, M.R. 1985: Interpersonal communication and the quest for personal competence. In Knapp, M.L. and Miller, G.R. (Eds.), *Handbook of interpersonal communication*. Beverly Hills, CA: Sage, 171–201.

Parten, M.B. 1932: Social participation among preschool children. *Journal of Abnormal Psychology* **27**, 243–69.

Patterson, C.J., Kupersmidt, J.B. and Griseler, P.C. 1990: Children's perceptions of self and of relationships with others as a function of sociometric status. *Child Development* **61**, 1335–49.

Patterson, G.R. 1982: *A social learning approach*, vol. 3: *Coercive family processes*. Eugene, OR: Castalia.

Patterson, G.R. and Cobb, J.A. 1971: A dyadic analysis of 'aggressive' behaviors. In Hill, J.P. (Ed.), *Minnesota symposia on child psychology*. Minneapolis, MN: University of Minnesota Press, vol. 5, 74–102.

Pearl, R., Farmer, T.W., van Acker, R., Rodkin, P.C., Bost, K., Coe, M. and Henley, W. 1998: The social integration of students with disabilities in general education classrooms: peer group membership and peer-assessed social behavior. *Elementary School Journal* **99**, 167–85.

Peel, M., Reed, L. and Walter, J. 2009: The importance of friends: the most recent past. In Caine, B. (Ed.), *Friendship: a history*. London: Equinox, 316–55.

Peery, J.C. 1979: Popular, amiable, isolated, rejected: a reconceptualization of sociometric status in preschool children. *Child Development* **50**, 1231–4.

Peery, J.C., Jensen, L. and Adams, G.R. 1985: The relationship between parents' attitudes toward child rearing and the sociometric status of their preschool children. *Journal of Psychology* **119**, 567–74.

Pelham, W.E and Bender, M.E. 1982: Peer relationships in hyperactive children: description and treatment. *Advances in Learning and Behavioral Disabilities* **1**, 365–436.

Pelham, W.E. Jr. and Fabiano, G.A. 2008: Evidence-based psychosocial treatments for attention-deficit/hyperactivity disorder. *Journal of Clinical Child and Adolescent Psychology* **37**, 184–214.

Pellegrini, A.D. 2004: *Observing children in their natural worlds: a methodological primer.* 2nd Edition. Mahwah, NJ: Lawrence Erlbaum Associates.

Pepler, D.J. and Craig, W.M. 1995: A peek behind the fence: naturalistic observations of aggressive children with remote audiovisual recording. *Developmental Psychology* **31**, 548–53.

Pepler, D.J., Craig, W.M. and O'Connell, P. 2010: Peer processes in bullying: informing prevention and intervention strategies. In Jimerson, S.R., Swearer, S.M. and Espelage, D.L. (Eds.), *The International Handbook of School Bullying*. Mahwah, NJ: Erlbaum, 469–80.

Peres, Y. and Pasternack, R. 1991: To what extent can the school reduce the gaps between children raised by divorced and intact families? *Journal of Divorce and Remarriage* **15**, 143–58.

Perlman, D. 2007: The best of times, the worst of times: The place of close relationships in psychology and our daily lives. *Canadian Psychology* **48**, 7–18.

Perret, P. and Faure, S. 2006: Les fondements de la psychopathologie développementale [The foundations of developmental psychopathology]. *Enfance* **584**, 317–33.

Perry, H.S. 1982: *Psychiatrist of America: the life of Harry Stack Sullivan*. Cambridge, MA: Harvard University Press.

Peter, J., Valkenburg, P.M. and Schouten, A.P. 2005: Developing a model of adolescent friendship formation on the internet. *Cyberpsychology and Behavior* **8**, 427–30.

Peterson, L. and Bell-Dolan, D. 1995: Treatment outcome in child psychology: realistic coping with the 'Ten commandments of methodology'. *Journal of Clinical Child Psychology* **24**, 149–62.

Petrina, N., Carter, M. and Stephenson, J. 2014: The nature of friendship in children with autism spectrum disorders: a systematic review. *Research in Autism Spectrum Disorders* **88**, 111–26.

Pettit, G.S., Brown, E.G., Mize, J. and Lindsey, E. 1998: Mothers' and fathers' socializing behaviours in three contexts: links with children's peer competence. *Merrill-Palmer Quarterly* **44**, 173–93.

Pettit, G.S., Dodge, K.A. and Brown, M.M. 1988: Early family experience, social problem solving patterns, and children's social competence. *Child Development* **59**, 107–20.

Pettit, G.S, Harrist, A.W., Bates, J.E. and Dodge, K.A. 1991: Family interaction, social cognition and children's subsequent relations with peers and kindergarten. *Journal of Social and Personal Relationships* **8**, 383–402.

PEW Institute 2013: *Teens and technology survey*. www.pewinternet.org/files/old-media/Files/Reports/2013/PIP_TeensandTechnology2013.pdf, retrieved March 3, 2015.

Philipsen, G. 1987: The prospect for cultural communication. In Kincaid, D. (Ed.), *Communication theory: Eastern and Western perspectives*. New York: Academic Press, 245–54.

Phillips, E.L. 1979: *The social skills basis of psychopathology*. New York: Grune and Stratton.

Piaget, J. 1932: *The language and thought of the child*. New York: Harcourt Brace and Company.

Pinto, G., Bombi, A.S. and Cordioli, A. 1997: Similarity of friends in three countries: a study of children's drawings. *International Journal of Behavioural Development* **20**, 453–69.

Piercy, M., Wilton, K. and Townsend, M. 2002: Promoting the social acceptance of young children with moderate–severe intellectual disabilities using cooperative-learning techniques. *American Journal on Mental Retardation* **107**, 352–60.

Pleck, Joseph H. 2007: Why could father involvement benefit children? Theoretical perspectives. *Applied Developmental Science* **11**, 196–202.

Plomin, R. 1990: The role of inheritance in behavior. *Science* **248**, 183–8.

Plomin, R., Foch, T.T. and Rowe, D.C. 1981: Bobo clown aggression in childhood: environment, not genes. *Journal of Research in Personality* **15**, 331–42.

Plomin, R., Pedersen, J.R., McClearn, N.L., Nesselroade, J.R. and Bergeman, C.S. 1988: Genetic influence on child family environment perceived retroactively from the last half of the life span. *Developmental Psychology* **24**, 738–45.

Plomin, R. and Rowe, D.C. 1979: Genetic and environmental etiology of social behavior in infancy. *Developmental Psychology* **15**, 62–72.

Plusquellec, P., Francois, N., Boivin, M., Perusse, D. and Tremblay, R.E. 2007: Dominance among unfamiliar peers starts in infancy. *Infant Mental Health Journal* **28**, 324–43.

Polloway, E.A., Patton, J.R., Smith, T.E.C. and Buck, G.H. 1997: Mental retardation and learning disabilities: conceptual and applied issues. *Journal of Learning Disabilities* **30**, 297–308.

Pontecorvo, C. and Arcidiacono, F. 2010: Development of reasoning through arguing in young children. *Historical and Cultural Psychology* **4**, 19–29.

Potier, R. 2007: De l'amitié en virtuel [Virtual friendship]. *Adolescence* **3**, 581–91.

Poulin, F., Cillessen, A.H.N., Hubbard, J.A., Coie, J.D., Dodge, K.A. and Schwartz, D. 1997: Children's friends and behavioural similarity in two social contexts. *Social Development* **6**, 224–36.

Poulin, F., Dishion, T.J. and Medici, N. 1998: Antisocial behaviour and stability of friendship networks: network structure, behavioural confluence, and relationship satisfaction. Poster session presented at the biennial meeting of the International Society for the Study of Behavioural Development, Berne, Switzerland, July.

Price, J.M. and Dodge, K.A. 1989: Reactive and proactive aggression in childhood: Relations to peer status and social context dimensions. *Journal of Abnormal Child Psychology* **17**, 455–71.

Prillaman, D. 1981: Acceptance of learning disabled students in the mainstream environment: a failure to replicate. *Journal of Learning Disabilities* **14**, 344–6.

Prinstein, M. and Cillessen, A.H.N. 2003: Forms and functions of adolescent peer aggression associated with high levels of peer status. *Merrill-Palmer Quarterly* **49**, 310–42.

Prior, M., Smart, D., Sanson, A. and Oberklaid, F. 2000: Does shy-inhibited temperament in childhood lead to anxiety problems in adolescence? *Journal of the American Academy of Child and Adolescent Psychiatry* **39**, 461–8.

Pryor-Brown, L. and Cowen, E.L. 1989: Stressful life events, support, and children's school adjustment. *Journal of Clinical Child Psychology* **18**, 214–20.

Pulkinnen, L. 1999: Social-emotional behaviour in childhood as a predictor of adult outcomes: gender differences. Paper presented at the ninth European Conference on Developmental Psychology, Spetses, Greece, September.

Putallaz, M. 1983: Predicting children's sociometric status from their behavior. *Child Development* **54**, 1417–26.

Putallaz, M. 1987: Maternal behaviour and children's sociometric status. *Child Development* **58**, 324–40.

Putnam, J., Markovchick, K., Johnson, D.W. and Johnson, R.T. 1996: Co-operative learning and peer acceptance of students with learning disabilities. *Journal of Social Psychology* **136**, 741–52.

Quinn, M.M., Kavale, K.A., Mathur, S.R., Rutherford Jr., R.B. and Forness, S.R. 1999: A meta-analysis of social skills interventions for students with emotional and behavioral disorders. *Journal of Emotional and Behavioral Disorders* **7**, 54–64.

Qvotrop, J. 1990: *Childhood as a social phenomenon*. Vienna: European Centre for Social Welfare Policy and Research.

Raabe, T. and Beelmann, A. 2011: Development of ethnic, racial, and national prejudice in childhood and adolescence: a multinational meta-analysis of age differences. *Child Development* **82**, 1715–36.

Rackham, H. 1945: *Aristotle's Ethics for English readers*. Oxford: Blackwell.

Radin, N., Oyserman, D. and Benn, R. 1991: Grandfathers, teen mothers and children under two. In Smith, P.K. (Ed.), *The psychology of grandparenthood: an international perspective*. Florence, KY: Taylor and Frances/Routledge, 85–99.

Radmacher, K. and Azmitia, M. 2006: Are there gendered pathways to intimacy in early adolescents' and young adults' friendships? *Journal of Adolescent Research*, **21**(4), 415–48.

Ramdoss, S., Machalicek, W., Rispoli, M. *et al*. 2012: Computer-based interventions to improve social and emotional skills in individuals with autism spectrum disorders: a systematic review. *Developmental Neurorehabitation* **15**, 119–35.

Ray, G.E. and Cohen, R. 1997: Children's evaluations of provocation between peers. *Aggressive Behaviour* **23**, 417–41.

Ray, G.E., Cohen, R., Secrist, M.E. and Duncan, M.K. 1997: Relating aggressive and victimization behaviours to children's sociometric status and friendships. *Journal of Social and Personal Relationships* **14**, 95–108.

Reddy, L.A. 2012: *Group play interventions for children: strategies for teaching prosocial skills*. Washington, DC: American Psychological Association.

Reese-Dukes, J.L. and Stokes, E.H. 1978: Social acceptance of elementary EMR pupils in the regular classroom. *Education and Training of the Mentally Retarded* **13**, 356–61.

Renshaw, P.D. 1981: The roots of current peer interaction research: a historical analysis of the 1930s. In Asher, S.R. and Gottman, J.M. (Eds.), *The development of children's friendships*. Cambridge: Cambridge University Press, 1–27.

Renshaw, P.D. and Asher, S.R. 1983: Children's goals and strategies for social interaction. *Merrill-Palmer Quarterly* **29**, 353–74.

Renshaw, P.D. and Brown, P.J. 1993: Loneliness in middle childhood: concurrent and longitudinal predictors. *Child Development* **64**, 1271–84.

Renshaw, P.D. and Parke, R.D. 1992: Family and peer relationships in historical perspective. In Parke, R.D. and Ladd, G.W. (Eds.), *Family–peer relationships: modes of linkage*. Hillsdale, NJ: Erlbaum Associates, 35–74.

Reuter, J. and Yunik, G. 1973: Social interaction in nursery schools. *Developmental Psychology* **9**, 319–25.

Richard, B.A. and Dodge, K.A. 1982: Social maladjustment and problem solving in school-aged children. *Journal of Consulting and Clinical Psychology* **50**, 226–33.

Richard, J. and Schneider, B.H. 2005: Assessing friendship motivation during pre- and early adolescence. *Journal of Early Adolescence* **25**, 367–85.

Riva, G. 2002: The sociocognitive psychology of computer-mediated communication: the present and future of technology-based interactions. *Cyberpsychology and Behavior* **5**, 581–98.

Rizzo, T.A. 1992: The role of conflict in children's friendship development. In Corsaro, W.A. and Miller, P.J. (Eds.), *Interpretive approaches to children's socialization*. San Francisco, CA: Jossey-Bass, 93–112.

Roazzi, A. and Bryant, P. 1998: The effects of symmetrical and asymmetrical social interaction on children's logical inferences. *British Journal of Developmental Psychology* **16**, 175–81.

Roberts, W.L. and Strayer, J. 1987: Parents' responses to the emotional distress of their children: relations with children's competence. *Developmental Psychology* **23**, 415–22.

Rodkin, P. and Ahn, H.J. 2009: Social networks derived from affiliations and friendships, multi-informant and self-reports: stability, concordance, placement of aggressive and unpopular children, and centrality. *Social Development* **18**, 556–76.

Rodkin, P.C., Farmer, T.W., Pearl, R. and Van Acker, R. 2006: They're cool: social status and peer group supports for aggressive boys and girls. *Social Development* **15**, 175–204.

Roff, J.D. 1992: Childhood aggression, peer status, and social class as predictors of delinquency. *Psychological Reports* **70**, 31–4.

Roff, J.D. and Wirt, R.D. 1984: Childhood aggression and social adjustment as antecedents of delinquency. *Journal of Abnormal Child Psychology* **12**, 111–26.

Roff, M., Sells, B.B. and Golden, M.M. 1972: *Social adjustment and personality development.* Minneapolis, MN: University of Minnesota Press.

Rogoff, B. 1991: Children's guided participation in planning imaginary errands with skilled adult or peer partners. *Developmental Psychology* **27**, 381–9.

Roopnarine, J.L. and Adams, G.R. 1987: The interactional teaching patterns of mothers and fathers with their popular, moderately popular, or unpopular children. *Journal of Abnormal Child Psychology* **15**, 125–36.

Rose, A.J. and Asher, S.R. 1999: Children's goals and strategies in response to conflicts within a friendship. *Developmental Psychology* **35**, 69–79.

Rose, A.J., Schwartz-Mette, R.A., Smith, R.L., Asher, S.R., Swenson, L.P., Carlson, W. and Waller, E.M. 2012: How girls and boys expect disclosure about problems will make them feel: implications for friendships. *Child Development* **83**, 844–63.

Rose, A.J., Swenson, L.P. and Waller, E.M. 2004: Overt and relational aggression and perceived popularity: developmental differences in concurrent and prospective relations. *Developmental Psychology* **40**, 378–87.

Rose, K., Hawes, D.J. and Hunt, C.J. 2014: Randomized controlled trial of a friendship skills intervention on adolescent depressive symptoms. *Journal of Consulting and Clinical Psychology* **82**, 510–20.

Rosenthal, M.J., Ni, E., Finkelstein, M. and Berkowitz, G.K. 1962: Father–child relationships and children's problems. *Archives of General Psychiatry* **7**, 360–73.

Ross, H. and Howe, N. 2009: Family influences on children's peer relationships. In Rubin, K.H., Bukowski, W.M. and Laursen, B. (Eds.), *Handbook of peer interactions, relationships, and groups.* New York: Guilford, 508–27.

Rotenberg, K.J. (Ed.) 2010: *Interpersonal trust during childhood and adolescence.* New York: Cambridge University Press.

Rotenberg, K.J. and Mann, L. 1986: The development of the norm of reciprocity of self-disclosure and its functions in children's attraction to peers. *Child Development* **57**, 1349–57.

Rotenberg, K.J. and Pilipenko, T.A. 1983: Mutuality, temporal consistency, and helpfulness in children's trust in peers. *Social Cognition* **2**, 235–55.

Rotenberg, K.J. and Sliz, D. 1988: Children's restrictive disclosure to friends. *Merrill-Palmer Quarterly* **34**, 203–15.

Rotheram, M.J. 1982: Social skills training with underachievers, disruptive, and exceptional children. *Psychology in the Schools* **19**, 532–39.

Rotheram, M.J., Armstrong, M. and Booraem, C. 1982: Assertiveness training in fourth- and fifth-grade children. *American Journal of Community Psychology* **10**, 567–82.

Rowe, D.C. 1994: *The limits of family influence: genes, experience, and behaviour.* New York: Guilford.

Rubin, K.H. 1993: The Waterloo Longitudinal Project: correlates and consequences of social withdrawal from childhood to adolescence. In Rubin, K.H. and Asendorpf, J.B. (Eds.), *Social withdrawal, inhibition and shyness in childhood.* Hillsdale, NJ: Erlbaum, 291–314.

Rubin, K.H. 1998: Social and emotional development from a cross-cultural perspective. *Developmental Psychology* **34**, 611–15.

Rubin, K.H., Bowker, J.C., McDonald, K.L. and Menzeer, M. 2013: Peer relationships in childhood. In Zelazo, P.D. (Ed.), *Oxford handbook of developmental psychology.* Oxford: Oxford University Press, vol. 2, 242–75.

Rubin, K.H., Bukowski, W. and Parker, J.G. 1998: Peer interactions, relationships, and groups. In Damon, W. and Eisenberg, N. (Eds.), *Handbook of child development*, vol. 3: *Social, emotional, and personality development*. 5th Edition. New York: Wiley, 619–700.

Rubin, K.H., Bukowski, W. and Parker, J. 2006: Peer interactions, relationships, and groups. In Eisenberg, N. (Ed.), *Handbook of child psychology: social, emotional, and personality development*. New York: Wiley, 571–645.

Rubin, K.H., Chen, X. and Hymel, S. 1993: Sociometric characteristics of withdrawn and aggressive children. *Merrill-Palmer Quarterly* **39**, 518–34.

Rubin, K.H., Chen, X., McDougall, P., Bowker, A. and McKinnon, J. 1995: The Waterloo Longitudinal Project: predicting internalizing and externalizing problems in adolescence. *Development and Psychopathology* **7**, 751–64.

Rubin, K.H., Coplan, R.J. and Bowker, J.C. 2009: Social withdrawal in childhood. *Annual Review of Psychology* **60**, 141–71.

Rubin, K.H., Daniels-Beirness, T. and Hayvren, M. 1982: Social and social-cognitive correlates of sociometric status in preschool and kindergarten children. *Canadian Journal of Behavioural Science* **14**, 338–49.

Rubin, K.H., Hymel, S., Lemare, L. and Rowden, L. 1989: Children experiencing social difficulties: sociometric neglect reconsidered. *Canadian Journal of Behavioural Science* **21**, 94–111.

Rubin, K.H., Hymel, S. and Mills, R.S.L. 1989: Sociability and social withdrawal in childhood: stability and outcomes. *Journal of Personality* **57**, 237–55.

Rubin, K.H. and Rose-Krasnor, L. 1986: Social-cognitive and social behaviour perspectives on problem-solving. In Perlmutter, M. (Ed.), *Minnesota symposium on child psychology*. Hillsdale, NJ: Erlbaum, vol. 18, 1–68.

Rubin, K.H. and McDonald, K.L. 2013: The development of relationships. In Pashler, H. (Ed.), *Encyclopedia of the mind*. Thousand Oaks, CA: Sage, 646–55.

Rubin, K.H. and Mills, R.S.L. 1988: The many faces of social isolation in childhood. *Journal of Consulting and Clinical Psychology* **56**, 916–24.

Rubin, K.H., Stewart, K.H. and Chen, X. 1995: Parents of aggressive and withdrawn children. In Bornstein, M.H. (Ed.), *Handbook of parenting*. Mahwah, NJ: Erlbaum, vol. 1, 255–84.

Rubin, K.H., Wojslawowicz, J.C., Rose-Krasnor, L., Booth-LaForce, C. and Burgess, K.B. 2006: The best friendships of shy/withdrawn children: prevalence, stability, and relationship quality. *Journal of Abnormal Child Psychology* **34**, 143–57.

Rubin, Z. 1975: Disclosing oneself to a stranger: reciprocity and its limits. *Journal of Experimental Social Psychology* **11**, 233–60.

Rubin, Z. and Sloman, J. 1984: How parents influence their children's friendships. In Lewis, M. (Ed.), *Beyond the dyad*. New York: Plenum Press, 223–50.

Rutter, M. 1979: Maternal deprivation, 1972–1978: new findings, new concepts, new approaches. *Child Development* **50**, 283–305.

Rutter, M. and Stevenson, J. 2010: Developments in child and adolescent psychiatry over the last 50 years. In Rutter, M., Bishop, D., Pine, D., Scott, S., Stevenson, J., Taylor, E. and Thapar, A. (Eds.), *Rutter's child and adolescent psychiatry*. Oxford: Blackwell, 1–17.

Ryan, A.S. 1985: Cultural factors in casework with Chinese-Americans: social casework. *Journal of Contemporary Social Work* **66**, 333–40.

Rys, G.S. and Bear, G.G. 1997: Relational aggression and peer relations: gender and developmental issues. *Merrill-Palmer Quarterly* **43**, 87–106.

Saarento, S.L., Boulton, A.J. and Salmivalli, C. 2015: Reducing bullying and victimization: student- and classroom-level mechanisms of change. *Journal of Abnormal Child Psychology* **43**, 61–76.

Sagi, A., Lamb, M.E., Estes, D., Shoham, R., Lewkowitz, K. and Dvir, R. 1982: Security of infant–adult attachment among kibbutz-reared infants. Paper presented at the meeting of the International Conference on Infant Studies, Austin, TX, April.

Sagi, A., van IJzendoorn, M.H., Aviezer, O., Donnell, F. and Mayseless, O. 1994: Sleeping out of home in a kibbutz communal arrangement: it makes a difference for infant–mother attachment. *Child Development* **65**, 992–1004.

Sainato, D.M., Zigmond, N. and Strain, P.S. 1983: Social status and initiations of interaction by learning disabled students in a regular education setting. *Analysis and Intervention in Developmental Disabilities* **3**, 71–87.

Sale, P. and Carey, D.M. 1995: The sociometric status of students with disabilities in a full-inclusion program. *Exceptional Children* **62**, 6–19.

Salmivalli, C., Huttunen, A. and Lagerspetz, K.M.J. 1997: Peer networks and bullying in schools. *Scandinavian Journal of Psychology* **38**, 305–12.

Salvas, M.C., Vitaro, F., Brendgen, M., Dionne, G., Tremblay, R.E. and Boivin, M. 2014: Friendship conflict and the development of generalized physical aggression in the early school years: a genetically informed study of potential moderators. *Developmental Psychology* **50**, 1794–1807.

Sandstrom, M.J. and Coie, J.D. 1999: A developmental perspective on peer rejection: mechanisms of stability and change. *Child Development* **70**, 955–66.

San Miguel, S.K., Forness, S.R. and Kavale, K. 1996: Social skills deficits in learning disabilities: the psychiatric comorbidity hypothesis. *Learning Disability Quarterly* **19**, 252–61.

Santana-Gonzalez, Y., Silot-Moreno, D. and Schneider, B.H. 2004: Friendship expectations of early adolescents in Cuba and Canada. *Journal of Cross-Cultural Psychology* **35**, 436–45.

Sasso, G., Melloy, K.G. and Kavale, K. 1990: Generalization, maintenance, and covariation associated with social skills training through social learning. *Behavior Disorders* **16**, 9–22.

Scarr, S. 1992: Developmental theories for the 1990s: developmental and individual differences. *Child Development* **63**, 1–19.

Scharf, M. and Hertz-Lazarowitz, R. 2003: Social networks in the school context: effects of culture and gender. *Journal of Social and Personal Relationships* **20**, 843–58.

Schaughency, E.A., Vannatta, K., Langhinrichsen, J., Lally, C. and Seeley, J. 1992: Correlates of sociometric status in school children in Buenos Aires. *Journal of Abnormal Child Psychology* **20**, 317–26.

Scherf, K.S., Smyth, J.M. and Delgado, M.R. 2013: The amygdala: an agent of change in adolescent neural networks. *Hormones and Behavior* **64**, 298–313.

Schmidt, L.A. and Coplan, R.J. 2014: The A, B, C's of recent work on shyness and social withdrawal: assessment, biology, and context. *Infant and Child Development* **23**, 217–19.

Schmitz, S. 1994: Personality and temperament. In DeFries, J.C., Plomin, R. and Fulker, D.W. (Eds.), *Nature and nurture during middle childhood*. Oxford: Blackwell, 120–40.

Schmitz, S., Cherny, S.S., Fulker, D.W. and Mrazek, D. 1994: Genetic and environmental influences on early childhood behaviour. *Behaviour Genetics* **24**, 25–34.

Schmitz, S., Saudino, K.J., Plomin, R., Fulkner, D. and DeFries, J.C. 1996: Genetic and environmental influences on temperament in middle childhood: analysis of teacher and tester ratings. *Child Development* **67**, 409–22.

Schneider, B.H. 1987: *The gifted child in peer group perspective*. New York: Springer-Verlag.

Schneider, B.H. 1992: Didactic methods for enhancing children's peer relations. *Clinical Psychology Review* **12**, 363–82.

Schneider, B.H. 1993: *Children's social competence in context: the contributions of family, school and culture*. Oxford: Pergamon.

Schneider, B.H. 1999: A multimethod exploration of the friendships of children considered socially withdrawn by their school peers. *Journal of Abnormal Child Psychology* **27**, 115–23.

Schneider, B.H. 2009: An observational study of the interactions of socially withdrawn/anxious early adolescents and their friends. *Journal of Child Psychology and Psychiatry* **50**, 799–806.

Schneider, B.H. 2014: *Child psychopathology: from infancy to adolescence*. Cambridge: Cambridge University Press.

Schneider, B.H. and Amichai-Hamburger, Y. 2010: Electronic communication: escape mechanism or relationship-building tool for shy, withdrawn children and adolescents? In Rubin, K.H. and Coplan, R.J. (Eds.), *The development of shyness and social withdrawal*. New York: Guilford, 236–61.

Schneider, B.H., Attili, G., Vermigli, P. and Younger, A. 1997: A comparison of middle class English-Canadian and Italian mothers' beliefs about children's peer-directed aggression and social withdrawal. *International Journal of Behavioural Development* **21**, 133–54.

Schneider, B.H., Atkinson, L. and Tardif, C. 2001: Child–parent attachment and children's peer relations. *Developmental Psychology* **37**, 86–100.

Schneider, B.H. and Byrne, B.M. 1985. Children's social skills: a meta-analysis. In Schneider, B.H., Rubin, K.H. and Ledingham, J.E. (Eds.), *Children's peer relations: issues in assessment and intervention*. New York: Springer-Verlag, 175–92.

Schneider, B.H. and Byrne, B.M. 1987: Individualizing social skills training for behavior-disordered children. *Journal of Consulting and Clinical Psychology* **55**, 444–5.

Schneider, B.H., Clegg, M.R., Byrne, B.M., Ledingham, J.E. and Crombie, G. 1989: Social relations of gifted children as a function of age and school program. *Journal of Educational Psychology* **81**, 48–56.

Schneider, B.H. and Daniels, T. 1992: Peer acceptance and social play of gifted kindergarten children. *Exceptionality* **3**, 17–29.

Schneider, B.H., Fonzi, A., Tani, F. and Tomada, G. 1997: A cross-cultural exploration of the stability of children's friendships and predictors of their continuation. *Social Development* **6**, 322–39.

Schneider, B.H., Fonzi, A., Tomada, G. and Tani, F. 2000: A cross-national comparison of children's behaviour with their friends in situations of potential conflict. *Journal of Cross-Cultural Psychology* **31**, 259–66.

Schneider, B.H., Lee, M.D. and Alvarez-Valdivia, I. 2011: Adolescent friendship bonds in cultures of connectedness. In Laursen, B. and Collins, W.A. (Eds.), *Relationship pathways: from adolescence to young adulthood*. Thousand Oaks, CA: Sage, 114–34.

Schneider, B.H., Richard, J.F., Younger, A.J. and Freeman, P. 2001: A longitudinal exploration of the continuity of children's social participation and social withdrawal across socioeconomic status levels and social settings. *European Journal of Social Psychology* **30**, 497–519.

Schneider, B.H., Udvari, S. and Dixon, K. 2007: Closeness and competition in the inter-ethnic and co-ethnic friendships of early adolescents in Toronto and Montreal. *Journal of Early Adolescence* **27**, 115–38.

Schneider, B.H. and Tessier, N. 2007: Close friendship as understood by socially withdrawn, anxious early adolescents. *Child Psychiatry and Human Development* **38**, 339–51.

Schneider, B.H., Tomada, G., Normand, S., Tonci, E. and deDomini, P. 2008: Social support as a predictor of school bonding and academic motivation following the transition to Italian middle school. *Journal of Social and Personal Relationships* **25**, 287–310.

Schneider, B.H., Woodburn, S., Soteras del Toro, M. and Udvari, S.J. 2005: Cultural and gender differences in the implications of competition for early-adolescent friendship. *Merrill-Palmer Quarterly* **51**, 163–91.

Schneider, J. 1971: On vigilance and virgins: honour, shame, and access to resources in Mediterranean societies. *Ethnology* **10**, 1–23.

Schwartz, C.E., Snidman, N. and Kagan, J. 1996: Early childhood temperament as a determinant of externalizing behavior in adolescence. *Development and Psychopathology* **8**, 527–37.

Schwartz, D., McFayden-Ketchem, S., Dodge, K.A., Pettit, G.S. and Bates, J.E. 1999: Early behaviour problems as a predictor of later peer group victimization: moderators and mediators in the pathways of social risk. *Journal of Abnormal Child Psychology* **27**, 191–201.

Schwartz, J.C. 1972: Effects of peer familiarity on the behavior of preschoolers in a novel situation. *Journal of Personality and Social Psychology* **24**, 276–84.

Schwartz, S.H. and Ros, M. 1995: Value priorities in West European nations: a cross-cultural perspective. In Ben-Shakar, G. and Lieblich, A. (Eds.), *Studies in psychology in honor of Solomon Kugelmass*. Jerusalem: Magnes Press, 322–47.

Sears, R.R. 1961: Relation of early socialization experiences to aggression in middle childhood. *Journal of Abnormal and Social Psychology* **63**, 466–92.

Sears, R.R., Maccoby, E.E. and Levin, H. 1957: *Patterns of child rearing*. Evenston, IL: Row-Peterson.

Sears, R.R., Whiting, J.W.M., Nowlis, V. and Sears, P.S. 1953: Some child rearing antecedents of aggression and dependency in. *Genetic Psychology Monographs* **47**, 135–234.

Selfhout, M.H.W., Branje, S.T., Delsing, M., ter Bogt, T.F.M. and Meeus, W.H.J. 2009: Different types of internet use, depression and social anxiety: the role of perceived friendship quality. *Journal of Adolescence* **32**, 819–33.

Selman, R.L. 1980: *The growth of interpersonal understanding: developmental and clinical understandings*. New York: Academic Press.

Selman, R.L. and Schultz, L.H. 1989: Children's strategies for interpersonal negotiation with peers: an interpretative/empirical approach to the study of social development. In Berndt, T.J. and Ladd, G.W. (Eds.), *Peer relationships in child development*. Wiley series on personality processes. New York: John Wiley and Sons, 371–406.

Selman, R.L. and Schultz, L.H. 1990: *Making a friend in youth*. Chicago, IL: University of Chicago Press.

Selman, R.L., Watts, C.L. and Schultz, L.H. (Eds.) 1997: *Fostering friendship: pair therapy for treatment and prevention*. New York: Aldine De Gruyter.

Selman, R.S., Levitt, M.Z. and Schultz, L.H. 1997: The friendship framework: tools for the assessment of psychosocial development. In Selman, R.S., Watts, C.L. and Schultz, L.H. (Eds.), *Fostering friendship for treatment and prevention*. New York: de Gruyter, 31–53.

Serbin, L.A., Peters, P.L., McAffer, V.J. and Schwartzman, A.E. 1991: Childhood aggression and withdrawal as predictors of adolescent pregnancy, early parenthood, and environmental risk for the next generation. *Canadian Journal of Behavioural Sciences* **23**, 318–31.

Seyfarth, R.M. and Cheney, D.L. 2012: The evolutionary origins of friendship. *Annual Review of Psychology* **63**, 153–77.

Shannon, K. and Kafer, N.F. 1984: Reciprocity, trust, and vulnerability in neglected and rejected children. *Journal of Psychology* **117**, 65–70.

Shantz, C. 1985: *Children's peer relations: sociometric status, dyads and triads*. Washington, DC: National Science Foundation.

Shapira, A. and Madsen, M.C. 1974: Between and within-group co-operation and competition among kibbutz and nonkibbutz children. *Developmental Psychology* **10**, 140–5.

Sharabany, R. 1982: Comradeship: peer group relations among preadolescents in kibbutz versus city. *Personality and Social Psychology Bulletin* **8**, 302–9.

Sharabany, R. 1994: Continuities in the development of intimate friendships: object relations, interpersonal, and attachment perspectives. In Erber, R. and Gilmour, R. (Eds.), *Theoretical frameworks for personal relationships*. Hillsdale, NJ: Erlbaum, 164–79.

Sharabany, R., Eshel, Y. and Hakim, C. 2008: Boyfriend, girlfriend in a traditional society: parenting styles and development of intimate friendships among Arabs in school. *International Journal of Behavioral Development* **32**, 66–75.

Sharabi, A. and Margalit, M. 2011: The mediating role of internet connection, virtual friends, and mood in predicting loneliness among students with and without learning disabilities in different educational environments. *Journal of Learning Disabilities* **44**, 215–27.

Shenkar, O. and Ronen, S. 1987: The cultural context negotiations: the implications of Chinese interpersonal norms. *Journal of Applied Behavioural Science* **23**, 263–75.

Shernoff, D.J. 2010: Engagement in after-school programs as a predictor of social competence and academic performance. *American Journal of Community Psychology* **45**, 325–37.

Shih T.A. 1998: Finding the niche: friendship formation of immigrant adolescents. *Youth and Society* **30**, 209–40.

Shin N., Vaughn, B.E., Kim, M., Krzysik, L., Bost, K.K., McBride, B., Santos, S., Peceguina, I. and Coppola, G. 2011: Longitudinal analyses of a hierarchical model of peer social competence for preschool children: structural fidelity and external correlates. *Merrill-Palmer Quarterly* **57**, 73–103.

Shure, M.B. 2001: *I can problem solve*. Champaign, IL: Research Press.

Siegelman, M. 1966: Loving and punishing parental behavior and introversion tendencies in sons. *Child Development* **37**, 985–92.

Sillars, A.L. 1991: Behavioural observation. In Montgomery, B.M. and Duck, S. (Eds.), *Studying interpersonal interaction*. New York: Guilford, 197–218.

Silver, J.M. and Yudofsky, S.C. 1991: The Overt Aggression Scale: overview and guiding principles. *Journal of Neuropsychiatry and Clinical Neurosciences* **3**, 522–9.

Simonton, D.K. 2011: Positive psychology in historical and philosophical perspective: predicting its future from the past. In Sheldon, K.M., Kashdan, T.B. and Steger, M.F. (Eds.), *Designing positive psychology: taking stock and moving forward*. New York: Oxford University Press, 447–54.

Sinha, J.B.P. and Tripathi, R.C. 1994: Individualism in a collectivistic culture: a case of coexistence of opposites. In Kim, U., Triandis, H.C., Kagitcibasi, C., Choi, S.C. and Yoon, G. (Eds.), *Individualism and collectivism: theory, methods, and applications*. Thousand Oaks, CA: Sage, 123–36.

Siperstein, G.N., Glick, G.C. and Parker, R.C. 2009: Social inclusion of children with intellectual disabilities in a recreational setting. *Intellectual and Developmental Disabilities* **47**, 97–107.

Siperstein, G.N., Leffert, J.S. and Widaman, K. 1996: Social behavior and the social acceptance and rejection of children with mental retardation. *Education and Training in Mental Retardation and Development* **31**, 271–81.

Skinner, B.F. 1948: *Walden two*. New York: Machultan.

Slanina, A.M. 1996: Factors that impact transitions between a regular-educational program and a gifted program: the perceptions of four African-American males. *Journal for the Education of the Gifted* **20**, 54–83.

Slavin, R.E. 1979: Effects of biracial learning teams on cross-racial friendships. *Journal of Educational Psychology* **71**, 381–7.

Slavin, R.E. 1987: Developmental and motivational perspectives on co-operative learning: a reconciliation. *Child Development* **58**, 1161–7.

Slavin, R.E. 1991: Co-operative learning and group contingencies. *Journal of Behavioral Education* **1**, 105–15.

Slavin, R.E. 2015: Cooperative learning in elementary schools. *Education 3–13: International Journal of Elementary and Early Years Education* **43**, 5–14.

Slee, P.T. 1999: Bullying amongst Australian primary school students: some barriers to help-seeking and links with sociometric status. In Slee, P.T. and Rigby, K. (Eds.), *Children's peer relations*. London: Routledge, 205–14.

Smahel, D., Brown, B. and Blinka, L. 2012: Associations between online friendship and internet addiction among adolescents and emerging adults. *Developmental Psychology* **482**, 381–8.

Smith, A. and Schneider, B.H. 2000: The inter-ethnic friendships of adolescent students: a Canadian study. *International Journal of Intercultural Relations* **24**, 247–58.

Smith, A.K., Rhee, S.H., Corley, R.P., Friedman, N.P., Hewitt, J.K. and Robinson, J.L. 2012: The magnitude of genetic and environmental influences on parental and observational measures of behavioral inhibition and shyness in toddlerhood. *Behavior Genetics* **42**,764–77.

Smith, J.D., Schneider, B.H., Smith, P.K. and Ananiadou, K. 2004: The effectiveness of whole-school antibullying programs: a synthesis of evaluation research. *School Psychology Review* **33**, 547–60.

Smith, L. 1996: The social construction of rational understanding. In Tryphon, A. and Voneche, J. (Eds.), *Piaget–Vygotsky: the social genesis of thought*. Hove: Psychology Press, 107–22.

Smith, M.C., Winningham, V. and Haro, L. 1999: Social and emotional competencies: contributions to young African-American children's peer acceptance. Paper presented at the Society for Research and Development in Child Psychology, Albuquerque, NM, April.

Smith, P.K. 1989: The role of rough and tumble play in the development of social competence: theoretical perspectives and empirical evidence. In Schneider, B.H., Attili, G., Nadel, J. and Weissberg, R.P. (Eds.), *Social competence in developmental perspectives*. Dordrecht: Kluwer, 239–55.

Smith, P.K. 1999: Introduction. In Smith, P.K., Morita, Y., Junger-Tas, J., Olweus, D., Catalono, R. and Slee, P. (Eds.), *The nature of school bullying: a cross-national perspective*. London: Routledge, 1–4.

Smith, P.K. In press: Bullying and theory of mind. *Current Psychiatry Reviews*.

Smith, P.K., Morita, Y., Junger-Tas, J., Olweus, D., Catalano, R.F. and Slee, P. 1999: *The nature of school bullying: a cross-national perspective*. New York: Routledge.

Smith, P.K., Salmivalli, C. and Cowie, H. 2012: Effectiveness of school-based programs to reduce bullying: a response. *Journal of Experimental Criminology* **84**, 433–41.

Smith, P.K. and Sharp, S. (Eds.) 1994: *School bullying insights and perspectives*. London: Routledge.

Smith, P.K. and Slonje, R. 2010: Cyberbullying: the nature and extent of a new kind of bullying, in and out of school. In Jimerson, S.R., Swearer, S.M. and Espelage, D.L. (Eds.), *The handbook of bullying in schools: an international perspective*. New York: Routledge, 249–62.

Smith, R.L. and Rose, A.J. 2011: The 'cost of caring' in youths' friendships: considering associations among social perspective taking, co-rumination, and empathetic distress. *Developmental Psychology* **47**, 1792–1803.

Solano, C.H. 1976: Teacher and pupil stereotypes of gifted boys and girls. Paper presented at the annual conference of the American Psychological Association, Washington, DC, September.

Spence, S.H. 1987: The relationship between social-cognitive skills and peer sociometric status. *British Journal of Developmental Psychology* **5**, 347–56.

Spieker, S.J. and Booth, C.L. 1988: Maternal antecedents of attachment quality. In Belsky, J. and Nezworski, T. (Eds.), *Clinical implications of attachment*. Hillsdale, NJ: Erlbaum, 95–135.

Spiel, C., Weixelbaum, E. and Spiel, C. 1999: The impact of dropouts in a longitudinal study of children at risk. Paper presented at the ninth European Conference on Developmental Psychology, Spetses, Greece, September.

Spies-Shapiro, L.A. and Margolin, A. 2014: Growing up wired: social network sites and adolescent psychosocial development. *Clinical Child and Family Psychology Review* **17**, 1–18.

Spivack, G. and Shure, M.B. 1974: *Social adjustment of young children*. San Francisco, CA: Jossey-Bass.

Spurgeon, P., Hicks, C. and Terry, R. 1983: A preliminary investigation into sex differences in reported friendship determinants amongst a group of early adolescents. *British Journal of Social Psychology* **22**, 63–4.

Sroufe, L.A., Duggal, S., Weinfield, N. and Carlson, E. 2000: Relationships, development, and psychopathology. In Sameroff, A.J., Lewis, M. and Miller, S.M. (Eds.), *Handbook of developmental psychopathology*. New York: Springer Science and Business Media, 75–92.

Stanton, M.E. 1995: Patterns of kinship and residence. In Ingoldsby, B.B and Smith, S. (Eds.), *Families in multicultural perspective: perspectives on marriage and the family*. New York: Guilford, 97–116.

Stark, K.D., Streusand, W., Arora, P. and Patel, P. 2012: Childhood depression: the ACTION treatment program. In Kendall, P.C. (Ed.), *Child and adolescent therapy: cognitive-behavioral procedures*. 4th Edition. New York: Guilford Press, 190–233.

Stattin, H. and Magnusson, D. 1989: The role of early aggressive behavior in the frequency, seriousness and types of later crime. *Journal of Consulting and Clinical Psychology* **57**, 710–18.

Steca, P., Bassi, M., Caprara, G.V. and delle Fave, A. 2007: Parents' self-efficacy beliefs and their children's psychosocial adaptation during adolescence. *Journal of Youth and Adolescence* **40**, 320–31.

Steinberg, L., Brown, B.B. and Dornbusch, S.M. 1996: *Beyond the classroom: why school reform has failed and what parents need to do*. New York: Simon and Schuster.

Stenhoff, D. and Lignugaris-Kraft, B. 2007: A review of the effects of peer tutoring on students with mild disabilities in secondary settings. *Exceptional Children* **74**, 8–31.

Stern, S. 2002: Sexual selves on the World Wide Web: adolescent girls' home pages as sites for sexual self-expression. In Brown, J.D., Steele, J.E. and Walsh-Childers, K. (Eds.), *Sexual teens, sexual media: investigating media's influence on adolescent sexuality*. Mahwah, NJ: Erlbaum, 265–85.

Stevahn, L., Johnson. D.W., Johnson, R.T. and Real, D. 1996: The impact of a cooperative or individualistic context on the effectiveness of conflict resolution training. *American Educational Research Journal* **33**, 801–23.

Stocker, C.M. 1994: Children's perceptions of relationships with siblings, friends, and mothers: compensatory processes and links with adjustment. *Journal of Child Psychology and Psychiatry* **35**, 1447–59.

Stokes, T.E. and Baer, D.M. 1977: An implicit technology of generalization. *Journal of Applied Behaviour Analysis* **10**, 349–67.

Stone, W.L. and La Greca, A.M. 1990: The social status of children with learning disabilities: a re-examination. *Journal of Learning Disabilities* **23**, 32–7.

Stoneman, Z., Brody, G.H. and MacKinnon, C. 1984: Naturalistic observations of children's activities and roles while playing with their siblings and friends. *Child Development* **55**, 617–27.

Stormshak, E.A., Bierman, K.L., Bruschi, C., Dodge, K.A. and Coie, J.D. 1999: The relation between behavior problems and peer preference in different classroom contexts. *Child Development* **70**, 169–82.

Storr, A. 1968: *Human aggression*. London: Penguin Press.

Strain, P.S., Schwartz, I.S. and Bovey, E. 2008: Social competence interventions for young children with autism. In Brown, W.H., Odom, S.L. and McConnell, S.R. (Eds.), *Social competence of young children: risk, disability, and intervention*. Baltimore, MD: Paul H. Brookes Publishing, 253–72.

Strassberg, Z., Dodge, K.A., Bates, J.E. and Pettit, G.S. 1992: The longitudinal relation between parental conflict strategies and children's sociometric standing in kindergarten. *Merrill-Palmer Quarterly* **38**, 477–93.

Strassberg, Z., Dodge, K.A., Pettit, G.S. and Bates, J.E. 1994: Spanking in the home and children's subsequent aggression toward kindergarten peers. *Development and Psychopathology* **6**, 445–61.

Strichart, S.S. and Gottlieb, J. 1975: Imitation of retarded children by their non-retarded peers. *American Journal of Mental Deficiency* **179**, 506–12.

Sturaro, C., van Lier, P.A, Cuijpers, P. and Koot, H.M. 2011: The role of peer relationships in the development of early school-age externalizing problems. *Child Development* **82**, 758–65.

Subrahmanyam, K., Greenfield, P.M. and Tynes, B. 2004: Constructing sexuality and identity in an online teen chat room. *Journal of Applied Developmental Psychology* **25**, 651–66.

Suchman, L. 2007: *Human–machine reconfigurations: plans and situation action*. 2nd Edition: Cambridge: Cambridge University Press.

Sugarman, D.B. and Willoughby, T. 2013: Technology and violence: conceptual issues raised by the rapidly changing social environment. *Psychology of Violence* **3**, 1–8.

Suler, J. 2004a: The online disinhibition effect. *CyberPsychology and Behavior* **7**, 321–6.

Suler, J. 2004b: The psychology of text relationships. In Kraus, R., Zack, J. and Stricker, G. (Eds.), *Online counseling: a handbook for mental health professionals*. San Diego, CA: Elsevier, 19–50.

Sullivan, D., Landau, M.J. and Rothschild, Z.R. 2010: An existential function of enemyship: evidence that people attribute influence to personal and political enemies to compensate for threats to control. *Journal of Personality and Social Psychology* **98**, 434–49.

Sullivan, H.S. 1953: *The interpersonal theory of psychiatry*. New York: Norton.

Sun, C.T.L. 2014: Psychology in Asia: an introduction. In Sun, C.T.L. (Ed.), *Culture and social behavior.* Boston, MA: Cengage Learning, 423–67.

Sutton, J., Smith, P.K. and Swettenham, J. 1999: Social cognition and bullying: social inadequacy or skilled manipulation? *British Journal of Developmental Psychology* **17**, 435–50.

Sutton-Smith, B. 1982: A performance theory for peer relations. In Borman, K. (Ed.), *The social life of children in a changing society*. Hillsdale, NJ: Erlbaum, 65–77.

Suzuki, L.K. and Calzo, J.P. 2004: The search for peer advice in cyberspace: an examination of online teen bulletin boards about health and sexuality. *Journal of Applied Developmental Psychology* **25**, 658–98.

Swenson, L.M. and Strough, J. 2009: Adolescents' collaboration in the classroom: do peer relationships or gender matter? *Psychology in the Schools* **87**, 715–28.

Symonds, P.M. 1939: *The psychology of the parent–child relationship*. New York: Appleton-Century.

Tabak, B.A., McCullough, M.E., Luna, L.R., Bono, G. and Berry, J.W. 2012: Conciliatory gestures facilitate forgiveness and feelings of friendship by making transgressors appear more agreeable. *Journal of Personality* **80**, 503–36.

Tajfel, H. and Turner, J.C. 1986: The social identity theory of inter-group behavior. In Worchel, S. and Austin, L.W. (Eds.), *Psychology of intergroup relations*. Chicago, IL: Nelson-Hall, 7–24.

Taki, M. 2010: Relations among bullying, stresses and stressors: a longitudinal and comparative survey among countries. In Jimerson, S.R., Swearer, S.M. and Espelage, D.L. (Eds.), *The handbook of bullying in schools: an international perspective*. New York: Routledge, 151–62.

Tarabulsy, G.M., Avgoustis, E., Phillips, J., Pederson, D. and Moran, G. 1997: Similarities and differences in mothers' and observers' descriptions of attachment behaviours. *International Journal of Behaviour Development* **21**, 599–619.

Tassi, F. and Schneider, B.H. 1997: Task-oriented versus other-referenced competition: differential implications for children's peer relations. *Journal of Applied Social Psychology* **27**, 1557–80.

Taylor, A.R., Asher, S.R. and Williams, G.A. 1987: The social adaptation of mainstreamed mildly retarded children. *Child Development* **58**, 1321–34.

Taylor, A.R. and Machida, S. 1994: The contribution of parent and peer support to Head Start children early school adjustment. *Early Childhood Research Quarterly* **9**, 387–405.

Terman, L.M. and Oden, M. 1959: *The gifted group at mid-life: thirty-five years' follow-up of the superior child*. Stanford, CA: Stanford University Press.

Terry, R. and Coie, J.D. 1991: A comparison of methods for defining sociometric status among children. *Developmental Psychology* **27**, 867–80.

Tesser, A., Campbell, J. and Smith, M. 1984: Friendship choice and performance: self-evaluation maintenance in children. *Journal of Personality and Social Psychology* **46**, 561–74.

Tessier, O., Tremblay, R.E. and Bukowski, W.M. 1994: Friendship, friendship quality and delinquency in an 'at risk' sample of boys between the ages of 10 and 15. Poster session presented at the biennial meeting of the International Society of Behavioural Development, Amsterdam, The Netherlands, June.

Thayer, S.M., Updegraff, K.A. and Delgado, M.Y. 2008: Conflict resolution in Mexican American adolescents' friendships: links with culture, gender and friendship quality. *Journal of Youth and Adolescence* **37**, 783–97.

Thrasher, F.M. 1927: *The gang: a study of 1,313 street gangs in Chicago*. Chicago, IL: University of Chicago Press.

Tian, L.M., Chen, G.H., Wang, S.Q., Liu, H.J. and Zhang, W.X. 2012: Effects of parental support and friendship support on loneliness and depression during early and middle adolescence. *Acta Psychologica Sinica* **44**, 944–56.

Tinbergen, N. 1963: On aims and methods of ethology. *Zeitschrift für Tierpsychologie* **20**, 410–33.

Tomada, G. and Schneider, B.H. 1997: Relational aggression, gender, and peer acceptance: invariance across culture, stability over time, and concordance among informants. *Developmental Psychology* **33**, 601–9.

Tong, V.M. 2014: Understanding the acculturation experience of Chinese adolescent students: sociocultural adaptation strategies and a positive bicultural and bilingual identity. *Bilingual Research Journal* **37**, 83–100.

Toupin, E.S.W.A. 1980: Counselling Asians: psychotherapy in the context of racism and Asian-American history. *American Journal of Orthopsychiatry* **50**, 76–86.

Townsend, M. and Hassall, J. 2007: Mainstream students' attitudes to possible inclusion in unified sports with students who have an intellectual disability. *Journal of Applied Research in Intellectual Disabilities* **20**, 265–73.

Triandis, H.C. 1990: Cross-cultural studies of individualism and collectivism. In Dienstbier, R.A. (Series Ed.) and Berman, J.J. (Ed.), *Nebraska symposium onmotivation 1989*. Lincoln, NE: University of Nebraska Press, vol. 37, 41–133.

Triandis, H.C., Bontempo, R., Villareal, M.J., Asai, M. and Lucca, N. 1988: Individualism and collectivism: cross-cultural perspectives on self-ingroup relationships. *Journal of Personality and Social Psychology* **52**, 323–38.

Troop-Gordon, W.P. and Asher, S.R. 2005: Modifications in children's goals when encountering obstacles to conflict resolution. *Child Development* **76**, 568–82.

Tseng, W.L., Banny, A.M., Kawabata, Y., Crick, N.R. and Gau, S.S.F. 2013: A cross-lagged structural equation model of relational aggression, physical aggression, and peer status in a Chinese culture. *Aggressive Behavior* **39**, 301–15.

Tseng, W.L., Kawabata, Y., Gau, S.S.F and Crick, N.R. 2014: Symptoms of attention-deficit/hyperactivity disorder and peer functioning: a transactional model of development. *Journal of Abnormal Child Psychology* **42**, 1353–65.

Tsui, P. and Schultz, G.L. 1988: Ethnic factors in group process: cultural dynamics in multi-ethnic therapy groups. *American Journal of Orthopsychiatry* **58**, 136–42.

Ttofi, M.M. and Farrington, D.P. 2012: Bullying prevention programs: the importance of peer intervention, disciplinary methods and age variations. *Journal of Experimental Criminology* **8**, 443–62.

Tuddenham, R.D. 1951: Studies in reputation III: correlates of popularity among elementary-school children. *Journal of Educational Psychology* **25**, 257–76.

Turkle, S. 2004: Whither psychoanalysis in computer culture? *Psychoanalytic-Psychology* **21**, 16–30.

Turkle, S. 2011: *Alone together: why we expect more from technology and less from each other.* New York: Basic Books.

Udvari, S.J. and Rubin, K.H. 1996: Gifted and non-selected children's perceptions of academic achievement, academic effort and athleticism. *Gifted Child Quarterly* **40**, 211–19.

Underwood, M.K. and Rosen, L.H. (Eds.) 2011: *Social development: relationships in infancy, childhood, and adolescence*. New York: Guilford Press.

Urberg, K.A., Değirmencioğlu, S.M., Tolson, J.M. and Halliday-Scher, K. 2000: Adolescent social crowds: measurement and relationship to friendships. *Journal of Adolescent Research* **15**(4), 427–45.

Vaillancourt, T., McDougall, P., Hymel, S. and Sunderani, S. 2010: Respect or fear? The relationship between power and bullying behavior. In Jimerson, S.R., Swearer, S.M. and Espelage, D.L. (Eds.), *The handbook of bullying in schools: an international perspective*. New York: Routledge, 211–22.

Valkenburg, P. M., Schouten, A.P. and Peter, J. 2005: Adolescents' identity experiments on the internet. *New Media and Society* **7**, 383–402.

van Aken, M.A.G. and Asendorpf, J.B. 1997: Support by parents, classmates, friends and siblings in preadolescence: covariation and compensation across relationships. *Journal of Social and Personal Relationships* **14**, 79–93.

Vandell, D.L. and Hembree, S.E. 1994: Peer social status and friendship: independent contributors to children's social and academic adjustment. *Merrill-Palmer Quarterly* **40**, 461–77.

van den Berg, Y.H.M., Lansu, T.A.M. and Cillessen, A.H.N. 2015: Measuring social status and social behavior with peer and teacher nomination methods. *Social Development*. http://onlinelibrary.wiley.com/doi/10.1111/sode.12120/abstract, retrieved May 22, 2015.

van der Horst, F.C.P, van der Veer, R. and van IJzendoorn, M.H. 2007: John Bowlby and ethology: an annotated interview with Robert Hinde. *Attachment and Human Development* **9**, 321–35.

van der Wal, R.C., Karremans, J.C. and Cillessen, A.H.N. 2014: It takes two to forgive: the interactive role of relationship value and executive control. *Personality and Social Psychology Bulletin* **40**, 803–15.

van der Watt, R. 2014: Attachment, parenting styles and bullying during pubertal years. *Journal of Child and Adolescent Mental Health* **26**, 251–61.

van IJzendoorn, M.H. and Kroonenberg, P.M. 1988: Cross-cultural patterns of attachment: a meta-analysis of the Strange Situation. *Child Development* **59**, 147–56.

van Ryzin, M.J. and Dishion, T.J. 2013: From antisocial behavior to violence: a model for the amplifying role of coercive joining in adolescent friendships. *Journal of Child Psychology and Psychiatry* **54**, 661–69.

van Salisch, M. and Uhlendorff, H. 1998: Peer rejection and angry, aggressive behavior in open-field situations and scorn during a cooperative task. Unpublished manuscript, Free University of Berlin.

Vaughn, B.E. and Langlois, J.H. 1983: Physical attractiveness as a correlate of peer status and social competence in preschool children. *Developmental Psychology* **19**, 561–7.

Vaughn, B.E. and Santos, A.J. 2009: Structural descriptions of social transactions among young children: affiliation and dominance in preschool groups. In Rubin, K.H., Bukowski, W.M. and Laursen, B. (Eds.), *Handbook of peer interactions, relationships, and groups*. New York: Guilford, 195–214.

Vaughn, S. and Haager, D. 1994: Social competence as a multifaceted construct: how do students with learning disabilities fare? *Learning Disability Quarterly* **71**, 253–66.

Vaughn, S., Haager, D., Hogan, A. and Kouzekanani, K. 1992: Self-concept and peer acceptance in students with learning disabilities: a four-to-five year prospective study. *Journal of Educational Psychology* **84**, 43–50.

Vaughn, S., Hogan, A., Kouzekanani, K. and Shapiro, S. 1990: Peer acceptance, self-perception and social skills of learning disabled students prior to identification. *Journal of Educational Psychology* **82**, 101–6.

Vaughn, S., McIntosh, R., Schumm, J.S., Haager, D. and Callwood, D. 1993: Social status, peer status and reciprocal friendships revisited. *Learning Disabilities Research and Practice* **8**, 82–8.

Vekiri, I. and Chronaki, A. 2008: Gender issues in technology use: perceived social support, computer self-efficacy and value beliefs, and computer use beyond school. *Computers and Education* **51**, 1392–1404.

Verissimo, M., Santos, A.J., Vaughn, B.R., Torres, N., Monteiro, L. and Santos, O. 2011: Quality of attachment to father and mother and number of reciprocal friends. *Early Child Development and Care* **181**, 27–38.

Verkuyten, M. and Martinovic, B. 2006: Understanding multicultural attitudes: the role of group status, identification, friendships, and justifying ideologies. *International Journal of Intercultural Relations* **30**, 1–18.

Verkuyten, M. and Thijs, J. 2002: Multiculturalism among minority and majority adolescents in the Netherlands. *International Journal of Intercultural Relations* **26**, 91–108.

Véronneau, M.-H., Vitaro, F., Pedersen, S. and Tremblay, R.E. 2008: Do peers contribute to the likelihood of secondary school graduation among disadvantaged boys? *Journal of Educational Psychology* **100**, 429–42.

Véronneau, M.-H., Vitaro, F., Brendgen, M., Dishion, T.J. and Tremblay, R.E. 2010: Transactional analysis of the reciprocal links between peer experiences and academic achievement from middle childhood to early adolescence. *Developmental Psychology* **46**, 773–90.

Verry, E.E. 1923: A study of mental and social attitudes in the free play of preschool children. Unpublished thesis for MA degree, State University of Iowa.

Vitaro, F., Gagnon, C. and Tremblay, R.E. 1990: Predicting stable peer rejection from kindergarten to Grade One. *Journal of Clinical Child Psychology* **19**, 257–64.

Vitaro, F., Gendreau, P.L., Tremblay, R.E. and Oligny, P. 1998: Reactive and proactive aggression differentially predict later conduct problems. *Journal of Child Psychology and Psychiatry and Allied Disciplines* **39**, 377–85.

Vitaro, F., Pedersen, S. and Brendgen, M. 2007: Children's disruptiveness, peer rejection, friends' deviancy, and delinquent behaviors: a process-oriented approach. *Development and Psychopathology* **19**, 433–53.

Vitoroulis, I., Schneider, B.H., Vasquez, C.C., Soteras de Toro, M.P. and Gonzales, Y.S. 2012: Perceived parental and peer support in relation to Canadian, Cuban, and Spanish adolescents' valuing of academics and intrinsic academic motivation. *Journal of Cross-Cultural Psychology* **43**, 704–22.

Volkan, V.D. 1988: *The need to have enemies and allies*. London: Jason Aronson, Inc.

Volling, B.L., Youngblade, L.M. and Belsky, J. 1997: Young children's social relationships with siblings and friends. *American Journal of Orthopsychiatry* **67**, 102–11.

Vosk, B., Forehand, R., Parker, J.B. and Rickard, K. 1982: A multimethod comparison of popular and unpopular children. *Developmental Psychology* **18**, 571–5.

Vygotsky, L.S. 1962: *Thought and language.* Cambridge, MA: Massachusetts Institute of Technology.

Wagner, E.F. and Austin, A.M. 2009: Problem solving and social skills training. In Springer, D.W. and Rubin, A. (Eds.), *Substance abuse treatment for youth and adults: clinician's guide to evidence-base practice*. Hoboken, NJ: Wiley, 57–107.

Walcott, E. 1932: Daydreamers: a study of their adjustment in adolescence. *Smith College Studies in Social Work* **2**, 283–335.

Waldrop, M.F. and Halverson, C.F. Jr. 1975: Intensive and extensive peer behavior: longitudinal and cross-sectional analyses. *Child Development* **46**, 19–26.

Walker, H.M. and Lamon, W.E. 1987: Social behavior standards and expectations of Australian and US teacher groups. *Journal of Special Education* **21**, 56–82.

Walker, H.M. and Rankin, R. 1983: Assessing the behavioral expectations and the demands of less restrictive settings. *School Psychology Review* **12**, 274–84.

Wallerstein, R.S. 1989: The psychotherapy research project of the Menninger Foundation: an overview. *Journal of Consulting and Clinical Psychology* **55**, 195–205.

Walters, J. M. and Kim-Spoon, J. 2014: Are religiousness and forgiveness protective factors for adolescents experiencing peer victimization? *Journal of Aggression, Maltreatment and Trauma* **23**, 1090–1108.

Wasserstein, S.B. and LaGreca, A. 1996: Can peer support buffer against behavioral consequences of parental discord? *Journal of Clinical Child Psychology* **25**, 177–82.

Waters, E. and Deane, K. 1985: Defining and assessing individual differences in attachment relationships: Q-methodology and the organization of behaviour in infancy and early childhood. In Bretherton, I. and Waters, E. (Eds.), *Growing points of attachment theory and research.* Monographs of the Society for Research in Child Development 50, Serial No. 209, 41–65.

Waters, E. and Sroufe, L.A. 1983: Social competence as a developmental construct. *Developmental Review* **3**, 79–97.

Watson, G. 1957: Some personality differences in children related to strict or permissive parental discipline. *Journal of Psychology* **44**, 227–49.

Way, N. 2013: Boys' friendships during adolescence: intimacy, desire, and loss. *Journal of Research on Adolescence* **23**, 201–13.

Weeks, M.S. and Asher, S.R. 2012: Loneliness in childhood: toward the next generation of assessment and research. In Benson, J.B. (Ed.), *Advances in child development and behavior*. San Diego, CA: Elsevier, vol. 42, 1–39.

Weinreich, P. 1983: Emerging from threatened identities: ethnicity and gender in definitions of ethnic identity. In Breakwell, G. (Ed.), *Threatened identities*. Chichester: Wiley, 102–21.

Weiss, B., Dodge, K.A., Bates, J.E. and Pettit, G.S. 1992: Some consequences of early harsh discipline: child aggression and maladaptive social information processing study. *Child Development* **63**, 1321–35.

Weissberg, R.P. 1981: Evaluation of a social-problem-solving skills training: a competence-building intervention with second- to fourth-grade children. *Journal of Consulting and Clinical Psychology* **49**, 251–61.

Weissberg, R.P., Gesten, E., Carnrike, C., Toro, P., Rapkin, B., Davidson, E. and Cowen, E.L. 1981: Social problem-solving training: a competence building intervention with second-to-fourth-grade children. *American Journal of Community Psychology* **9**, 411–23.

Weissman, M.M., Rabinovich, A.E. and Verdell, H. 2013: Interpersonal therapy. In Mann, J.J., McGrath, P.J. and Roose, S.P. (Eds.), *Clinical handbook for the management of mood disorders*. New York: Cambridge University Press, 270–9.

Weisz, J.R., Suwanlert, S., Chaiyasit, W., Weiss, B., Walter, B.R. and Anderson, W.W. 1988: Thai and American perspectives on over and undercontrolled child behaviour problems: exploring the threshold model among parents, teachers, and psychologists. *Journal of Consulting and Clinical Psychology* **56**, 601–9.

Weller, M.P.I. 1993: Where we come from: recent history of community provision. In Weller, M.P.I. and Muijen, M. (Eds.), *Dimensions of community mental health care*. London: Saunders, 1–19.

Wentzel, K.R. 1991: Relations between social competence and academic achievement in early adolescence. *Child Development* **62**, 1066–78.

Wentzel, K.R. and Asher, S.R. 1995: The academic lives of neglected, rejected, popular, and controversial children. *Child Development* **66**, 754–63.

Wentzel, K.R., McNamara-Barry C. and Caldwell K. 2004: Friendships in middle school: influences on motivation and school adjustment. *Journal of Educational Psychology* **96**, 195–203.

Werebe, M.J. and Baudonniere, P.M. 1991: Social pretend play among friends and familiar peers. *International Journal of Behavioural Development* **14**, 411–28.

Westen, J.H.A. 1995: Interpersonal relationship networks of Canadian children of East Indian origin. Unpublished master's thesis, University of Toronto.

Westman, A.S. 1990: Do people's presence more than their presents makes children happy? *Perceptual and Motor Skills* **71**, 674.

White, K.J. and Kistner, J. 1992: The influence of teacher feedback on young children's peer preferences and perceptions. *Developmental Psychology* **28**, 933–40.

Whiting, B.B. and Edwards, C.P. 1988: *Children of different worlds: the formation of social behaviour*. Cambridge, MA: Harvard University Press.

Whiting, B.B. and Whiting, J.W.M. 1975: *Children of six cultures: a psychocultural analysis*. Cambridge, MA: Harvard University Press.

Wiener, J.R. 1987: Peer status of learning disabled children and adolescents: a review of the literature. *Learning Disabilities Research* **2**, 62–79.

Wiener, J.R. and Schneider, B.H. 2002: A multi-source exploration of the friendship patterns of children with and without learning disabilities. *Journal of Abnormal Child Psychology* **30**, 127–41.

Williams, M.-J. 2013: Life skills all teens should have before graduating from high school. *Washington Post*, January 23. www.washingtonpost.com/lifestyle/on-parenting/life-skills-all-teens-should-have-beforegraduating-from-high-school/2013/01/22/bf32fcb8-5c0e-11e2-beee-6e38f5215402_story.html, retrieved April 27, 2015.

Williams, S.K. and Kelly, F.D. 2005: Relationships among involvement, attachment, and behavioral problems in adolescence: examining father's influence. *Journal of Early Adolescence* **25**, 168–96.

Williams, S.T., Ontai, L.L. and Mastergeorge, A.M. 2010: The development of peer interaction in infancy: exploring the dyadic processes. *Social Development* **19**, 348–68.

Windle, M. 1994: A study of friendship characteristics and problem behaviors among middle adolescents. *Child Development* **65**, 1764–77.

Wiseman, J.P. and Duck, S. 1995: Having and managing enemies: a very challenging relationship. In Duck, S. and Wood, J.T. (Eds.), *Confronting relationship challenges.* Thousand Oaks, CA: Sage, 43–72.

Wolfensberger, W. 1972: *The principle of normalization in human services.* Toronto: National Institute on Mental Retardation.

Wolfensberger, W. and Tullman, S. 1982: A brief outline of the principle of normalization. *Rehabilitation Psychology* **27**, 131–45.

Wolman, B.B. 1973: *Dictionary of behavioural science.* New York: Van Nostrand Reinhold.

Wolters, N., Knoors, H., Cillessen, A.H.N. and Verhoeven, L. 2014: Behavioral, personality and communicative predictors of acceptance and popularity in early adolescence. *Journal of Early Adolescence* **34**, 585–605.

World Internet Project 2010: Unpublished report. Los Angeles: University of Southern California, Annenberg School Center for the Digital Future.

Wright, J.C., Giammarino, M. and Parad, H.W. 1986: Social status in small groups: individual-group similarity and the social 'misfit'. *Journal of Personality and Social Psychology* **50**, 523–36.

Yang, A. and Salmivalli, C. 2015: Effectiveness of the KiVa antibullying programme on bully-victims, bullies and victims. *Educational Research* **57**, 80–90.

Yang, K.S. 1981: Social orientation and individual modernity among Chinese students in Taiwan. *Journal of Social Psychology* **113**, 159–70.

Ybarra, M.L., Boyd, D., Korchmaros, J.D. and Oppenheim, J.K. 2012: Defining and measuring cyberbullying within the larger context of bullying victimization. *Journal of Adolescent Health* **51**, 53–8.

Ybarra, M.L., Kiwanuka, J., Emenyonu, N. and Bangsberg, D.R. 2006: Internet use among Ugandan adolescents: implications for HIV intervention. *PLoS Medicine* **3**, 2104–12.

Ybarra, M.L. and Mitchell, K.J. 2004: Online aggressor/targets, aggressors, and targets: a comparison of associated youth characteristics. *Journal of Child Psychology And Psychiatry* **45**, 1308–16.

Yeager, D.S., Fong, C.J., Lee, H.L. and Espelage, D. 2015: Declines in efficacy of anti-bullying programs among older adolescents: theory and a three-level meta-analysis. *Journal of Applied Developmental Psychology* **37**, 36–51.

Young, M.R.R. and Bradley, M.T. 1998: Social withdrawal: self-efficacy, happiness, and popularity in introverted and extroverted adolescents. *Canadian Journal of School Psychology* **14**, 21–35.

Younger, A., Gentile, C. and Burgess, K. 1993: Children's perceptions of social withdrawal: changes cross age. In Rubin, K.H. and Asendorpf, J.B. (Eds.), *Social withdrawal, inhibition, and shyness in childhood*. Hillsdale, NJ: Erlbaum, 215–35.

Yu, G., Zhang, Y. and Yan, R. 2005: Loneliness, peer acceptance, and family functioning of Chinese children with learning disabilities: characteristics and relationships. *Psychology in the Schools* **42**, 325–31.

Zahn-Waxler, C., Schmitz, S., Fulker, D. and Robinson, J. 1996: Behavior problems in 5-year-old monozygotic and dizygotic twins: genetic and environmental influences, patterns of regulation, and internalization of control. *Development and Psychopathology* **8**, 103–22.

Zao H., Zhang, D.J. and Yu, L. 2011: Development of and experimental research on improving peer relationship with computer assistance. In Zhang, D.J., Wang, J.L. and Yu, L. (Eds.), *Methods and implementary strategies on cultivating students' psychological suzhi*. Hauppauge, NY: Nova Science, 471–522.

Zigler, S. 1981: The effectiveness of cooperative learning teams for increasing cross-ethnic friendship: additional evidence. *Human Organization* **40**, 264–68.

Zigler, S. and Trickett, P.K. 1978: IQ, social competence, and evaluation of early childhood intervention programs. *American Psychologist* **33**, 789–98.

Zimmer-Gembeck, M.J., Nesdale, D., McGregor, L., Mastro, S., Goodwin, B. and Downey, G. 2013: Comparing reports of peer rejection: associations with rejection sensitivity, victimization, aggression, and friendship. *Journal of Adolescence* **36**, 1237–46.

INDEX

For Product Safety Concerns and Information please contact our EU representative GPSR@taylorandfrancis.com Taylor & Francis Verlag GmbH, Kaufingerstraße 24, 80331 München, Germany